Children and Society

The Sociology of Children and Childhood Socialization

Gerald Handel
*The City College and The Graduate Center,
City University of New York*

Spencer Cahill
University of South Florida

Frederick Elkin
York University, Toronto

New York   Oxford
OXFORD UNIVERSITY PRESS

Oxford University Press, Inc., publishes works that further Oxford University's
objective of excellence in research, scholarship, and education.

Oxford   New York
Auckland   Cape Town   Dar es Salaam   Hong Kong   Karachi
Kuala Lumpur   Madrid   Melbourne   Mexico City   Nairobi
New Delhi   Shanghai   Taipei   Toronto

With offices in
Argentina   Austria   Brazil   Chile   Czech Republic   France   Greece
Guatemala   Hungary   Italy   Japan   Poland   Portugal   Singapore
South Korea   Switzerland   Thailand   Turkey   Ukraine   Vietnam

Copyright © 2007 by Oxford University Press, Inc.

Published by Oxford University Press, Inc.
198 Madison Avenue, New York, New York 10016
http://www.oup.com

Oxford is a registered trademark of Oxford University Press

ISBN 978-0-19-533078-6

Printed in the United States of America
on acid-free paper

This book is dedicated to
Ruth, Jonathan, and Michael —G. H.
Doni —S. C.
Sylvia —F. E.

Contents

PART I
INTRODUCTION
Understanding Childhood
Socialization

PART II
Agencies of Socialization

PART III
Diversities of Socialization

PART IV
Continuities With and Discontinuities From Childhood

Preface

This book, with the addition of a third author, is a successor to *The Child and Society*, which was published in five editions, the last in 1989. *The Child and Society* has continued to find an audience, but with many new developments in knowledge, interpretation, and research, a new volume has long been called for.

Our objective in this volume, however, remains the same as that of the earlier work: to provide a coherent account, from a sociological perspective, of how children are socialized into modern society. We are interested in how children, as active and interpreting beings, incorporate a constantly changing society into their very selves. The book is focused on children from birth to the beginning of adolescence. In the last chapter, we briefly discuss adolescence in order to indicate continuities and discontinuities between childhood, adolescence, and later life, but we have made a focused effort to devote the book to the earlier years. There are many sociological works on adolescence, but few on childhood. Also, we know of no other sociological work that attempts, as does this one, to present an overview of the major factors affecting socialization during childhood.

We cover the basic sociological theories and areas of study that explain how children grow up to be participating members of their society. We bring into our review and discussion recent perspectives and research that have added to and become intertwined with earlier data and areas of emphasis.

Our first chapter reviews some basic differences in how children have been and are viewed, differences in theoretical understanding of the nature of children. It also introduces the concept of socialization and some of its complexities, which are further described and explained throughout the book. The chapter also includes a brief overview of methods for studying children. In the next chapter, beginning with the biological and early social foundations of socialization, we introduce newer developments in brain research along with studies that reinforce the importance of early childhood experience. Inevitably these two foundations mesh in the social development of children, and we have incorporated available information on the complicated relationships between the two.

In developing into social beings, children experience and are influenced by many interrelated institutions, which we call *agencies of socialization*. Our discussion focuses on families, daycare and schools, peer groups, and media of mass communication. In discussing these agencies, we note new materials on the significance of early family upbringing, the independence and creativity of peer groups, the shaping effects of schools, and the growing use of home computers and video games.

Inevitably, in our complex world, any child is a member of only certain segments of the society, segments that we identify as subcultural groups. We discuss the major social groupings of which children are members, including gender, social class, ethnic group and racial group, and neighborhood of residence. Discussion of them adds specific detail to the preceding chapters that deal with children generally in our society and in others that are similar. These groupings, of course, are closely interrelated, but for purposes of analysis, we distinguish the crucial aspects of each. The changes in these areas in recent years that affect the socialization of children have been momentous, and research has been extensive, especially in the areas of gender relationships and, with Asian and Hispanic immigration, ethnic identity. Neighborhoods, once a major area of research but neglected for years, are once again being recognized as significant in their impact on children, and we discuss some key studies. Social stratification, as always, is a crucial element in socialization, and here, too, we consider important new work.

In addition to paying close attention to variations in childhood experience in our own society, we include a new chapter, Chapter 3, devoted first to variations across cultures and then to historical changes in our own society. Additional cross-cultural examples are offered at other points in the book. These discussions alert the reader to the fact that childhood is defined differently in different places and times, and socialization varies accordingly.

Theories of socialization have had to take into account the new knowledge, modified perspectives, and trends in society. Our new work gives greater emphasis than did its predecessors to children's agency, activity, and distinctive interpretive outlook, while also not losing sight of the fact that children are embedded in a world governed by adults. Children are engaged both in trying to understand adult definitions of situations and in trying to assert their own definitions. Adult definitions and children's own definitions are both consequential in socialization, and we try to illuminate their respective significance.

While we have sought throughout to be cognizant of recent trends, we have not hesitated to retain discussions of less recent research and concepts where we believe they have merit. Many of these earlier works continue to provide a basic foundation for our current knowledge and understanding. Later work often builds on them directly or must take them into account in order to provide a different view. Sometimes there is no later work that covers the same ground, or more recent work does not do it as well.

Many of the most important topics in the study of socialization continue to be controversial. We have attempted, citing the evidence, to present the issues clearly and fairly. In some instances we indicate our evaluation of the evidence and view of the controversy; in others, we leave the matter open because we do not believe the evidence is sufficiently definitive to justify a conclusion. We are more interested in identifying major issues and stimulating thought in the student than in promulgating particular points of view or reinforcing the "correctness" of certain views. ✦

Acknowledgments

The authors would like to thank several anonymous reviewers who offered a great variety of suggestions on two drafts of the manuscript. We found many of these very helpful, and we incorporated them into the text. We also express our appreciation to the following people who assisted us: Jonathan Handel gave us some carefully considered advice as we were getting underway. Michael Handel brought some important material to our attention. Ruth D. Handel provided unfailing moral support as well as some practical computer guidance to her husband, who needed it. We thank Sandy Roscoe, reference librarian at The University of Chicago, who quickly tracked down two elusive references. We also want to thank our publisher, Claude Teweles, and the others at Roxbury Publishing Company, especially Carla Plucknett and Scott Carter, who have worked on this book and brought it to fruition. ✦

About the Authors

Gerald Handel earned his Ph.D. in human development at The University of Chicago. He is the author of *Making a Life in Yorkville*, a symbolic interactionist study of the life course; and coauthor of *Family Worlds*, the first study of families based on interviews with all the children and both parents of intact families, and of *Workingman's Wife*, a pioneering study of working-class women. The second edition of his anthology, *Childhood Socialization*, was published in 2006. In addition to some 20 journal articles and book chapters, his work includes *The Psychosocial Interior of the Family* (editor, three editions; coeditor, fourth edition), *The Child and Society* (coauthor), *Qualitative Methods in Family Research* (coeditor), *The Apple Sliced: Sociological Studies of New York City* (coeditor), and *Social Welfare in Western Society* (author). He has served as associate editor of *The Journal of Marriage and Family* and of *Sociological Inquiry*. He recently retired as professor of sociology at The City College and The Graduate Center of the City University of New York.

Spencer Cahill received his Ph.D. from the University of California, Santa Barbara, and is currently professor of sociology at the University of South Florida. He is the immediate past editor of *Social Psychology Quarterly*, former coeditor of *The Journal of Contemporary Ethnography*, and former chair of the American Sociological Association's Section on Children and Youth. He also is editor of *Inside Social Life: Readings in Sociological Psychology and Microsociology* (also published by Roxbury), and of *Sociological Perspectives on Child Development, Volume 4: Perspectives of and on Children*. His articles and essays, many dealing with children and youth, have appeared in such journals as *Contemporary Sociology*, *Social Problems*, *Social Psychology Quarterly*, and the *Sociological Quarterly*.

Frederick Elkin is Professor Emeritus, York University, Toronto. He received his Ph.D. from the University of Chicago and has taught at the University of Missouri, McGill University, and the University of Montreal. He is author of *The Family in Canada* and *Rebels and Colleagues: Advertising and Social Change in French Canada*, and coeditor of *Volunteers, Voluntary Associations and Development*. He is first author of *The Child and Society* and coauthor of four subsequent editions. In addition, he has written reports for public organizations and made numerous contributions to academic journals and edited works. He has served as president of the

Canadian Sociology and Anthropology Association and is an honorary member of the Vanier Institute of the Family. ✦

PART I
INTRODUCTION
Understanding Childhood Socialization

Introduction

As human beings age, they change in many ways. Over the early years of our lives, we grow in physical strength and stature. Most of us start to walk, talk, and perform other feats that were previously beyond our physical capabilities. The onset of what we call *puberty* initiates radical bodily changes that may both fascinate and frighten us. Much later in life, our physical strength and capacities may decline. Although we tend to pay less attention to physical changes during our middle years of life, they never cease.

Our social lives are at least as dynamic as our bodily being. The ever changing character of our social lives sometimes parallels bodily changes. In many past and some societies still today (see Chapter 3), the young are expected to take on more and more physically demanding tasks as they grow in physical strength and stature. Visible signs of puberty such as menarche, or first menstruation, may occasion elaborate rituals marking a dramatic change in social status, expectations, and obligations. As our physical capacities decline during later years, we may lose much of the autonomy that we had long taken for granted.

Yet, the changing contours of our lives are largely a matter of social definition and convention. This is particularly apparent in contemporary, technologically advanced societies like our own. In most cases, our early lives are largely confined to our immediate family and its place of residence. The social, relational, and organizational contexts of our lives then gradually expand. We enter into new relationships with similarly aged peers and with elders outside of our family, such as paid care providers and teachers. Over our early years we move from preschools to elementary, middle, and high schools, often on to college or university, and eventually out of school, changing teachers and often friends as we do. More and more of us move in and out of jobs and from one employer to another in the course of our working lives. We end social relationships and begin others. Even those social relationships that endure are commonly transformed over time. Close friends may become distant and occasional ones, while former strangers become close friends. The birth or adoption of a child and the departure of that child from the family home may profoundly alter our relationship with our spouse. Many of us marry, divorce, and remarry over the course of our lives, and some are widowed.

The ever changing character of our social lives requires continual learning and adaptation. Social scientists have coined the term *socialization* to refer to this continual process of learning and adaptation. It refers to *the processes by which we learn and adapt to the ways of a given society or social group so as to ade-*

2

quately participate in it. Adequate participation in a social group clearly requires understanding of the social expectations and obligations associated with our particular position within that group, such as daughter or son, student, retail clerk or physician, mother or father, and so on. However, it does not necessarily imply conformity to prevailing social expectations but adaptation to them. Such adaptation may involve strategically circumventing social expectations or altering them. In any case, knowledge and practical skills must be acquired in order to follow, evade, or alter the ways of a social group and the expectations associated with a given position within it.

Socialization is clearly a lifelong process. In societies like our own, young children first learn the ways of their family. When they attend preschool or a daycare center, they must learn how to deal and play with similarly aged peers from varied family backgrounds. As students, they learn the procedures and conventions of the different schools they attend and the peer cultures of the student body. When they become employees, they are socialized to the formal and informal operations of the factory, store, or office. Later in life, they may have to learn and adapt to the peculiar ways of a nursing home.

Although we must continually acquire new knowledge and skills in response to the changing contexts of our social lives, socialization tends to have a cumulative character. That is, later socialization tends to build upon already acquired social skills, knowledge, and capacities to regulate our own conduct in relation to the actions of others. That is why the socialization that occurs early in life is often called *primary*, and later socialization *secondary*. Successful secondary socialization must either build upon the foundation laid by primary socialization or dismantle it. Building upon primary socialization is obviously far less challenging than attempting to purge an individual of previously acquired and often deeply ingrained ways of feeling, thinking, and acting. Although primary socialization is not irreversible, it typically has a continuing influence over later life (Berger and Luckmann 1966, 140; Handel 2003, 104–107). Because of that continuing influence, understanding primary socialization is essential to explaining how people become the kinds of social beings they do and how human societies endure and change.

This book concerns primary, or childhood, socialization. As we will discuss later (see Chapter 3), the duration of childhood is a matter of social definition and varies over time and among different human societies. However, for the sake of convenience, we follow the social convention of contemporary Western societies and define childhood as the period of life from birth to puberty. This definition of childhood is admittedly somewhat arbitrary, but such arbitrariness is unavoidable. The character and duration of childhood socialization are as varied as the human societies that populate and have populated the earth. Yet, however childhood is defined, processes of primary socialization shape the kind of people who will populate a society and, thereby, its future. Understanding childhood socialization is, therefore, essential to understanding human social life and experience.

Complexities of Childhood Socialization

Initiates into a society, whether newborns or new immigrants, must acquire considerable knowledge and skill in order to participate in it adequately. They must learn what utensils, if any, to use when eating specific foods; how to greet strangers and acquaintances; in what situations to express and conceal different emotions; and when to speak and when to remain silent. In our society, they must learn to expect different things from a doctor and a store clerk and the difference between acceptable behavior at a football game and in a church. They must learn these and countless other lessons from observation and interaction with others. The ways of the society from which immigrants come may both facilitate and interfere with their learning of the ways of the society that they are joining. In comparison, a newborn starts from scratch.

As we discuss in more detail later (Chapter 2), infants are born with the potentialities to acquire the knowledge and skills required for adequate participation in human society. Yet, those potentialities are wide and varied and are only realized through interaction with others. For example, all children are born with the biological capacity to speak any language, but learn to speak only the language (or, in some cases, languages) they hear from others. In one social setting, they may learn to speak English; and in another, Japanese. Similarly, in one setting a child may learn to eat rice with chopsticks; in another, with a fork. In one, they will learn to value personal independence; and in another, the interest of the group. In one setting, a boy will learn to be deeply respectful of his father; and in another to treat his father as a "pal" or "buddy." In one social setting, a girl will learn that her future social acceptability and well-being require marriage as a virgin and childbearing; while in another, she will learn that she can choose whether to marry or not and whether to have children or not.

Childhood socialization is concerned with complex matters such as these. Some are matters of everyday custom, such as whether to eat rice with chopsticks or a fork. Others have lifetime consequences, such as whether a girl learns that she must marry a man her parents choose or is encouraged to choose whether and whom to marry. Some of what children learn in the course of their socialization is overt and visible, such as what clothes are appropriate for different kinds of occasions. Yet, even such overt behaviors depend on a more generalized learning, the effects of which are not directly visible but must be inferred.

Over time, children acquire common sense understandings of how their social environments are organized. They come implicitly to recognize that it is made up of different kinds of people, such as doctors and store clerks, and different kinds of situations, like football games and church services. They learn to be concerned with "appropriateness" as a general guide to conduct. They develop a "sense of propriety," which not only governs behavior in situations comparable to those that they have already experienced but also guides them in dealing with new situations. Hence, when they enter a novel situation they do so with some sense of how to act because they have learned how to define varied situations and to be concerned with acting appropriately in them. For example, when they get their first job, they are not at a total loss. They have experienced other situations that have the general quality of "being supervised by someone with authority to supervise." They know they are expected to listen to the boss and undertake the tasks she or he assigns them. They then go on to learn the specific requirements of being supervised as an employee, which are different from the supervision they received as children from their parents and as pupils from teachers.

Children also learn to experience specific emotions in particular kinds of situations. Depending on their social environment, they may learn to feel possessive with personal property or feel indifferent to it. They may learn to react angrily to apparent slights or to dismiss them as unimportant. They may learn to feel proud at embarrassing a rival, ashamed of having done so, or a mixture of the two.

Some of what children learn in the process of socialization, as when they learn to say "please" and "thank you" or arithmetic, is explicitly taught by people who are socially responsible for teaching them. In many societies, parents and teachers are specifically entrusted with the responsibility to prepare the young to participate in adult society. Of course, children do not always respond as these adults would wish, and children's responses may influence adults to change what they expect of and how they treat those children. Socialization is an interactive process, a process of mutual influence. Adults socialize children, and children socialize adults. For example, as children learn from one another, they often bring expressions and practices home that are unfamiliar to their parents. Children also learn to keep aspects of their distinctive peer cultures secret from parents and other adults, especially those that they know or suspect would meet with adults' disapproval. Yet, that too is part of their socialization. Learning to keep secrets is an important social skill, requiring an understanding of social expectations and a capacity for self-regulation.

Some of what children learn in the course of their socialization is self-motivated. Children actively attempt to understand the social world around them, to recognize the types of people and types of situations that constitute it. Parents who are overwhelmed by young children's endless "why" questions are well aware of their social curiosity. They want to know why a lighter- or darker-skinned child looks different from them, why "that man" is dressed "like that," why "that woman" is "doing that," and so on. Partly, through such questioning, children learn about the dimensions and methods of social classification that organize their social world.

On their own initiative, children also look to others for guidance in how they should act. Having first become responsive to their parents or other adult caregivers, children are prepared to be responsive to others. Early on, children begin to see other people as models for what they might like to do and become. At home, they are apt to take their parents as models of behavior. For example, if a mother wears high-heeled shoes, her 3-year-old daughter may sneak into her closet, put on the oversized shoes, and shuffle around the house "like mommy." Sports celebrities are early heroes of many young boys who see them, at least for a time, as models for their own behavior.

Children also learn much about social life from one another. Although children often view adults as models and knowledgeable authorities, they learn many subtle lessons about the negotiated character of social relationships from similarly aged peers. They teach each other what it means to be a friend, how to manage others' impression of them, how to circumvent formal rules with relative impunity, and many other practical lessons about social life. And, children not only learn from age-mates but also pick up many pointers and practices from older peers who are more like themselves than are adults, yet more knowledgeable, skilled, and "cool" than they themselves are.

These different varieties of socialization take place in many settings—at home and in school, in front of televisions and on playgrounds. Childhood socialization can also be fairly readily observed in public places, as the following example that occurred in a neighborhood bank illustrates.

> After a young woman finishes her transaction at a teller's window, she and her approximately 2-year-old son head toward the door of the bank. The boy runs ahead of her and sits on a swivel chair near the door, turning from side to side. When the mother urges him to come along, he says, "No, I like it." She replies in an even, matter-of-fact tone, "Goodbye, I'm leaving," and walks out the door without looking back. The boy jumps off the chair and quickly follows.

This brief episode illustrates how adults draw upon their power over children in an attempt to influence children's current behavior and thereby socialize them. First, the mother uses the threat of abandonment (although it seems virtually certain that she would not have left the boy in the bank if he had not followed her out) in an attempt to alter her son's behavior. Adults often use threats of *negative sanctions* in an attempt to influence children's behavior. They may even carry out such threats. Other times, adults may promise a reward—a *positive sanction*—if children will act as the adult wishes. For example, another mother might have offered the boy some ice cream if he would come with her. In either case, adults routinely draw upon their power of potential punishment and reward to impose their *definition of a situation* on children. Children may challenge adults' definitions of situations, but adults often act so that their definition prevails. For example, by proceeding to leave right away, the mother in the above episode obliges the boy to sacrifice his immediate pleasure to her schedule and projects or face possible abandonment. This is but one example of how adults impose definitions of situations on children and thereby create the social reality to which children must respond.

The definitions of situations that adults attempt to impose upon children often include definitions of appropriate conduct in different situations. For example, the following conversation between an approximately 5-year-old girl and her mother was overheard in a busy laundromat:

> The girl asks her mother, "Mommy, do you see that baby?" When the mother does not respond, the girl continues, "His face is so fat. . . ." Before she can finish, her mother emphatically interrupts, "*Don't* talk so loudly about other people. They might hear you." The girl giggles and points out

that "the baby won't understand." Her mother replies, "That's not the point. It's not polite. You have to keep your voice down." (Adapted from Cahill 1987, 316–317)

In this episode, the mother instructs her daughter about an important and complex rule of social propriety: Do not publicly make comments about others. When the girl objects that "the baby won't understand," the mother elaborates that it does not matter whether the subject of the remark understands or hears the remark. The implication seems to be that others might hear, understand, and judge you harshly for such an impolite remark. However, note that the mother does not object to the daughter calling the baby fat, but to doing so loudly. The mother thereby subtly conveys that what might be appropriate in a private conversation among intimates can be quite inappropriate in a more public situation. Whether or not the girl recognizes this subtle distinction at the time, it is a lesson she will undoubtedly hear repeated in different ways and on many occasions. Socializing lessons such as this often occur when a child inadvertently violates a standard of social appropriateness. Parents or other adult caretakers attempt both to alter the child's immediate conduct and to prevent its recurrence in the future. In the process, they teach the child general standards of social appropriateness, which the child may then gradually adopt as her or his own.

Socializing lessons often are even less direct. For example, a simple request to explain or account for one's conduct or appearance suggests that it requires explanation—that it is not socially expected or appropriate under the circumstances. For example, when one kindergartner asks another boy, "Why do you always dress up the same?" he sends a message that day-to-day changes of costume are socially expected. The fact that the second boy always dresses "the same," in the words of the first, requires explanation. The second boy apparently understands the message and denies the implied accusation by noting that "no, I sometimes wear blue" (adapted from Much and Shweder 1978, 27). Yet, by claiming that he does not always dress like that, the second boy acknowledges the general convention that one should not "always dress up the same." If he did not already know it, he has learned a lesson about social conventions.

Socialization is a complex process that takes many different forms. It occurs through simple observation, imitation, direct and indirect instruction, applications of positive and negative sanctions, trial and error, and continual participation in social interaction. Social rules and standards of appropriateness are general guidelines and not elaborate instructions for how to conduct oneself under every conceivable circumstance. Individuals must learn how to apply and adapt social rules and standards to different situations and how to align their actions with those of others. These are practical skills and are acquired through practice, the practice of social interaction.

The complex and varied process of socialization helps explain two different kinds of phenomena. On the one hand, it helps to explain how a person becomes capable of adequate participation in a human society, as we have emphasized and will continue to do throughout this book. On the other hand, it helps explain how ongoing human societies are possible at all. Although some other animals have rudimentary societies, none of them approaches the complexity or wide variety of human societies. The continuation of such complex societies across generations requires explanation of how human beings can finely attune their actions to one another in ways that make possible ongoing, relatively orderly social life. Although a full explanation, if one is possible, is beyond the scope of this book, the socialization process is a key element to such an explanation. Ongoing, orderly human social life is possible because individuals learn to be self-regulating participants in social life. They learn to recognize different socially defined categories of people and situations, to regulate their actions in accordance with varied standards of social appropriateness, to align their actions with those of others, and to negotiate collective definitions of social situations. They thereby come to reproduce the orderly social worlds into which they are born.

This does not imply that socialization is a guarantee against social disorder. The traditional ways of a society may prove ineffective in dealing with new challenges, including challenges that are caused by those traditional ways. For example, some agricultural techniques may result in environmental damage that then makes them ineffective for feeding the population, resulting in growing conflict over increasingly scarce resources. Political leaders may act in capricious or tyrannical ways that excite widespread rebellion. Different groups within a society may have or develop diametrically opposed conventions and customs that engender intergroup conflict, as the many civil conflicts of the past and present attest. Yet, even under such extraordinary circumstances, people tend to band together, negotiating collective definitions of their common situation, if only of a common foe, and act in concert. They are able to do so because of the social knowledge and skills that they have acquired through prior socialization. The process of socialization is as central to explanations of social collapse, rebellion, and civil conflict as it is to explanations of more orderly social life.

Limitations of the Study of Socialization

The study of childhood socialization does not address a number of topics that are of social scientific interest. Its principal focus is on the process through which the young learn the ways of a society and social groups. Although, as previously argued, it must necessarily attend to the ways that children influence adults, its interest in such influence is limited to how it may affect children's socialization rather than how it may socialize adults. The study of childhood socialization is principally concerned with the likely influence of socializing interactions on the young's subsequent participation in social life, and not that of adults.

Second, the study of childhood socialization does not speculate or attempt to explain how a society or social group came to be. The society into which a child is born, with its common understandings, ways of doing things, standards of appropriateness, and current issues, is a product of a unique history and exists before the child enters it. The study of socialization begins with that ongoing, preexisting society and asks how the young are recruited into self-regulated participation, and different kinds of participation, in it.

Third, the study of childhood socialization does not try to explain the uniqueness of individuals. Although no two individuals are alike and each person has a singular genetic inheritance, distinctive experiences, and personal characteristics, the study of childhood socialization focuses not on such individualizing factors and processes but on how individuals learn of and adapt to a shared culture and society. As children age, they develop both distinguishing personal characteristics and shared cultural and social characteristics. They inevitably develop some sense of individual identity, but the particular aspects of their uniqueness—be they distinctive physical characteristics, special ways of acting, or tastes—and how those aspects are judged are matters of social definition and consequences of a socialization process. Even a person's sense of individuality bears the mark of their social experiences.

Finally, the study of socialization is ill suited to prescribe what a human society should be or the type of child rearing necessary to achieve it. Its concern is with how children learn the ways of a given society or social group as it is, however harmonious or turbulent, peaceful or violent, and just or unjust it may be. Its findings can certainly be used to praise or condemn a particular society, social group, or type of child rearing, but such evaluations are beyond its scope. Similarly, its findings can be used to argue against one or another social policy proposal, but it does not specify what the goals of public policy should be. That is a matter for public debate and discussion, hopefully debate and discussion that are informed by an understanding of the complexities of children's social lives and socialization.

Organization of the Book

The remainder of this book provides a detailed overview of childhood socialization. We will use a wide range of illustrations, although most of them are from contemporary North America, with which we are most familiar. However, we will give some attention to patterns of socialization in other places, at other times, and among varied social groups. Part I consists of four chapters. Chapter 1 summarizes varied approaches to and methods of studying children and childhood socialization, and briefly presents our own integrative approach. Chapter 2 discusses the biological and social foundations of childhood socialization and is followed in Chapter 3 by some illustrations of cross-cultural and historical variations in conceptions of and the treatment of children. Chapter 4 considers the processes, mechanisms, and techniques through which socialization occurs, as well as its major outcomes. There are also four chapters in Part II, 5 through 8, that discuss the primary socializing agencies in North American and similar societies. They are, respectively, families, schools, peer groups, and media of mass communication. Although we consider diverse patterns of childhood socialization both between and within human societies throughout the book, Part III focuses specifically on the most fundamental sources of such diversity within societies. Chapter 9 discusses social class variations. Chapter 10 deals with diverse patterns of socialization among ethnic and minority groups and across neighborhoods. Chapter 11 addresses issues of sex and gender socialization. Finally, in Part IV, Chapter 12 offers a brief concluding overview of childhood socialization and discussion of adolescence and continuing socialization throughout the life course.

We hope that this book will sensitize readers to the complexity of children's social lives and socialization. The knowledge and social skills that children acquire through processes of socialization and how they acquire them shape the kind of people they become and, thereby, the future of the society into which they are born. Hence, the study of childhood socialization is essential for understanding human social life and experience.

Over the years, as we discuss in Chapter 1, different approaches to the study of children have emphasized one or another aspect of children's social development or socialization to the neglect of others. That has led some who study children to reject the very idea of childhood socialization. We argue, in Chapter 1, that this is an overreaction. Adequate understanding of childhood socialization requires appreciation of the variability of childhoods, children's influence over adults, their peer cultures, and current concerns. Yet, adequate participation in a human society requires the acquisition of considerable knowledge and skills. It requires socialization. This book provides an overview of that most fundamental process of human being during childhood, in all its fascinating but challenging complexity.

References

Berger, Peter, and Thomas Luckmann. 1966. *The Social Construction of Reality*. New York: Doubleday.

Cahill, Spencer. 1987. "Children and Civility: Ceremonial Deviance and the Acquisition of Ritual Competence." *Social Psychology Quarterly* 50: 312–321.

Handel, Gerald. 2003. *Making a Life in Yorkville: Experience and Meaning in the Life Course Narrative of an Urban Working-Class Man*. New York: Aldine de Gruyter.

Much, Nancy, and Richard Shweder. 1978. "Speaking of Rules: The Analysis of Culture in Breach." In William Damon (ed.), *Moral Development*, 19–39. San Francisco: Jossey-Bass. ✦

Chapter 1
Studying Children

Human social life is widely diverse and highly complex, and children's social lives and socialization are no less so than adults'. Those who attempt to better understand children's social lives and socialization cannot study them in all their diversity and complexity simultaneously. They must selectively focus on those factors they consider most important and most revealing. They are guided in that selection by general theoretical perspectives or approaches, each with its own assumptions about the nature of children, their development, and the proper goals of their study. There has been and continues be much debate among social scientists over how best to approach the study of children's social lives and socialization. In this chapter we review some of the major social scientific approaches to the study of children and childhood socialization and briefly present our own approach.

However social scientists approach the study of children's social lives and socialization, they must also choose how best to gather information that might answer the questions that approach suggests are important. That is, they must choose particular research methods that will provide the best evidence possible regarding their particular research questions. Social scientists employ a variety of research methods and often argue among themselves about which is "best." We maintain that those arguments have been and are largely fruitless. Every research method has its advantages and disadvantages, and each is better or worse suited for addressing different kinds of research questions. In this chapter, we also briefly review the most prominent research methods that have been and are used to study children's social lives and socialization, and some of the advantages and disadvantages of each.

Competing Images of Children and Childhood

The character of children, their development, and their preparation for adult social life have long been subjects of debate in Western and probably other societies as well. Some have argued that the young are born with original sin and literally need to have the "devil beaten out of them." Others argued that children, like plants, will naturally grow and flourish with proper nourishment. Still others have argued that children are like soft lumps of clay that must be carefully shaped before they harden with age (see Chapter 3). The development of modern Western thought did little to quiet these debates. In the late nineteenth century, many Western thinkers became convinced that science, which had proved so successful in unraveling the mysteries of the natural world, could also unravel the mysteries of human social life. More than a few of them turned their attention to the scientific study of children in the hope of resolving debates over children's character, development, and appropriate preparation for later life. However, the scientific study of children that mushroomed over the next century did little to resolve such debates. It merely shifted the terms of those debates.

The Natural Development of Children

In the late nineteenth century, when the scientific study of children began in earnest, evolutionary thought dominated Western science, including the social sciences. Many social scientists concluded that the evolution of the species, as described by Charles Darwin and others, provided a template for understanding the evolution of human social life. They also believed that evolution, both natural and social, was intrinsically progressive, moving from "primitive" and simple to more advanced and complex forms of life. Not surprisingly, they assumed that the industrializing societies of Western Europe and North America in which they lived were the most highly evolved and advanced form of human society in history and of their time.

What became known as *recapitulation theory* translated this progressive view of human social evolution into a model for understanding individual human development (Gould 1977, 135–147; Lesko 2001, 30–35). The catchphrase of recapitulation theory, coined by the German zoologist Ernst Haeckel in 1866, was "Ontogeny recapitulates phylogeny" (Gould 1977, 76–77). That is, the development of the individual organism retraces or parallels the evolutionary developmental of its species. Haeckel and other biologists were primarily interested in how the physical development of the individual organism from fertilized egg to fully mature being retraces or parallels the evolution of species from simple, single-celled organisms to anatomically and physiologically complex animals, such as humans. However, psychologists and other social scientists soon extended the notion of recapitulation to the study of child development. They reasoned that the intellectual and moral development of the human child retraced or paralleled what they considered the intellectually and morally progressive evolution of human societies.

The American psychologist Granville Stanley Hall (1844–1924) was one of the first to build a theory of child development upon this expanded notion of recapitulation. Like others of his time, he assumed that industrializing Western societies were the most highly evolved of human societies and that their adult members were the most intellectually and morally advanced humans. He therefore reasoned that children in Western societies resembled adults in purportedly more "primitive" societies. According to Hall, the early years of a child's life are dominated by primitive instincts, similar to what he called "the pre-savage stage of evolution." "Then, at about age six or seven, the child experiences crises that lead into the preadolescent years of six to twelve, when individualistic and unimaginative behavior harken back to the world of . . . so-called savages" (Chudacoff 1989, 67). A new period of crises then moves the child into what Hall considered the crucial stage of adolescence, between the ages of 13 to 18, characterized by emotionalism, idealism, and group identification reminiscent, according to Hall, of ancient and medieval civilizations

(Chudacoff 1989, 67). According to Hall, the treatment and education of children must be carefully harmonized with their stage of development to avoid retarding or dangerously rushing their "natural" progress.

Although Hall's theory of child development has few adherents today, it was highly influential in its day with consequences for the present. Hall is generally credited with inspiring the "child study movement" in North America that made children objects of extensive scientific study. His proposed stages of development provided the intellectual justification for the sequential organization of schooling into primary grades beginning around age 6, middle or junior high, and then high school that continues to characterize education in North America today (Chudacoff 1989, 67–72). Many subsequent and still influential theories of child development share Hall's basic framework. These theories are not as explicit as Hall was in drawing parallels between children in contemporary Western societies and adults in purportedly more "primitive societies," but such parallels are often implied. They depict child development as a natural sequence of discrete stages. Children progress from one stage to the next by surmounting some kind of crisis or challenge. They advise that adults' treatment and education of children must be carefully fitted to their stage of development so as not to hinder them or prematurely place impossible and potentially dangerous demands upon them.

Jean Piaget's (1896–1980) theory of cognitive development is probably the most familiar and influential theory of this kind today. Piaget was primarily interested in the evolution of human intelligence. Drawing inspiration from recapitulation theory, Piaget believed that there must be parallels "between the progress made in the logical and rational organization of knowledge and the corresponding formative psychological processes." He therefore concluded that "in studying children . . . we have the best chance of studying the [historical] development of logical knowledge, mathematical knowledge, physical knowledge, and so forth" (Piaget 1969, 4).

Piaget's study of children led to his proposal of four stages of cognitive development (as well as a number of less familiar substages), now memorized by countless college students in introductory psychology courses. Piaget called the first of these stages, from birth to around 2 years of age, the *sensorimotor*, during which the child learns about her or his world through the coordination of perceptions (*sensori-*) and motions (*motor*) into plans of action (Piaget 1973, 11). The practical understandings the child thereby acquires constitute what Piaget described as "an intelligence" that precedes "thought" (Piaget 1973, 11). For example, through physical exploration of her or his environment, the infant comes to understand that objects continue to exist even when he or she cannot see or immediately perceive them, as when they are covered by a blanket, and, around 9 or 10 months of age, searches for "lost" objects under blankets or hidden behind other objects. As Piaget (1973, 12) argues, "[T]his seems quite simple, but is a very complex act of intelligence." It presupposes a notion of object permanence, of the localization of objects, and, hence, of spatial organization.

Yet, this early sensorimotor or practical intelligence is not the same as thought, which requires the mental or symbolic representation and *interiorization of action* that Piaget (1973, 17) termed *operations*. Hence, according to Piaget, it is not until the child begins to acquire speech, the symbols of language, that she or he begins to "think," to represent objects and actions to herself or himself, and enters what he termed the *preoperational* stage of cognitive development, lasting from around 2 to 6 years of age. This initiates a long process of not simply translating but also reconstructing the practical knowledge acquired through sensorimotor manipulation into symbolic forms. During the preoperational stage, the child's symbolic or mental representations of objects and plans of action are disconnected. The child then enters what Piaget (1973, 20–21) called the stage of *concrete operations*, lasting from around 6 or 7 to 11 or 12 years of age, when the child begins to integrate his or her previously fragmented understandings into systems of thought based on the classification of objects, relations among them, and their number. However, these systems of thought are directly tied to the direct manipulation of objects. It is not until around age 12 that the child enters what Piaget (1973, 59) called the stage of *formal operations*, when the child begins to think in terms of verbal statements, or propositions, divorced from the manipulation of concrete objects. According to Piaget (1973, 24), this "superimposes" a new logic, "a whole set of specific operations . . . on preceding ones," resulting in a kind of system or systems of thought.

For Piaget, these stages of cognitive development (and their substages) constitute a natural developmental sequence (paralleling the historical evolution of human intelligence). That is, each successive stage of development necessarily builds upon prior stages. Yet, Piaget maintained that movement from one stage (or substage) of development to the next was not an automatic outcome of aging. In his words, the timing of movement from one stage (or substage) to the next "depends on the individual's previous experience, and not only on his [or her] maturation; and it depends above all on the social milieu which can hasten or delay the appearance of a stage, or even prevent the manifestation" (Piaget 1973, 50). According to Piaget, each stage (and substage) of cognitive development is characterized by a cognitive schema or structures. The child processes or makes sense of experience in terms of the characteristic cognitive structures of his or her stage of development. Piaget (1973, 166) called this process *assimilation*. However, novel experiences that cannot be readily assimilated to existing forms of understanding disturb the "equilibrium" between the child's experience and cognitive structures, resulting in the child's active *accommodation*, or adaptation, of his or her existing cognitive structures to that experience (Piaget 1973, 166). Through such accommodation, the child achieves a new "equilibrium" between experience and thought. According to Piaget, this active and progressive *equilibration* of experience and cognitive structures propels the child's cognitive development.

Piaget also implied that the child's cognitive development is a kind of socialization. The child progressively moves from more egocentric to more socially shared perspectives and forms of thought (Piaget 1959). Subsequent scholars who applied Piaget's framework to children's development of moral reasoning (Kohlberg 1984) and social cognition or understanding (Damon

1977) are even more explicit in this regard. Although Piaget and his followers stress the child's active role in her or his own intellectual and social development, their focus is on the individual child's adaptation to a fixed and autonomous world. They therefore neglect the variability of children's social environments, both within and among human societies, and how children, in concert with others, may shape the very social environments to which they accommodate their understandings. The idea that individual development paralleled humans' purportedly progressive adaptation to the physical environment seemed to blind them to the largely constructed character and variability of children's social environments.

The Social Inculcation of Children

At the same time that developmental psychologists like Hall and Piaget were proposing supposedly universal models of individual child development, many social psychologists and sociologists turned their attention to childhood with a much different goal in mind. They were far less interested in possible parallels between purported patterns of social evolution and individual development than in questions of how any human society, and its continuation across generations, was possible. Many assumed that "the moral demands of society are incompatible with the individual's needs and desires for immediate gratification" (Maccoby 1968, 229) and thought of childhood socialization as a "struggle" between the individual's "innate self" and "the society in which he [or she] will participate as an adult" (Inkeles 1968, 75). These social scientists concluded that because human societies tend to endure, society commonly prevails in this struggle. They argued that it does so by, to use one of their favorite expressions, "inculcating" individuals with a set of social demands (Inkeles 1968, 89) or expectations (Parsons 1951, 258). In other words, they argued that, through socialization, individuals *internalize* social demands and expectations and voluntarily attempt to meet them. Ironically, these social scientists turned to then prevailing theories of individual psychology to explain this supposed inculcation or internalization of social norms and expectations.

For example, Talcott Parsons (1902–1979), one of the most influential sociologists of the mid-twentieth century, drew upon Sigmund Freud's (1856–1939) then popular psychoanalytic theory to explain what Parsons often referred to as the "interpenetration" of the social system and personality system. Like Freud, Parsons (Parsons and Bales 1955, 16) considered nuclear families the " 'factories' which produce human personalities." According to Parsons (Parsons and Bales 1955, 54), the child's early experiences in the family lead her or him to internalize a "system of social objects," or pattern of complementary roles such as mother and child, mother and father, parent and child, and the like. Moreover, first the mothers' and then both parents' changing gratification and frustration of the child's desires result in what Parsons (1951, 249) called "motivational structures" that encourage either voluntary conformity to "social normative expectations" or, in some cases, "resistances" to such conformity. According to Parsons (1951, 227), the child's subsequent social experiences outside the family elaborate on these "broad fundamental patterns of 'character' laid down" during early childhood within the nuclear family. For example, the child generalizes her or his orientation to the father's authority to other authoritative roles like teacher or political leader in the future. And, the "structures of motivation" built up in the family during early childhood lead to lifelong tendencies toward either compliance with or resistance to social normative expectations. Of course, for Parsons (Parsons and Bales 1955, 358), the continuation and stability of a society depend on young children's internalization of and motivated commitment to the values that mirror the "institutionalized values" governing that society.

Other social scientists who attempted to explain children's socialization drew upon another dominant psychological theory of the time—*behaviorism*. Behaviorism based its account of human conduct on the simple principle that animals, including humans, tend to repeat behavior that brings rewards and refrain from behavior that results in punishment. According to behaviorists, an individual's current conduct is simply a product of immediate environmental stimuli and her or his past history of rewarding or punishing reinforcement. Hence, socialization resulted from rewarding individuals for socially desirable behaviors and punishing them for socially undesirable behavior. The most prominent proponent of behaviorist psychology, B. F. Skinner (1904–1990), once defined human culture as "a set of contingencies of reinforcement [i.e., of rewards and punishments contingent upon certain kinds of behavior] maintained by a group, possibly formulated in rules or laws," that "*controls the behavior of the members of the group that practice it*" (Skinner 1974, 223; emphasis in original). According to Skinner and other behaviorists, a society endures across generations not because it implants itself into the personalities of its members but because it maintains a set of contingencies of reinforcement that shapes and continually controls their behavior. In Skinner's (1974, 164) words, "[A] personality . . . is at best a repertoire of behavior imparted by an organized set of contingencies."

Yet, some social scientists who were influenced by behaviorism acknowledged that socialization may result in a kind of internalization of social expectations. First, based on past experience, the individual may anticipate social rewards or punishments for certain behaviors and act accordingly even when those anticipated rewards or punishments are not immediately forthcoming. For example, a child may endure the punishing taunts of peers in anticipation of the future rewards of parental approval for "standing up for what you believe." Or, the child may endure parental punishments in anticipation of the rewarding future admiration of peers for asserting her or his independence. Second, the individual may adopt standards of self-reward and self-punishment, of self-congratulation and self-condemnation, that mirror prior patterns of external reward and punishment (Maccoby 1968, 258–260). For example, the child who is repeatedly praised by parents and teachers for academic achievements may come to congratulate herself or himself, to feel a rewarding sense of pride, when receiving good grades that may at least partially offset the punishment of being considered a "nerd" by her or his peers.

Despite their differences, these two views of childhood socialization are similar in a fundamentally important respect. Both argue that the social environment exerts a determining or controlling influence over children by either molding their personalities or shaping their behavior. Unlike the emphasis of Piaget's model of child development on the child's *active* accommodation to the external environment, these two views of childhood socialization depict the child as a mostly passive product of social forces. Although these traditional views of socialization focused much needed attention on the social environments of childhood, they did so to the neglect of children's active participation in social life and in their own socialization. The emphasis was on society's inculcation of children, rather than on children's active appropriation and exercise of social knowledge and skills.

The Social Construction of Children

Beginning in the 1970s (e.g. MacKay 1974) and in growing numbers during the 1980s and 1990s, social scientists began to question the very notions of child development and socialization. Models of child development like Piaget's were criticized for treating childhood as both natural and universal, ignoring the wide variability among children and childhoods over time, across cultures, and even within particular societies (e.g., Prout and James 1997, 13). Although Piaget and other developmental psychologists concede that social environments can influence the pace of and limit children's development, they clearly suggest that there is a natural sequence of development with a preferred goal. That preferred goal is to talk, think, and make moral decisions like a highly educated, Western adult. The very term *development* implies advancement and improvement, thus the expression *child development* implies biographical advancement toward an improved state. Hence, studies of child development tend to focus on how children's knowledge and understanding do not measure up to that of highly educated (Western or Westernized) adults and on the factors that either promote or impede their advancement to this end.

Many social scientists level similar criticisms at the concept of socialization. They argue that this concept has "the more or less inescapable implication" of viewing children "as a defective form of adults, social only in their future potential but not in their present being" (James, Jenks, and Prout 1998, 6). The obvious target of such criticisms is traditional models of socialization, like those of Parsons and the behaviorists, which treat children as passive products of society's inculcation of social norms or reinforcing control of behavior. Such models of socialization focus attention on possible associations between parents' and other adults' treatment of children and children's subsequent behaviors or attitudes. The critics of socialization contend that such a focus neglects children's agency and voice (Pufall and Unsworth 2004, 8–9). That is, it disregards children's active contributions to the construction of their own social environments and their perspectives on their current and future social lives.

The critics of socialization propose a new sociology or social studies of childhood as an alternative to traditional developmental or socialization approaches. That alternative approach treats childhood as a "social construction" and a kind of social status or position, defined as "the life period during which a human being is regarded as a child" (Qvortrup 1994, 148). This view of childhood as largely a matter of social definition also directs attention to the variability of childhoods historically, cross-culturally, and among different groups within a society. It also stresses that children, however socially defined, are serious social actors who influence their own social lives, the social lives of those around them, and the societies in which they live (Prout and James 1997, 8). As such, it maintains that children's perspectives, current concerns, relations, and peer cultures are worthy of study "in their own right," independent of the perspective or concerns of adults, including concerns about the future course of those children's social lives.

Appreciating the Complexities of Childrens' Lives

Critics of traditional developmental and socialization approaches to the study of children and childhood do have valid points. Developmental models like that of Piaget do tend to imply that human development follows a similar path everywhere and at all times, neglecting the possibly divergent developmental challenges children face in different social and cultural contexts. Such models also imply that child development is a largely individual process of accommodation to an autonomous world, ignoring its largely collective and communal character. Children do not acquire knowledge and skills alone but with the help and cooperation of (and, often, in concert with) others. On the other hand, traditional models of childhood socialization have tended to treat children as passive products of social forces, whether through the social structuring of their personalities or control of their behavior. Yet, as anyone who has spent time with children knows, they do not simply react but also act. They actively attempt to make sense of their environments, to influence others, to adjust their actions to those of others, and to find both individual and collective solutions to the varied challenges that they face.

However, we maintain that many critics of traditional models of child development and socialization have overreacted to those approaches' shortcomings. Although childhood is in part a matter of social definition, and the lives of those called *children* quite variable, societies and social groups everywhere demand that the young acquire certain knowledge and skills before assuming the rights and responsibilities of adults. However varied their experiences, it seems likely that children everywhere face some similar challenges in gaining social recognition as full-fledged members of the social groups and society into which they are born. Children address those challenges with assistance from, and in collaboration with, others and thereby acquire personal knowledge, skills, and predispositions that they draw upon in future situations. Children do actively shape their own social environments, but they are also deeply influenced by them.

We contend that recent debates over the proper approach to the study of children and childhood have created a set of false dichotomies that detract from our understanding of children's social lives and socialization. The important question is not whether childhood is a natural stage of life or socially constructed and variable, but to what extent and how children's experiences are similar and different across time and cultures, and within particular societies. It is not whether human development is primarily an individual or communal process, but how children acquire knowledge and skills through interaction with their environment, including others, and use such knowledge and skills in dealing with novel situations. It is not whether children are socially determined or determining, but how and to what extent children, and children of varying ages, are influenced by and influence their social environments. These are complicated issues that cannot be resolved through scholarly debate. They are issues that require thorough and careful investigation with an always open mind, as at least some proponents of the new sociology or social studies of childhood recognize (e.g., Smart, Neale, and Wade 2001).

Moreover, many of those who study children and childhood were moving beyond the limitations of traditional developmental and socialization approaches before those approaches became popular targets of scholarly criticism. For example, the translation into English during the 1960s of the work of the late Russian psychologist Lev Vygotsky (1896–1934) led many developmental and child psychologists to question the implied universalism and individualism of Piaget's model of child development. Beginning in the late 1970s, some sociologists began to document how children acquire essential social skills through participation in cultural routines and in the collective creation of peer cultures. And, the last quarter of the twentieth century brought a revival of interest in the study of children and childhood from a symbolic interactionist perspective that stresses the centrality of communication, interpretation, negotiation, and self-direction to social life, including childhood socialization (Cahill 2003).

As early as the 1920s, Vygotsky challenged Piaget's and related models of child development. For example, Piaget had proposed that children's thought is initially "autistic," or idiosyncratic and fantastic, and then became largely "egocentric," or self-centered, as indicated by preschool-aged children's tendency to talk to themselves or engage in what Piaget called *egocentric speech*. However, in a series of ingenious experiments, Vygotsky (1986, 12–38) demonstrated that young children tend to talk to themselves more, to engage in more of what Piaget called egocentric speech, when confronted by a problem. According to Vygotsky, these findings suggest that children initially acquire speech to communicate with others and then subsequently use it to talk themselves through problems in much the same way that others had previously talked them through similar problems. Hence, Vygotsky concluded that what Piaget termed *egocentric speech* is more accurately described as self-directed and directing speech. Moreover, he argued that such self-directed speech does not simply disappear, as Piaget proposed, but becomes inner speech or thought. In general, as in this example, Vygotsky (1978, 57; emphasis in the original) proposed that

... every function in the child's cultural development appears twice: first, on the social level, and later, on the individual level; first, *between* people (*interpsychological*) and then *inside* the child (*intrapsychological*).

That is, the child actively appropriates cultural resources, such as language, from her or his interaction with others or ongoing participation in social life, and subsequently draws upon and creatively employs those resources to make sense of and deal with new situations and challenges.

Vygotsky argued that it was not so much the individual child's accommodation to an autonomous environment that propelled her or his development but the child's interactions with others. Vygotsky (1987, 208) faulted developmental psychologists of his time for limiting their attention to tasks that a child can solve independently or the establishment of what he called the child's actual level of development. He argued that it was equally important to investigate what he called the child's *zone of proximal development*, or what she or he could accomplish through imitation of, with direction from, or in collaboration with adults or older peers (Vygotsky 1987, 209). In Vygotsky's (1987, 211) words,

> What lies in the zone of proximal development at one stage is realized and moves to the level of actual development at a second. In other words, what the child is able to do in collaboration today he [or she] will be able to do independently tomorrow.

This is because, according to Vygotsky (1987, 210), "development based on collaboration and imitation is the source of all the specifically human characteristics of consciousness that develop in the child."

Inspired in part by Vygotsky, the sociologist William Corsaro began documenting the complex collaborative character of childhood socialization in the mid-1970s. Since that time, Corsaro and others have shown how "kids creatively take information from the adult world to produce their own unique childhood cultures" (Corsaro 2003, 4). According to Corsaro (1992, 169), children's interactions with adults expose them to varied aspects of adult culture. However, children do not simply internalize the information and understandings they acquire through interaction with adults but attempt to make sense of and creatively use such information and understandings in their interactions with peers. Through their production of and participation in childhood cultures, children gain practical social understandings and skills that are essential for adequate participation in the adult society and social groups into which they are born. According to Corsaro (1992, 162), "[W]ith the creation of an initial peer culture, other children become as important as adults in the socialization process." Hence, adequate understanding of childhood socialization requires "documentation and study" of children's peer cultures "in their own right" (Corsaro 1992, 168).

There was also, as mentioned above, a revival of interest during the last quarter of the twentieth century in the study of childhood and children from a symbolic interactionist perspective. This perspective had its roots a half century earlier in the ideas of George Herbert Mead (1863–1931), who, like Vygotsky, emphasized the social character of children's development. Mead recognized that children initially learn to participate in society through perceiving the actions and words of others but also recognized that children play an active part in their own socialization and are not passive recipients of others' action. Several scholars contributed ideas to the development of this approach (Clausen 1968). None of them developed a comprehensive and systematic statement of it, as Parsons and Skinner did for theirs, but they contributed ideas that were blended by later writers into a coherent approach. A student of Mead's, Herbert Blumer (1969, 1), further elaborated Mead's ideas and, in 1937, named this approach *symbolic interactionism*, the name by which it is known today.

Mead (1934) proposed that children acquire a "self" that is built partly out of the actions of others toward the child and partly from the child's own impulses in interactions with others. The child's actions arise from the self, the attitudes of others that the child takes toward herself or himself, but they do not simply conform to what has been absorbed from others because every action also involves an impulse. Mead thus insisted on the unusual and important point that actions and interactions result in novelty, something that was not there before. Mead did not elaborate on the concept of novelty so as to distinguish major from insignificant novelties, but introduced the principle that, while the actions of children (and adults) always take place within a framework of social conformity, they are not understandable as manifesting only conformity. They also manifest what we now commonly call *agency*. We will describe the ideas of Mead and other symbolic interactionist thinkers in more detail in Chapter 4.

Symbolic interactionism stresses the centrality of communication, interpretation, and the *self*, the individual's view of herself or himself, to human social life. This perspective refocused attention from broad characterizations of parents' and adults' treatment of children to detailed observation of interactions between adults and children and among children. For example, in the 1970s, the sociologist Norman Denzin (1977) illustrated how parents incorporate young children into a local "universe of discourse" or communication by responding to their children's gestures and vocalization as meaningful communications. Children thereby learn how to influence others through the communication and negotiation of shared meanings, basic social skills upon which subsequent interactions with a broader range of people gradually build. As the sociologist Nancy Mandell (1984; 1986) showed nearly a decade later, preschool-aged children carefully study one another's activities, make strategic moves to join those activities or invite others to join theirs, and cooperatively fit their separate activities together through negotiations of shared meaning. Studies such as these demonstrate that even as children learn and adapt to the ways of social groups, they are serious social actors who are both influenced by and influence those with whom they interact.

Some critics of the very notion of childhood socialization concede that the symbolic interactionist perspective provides a "softer version" of socialization than more traditional approaches, but argue that it still belittles children's agency and voice (James, Jenks, and Prout 1998, 25). We disagree. We contend that the general perspective of symbolic interactionism (see Chapter 4) is open and comprehensive enough to incorporate the insights of other approaches to the study of children and childhood without falling prey to their often one-sided emphases.

First, the symbolic interactionist perspective recognizes that childhood, like all meaningful social categories and objects, is a matter of social definition. Yet, it appreciates that there are limits to how children and childhood are and probably can be socially defined. Human infants and young children are not capable of survival on their own. They require care from those who are more physically capable and experienced than they are. Such dependency distinguishes children from adults in all human societies, even though the length and extent of that dependency may vary widely among societies. Similarly, all human infants must learn the ways of the society into which they are born in order adequately to participate in it. Although newborn infants are especially attentive and responsive to other humans (see Chapter 2), it seems fair to say that they know nothing of the ways of human society. They may well have the potentialities to acquire such knowledge but those potentialities can only be realized through interaction with others, through some form of primary socialization. The character and duration of childhood do vary widely across time and cultures, and even within particular societies, but that does not imply a *radical relativism*. A human society cannot define and treat its youngest members in just any way if it hopes to continue across generations. Rather, it must recognize that its youngest members require more extensive care, instruction, and practice than its older members typically do.

Second, children do influence those who live around them, but that does not diminish the influence that adults have over children. Parents are responsive to their infants' cries and coos and to older children's questions and protests, and teachers are responsive to their students' deference and defiance. In these and many other ways, children influence and, in an important sense, socialize adults. Yet, almost by definition, children are dependent on adults, which gives adults power over them. Children may attempt to circumvent and even defy adults' authority, but even then they do not ignore it. They must adjust their actions to adults' actions and anticipated actions. Socialization is an interactive process, one of mutual or reciprocal influence. Adults adjust their actions in response to the actions of children, and children adjust their actions in response to adults' actions. They thereby learn from one another how to engage in meaningful interaction with one another.

Third, children's interactions with peers and production of peer cultures are integral to their socialization. As we document in some detail later (see Chapter 7), peers are important agents of children's socialization. Adequate understanding of childhood socialization requires careful study of children's peer interactions and cultures "in their own right." Yet, children's peer interactions, concerns, and cultures cannot be fully understood apart from their interactions and relations with adults. As Corsaro (1992, 171) has noted, "[I]mportant features of peer culture arise and develop as a result of children's attempts to make sense of the adult world, and to a certain extent resist it." In many societies today, children continually move between peer and adult social worlds, carrying information and confusions from one to the other. It is unlikely that either children's current or future lives can be adequately understood apart from this continual cross-fertilization.

We believe that the general perspective of symbolic interactionism is broad enough to address these and the many other complexities of children's lives, and we draw upon it throughout this book. Although the concept of socialization does focus attention on the future consequences of children's current social lives, the perspective of symbolic interactionism suggests that it need not and often does not do so to the neglect of the variability of children's experience, their influence over adults, their complex peer interactions, or current concerns. On the contrary, it suggests that an adequate understanding of childhood socialization requires attention to the variability of childhood and children's experience. It demands careful attention to the reciprocal influence of adults on children and children on adults. It necessitates respectful study of children's interactions with one another and of their distinctive and rich peer cultures. And, it requires that we respectfully listen to children and take their perspectives and concerns seriously. A prominent sociologist of childhood, Barrie Thorne (1993, 3), once wrote that "children's interactions are not preparations for life" but "life itself." The perspective we adopt in this book implies that those interactions, like all social interactions, are *both* life itself and preparations for future life. Childhood is not simply a period of preparation for adulthood, and it deserves study and understanding in its own right. Yet, we should not stop there. We should also attempt to understand the likely future consequences of children's current lives both for them and for the society into which they born.

Methods of Studying Children

Understanding the complexities of children's lives and socialization is necessarily a complex pursuit. It requires answers to countless questions that must be addressed with appropriate empirical information or evidence. Research methods are ways of obtaining that information or evidence. Like other social scientists, those who study children and childhood socialization use different research methods such as experimentation, survey research, unstructured interviewing, and observation. They also employ different variations on these more general research strategies. No research method or technique yields complete and definitive information. Each is better or worse suited for addressing different kinds of questions, and each has its advantages and disadvantages. Periodically throughout this book, and especially in regard to the effects of media on children (see Chapter 8), we mention how the use of particular methods may influence the character and quality of resulting research information. Here we provide some necessary background. We briefly review research methods commonly used in the social sciences, some variations on those general research strategies, and the advantages and disadvantages of each, especially for studying children and their socialization.

The *experiment* is generally considered the prototype of rigorous scientific research. Ideally, the experimenter randomly assigns similar research subjects to at least two groups—a treatment or experimental group, and a control group. Attempting to control all other possibly influential factors, the experimenter then exposes the treatment group but not the control group to an experimental manipulation or treatment (often called the *independent variable*). After the experimental manipulation, the experimenter then compares the treatment and control group on the behavior, belief, or other factor of interest (often called the *dependent variable*). Any difference between the treatment and control groups in that factor of interest is considered the experimental effect. That is, such a finding suggests that the experimental treatment or independent variable caused the difference between the two groups on the factor of interest, or dependent variable.

For example, in a classic experiment that we discuss again later (Chapter 8), the social psychologist Albert Bandura and his associates (Bandura, Ross, and Ross 1961) were interested in whether children imitated or modeled aggressive behavior that they observed, such as on television. To address that question, Bandura and his associates showed one group of preschool-aged children (the treatment group) a short film of an adult hitting an inflated doll. Another group of children (the control group) was not shown the film. The children were subsequently put in a playroom with a number of toys, including an inflatable doll like the one the adult actor had repeatedly hit in the film. Observation revealed that the children in the treatment group who had watched the film not only hit and punched the inflatable doll more than the children in the control group who had not watched the film but also engaged in other forms of aggressive behavior more than the children in the control group. Based on these findings, Bandura and his associates concluded that children's observation of aggression, especially by an apparent role model like an adult, encourages them to engage in aggressive behavior themselves.

Yet, even the findings of a well-designed experiment such as this are subject to alternative interpretations (see Chapter 8) and dispute. As with all laboratory experiments, it is impossible to know whether the results obtained under such highly controlled and artificial conditions represent what usually occurs in everyday social life. This is commonly called the issue of *external validity*: Do the results have any validity external to, or outside of, the carefully controlled conditions of the experiment? Although the control provided by laboratory experimentation allows researchers to isolate the effect of particular factors or treatments, everyday social life commonly exposes children to varied influences simultaneously that may reinforce or counteract each other in complex ways. Moreover, there are reasons to suspect that children may act quite differently in strange situations, like experimental laboratories, than they do in more familiar surroundings like their homes, schools, and neighborhoods.

A variation on the experimental method designed to address the issue of external validity raised by the artificiality of laboratory experiments is the *field experiment*. As in laboratory experimentation, field experiments attempt to investigate the influence of a particular factor by manipulating it while controlling for other factors, but in more naturalistic surroundings. A classic example of a field experiment was the so-called Robbers' Cave study conducted by the social psychologist Muzafer Sherif (1956) and his associates in the 1950s to investigate intergroup dynamics. The researchers invited a number of 11- to 12-

year-old boys who were unaware that they were part of a study to a summer camp called Robbers' Cave. At first the boys engaged in the usual activities of a summer camp and freely made friends. Then, the boys were separated into teams that intentionally separated former friends. The teams were then pitted against each other in a tournament of competitive events with prizes for the winning team at the end of the competition. As a result of this manipulation, solidarity among team members and hostility between teams rose. Fights broke out between members of the different teams, including between former friends, and the researchers eventually had to intervene to prevent injury and property damage.

The Robbers' Cave study clearly illustrated that group competition encourages negative attitudes, aggression, and hostility toward members of "out-groups" as well as "in-group solidarity," but also illustrated some of the limitations of field experiments. First, it is nearly impossible to achieve the level of control in more "natural" settings like summer camps that is possible in the laboratory. For example, Sherif and his associates (1956) did not compare a treatment group that was exposed to an experimental manipulation with a control group that was not so exposed. Hence, there was no control over the possible effect of prolonged contact on in- and out-group relations. Moreover, as the Robbers' Cave study suggests, field experiments often require a far greater investment of researchers' time and effort, not to mention money, than laboratory experimentation. Last but certainly not least, field experiments often expose participants to more risks, such as psychological and physical injury in the case of the Robbers' Cave study, and raise more ethical concerns and questions than do more controllable laboratory situations. Today, governmental and university regulators would be unlikely to approve a field experiment like the Robbers' Cave study because of the potential dangers it posed to children, who are considered a protected population under current ethical guidelines and rules governing research with human subjects.

Perhaps the most revealing variation of experimentation is the *natural experiment* when events not explicitly designed for research occur that create a kind of experimental situation under naturally occurring circumstances. For example, as we discuss in detail later, the coming introduction of television to an isolated town that had not previously received television transmissions provided a group of Canadian researchers the opportunity for just such a natural experiment (Williams 1986). They located a nearby, comparable town that received only one television channel and another town that received multiple channels, which could serve as kinds of control or comparison groups. The researchers both questioned and observed children in all three towns both before the introduction of television to the community they dubbed Notel and then again three years later. Among other things, they found children in Notel engaged in more physical and verbal aggression after two years of exposure to television than they had before, while there was little increase in children's aggression in the other two towns during that same two-year period. They also found that views of gender-appropriate activities became more stereotypical among children in Notel after two years of exposure to television and more similar to those of children in the other two towns (see Chapter 11).

The advantages of a natural experiment such as this are clear. They allow researchers to investigate the influence of a particular factor, like exposure to television, on other factors, such as aggression and gender stereotypes, in everyday social life. Hence, the results are externally valid by definition. They also do not raise the ethical concerns and questions that field and some laboratory experiments do because researchers do not manipulate situations, potentially exposing people to risks that they normally would not face. On the other hand, that is why natural experiments are so rare. The occurrence of events that might create the conditions for a natural experiment is, for researchers, largely a matter of luck. Moreover, researchers need to learn of the anticipated events enough in advance to exploit them for research purposes. Although often particularly revealing, natural experiments depend on fortuitous and highly unusual circumstances. There would be little research if it was limited to such circumstances.

Survey research is a more common method for investigating relationships between various factors in everyday social life, such as between a particular parenting style and children's attitudes or behaviors. Surveys usually ask a large number of people individually to answer questions, usually of a "forced-choice" variety such as yes/no or multiple-choice questions, either during an interview or on a written questionnaire. The researchers typically assign different numerical values to the different responses to each question and then use a variety of statistical techniques to investigate possible relationships among the factors the questions are designed to measure or gauge. For example, the developmental psychologist Susan McHale and her associates (McHale, Crouter, and Tucker 1999) were interested in the relationship between family context and gender socialization. They asked 200 fathers with a child in the fourth or fifth grade and another child one to three years younger a series of questions designed to measure the fathers' gender role attitudes. About an equal number of the fathers had two daughters, two sons, an older daughter and younger son, or an older son and younger daughter. Among other questions, McHale and her associates asked the children of these fathers a series of questions about their interest and involvement in different activities often considered gender stereotypical, such as playing with dolls or playing with toy trucks. Statistical analyses indicated that children whose fathers had more traditional gender role attitudes and who had a differently sexed sibling were more likely to be interested and engage in gender-stereotypical activities than children with less traditional fathers, a same-sexed sibling, or both. These findings suggest that the interaction, or combination, of fathers' traditional gender attitudes and the example of a differently sexed sibling is more strongly associated with traditional gender interests among children than either alone.

One of the primary advantages of survey research is that its results are commonly more *generalizable* to populations beyond those directly studied than the results of other types of research, including experimentation. Surveys can be efficiently administered to relatively large numbers of people randomly chosen from a larger population. That makes it more likely that the study's participants are representative of the larger population than are the smaller and often less systematically selected participants in other kinds of research.

However, there are almost always questions about whether answers to survey questions accurately reflect the behaviors, attitudes, or state of affairs that they are intended to measure. First, what people say they do or might do is often different from what they actually do. Oftentimes, people simply do not recognize discrepancies between what they profess and what they do. Other times, participants in survey research may provide what they think are socially desirable answers rather than honestly report their own less socially desirable behaviors and attitudes. Finally, respondents to survey questions may misunderstand them or not interpret them in the way that the researcher intended, resulting in the researcher misinterpreting the meaning of the results.

The latter problem seems particularly likely in surveys of younger children with more limited language skills and less familiarity with this form of questioning than older children and adults. For example, research indicates that young children tend to answer forced-choice questions like those usually used in surveys even when they do not understand them, and are far more likely to answer nonsensical questions than are adults (Greene and Hill 2005, 9). Children also may not understand metaphorical expressions that adults consider self-evident, resulting in misinterpretation of their responses to questions containing such expressions. For example, the following question-and-answer sequence occurred during a study designed to investigate the relative strength of children's family relationships.

Q: How close are you to your grandfather?

A: Well, not very close really: I live in Dublin and he lives in Offaly. (Greene and Hill 2005, 10)

It is highly likely that if this child had not elaborated on his initial answer—"Well, not very close really"—the adult researcher who was questioning the boy would have concluded that he was not very emotionally close to his grandfather. However, the boy clearly interpreted the question as inquiring about his physical proximity to his grandfather.

Some researchers have used props such as dolls and pictures in an attempt to get more accurate information about children's understandings than direct questioning might yield. For example, the development psychologists Spencer Thompson and P. M. Bentler (1971) first asked preschool children how you tell a boy from a girl. Most answered that it depended on the genitals, saying things along the lines of "Boys have pee-pees and girls don't." However, when the researchers then asked these children to identify a set of anatomically correct dolls with different hair lengths as either boys or girls, the children generally identified the longer haired dolls as girls and the shorter haired dolls as boys regardless of the dolls' genitals. These results suggest that while these children knew the "correct" answer, it did not accurately reflect how they actually decided whether a doll, and perhaps a person, was a boy or girl. The use of props not only may help in obtaining more accurate information but also offers more complex information than direct verbal questioning might provide. For example, in a study of fourth graders' understandings of the prestige and relative income of different adult occupations, the sociologists Jeanne McGee and Jean Stockard (1991) used decks of cards with drawings of people engaged in different occupations, such as a doctor operating on a patient or a carpenter sawing a board. Rather than ask the children long series of questions about whether a particular occupation was more important than another or whether someone in that kind of job made more than someone in another, they asked the children to sort the cards into five different boxes depending on "how much you think people admire or respect people who work at that job" or "how much money you think a person makes for doing that job."

Many other researchers have simply assumed that children, especially younger ones, will not understand survey questions as intended and instead have relied on parents' or teachers' reports of children's behaviors, attitudes, and understandings. However, there are as many reasons to be skeptical of parents' and teachers' answers to survey questions about children's behaviors, attitudes, and understandings as there are to be skeptical of children's own answers. First, how children behave in the presence of their parents or teachers may be quite different from how they behave when not under the scrutiny of adults. They may also tell parents and teachers what they think they want to hear rather than what they actually feel or believe. Second, adults' reports of children's behaviors and attitudes are seldom based on systematic observation but, more often, are based on vague impressions. Moreover, those impressions may be products of selective attention. We all tend to typify people we know as passive or active, compliant or rebellious, and the like, and then are more attentive to behaviors and comments that tend to verify that typification than to those that do not. It is unlikely that parents and teachers are exceptions to this general tendency when reporting on children.

Some researchers survey children's own peers, usually classmates, for information about one another's behavior. This is particularly common in studies of children's aggressive behavior (e.g., Grotpeter and Crick 1996). These researchers reason that a child's classroom peers have more complete and accurate knowledge than teachers of whether he or she "starts fights," "tells friends they will stop liking them unless friends do what they say," "does nice things for others," and the like. Moreover, such "peer reports" allow researchers to assess the degree of agreement among classroom peers' responses to such questions. When those classroom peers' reports are similar, as they tend to be, there are stronger grounds for confidence in their accuracy than the reports of a single teacher or even two parents can provide. Yet, even with peer reports, researchers cannot be certain that survey respondents have interpreted the question as they intended.

Unstructured or *conversational interviews* are another method for obtaining information by questioning people but without many of the constraints of more highly structured survey questions. Researchers using this method commonly start with a set of topics that they want to talk about, but not with exactly worded, prewritten questions or sets of predetermined, forced-choice responses. Rather, the interviewer simply attempts to get the respondent to talk about the topic or topics of interest. This more flexible format allows the respondent to elaborate on her or his answer and allows the interviewer to clarify ambiguous responses, to correct possible misunderstandings, and to probe for more information. Hence, the information obtained from unstructured interviews is generally more complete, richer, and less subject to possible misinterpretation than respondents' answers to structured survey questions.

On the other hand, unstructured interviews, as with surveys, do little to address concerns about the accuracy of respondents' reports. Participants in open-ended interviews would seem as likely to give socially desirable answers, rather than honestly report their less desirable behavior or attitudes, as respondents to survey questions. Children would seem as likely to tell an adult what they thought that adult wanted to hear, and avoid revealing anything that they thought the adult might disapprove of, in an unstructured interview as in a more structured interview. A few researchers have tried to address these problems by having children rather than adults interview other children. For example, in a study of how free children were to move about their neighborhoods, the sociologist Sarane Spence Boocock (1981) had 10- to 12-year-old children conduct half the interviews with the studied children. She found that the interviewed children were more likely to report forbidden activities to the child interviewers than to the adult interviewers. Although it might first appear that the interviewed children were being more honest with the child interviewers than they were with the adult interviewers, they might just as well have been trying to impress the child interviewers by overreporting forbidden activities to them. In either case, children do seem to respond differently to interviewers of a similar age than they do to adult interviewers.

In recent years, it has become increasingly popular to interview groups of people together—so-called *focus groups*—rather than individually. Those who use focus groups claim that the support offered by the group encourages greater openness and counteracts the tendency for respondents to tell the interviewer what they think he or she wants to hear. Those who study children claim this is particularly true when groups of already acquainted peers are interviewed together. Children may well feel less intimidated by an adult interviewer in a supportive peer environment than when interviewed alone, especially if the interviewer acts more like a facilitator of group discussion than a questioner. On the other hand, the interpersonal dynamics of focus groups may have as many disadvantages as advantages. Higher status and more assertive members of the group may dominate the conversation and discourage other members from talking. And, children would seem at least as likely to say things to impress their peers, however honest or accurate, as they are to tell an adult interviewer what they think he or she wants to hear (Hennessy and Heary 2005).

Although unstructured interviews do not avoid all the potential disadvantages of survey research, they do provide more complete and richer information that is probably less subject to misinterpretation than structured, forced-choice survey questions. However, this advantage is purchased at a price. Unstructured interviews commonly take much longer, usually an hour or more, than it takes to conduct a structured survey interview or complete a questionnaire. Hence, it is seldom possible to study as many people with unstructured interviews as can be studied with the structured, forced-choice questions of survey research, and the fewer people involved in a study, the more questionable it is that the results can be generalized to a larger population. Moreover, it is far more difficult to justify assigning numerical values to the complex answers to unstructured interviews than it is to assign numerical values to the forced-choice responses to survey questions. Instead, researchers commonly go over the lengthy transcripts of interviews looking for common themes and contrasts. This raises serious questions about the *reliability* of the conclusions. That is, would other researchers looking at the same information reach the same conclusions? Researchers generally consider the results of survey research more reliable because different researchers analyzing numerical data with similar statistical techniques are likely to reach the same conclusions. It seems far more likely that different researchers would find different themes and contrasts in the lengthy transcripts of unstructured interviews and, therefore, reach somewhat different conclusions.

Of course, the most direct way to study people, including children, is to observe them in the course of their everyday social lives. Although researchers sometimes attempt to observe people unobtrusively, without those under observation knowing they are being observed, a more common research method is *participant observation*, or what is often called *ethnographic observation*. In this case, the researcher observes while participating to some extent in the activities of those being studied. This allows the researcher to become well acquainted with those being studied, to observe them under different circumstances, to question them about their activities, and to better understand the contexts of their activities. The participant observer generally writes short field notes to herself or himself while conducting observation and then uses those brief notes to write far more extensive and elaborate field notes later. Observation is sometimes supplemented by audio and video recording to provide more exact records of what is seen and heard than written field notes can provide (e.g., Corsaro 1985). Participant observation generally takes place over months so as truly to get "inside" the social life of those being studied.

A central issue in the conduct of participant observation research is just how much the researcher should participate in the activities of the group being studied and attempt to become a full-fledged member of the group (e.g., Adler and Adler 1987). On the one hand, the more actively engaged in the group and accepted as a member the researcher is, the more the researcher is likely to learn. On the other hand, the more actively the researcher participates, the more likely she or he will influence the activities of the group and, in a sense, contaminate the findings. Although this issue is often hotly debated among researchers who conduct participant observation, it is probably best decided in relation to the particular research project. The character of the group being studied and the characteristics of the researcher often determine just how much of an insider the researcher can and should become.

This is clearly the case when adult researchers conduct participant observation of children. Among other things, the sheer difference in physical size makes it unlikely that children will fully consider an adult researcher just another peer. This is an inherent problem in participant observation research of children because children are used to dealing with adults as authority figures who issue directives and reprimands and who generally intervene in their affairs. Hence, children are likely to alter their conduct when being observed by an adult, attempt to conceal activities and information of which they think an adult would disapprove, and ask the researcher to intervene on their behalf in their disputes and conflicts with one another.

Researchers who conduct participant observation of children have responded to this problem in a variety of ways. A few simply attempt to conduct research from their authoritative adult position, as when teachers conduct observational research of their own classroom and students (e.g., Gallas 1998). A few others take the opposite tack, such as the sociologist Nancy Mandell (1988), who, in her study of preschools, attempted to adopt what she called "the least adult role." Mandell claims that by refusing to direct or correct the children, waiting to be invited to engage in their activities, and then fully participating in them as a "learner," she was able to become a kind of honorary child. However, most researchers who conduct participant observation of children adopt a strategy somewhere between these two extremes. They accept that size difference and children's expectations about adults prevent them from ever being fully accepted as just "another kid" but attempt to reduce this problem by gradually convincing the children to accept them as a "big friend." They do so by not directing or correcting the children or reporting their forbidden activities to other adults, by accepting the children's directions when invited to engage in their activities, by listening to them without being judgmental, and by refusing to intervene in their disputes or activities, except when physical injury seems likely (see Fine and Sandstrom 1988). This is the strategy adopted by most of the participant observers of children whose research is discussed in this book.

Participant observation arguably yields the richest and most complete information of any research strategy, but it is limited to small groups of children. It is always a kind of case study, the results of which may not be generalizable to other groups of children. However, when participant observation research on different groups of children yields similar results, as it often does, confidence in the generalizability of the findings is increased. Perhaps a more serious disadvantage is that the extensive information that participant observation yields can be interpreted in a variety of ways. Like transcripts of unstructured interviews, it is difficult and probably ill-advised to attempt to convert the information recorded in extensive field notes to numerical values that can be statistically analyzed. Instead, researchers look for common themes and contrasts, yielding what is often termed *qualitative* (as opposed to *quantitative*) analyses of the findings. Again as with unstructured interview studies, this raises concerns about reliability or whether other researchers would reach the same conclusions based on the same information. Researchers attempt to allay this concern by reporting numerous excerpts from unstructured interview transcripts or their field notes so that others can assess the researcher's interpretations against their own, but this does not allow others to assess the selection of such illustrative examples.

As the above brief discussion of research methods indicates, no research method yields definitive information. Each method has its own particular advantages and disadvantages. No single study, regardless of its method, yields definitive information but tentative and incomplete findings. Social scientific knowledge, including about children and childhood socialization, consequently advances step by step, study by study, as findings are compared, conclusions revised, and new research conducted to answer questions raised by earlier research. This gradual advancement of understanding is not promoted by arguing over which research method is best but through the use of different methods and attempts to integrate the different kinds of information each yields into a more complete picture. The advantages of one research method can often help compensate for the disadvantages of another. For example, survey research on a large number of people can provide information about broad patterns, while a participant observational case study can provide insights into the concrete social processes that produce those patterns. This is but one example of how information obtained through different research methods can complement each other and provide greater understanding than either could provide alone. Better understanding of children's complex and diverse social lives and socialization requires different kinds of information. Different research methods provide such different kinds of information that, when combined and integrated, advance such understanding.

* * *

Throughout this chapter, we have stressed the diversity and complexity of children's social lives and socialization. We maintained that understanding them requires a theoretical perspective that is comprehensive enough to capture their diversity and complexity and open enough to incorporate the insights of other theoretical perspectives. We proposed that symbolic interactionism provides such a comprehensive and flexible perspective and draw upon it throughout this book. We also review the findings of studies using a variety of different research methods, in recognition that each research method yields important, although always tentative and limited, information. Our goal is to provide as comprehensive a view of children's social lives and socialization as possible. We do so by incorporating the insights of varied theoretical perspectives into our general symbolic interactionist approach and by drawing upon findings from varied kinds of studies.

References

Adler, Patricia, and Peter Adler. 1987. *Membership Roles in Field Research.* Newbury Park, CA: Sage.

Bandura, Albert, Dorothea Ross, and Shelia Ross. 1961. "Transmission of Aggression Through Imitation of Aggressive Models." *Journal of Abnormal and Social Psychology* 63: 575–582.

Blumer, Herbert. 1969. *Symbolic Interactionism*. Englewood Cliffs, NJ: Prentice Hall.

Boocock, Sarane Spence. 1981. "The Life Space of Children." In Susanne Kellner (ed.) *Building for Women*, 93–116. Lexington, MA: Lexington Books.

Cahill, Spencer. 2003. "Chapter 35. Childhood." In Larry Reynolds and Nancy Herman (eds.), *Handbook of Symbolic Interactionism*, 857–874. Walnut Creek, CA: Alta Mira.

Chudacoff, Howard. 1989. *How Old Are You? Age Consciousness in American Culture*. Princeton, NJ: Princeton University Press.

Clausen, John. 1968. "A Historical and Comparative View of Socialization Theory and Research." In John Clausen (ed.) *Socialization and Society*, 18–72. Boston: Little, Brown.

Corsaro, William. 1985. *Friendship and Peer Culture in the Early Years*. Norwood, NJ: Ablex.

———. 1992. "Interpretive Reproduction in Children's Peer Cultures." *Social Psychology Quarterly* 55: 160–177.

———. 2003. *We're Friends Right? Inside Kids' Culture*. Washington, DC: Joseph Henry Press.

Damon, William. 1977. *The Social World of the Child*. San Francisco: Jossey-Bass.

Denzin, Norman. 1977. *Childhood Socialization*. San Francisco: Jossey-Bass.

Fine, Gary Alan, and Kent Sandstrom. 1988. *Knowing Children: Participant Observation with Minors*. Newbury Park, CA: Sage.

Gallas, Karen. 1998. *Sometimes I Can Be Anything: Power, Gender, and Identity in a Primary Classroom*. New York: Teachers College Press.

Gould, Stephen Jay. 1977. *Ontogeny and Phylogeny*. Cambridge, MA: Harvard University Press.

Greene, Sheila, and Malcolm Hill. 2005. "Researching Children's Experience: Methods and Methodological Issues." In Sheila Greene and Diane Hogan (eds.), *Researching Children's Experience: Approaches and Methods*, 236–252. London: Sage.

Grotpeter, Jennifer, and Nicki Crick. 1996. "Relational Aggression, Overt Aggression, and Friendship." *Child Development* 67: 2328–2338.

Hennessy, Ellis, and Caroline Heary. 2005. "Exploring Children's Views Through Focus Groups." In Sheila Greene and Diane Hogan (eds), *Researching Children's Experience: Approaches and Methods*, 236–252. London: Sage.

Inkeles, Alex. 1968. "Society, Social Structure, and Child Socialization." In John Clausen (ed.) *Socialization and Society*, 73–129. Boston: Little, Brown.

James, Allison, Chris Jenks, and Alan Prout. 1998. *Theorizing Childhood*. New York: Teachers College Press.

Kohlberg, Lawrence. 1984. *The Psychology of Moral Development*. San Francisco: Harper & Row.

Lesko, Nancy. 2001. *Act Your Age! A Cultural Construction of Adolescence*. New York: Routledge Falmer.

Maccoby, Eleanor. 1968. "The Development of Moral Values and Behavior in Childhood." In John Clausen (ed.) *Socialization and Society*, 227–269. Boston: Little, Brown.

Mackay, Robert. 1974. "Conceptions of Children and Models of Socialization." In Roy Turner (ed.) *Ethnomethodology*, 180–191. Baltimore, MD: Penguin.

Mandell, Nancy. 1984. "Children's Negotiation of Meaning." *Symbolic Interaction* 7: 191–211.

———. 1986. "Peer Interaction in Day Care Settings: Implications for Social Cognition." In Patricia Adler and Peter Adler (eds.) *Sociological Studies of Child Development: Volume 1*, 55–79. Greenwich, CT: JAI Press.

———. 1988. "The Least Adult Role in Studying Children." *Journal of Contemporary Ethnography* 16: 433–467.

McGee, Jeanne, and Jean Stockard. 1991. "From a Child's View: Children's Occupational Knowledge and Perceptions of Occupational Characteristics." In Spencer Cahill (ed.) *Sociological Perspectives in Child Development: Volume 4*, 113–136. Greenwich, CT: JAI Press.

McHale, Susan, Ann Crouter, and Corinna Tucker. 1999. "Family Context and Gender Role Socialization in Middle Childhood." *Child Development* 70: 990–1004.

Mead, George Herbert. 1934. *Mind, Self, and Society*. Chicago: University of Chicago Press.

Parsons, Talcott. 1951. *The Social System*. Glencoe, IL: Free Press.

Parsons, Talcott, and Robert Bales. 1955. *Family, Socialization and Interaction Process*. Glencoe, IL: Free Press.

Piaget, Jean. 1959. *The Language and Thought of the Child*. London: Routledge and Kegan Paul.

———. 1969. "Genetic Epistemology." *Columbia Forum* 12: 4–11.

———. 1973. *The Child and Reality: Problems of Genetic Psychology*. New York: Viking Press.

Prout, Alan, and Allison James. 1997. "A New Paradigm for the Sociology of Childhood? Provenance, Promise, and Problems." In Allison James and Alan Prout (eds.), *Constructing and Reconstructing Childhood*, 7–33. London: Falmer Press.

Pufall, Peter, and Richard Unsworth. 2004. "Introduction: The Imperative and the Process of Rethinking Childhood." In Peter Pufall and Richard Unsworth (eds.), *Rethinking Childhood*, 1–21. New Brunswick, NJ: Rutgers University Press.

Qvortrup, Jens. 1994. "Childhood Matters: An Introduction." In J. Qvortrup, M. Bardy, G. Sgritta, and H. Wintersberger (eds.), *Childhood Matters: Social Theory, Practice, and Politics*, 1–23. Brookfield, VT: Avebury.

Sherif, Muzafer. 1956. "Experiments in Group Conflict." *Scientific American* 195(5): 54–58.

Skinner, B. F. 1974. *About Behaviorism*. New York: Random House.

Smart, Carol, Bren Neale, and Amanda Wade. 2001. *The Changing Experience of Childhood: Families and Divorce*. Cambridge: Polity Press.

Thompson, Spencer and P. M. Bentler. 1971. "The Priority of Cues in Sex Discrimination by Children and Adults." *Developmental Psychology* 5: 181–185.

Thorne, Barrie. 1993. *Gender Play*. New Brunswick, NJ: Rutgers University Press.

Vygotsky, Lev. 1978. *Mind in Society*. Cambridge, MA: Harvard University Press.

———. 1986. *Language and Thought*. Cambridge, MA: MIT Press.

———. 1987. *The Collected Works of L. S. Vygotsky: Volume 1, Problems of General Psychology*, edited by Robert Rieber and Aaron Carton. New York: Plenum.

Williams, Tannis MacBeth (ed.). 1986. *The Impact of Television: A Natural Experiment in Three Communities*. Orlando, FL: Academic Press. ✦

Chapter 2

Foundations of Socialization

While a building can have only one foundation, childhood socialization is based on two foundations: (1) the biological nature of the human organism, and (2) the organization of the ongoing society into which the child is born. Human beings are biological creatures, and they are social creatures. *Indeed, their biological nature requires that they can survive as recognizably human beings only if they become social creatures.* A newborn baby cannot survive unless it is nurtured and cared for by someone more physically capable and socially experienced. That caregiver participates in society to obtain food, clothing, and shelter, as well as other forms of social support. The baby's *dependency* on others for survival, and then for growing and developing, is both a biological condition and a social condition. Through being cared for or nurtured, the baby will be transformed as an organism into a biological child and then a biological adult through a process of *biological maturation*. Over the same time, the newborn baby will be transformed from a socially ignorant creature into a socially competent participant in his or her society through a process of *socialization*. Biological maturation and socialization proceed concurrently.

For centuries, there has been an ongoing debate concerning the relative importance of the biological nature of the human organism compared to the importance of experience and socialization in shaping the abilities and personality of the human adult. This long-running debate is referred to by the shorthand phrase "nature versus nurture," as though one or the other were the sole determinant. As knowledge has increased in both biology and the social sciences, there is growing recognition that (1) most human characteristics result from complex interactions of biological nature and socialization, and (2) many characteristics once attributed exclusively to biological nature are clearly influenced by social experience. Individual human beings are born with potential talents. Those talents can never be discovered or developed unless the society into which the child is born is organized in such a way as to recognize those talents. Women scientists have won Nobel Prizes. None came from societies that believe girls don't need much education. Babe Ruth became a baseball legend when he became the first player to hit 60 home runs in one season, but what would have become of his talent if he had been born into a society that doesn't play baseball? A talent is a potential; it can become actualized only through participation in a society that recognizes such a talent.

Commonplace activities as well as those that require uncommon talents similarly involve the interplay of biological maturation and socially available opportunities for action. A 3-year-old child cannot acquire the capability to drive an automobile. In today's world, that is due entirely to the child's biological immaturity. But before automobiles were invented, biological adults never acquired the capability to drive automobiles because none existed. Inventing, producing, and distributing automobiles are socially organized activities. The biological capability for driving a car became a meaningful reality only after these socially organized activities came into existence.

In this chapter, we sketch some of the basic aspects of the biological nature of the human organism that make socialization both necessary and possible. We also provide here a brief introduction to concepts commonly used to describe and understand the organization of the ongoing society into which children are born. Later chapters will relate these concepts to particular aspects of socialization. They are discussed here as necessary preparation for understanding what follows. First, however, we briefly review some cases of socially isolated or so-called wild or feral children. Such children have attracted much attention. Many scholars hoped that these children would reveal what is "natural" about what we consider human nature and what is a product of socialization. Yet, as our review suggests, documented cases of socially isolated children and their attempted socialization after discovery raise as many questions as they answer.

Isolated Children

We take it for granted that a child is born into a family (or foster care) and an ongoing society that cares for it. Without continuing care in the early years, a human infant cannot survive, and, in contemporary societies, we believe that children need adult care well into their teenage years. As far back as the late Middle Ages, however, reports have appeared from time to time of young children who had been isolated from society and who, in one fashion or another, lived in a "wild" state. In some cases, supposedly, they had been reared by or at least lived in the company of such animals as wolves, wild dogs, and monkeys (Newton 2002). One study compiled a list of 53 cases of isolated children, beginning with "the Hesse wolf-child," discovered in Germany in 1344, through the "Teheran ape-child," discovered in Iran in 1961 (Malson 1972, 80–82). Occasional reports of newly discovered isolated or "wild" children continue to surface (Newton 2002).

One of the best documented and most celebrated of these cases is that of the *sauvage d'Aveyron*, or "wild boy of Aveyron." The boy was first seen in south-central France in 1797, "a naked child, running free in the woods" (Newton 2002, 98). Locals soon captured him, but he escaped, was captured by hunters 15 months later, and escaped yet again. Then, in early 1800, he sought shelter in a house in the region of Aveyron, where he was recaptured (Newton 2002, 99). He was passed from one local governmental authority and hospital to another before being sent to Paris for "medical inspection" and housed in the National Institute for Deaf-Mutes (Newton 2002, 100–101).

The "wild" boy was judged to be about 11 or 12 years old when he was taken to Paris. He had numerous scars on his body but was apparently free of any serious physical deformity. Of particular significance was the fact that he was, according to one of the reports of the time, "entirely without the gift of speech and makes himself heard only by cries and inarticulate sounds" (Lane 1976, 37), although later evidence indicated that his hearing was not impaired. A committee of experts, including Philippe Pinel, who is sometimes referred to as the first psychiatrist and is renowned for removing the chains from inmates of insane asylums, delivered an extensive report to the Society of Observers of Man, a leading scholarly association of the time, in which they concluded that the boy was mentally retarded and ineducable. Pinel thought that the boy "was not an idiot because he was abandoned in the woods; he was abandoned in the woods because he was an idiot . . . recognized by heartless parents for what he was" (Lane 1976, 56).

However, 25-year-old Jean-Marc-Gaspard Itard, a disciple of Pinel's who was appointed resident physician at the Institute for Deaf-Mutes soon after the "wild boy's" arrival in Paris, strongly disagreed (Newton 2002, 103). He set out to train or civilize the boy, whom he later named Victor. Itard ([1801] 1962, 10–11) hoped to achieve five "principle aims" in "the mental and moral education of the Wild Boy of Aveyron": (1) "To interest him in social life"; (2) "To awaken his nervous sensibility by the most energetic stimulation, and occasionally by intense emotion"; (3) "To extend the range of his ideas by giving him new needs and increasing his social contacts"; (4) "To lead him to use speech"; and (5) "To make him exercise the simplest mental operations" and apply "these mental processes to objects of instruction."

Itard, who is considered the founder of what is known today as special education, reported his painstaking instructional efforts and Victor's progress in a short book first published in 1801 (Newton 2002, 112) and later, in 1806, in a report requested by the French Ministry of Interior that provided funds for Victor's care and education. There was much progress to report. Victor soon learned to dress himself and get up in the night "to satisfy his needs" so as not to pass "the night in a cold wet bed" (Itard [1801] 1962, 16). He learned to sit at a table, wait for food to be served, and eat with utensils. He came to express recognizable human emotions, at times embracing Itard and, even more often, Madame Guérin, the housekeeper who took Victor on daily walks to local parks and often provided a warm counterpoint to Itard's stern manner. Gradually, Victor also learned to communicate with others through what Itard ([1801] 1962, 36) called "a pantomime language." For example, when the time for his walk came, he would bring Madame Guérin her coat and hat, and when she wanted Victor to fetch water she would hold the empty pitcher upside down and Victor would take it from her and fill it at the well (Itard [1801] 1962, 36). Eventually, Victor also learned to read and write simple sentences.

Yet, to Itard's great disappointment, Victor never learned to speak. After six years of tireless efforts that "brought about no change," Itard ([1806] 1962, 86) resigned himself "to the necessity of giving up any attempt to produce speech, and abandoned [his] pupil to incurable dumbness." Itard subsequently spent less and less time with Victor. In 1810, Victor and Madame Guérin moved out of Itard's quarters at the Institute and into a small house nearby, where Victor lived until his death in 1828, when he was around 40 years old (Newton 2002, 127).

Diverse experts have proposed various reasons why Victor never learned to speak. Perhaps Pinel was right that Victor was mentally retarded, although his many accomplishments would seem to suggest otherwise. When Victor was first captured, he did have "a very extended scar" on his throat (Itard [1801] 1962, 29), suggesting that his vocal organs might have been injured. Yet, Itard ([1801] 1962, 29–30) concluded from the "linear appearance" of the scar that the wound "had only been a superficial one" and had not damaged the vocal organs. It is also possible that Victor developed a serious psychological disturbance either before or because of his abandonment that resulted in his continuing muteness. Others have criticized Itard for what they consider his overly rigid and sometimes traumatic instructional methods that may have contributed to Victor's failure to acquire speech (e.g., Goode 1994, 176–181; Shattuck 1980, 165–170). Itard provided Victor few opportunities to learn for himself and sometimes used intimidation to get Victor to attend to his lessons. For example, having learned that Victor feared heights, on one occasion when Victor refused to continue his lessons, Itard ([1801] 1962, 44) grabbed him "forcibly by the haunches" and "held him out" a fourth-story window for "some seconds."

Yet others agree with Itard that Victor's failure to speak was a result of his extended social isolation. For example, after a thorough review of relevant documents, the psychologist Harlan Lane (1976, 182) concluded that Victor's "prolonged isolation deprived him of the crucial skill . . . of imitation," which both Lane and Itard (Itard [1801] 1962, 30) considered essential to the acquisition of speech. Others would argue that Victor's inability to speak is evidence that there is a biologically determined "critical" or "sensitive period" for learning spoken language. As we will discuss in more detail later in this chapter, they maintain that a child who is not exposed to spoken language during this "critical" phase of biological maturation will never learn to speak or to speak proficiently thereafter (e.g., Lenneberg 1967).

In more recent times, the best documented cases of socially isolated children are those of Anna, Isabelle, and Genie. Because Anna was considered "illegitimate," an expression seldom used today but a source of great shame until recently, she was confined to one room from infancy, with only minimal human contact. Her mother did bring her milk but otherwise paid little attention to her. When Anna was found, at the age of six, she was malnourished, immobile, expressionless, and seemingly indifferent (Davis 1940). She was believed to be deaf and dumb. She lived for another five years, first in a country home and later in a foster home and school for retarded children. According to the final report from the school, Anna had learned to follow directions, identify a few colors, walk, and repeat words (Davis 1947) but remained developmentally far behind other children her age. Whether that lack of development was due primarily to mental deficiency, the deprivations of her early life, or some combination of the two remains an open question. What is beyond question is that, by contemporary standards, this was a case of extreme child neglect, if not abuse.

Isabelle's circumstances were relatively more favorable than Anna's. She, too, was a so-called illegitimate child who was kept in seclusion. However, her deaf-mute mother was shut off in a dark room with her, and the two apparently communicated with gestures. When Isabelle was discovered, also at the age of six, "her behavior toward strangers, especially men, was almost that of a wild animal" (Davis 1947, 435). She did not speak but made only a strange croaking sound. In contrast to Anna, Isabelle received a "systematic and skillful program of training" (Davis 1947, 435), and, after a slow beginning, "she went through the usual stages of learning characteristic of ages one to six . . . far more rapidly than usual" (Davis 1947, 435). By the time Isabelle was eight and a half years old, she had reached a "normal" educational level for children of her age and was described as a "very bright, cheerful, energetic little girl" (Davis 1947, 436). That Isabelle attained this level of socialization suggests that she had the intellectual potential to do so but that its realization required intensive and focused social interaction. It is also notable that Isabelle, in contrast to Anna, did have close human contact with her mother during her early years.

The most recent well-documented case of a socially isolated child is that of Genie, a 13-year-old girl discovered in 1970 near Los Angeles, California (Curtiss 1977; Pines 1981). From the age of 20 months, Genie lived in nearly total isolation. She was kept in a room in the rear of her family's small house, tied to a potty seat, naked and restrained by a harness that her father had made, and only able to move her hands and feet. "At night, if her parents remembered (they didn't always remember)," she was put into a sort of straitjacket and placed in "a crib caged in wire mesh" (Newton 2002, 209). Her father forbade her mother and brother from speaking to her, and he only growled, snarled, or barked like a dog at her (Newton 2002, 209). If Genie made any noise, her father beat her with a piece of wood that he kept in her room especially for that purpose. Hence, Genie was not simply isolated or neglected but also severely abused.

Finally, in 1970, Genie's mother fled the family home with her daughter. A few months later Genie's mother sought assistance at a local welfare office, and a worker there noticed the "strange" girl with her and started asking questions. Based on what she learned, child welfare officials immediately removed Genie from her mother's care. Both Genie's father and mother were charged with willful abuse of a minor, but on the day her father's trial was to begin, he committed suicide and the charges against her mother were subsequently dropped (Newton 2002, 213).

Genie was placed in the care of a team of physicians, psychiatrists, psychologists, and linguists at Children's Hospital of Los Angeles. Inspired in part by a recently released film about "The Wild Boy of Aveyron" (Truffaut 1970), they launched a complex program of therapy and research on Genie (Newton 2002, 216–217). Under their care, Genie's progress was slow. During her first seven months at the hospital, she did learn to walk with a jerky motion and become more or less toilet trained. Yet, she still had many disconcerting habits, especially salivating, continually spitting, and incessantly masturbating (Newton 2002, 215).

A major focus of the research on Genie was on her language development. In spite of special attention by therapists, her speech development was painfully slow. After some months, she began to string two words together, but, unlike the language development of normal children, this was not followed by a rapid and explosive development of speech. Four years later, Genie understood little grammar, and her speech was like a garbled telegram. Those who studied Genie argued that her lack of language development was evidence that there was a "critical" or "sensitive" period for language learning. They concluded that her limited understanding of grammatical principles—for example, not distinguishing among pronouns or verb tenses—was probably permanent. We will never know whether that would have been the case with continued training. In 1975, when Genie turned 18, guardianship reverted to her mother, who was unable to cope with her. Genie passed from one foster home to another, while contending factions fought court battles over her custody. Her therapy ceased, and what progress she had made was largely undone by her experiences in foster care. At last report in 2002, Genie was living in a private adult care home (Newton 2002, 227).

For years, scholars hoped that isolated children would enable them to observe the separate influence of nature and nurture on human development. Those hopes have gone largely unfulfilled. Isabelle's case clearly suggests that social interaction is necessary to unlock humans' potentials. Yet, it is impossible to know if the lack of success of Victor, Anna, and Genie in mastering spoken language was, among other things, due to inherited deficiencies, early malnutrition or other physical insult, abuse, social isolation, inadequacies in their subsequent training, or some combination of these varied factors. Nonetheless, these cases and research that we discuss in the next section of this chapter do suggest the following: (1) the acquisition of language, of recognizable human emotions, and of social understanding—the defining characteristics of what we consider human nature—require suitable interaction between very young children and more socialized humans; (2) when such interaction is missing in the early years, a child is damaged in developing her or his human potential; and (3) later efforts to compensate for such damage require intensive and extensive effort, and success is uncertain. In short, human nature requires nurture for its realization. Then again, nurture depends on a supporting natural foundation.

The Human Organism

Socialization into any society or human group must build upon a biological foundation. For example, adequate socialization requires that individuals have the biological capacity to acquire human language since much of the information necessary for adequate participation in a society is transmitted from one generation to the next through language. Adequate socialization may also depend on an innate or natural responsiveness to human stimulation. Newborns who ignore or cry in response to the touch, smiles, and speech of their human caregivers, as may be the case with many babies who are later diagnosed with "infantile autism" (Greenspan 1997, 14–15), may never make the kind of human connections necessary to learn the ways of a society. Most fundamentally, adequate socialization depends on a biological capacity for much learning. An organism that simply enacts instinctive behavior could never acquire the remarkable amount of information and considerable skills necessary for participation in a human society. That requires an organism that is highly responsive to environmental influence—one that is biologically quite flexible, or "plastic."

Until recently, social scientists could only point to the wide variability among human societies as evidence of the biological plasticity of the human organism. However, recent discoveries of neurological research provide more direct evidence of humans' remarkable degree of *neural plasticity* (Huttenlocher 2002). These research findings suggest that the biological development, structure, and functioning of the human brain are "largely environmentally regulated" (Huttenlocher 2002, 189).

The development of the brain does occur within what many neurologists call "a particular genetic envelope" (Johnson 1997, 182). For example, all of the neurons or nerve cells that will make up the human brain have been produced, and most moved or migrated into what will be their permanent location in the brain, halfway through gestation or fetal development. However, "the real business of brain development is in synapse formation," or *synaptogenesis* (Eliot 1999, 26). A synapse is a junction that links one neuron to another. Once neurons are in their permanent location, they sprout branches called *dendrites* and a kind of trunk called an *axon*. Every place where a dendrite comes close to an axon, there is a potential for synapse formation. If stimulated, the axon releases a "chemical messenger," or neurotransmitter, that may then "bind" to a receptor chemical of a nearby dendrite of another neuron, forming a synapse (Eliot 1999, 23). This is the means through which neurons "communicate" or transfer information, leading to the coordinated functioning of systems of neurons (Barnet and Barnet 1998, 17). The development of such functioning neural systems apparently underlies the acquisition and retention of varied skills and abilities. In humans some synapses are formed before birth, but over 80 percent of the growth of dendrites and consequent formation of synapses occurs after birth when neurons are subject to the influence of sensory stimulation or experience (Eliot 1999, 27). Genes may lay the foundation for the functioning human brain, but experience largely determines what is built upon that foundation.

Most of the regulation of human intellect, emotions, as well as sensory and motor processes in humans takes place in the cerebral cortex, or outer layer, of the brain. Yet, at birth, there are few synaptic connections in that "rumpled gray mantle that covers the brain" (Barnet and Barnet 1998, 17). Most synaptic connections there form during the first year of life, when the size of the brain rapidly expands to near adult size (Huttenlocher 2002, 41), and an estimated 1.8 million new synapses form each second (Eliot 1999, 27). However, these synapses are not "hard-wired." Those that are routinely stimulated and activated are stabilized or strengthened, while less active ones are weakened (Eliot 1999, 30). Hence, the initial burst of synaptic formation over the first one or two years of life is followed by "a much longer period of elimination or pruning of . . . synaptic connections."

It is generally believed that this early "overproduction" and subsequent pruning of synaptic connections account for humans' remarkable neural plasticity and capacity to learn. For example, the brains of human infants and young children have a remarkable capacity for functional self-repair. In an infant or young child with localized brain damage from stroke or injury, the undamaged parts of the cerebral cortex commonly "take over" functions normally carried out by the damaged region (Huttenlocher 2002, 2). For example, language processing is normally localized in certain regions of the left side, or hemisphere, of the brain. However, language processing is often taken over by the right hemisphere if those regions of the left hemisphere are damaged or removed for medical reasons at a young age (Huttnelocher 2002, 136). Hence, individuals with such early brain damage can become as proficient in language use as those whose brains are fully intact, although there are limits to such neural plasticity. Extensive brain injury or damage can result in the crowding of neurological functions into smaller than normal areas of the brain, resulting in impairment of those functions and the associated abilities. Yet, the human brain has a remarkable capacity to "rewire" itself, especially early in life, and commonly does so in response to environmental inputs, especially those from the social environment.

Varied research suggests that human infants seem biologically "primed" to attend to other people. For example, research shows that within two to four months of birth, infants tend to look significantly more at a schematic drawing of a human face than at either an empty circle or a circle containing scrambled facial features (Johnson 1997, 99–117). Two-month-old infants also "show signs of becoming attuned to the eyes as a privileged communicative feature" (Rochart 2001, 138), and by six months of age they smile significantly more at an adult who looks directly at them compared to one who slightly averts her or his gaze (Hains and Muir 1996). Similarly, infants seem inherently responsive to human facial expressions of emotions. For example, in one study, newborns were observed while facing an experimenter who displayed, in succession, exaggerated expressions of happiness, sadness, and surprise. The newborns tended to widen their lips in response to the display of happiness, protrude their lower lips during the expression of sadness, and increase the opening of their eyes and mouth when the experimenter looked surprised (Feld et al. 1982). Such seemingly innate responsiveness to human stimulation arguably invites human interaction and thereby helps initiate the complex interplay of biological processes and social experience involved in human socialization.

Unfortunately, not all human newborns seem biologically primed to encourage social interaction and, thereby, their own socialization. For example, research suggests that some newborns who are later diagnosed with infantile autism tend to find novel forms of stimulation, including human stimulation, aversive that other newborns find pleasurable. That may be why autistic children tend to withdraw into so-called stereotypic forms of self-stimulation such as repeatedly rocking back and forth, flipping a light switch, or persistently rubbing a piece of carpet. However, the developmental psychologist Stanley Greenspan (1997, 159) and his colleagues have dramatically illustrated that autistic children's apparent aversion to human stimulation need not be an insurmountable barrier to adequate socialization. In their therapy with autistic children, Greenspan and his colleagues treat these children's stereotypic behavior not merely as symptoms but as opening wedges for human connection and, later, socialization. For example, they instructed the mother of a 2-year-old girl who repeatedly rubbed a favorite piece of carpet to lie down on the floor and place her hand next to her daughter's. The girl pushed her mother's hand away, but each time she did so, her mother gently returned it. After three days, the girl began to smile at her mother when pushing her hand away, and, from that small beginning, their play and interactions became progressively richer until, before long, the girl began to speak to her mother. At age 7, the girl had "a range of age-appropriate emotions, warm friendships and . . . score[d] in the low superior IQ range" (Greenspan 1997, 17). According to Greenspan (1997, 159), the crux to adequate socialization in such cases is finding the "environmental keys" that will unlock biological doors.

There are undoubtedly biological conditions that make socialization virtually impossible, but, because of human neural plasticity, they may be far fewer than previously thought. For example, a condition like congenital deafness could prove a major barrier to socialization if we relied on verbal sounds and language to communicate with deaf children. Yet, nonverbal languages such as American Sign Language can easily overcome such a biological barrier to human interaction, communication, and, thereby, socialization. Such languages are environmental keys that unlock biological doors to adequate socialization. They can unlock those doors because of the remarkable neural plasticity of the human brain. For example, among humans who are born deaf, the processing of visual information "appears to expand into" regions of the brain usually used for "auditory functions" (Huttenlocher 2002, 101).

Like hearing children, children who are born or "congenitally" deaf seem biologically "primed" to acquire language. The most compelling evidence for humans' biological propensity for language is that children learn whatever language to which they are exposed, spoken or signed, without specific instruction and in a remarkably regular way.

> A baby goes from speaking no words at birth, to 50 to 100 words and two-word phrases at eighteen moths or thereabouts, to nearly 600 words by age two and a half, to intricate and wordy constructions by three or four. A first-grader can understand 13,000 words and expertly deploys tenses, embedded clauses, compounds, and combinations using rules only a grammarian could explicate. (Barnet and Barnet 1998, 36)

Yet, the door to this remarkable human potential for language acquisition does not open automatically. It requires the environmental key of exposure to human language, and that exposure is always to a particular language or, in some cases, languages.

Although human infants apparently have the capacity to learn any human language, they end up proficiently speaking and understanding only the language or languages to which they are exposed relatively early in life. Research suggests that newborns can recognize differences between all the possible phonemes, or distinctive vocal units of speech, of all human languages. Yet, by the time they are around a year old, they have lost that ability and recognize only those sound combinations and contrasts that occur in the language to which they have been exposed, or what is commonly called their "native language." For example, research indicates that Japanese babies can distinguish between the sounds *ra* and *la*, but, a year later, they have lost this ability, apparently because these sounds are equivalent in Japanese (Barnet and Barnet 1998, 47).

Research findings such as these suggest that there may well be a critical or "sensitive" period for language learning, as previously discussed. That is, humans' capacity to acquire a language and speak it proficiently may decline with age. Grammatical aspects of language and proficient pronunciation may be most "sensitive" to the timing of language acquisition. For example, 90 percent of deaf children in the United States are born to hearing parents and differ greatly in the age at which they are first exposed to American Sign Language. As such, they provide important insights into the possible effects of learning a first language at varying ages (National Research Council and Institute of Medicine 2000, 134). Much of the research on language acquisition in deaf children has focused on their use of grammar because it seems especially sensitive to early experience. Among fluent users of American Sign Language, "subtle differences in hand-shape, as well as the spatial location and movement of individual signs," denote similar logical relations as word endings and order, articles, prepositions, and pronouns in spoken languages (Eliot 1999, 361). However, research indicates that only "native signers," or children who are exposed to sign language within the first two or three years of life, make full use of these grammatical capabilities of American Sign Language. Those who learn American Sign Language when they are between 4 and 6 perform well but not as fluently as "native" signers, and those who do not learn American Sign Language until after they are 12 consistently sign in ungrammatical ways even after using it for 30 years or more (Eliot 1999, 362).

Studies of second language learning reveal similar patterns. The earlier in life individuals acquire a second language, the more likely they are to speak it proficiently and accent free. For example, one study asked Chinese and Korean immigrants to the United States to listen to a few hundred English sentences, about half of which were ungrammatical, and indicate whether the sentences sounded "correct." "Only those who had immigrated by the age of seven performed as well as native English speakers, which is to say almost flawlessly." Among the rest, performance steadily declined in relation to the age at which they had immigrated and learned English (Eliot 1999, 362–363; National Research Council and Institute of Medicine 2000, 134–135). Other research indicates that the ability to speak a second language accent free is also related to the age at which that second language is acquired. For similar languages, like English and German, this window of opportunity for accent-free speech may extend into early adolescence, but for dissimilar languages, like English and Korean, it may close much earlier (Huttenlocher 2002, 149).

Research on the timing of language acquisition and subsequent fluency in its use suggests a more general lesson about the interplay of nature and nurture in human socialization: There may be temporal or chronological constraints on the experientially shaped "circuitry" of the human brain. The countless synaptic connections and potential connections in young children's brains enable the formation of varied neural circuits and, hence, the learning of varied skills and information. Yet, the formation of neural circuits in response to environmental stimulation tends to localize different neural functions into specific areas of the brain, and the associated loss or pruning of synaptic connections that are not stimulated limits the subsequent plasticity of the brain. As the brain's neural circuitry becomes more organized and specialized, it becomes more inflexible. Consequently, skills and abilities that might be easily acquired at an earlier age may be quite difficult or even impossible to acquire at a later age.

However, if there are critical or "sensitive" periods for acquiring different skills and capabilities, it would be misleading to consider them solely a matter of biological maturation. Whatever children experience, synaptic connections are being activated, strengthened, and stabilized while others are being weakened. The consequent neural circuitry of their brains is organized and specialized to process the kind of environmental stimulation to which they have been exposed. That circuitry may be ill suited to process other kinds of environmental stimulation and may interfere with the acquisition of new and different skills and abilities. For example, areas of the brain that normally process language may become devoted to other neural functions in children who are not exposed to human language earlier in their lives. If so, then their ability to process and proficiently use human language has not so much been lost as replaced by some other, experientially regulated neurological capability. Even the limits of our neural plasticity and capacity to learn are arguably products of the continual interplay of nature and nurture in our lives.

Moreover, the retention of acquired skills and capabilities also depends on this intricate dance between biology and experience in human life. Synaptic transmissions are facilitated by frequent activation, resulting in increased speed and accuracy in the performance of associated skills and abilities, while lack of activation can lead to the loss of neural pathways and the associated skills and abilities. For example, young children who learn to use a second language proficiently will rapidly lose that ability if they are not continually exposed to and use it. Experience not only shapes the neural circuitry of the human brain, but also sustains it. The biology of the brain organizes our experience, but experience just as profoundly organizes the biology—the functioning neurological circuitry—of our brains.

This complex interplay of nature and nurture is likely implicated in humans' acquisition of not only socially shared characteristics, such as a particular language, but personal ones as well. For example, research indicates that infants tend to react with more or less inhibition when encountering novel situations such as a strange human or a mechanical toy that moves toward them (see Kagan 1994). These early differences in "temperament" are apparently inborn and may well be genetically determined. They also tend to be long lasting. Relatively fearful infants tend to become timid children and shy adults, and relatively fearless infants tend to become bold children and outgoing adults. Yet, it is doubtful that the persistence of such traits is simply a matter of genetic inheritance.

As previously noted, socialization is an interactive process of mutual influence. Infants' behaviors influence how parents and other caregivers respond to them, and those responses, in turn, influence infants. For example, parents are likely to expose babies to novel stimulation who seem to delight in it and to avoid irritating babies who find such stimulation upsetting. They consequently and quite inadvertently may perpetuate and even deepen infants' inherent boldness or timidity. On the other hand, research conducted by the child psychologist Jerome Kagan (1994) indicates that about a third of inhibited babies outgrow their timidity by kindergarten. He speculates that they do so because their parents made a conscious effort to "engineer emboldening experiences" by expressing interest in unfamiliar objects and new experiences and by encouraging their child to do the same. Genes undoubtedly influence what human infants are and what they may become, but what humans most fundamentally are is biologically plastic or flexible.

Human biology, especially the neural plasticity of the human brain, provides the necessary foundation for human socialization. In turn, socialization shapes the very biological functioning of the human organism. In that sense, humans have not a single but a dual nature. We are born with a biological nature that enables and even requires the acquisition of a second nature through nurture. The ongoing society into which humans are born largely determines what that second nature will be.

An Ongoing Society

Children are born into a world that already exists. They are "raw recruits" into an ongoing society. They have no wish to be there and no knowledge of how to get along in it. From the point of view of society, the function of socialization is to transmit to new members the culture of the society and the motivation to participate in established social relationships. The society has a patterned consistency, so that one can predict, *within limits*, how people will behave, think, and feel.

A society can be defined as a group of people who occupy a specified territory and regard themselves as a recognizable group. In the modern world, most societies are organized as nation-states, which means that each has a government that is the only organization that can legally use violent force. Many models have been proposed for analyzing ongoing societies. Some stress the continuity and adaptability of established institutions, while others focus on fundamental conflict between groups within a society; some stress evolutionary change, and others the necessity of stages and revolutions; some stress political and economic spheres, and others the social, cultural, and religious. Rather than considering particular models to understand our society, each with its unique set of concepts, it seems more useful for our purpose to introduce certain general—and widely accepted—social concepts, each of which provides a useful vantage point for thinking about how a society is organized and operates.

We begin with the concepts of *norms* and *values*. A norm is an implicit rule defining the appropriate and expected pattern of behavior in a recurring situation. Being clothed is the norm when presenting oneself in a public place. This example indicates that a norm is both a standard by which behavior is judged and also a prediction of what behavior is likely to occur. People are supposed to be clothed in public, and one may predict that in any public place, the people one encounters will probably be clothed. Such convergence of the two meanings of *expected* (what should happen and what is predicted to happen) is never fully realized. In the late 1960s and early 1970s, for a time, there was a fad called *streaking*: Naked men (and occasionally women) would run rapidly through a crowd in a public place. Their point was to surprise people by violating the norm. More mundanely, students are expected to study throughout the term—that is, they should do so. But it is also expected that some will do no more than cram before an examination—that is, one may predict that this is how they will study. The two meanings of expectation are not always carefully distinguished, and for many purposes it is sufficient to make the rough assumption that what should be done is what generally is done. We organize much of our lives on the basis of social expectations—what we expect of others, and what we believe others expect of us. Many social problems, however, arise from divergence of what happens from what is supposed to happen, and it is then necessary to distinguish between ideal norms and behavioral norms.

Values are more general than norms. They are best thought of as conceptions of the desirable that serve as criteria for norms. A society in which freedom, for example, is a salient value will *tend* to develop norms consistent with that value in its economic practices, its educational methods, the relations between the sexes, the ways it rears its children, and other areas of life. This is not to say that all the norms in these situations are entirely consistent with freedom, for they are not. Other values tend to generate norms inconsistent with those of freedom, so that the norms governing any situation are not simple derivatives from a single value. Further, values are not perfectly compatible. In the United States, for example, equality of opportunity is also a value. Because it is a value, some people believe that it is an actuality, but abundant research, some of which we cite later in this book, shows that it is not. It is not possible to increase equality of opportunity for those who are disadvantaged without limiting in some way, usually financially, the freedom of the more advantaged. If, for example, a government seeks to provide medical care for people who cannot afford to pay for it, the government must tax people who have money, thus limiting their freedom to use all of their money as they wish. The tension between freedom and equality is a continuing issue in American society. This issue is often a focus of political debate and political competition for elective office. It affects children directly, for example, in the matter of school funding. Some schools get more tax money than others, and the children in the better funded schools usually have better qualified teachers and richer educational opportunities.

A second pair of related concepts is that of *status* and *role*. A status is a position in a particular organization or in the society as a whole. *Mother* and *daughter* are two statuses in a family organization. *Teacher* and *pupil* are statuses in an elementary school. *Branch manager* is a status in a business organization. *Registered voter* is a status in the political system. *Illegal immigrant* is another status in the political system. One can also speak of statuses in society as a whole. A billionaire and a celebrity both have high status (also called *prestige*) in the society as a whole, while people who clean office buildings at night have low status. A role is the expected behavior of someone who has a given status. One needs to recognize that there are layers of expectation. For example, there are general ideas of what is expected of mothers and daughters or of teachers and pupils, but these are *interpreted* and *defined* specifically in each family or in each classroom. Role expectations for the status of billionaire or celebrity are amorphous. Billionaires are appreciated if they donate generously to charities, and celebrities are appreciated if they don't try to hide from the public, but these are not well-defined role requirements. Each person has many statuses. A mother can be a branch manager and a registered voter and hold many other statuses as well.

Another basic concept for understanding society is *institutions*, each of which focuses on a segment of life and consists of relatively stable patterns of norms, values, and statuses. One such institution is the school, whose primary function is to transmit a large share of the intellectual heritage of the society, beginning with the skills of reading, writing, and doing arithmetic. Within the school there is the value of learning and norms relating to attendance, courses, sports events, and holiday celebrations; and there are patterned status relationships among the teachers, pupils, principal, and cleaning staff. There are economic institutions such as banks, insurance companies, and stock markets. There are medical institutions such as hospitals and clinics. There are religious institutions such as churches, synagogues, and mosques. There are political institutions, including executive offices, legislatures, and, indeed, elections that put people in those offices. Despite a regular turnover in personnel, these institutions continue to operate over a period of many years, in great part because each new generation is socialized into the appropriate patterns.

Yet another fundamental aspect of society is *social stratification*, or *social class*. *Social stratification* refers to the fact that people in a society are ranked according to how much of a socially desired benefit they possess. Some are on top, some are on the bottom, and some are in between. Three categories of benefit are those most often ranked: (1) economic benefits, specifically, *income, wealth*, and *occupation*; (2) social benefit, known as *prestige* or *social honor*; and (3) political benefit, known as *power*. A person's rank in any of these categories is often regarded as an individual accomplishment, but it is important to note that individual accomplishments occur in a framework of institutions and must be socially recognized and accepted. A person who gains great wealth illegally and is caught, convicted, and punished often forfeits that wealth. Each of these bases of ranking people is both somewhat independent of the others and somewhat influenced by the others. That is, a person can have great prestige without being very wealthy, and vice versa. Similarly, power, the ability to influence the actions of others, does not necessarily go hand in hand with great prestige or high income. Having said this, it is also necessary to say that these three types of benefit are somewhat associated. This is expressed in statistical language by saying they are *correlated*, but they are *not perfectly correlated*. (A familiar example of correlation is the association between height and weight. Taller people tend to be heavier than shorter people, but height and weight are not perfectly correlated, as there are some tall people who weigh less than some shorter people.)

People who have a similar amount of wealth, income, prestige, and power are said to be a *social class*. They recognize each other as approximate equals, and as somewhat different from those who have either more or less of these social benefits. Although members of a social class necessarily have some dealings with members of other social classes in work situations, in their private social lives they are likely to associate primarily with members of their own social class. A dentist and a dental assistant work together in the office, but after work they are likely to go their separate ways. They do not recognize each other as social equals, even though they are equal in legal terms; their differences in education, income, and prestige are too great. Such differences in rank are pervasive, and people generally segregate themselves in their private social lives according to their understanding of their social rank. The president of a bank and the teller at the window who serves customers paying bills or making deposits are at different levels in the organization, a difference that carries over into private social life.

Because people tend to choose their friends and intimates from among their social equals, they tend to create what can be considered *class subcultures*. These are contexts in which children are socialized, and we shall discuss them in Chapter 9. Here we want to identify the social classes. There are various ways of dividing up the classes, as well as various terms to label them. There has been a long tradition of identifying six social classes in the United States, and we present here one recent version that would find wide acceptance and that we believe is useful for our purposes (Gilbert 2003, 16–37). This set of classes is presented graphically in Figure 2-1. Each class is identified as a percentage of the total population, with some typical occupations of members of the class, and a typical income for members of the class.

At the top of the class structure is what Dennis Gilbert and Joseph Kahl call the capitalist class; it is also known as the upper class. This class includes about 1 percent of the population. It is made up of people who have inherited vast amounts of money or who are top executives of major companies. An income of $2 million or more a year is not uncommon in this group. Below them is the upper-middle class, consisting of people who work as upper-level managers, as professionals, or as owners of medium-sized businesses. Almost all are likely not only to be college graduates but to have advanced graduate degrees as well. They are said to be about 14 percent of the population. A typical income is given as $120,000 a year, although some earn two or three times that much. Next in rank is the middle class, comprising 30 percent of the American population. Occupations include lower managers, semi-professionals, and nonretail sales personnel among white-collar occupations, and craftsmen and foremen in blue-collar occupations. A typical income is $55,000 per year. Another 30 percent of the population is in the working class. Typical occupations include low-skilled manual workers, clerical workers, and retail salespersons, with a typical income of $35,000. The working poor, 13 percent of the population, work at the lowest-paid manual jobs and retail and service work, for a typical income of $22,000. At the bottom of the ranking is the underclass, 12 percent of the population, whose members are chronically unemployed, work part-time in menial jobs, or receive public assistance for an income of about

Figure 2.1   Gilbert-Kahl Model of the Class Structure

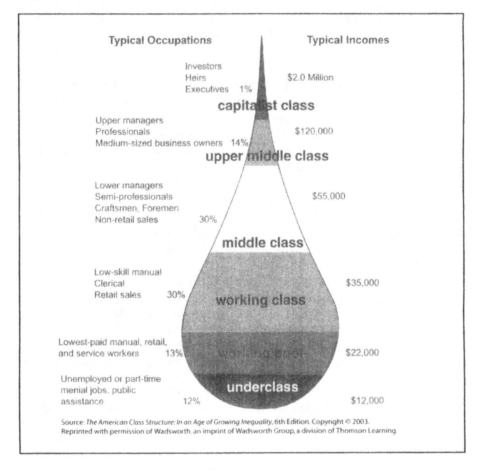

Source: *The American Class Structure: In an Age of Growing Inequality*, 6th Edition. Copyright © 2003. Reprinted with permission of Wadsworth, an imprint of Wadsworth Group, a division of Thomson Learning.

$12,000.

Children are socialized into their social class of origin, which establishes their initial level of what sociologist Max Weber called their *life chances*. However, the American class system (and some others) allows for *social mobility*, the chance to rise or fall in the social class ranking. For technical reasons, social mobility is usually studied in terms of general occupational levels. Best current evidence shows that the largest number of men at a particular occupational level are at the same level as their fathers, but substantial numbers end up at either a higher or lower level. For example, 60 percent of the sons of professionals, managers, and officials ended up at the same level, but 14 percent of them ended up as service workers, machine operators, and laborers. In contrast, 37 percent of the sons of workers, operators, and laborers ended up at the same level, but 27 percent of them ended up as professionals and managers

(Gilbert 2003, 143, Table 6-1). Results for daughters are similar (Gilbert 2003, 144–145). The social class into which a child is born sets an initial level of life chances for that child, but the class system does allow for some social mobility. Even so, it is evident that the son or daughter of a professional or manager has a better chance of ending up at that level than the son or daughter of a worker or laborer.

A capitalist is someone who has capital, that is, wealth that can be invested in companies that manufacture products or provide services that generate more wealth. Ownership of capital also leads to power, because it is a resource that gives its owner the ability to influence others. As the common expression puts it, "Money talks." The concept of capital has, however, been expanded beyond this original financial idea, without abandoning the original meaning. While there are several expansions, the most relevant for this book is the concept of *cultural capital*, introduced by sociologist Pierre Bourdieu (1984). Each social class has its own culture or subculture that characterizes the adults and children of that class. In the words of a scholar who has examined all of Bourdieu's extensive writings, "Bourdieu's concept of cultural capital covers a wide variety of resources, such as verbal facility, general cultural awareness, aesthetic preferences, scientific knowledge, and educational credentials. His point is to suggest that culture (in the broadest sense of the term) can become a power resource" (Swartz 1997, 43). In a slightly different formulation that overlaps Bourdieu's, sociologist Ann Swidler refers to the resources that distinguish one group from another as "culturally-shaped skills, habits, and styles" (Swidler 1986, 275; quoted in Farkas 1996, 12). Class differences in skills, habits, and styles affect the way children are socialized, as we shall discuss in Chapter 9.

American society, like many societies, is made up of different *ethnic groups*. An ethnic group is a group of people who originally came from the same foreign geographic area and brought with them a language, distinctive customs, and historical memories. The term today is used to identify groups whose origins are seen as distinctive from those of the dominant group. Leaving aside the native North American aboriginals, the 13 original American colonies were settled predominantly by people from England (whose distant ancestors were Celts as well as Germanic tribes, Anglos and Saxons). They became the dominant group in establishing the United States, and social commentators came to refer to them as White Anglo-Saxon Protestants, or WASPs. Their initial dominance persists in many ways—the national language is English, and the U.S. Constitution and the design of the political system are primarily their handiwork. However, while still strong, WASP dominance became diluted after World War II ended in 1945 and other ethnic groups became more socially accepted and less subject to discrimination. Immigration of people of other ethnic groups began during the colonial period and has continued ever since. In San Antonio, Texas, there is a museum, the Institute of Texan Cultures, presenting exhibits about the 22 ethnic groups that contributed to establishing the State of Texas. Although most early immigrants came from European countries, recent immigration has become much more diverse and includes, among others, Bangladeshis, Cubans, Dominicans, Ethiopians, Haitians, South Asian

Indians, Nigerians, Pakistanis, Vietnamese, and many others. At the City College of New York, where more than half of the students are foreign-born, students' native languages number about 60. The *Harvard Encyclopedia of American Ethnic Groups* (Thernstrom 1980) lists 106 ethnic groups. We shall provide some illustrative material to show how ethnic group membership affects the socialization of children, but, obviously, we shall not be able to discuss more than a few. In Canada, leaving aside the native aboriginal and Inuit population, the original settlers were French and English, and correspondingly both are official languages. Also, as in the United States, ethnicity has become much more diverse since 1945, with multiculturalism being official Canadian government policy.

North American society includes, as do numerous others, *racial minorities*. A racial minority consists of people who believe they have and are believed by others to have a distinctive biological lineage. They are considered a minority not necessarily because they make up a numerical minority of the population but because they have less power and influence than the dominant racial group. In the United States, a person who has at least one known forebear from Africa is considered African American, or black. People whose forebears came from Asia are often considered to be members of an Asian racial minority, although there is great physical and cultural diversity among people from different Asian countries, and people from these diverse countries do not consider themselves as belonging to a single racial group. People from Spanish-speaking countries have been grouped together by the U.S. Census in a category called *Hispanics* that is sometimes treated as a racial minority, sometimes as one ethnic group.

Biologists have found the concept of race to be so inaccurate in describing the results of biological inheritance that the concept is biologically meaningless. Nevertheless, many nonbiologists tend to believe that races are real subdivisions of humanity. The late anthropologist Robert Redfield took account of this belief and in his teaching used to refer to "the socially supposed races." People sometimes act on this belief and engage in discriminatory behavior against people in these minority groups, action that comes under the heading of *racism*. To the extent that institutions function in ways that discriminate against racial minorities, they practice *institutional racism*. As we shall see later in the book, racism is a factor in the socialization of children from racial minorities.

All of the basic dimensions of society that we have discussed are influenced in one way or another by *gender*, a term that refers to a society's beliefs about and practices concerning maleness and femaleness. In most societies, the care of young children is thought to be—and is—primarily the responsibility of women. Until about 40 years ago, mothers of young children in the United States were expected to—and most did—stay out of the labor market and at home to take care of their children. This meant that their status in society—their prestige—derived largely from their husband's status. Currently, mothers of young children work outside the home and can attain a status and prestige in their own right. Not many fathers ever were or are now full-time, stay-at-home fathers, although there is greater social acceptance today of those who do than there was 40 years ago. Although about half the American population is female, only 11 of the 100 U.S. senators are, at this writing, female. But this number is higher than ever before and indicates women's increasing, though far from equal, political power. Interestingly, in three states (California, Maine, and Washington), both senators are women, indicating that voters in those states do not seem concerned about "gender balance." These brief examples suggest some of the ways in which gender is interwoven with family, work, social status, and political power. Thus, gender does not refer to maleness and femaleness but to societies' values, norms, and practices about what is expected and what is possible for persons of each sex. Persons are born with a sex, but not with a gender. They are socialized to gender, and the outcomes of that socialization may either reinforce or challenge prevailing values, norms, and practices. In Chapter 11 we discuss gender socialization.

Societies are not static. While they have traditions, and they have institutions that continue to operate over years or decades, there is also an ongoing process of *social change*. Sometimes it is the result of social movements. A *social movement* is a concerted and organized effort by a group of people to change some aspect of society. In the 1960s and 1970s, the civil rights movement worked to eliminate institutional racism and gain legal and social equality for African Americans. In those same years, the women's movement worked to eliminate gender discrimination and gain equality for women in a society dominated by men. The gay liberation movement seeks legal equality for people whose sexual orientation is homosexual. To the extent that such social movements are successful, they affect the socialization of children. In addition to social movements, new technology changes society. The inventions of television and computers have affected society in many ways. Values and norms change for many reasons. One of the significant shifts is the change in values concerning families. Whereas once Americans strongly believed that marriages should remain intact no matter how strained, there is now widespread acceptance of divorce as a solution to marital strain. The women's movement, which sought equality for women in the workplace, made it easier for women to be self-supporting after divorce.

Children are born into a world that is organized in complex ways and continuously changing, sometimes dramatically. In order to function within it, whether primarily as conformist, as rebel, or in some way in between, they must have at least a minimum of knowledge about this world and a minimum of what the culture defines as appropriate behavior and feelings. They must know what to expect from people of given statuses, how they themselves fit in with the various groupings, what is considered proper and improper in various situations, and the range of alternative behaviors possible in those segments of social life that are rapidly changing. This is the world that the socializers, knowingly or unknowingly, pass on to the newcomers.

* * *

Childhood socialization is an intricate process, involving a variety of factors. It involves an intricate dance between biology and experience. Biological factors influence how newborns and children respond to others and how others respond to them. On the other hand, their social experience shapes the very biological processes that then organize their experience. Their social experience is subject to varied influences. Children are exposed to different norms and values and are recruited into different statuses and roles in an expanding range of institutions as they age. The social class, ethnic and racial groups, and sex into which children are born shape their social experiences and the cultural capital that they acquire through socialization. Childhood socialization may build on a largely shared biological human nature, but, because of the very plasticity of that biological nature, it results in varied second natures. Childhood socialization varies greatly within human societies, especially contemporary ones, and also across different ones. In the next chapter, we focus on the historical and cross-cultural variability of childhood socialization.

References

Barnet, Ann, and Richard Barnet. 1998. *The Youngest Minds*. New York: Simon & Schuster.

Bourdieu, Pierre. 1984. *Distinction: A Social Critique of the Judgment of Taste*, translated by Richard Nice. Cambridge, MA: Harvard University Press.

Curtiss, Susan. 1977. *Genie: A Psycholinguistic Study of a Modern-Day "Wild Child."* New York: Academic Press.

Davis, Kingsley. 1940. "Extreme Social Isolation of a Child." *American Journal of Sociology* 45: 554–565.

——. 1947. "Final Note on a Case of Extreme Isolation." *American Journal of Sociology* 52: 432–437.

Eliot, Lise. 1999. *What's Going on in There: How the Brain and Mind Develop in the First Five Years of Life*. New York: Bantam Books.

Farkas, George. 1996. *Human Capital or Cultural Capital?* Hawthorne, NY: Aldine de Gruyter.

Feld, T. M., R. Woodson, R. Greenberg, and D. Cohen. 1982. "Discrimination and Imitation of Facial Expression by Neonates." *Science* 218: 149–181.

Gilbert, Dennis. 2003. *The American Class Structure*, 6th ed. Belmont, CA: Wadsworth.

Goode, David. 1994. *A World Without Words*. Philadelphia: Temple University Press.

Greenspan, Stanley. 1997. *The Growth of the Mind*. Reading, MA: Addison-Wesley.

Hains, S. M., and D. W. Muir. 1996. "Infant Sensitivity to Adult Eye Direction." *Child Development* 67: 1940–1951.

Huttenlocher, Peter. 2002. *Neural Plasticity: The Effects of Environment on the Development of the Cerebral Cortex*. Cambridge, MA: Harvard University Press.

Itard, Jean-Marc-Gaspard. [1801] 1962. "First Development of the Young Savage of Aveyron." In George and Muriel Humphrey (trans.) *The Wild Boy of Aveyron,*, 3–51. Englewood Cliffs, NJ: Prentice Hall.

——. [1806] 1962. "A Report Made to His Excellency the Minister of the Interior." In George and Muriel Humphrey (trans.) *The Wild Boy of Aveyron,*, 52–101. Englewood Cliffs, NJ: Prentice-Hall.

Johnson, Mark. 1997. *Developmental Cognitive Neuroscience*. Cambridge, MA: Blackwell.

Kagan, Jerome. 1994. *Galen's Prophecy: Temperament in Human Nature*. New York: Basic Books.

Lane, Harlan. 1976. *The Wild Boy of Aveyron*. Cambridge, MA: Harvard University Press.

Lenneberg, E. 1967. *Biological Foundations of Language*. New York: John Wiley.

Malson, Lucien. 1972. *Wolf Children and the Problem of Human Nature*. New York: Monthly Review Press.

National Research Council and Institute of Medicine. 2000. *From Neurons to Neighborhoods: The Science of Early Childhood Development*, edited by Jack Shonkoff and Deborah Phillips. Washington, DC: National Academy Press.

Newton, Michael. 2002. *Savage Girls and Wild Boys: A History of Feral Children*. New York: St. Martin's.

Pines, Maya. 1981. "Civilizing of Genie." *Psychology Today* 51 (September): 28–34.

Rochart, Philippe. 2001. *The Infant's World*. Cambridge, MA: Harvard University Press.

Shattuck, Roger. 1980. *The Forbidden Experiment: The Story of the Wild Boy of Aveyron*. New York: Farrar, Straus & Giroux.

Swartz, David. 1997. *Culture and Power. The Sociology of Pierre Bourdieu*. Chicago: University of Chicago Press.

Swidler, Ann. 1986. "Culture in Action: Symbols and Strategies." *American Sociological Review* 51: 273–286.

Thernstrom, Stephan (ed.) 1980. *Harvard Encyclopedia of American Ethnic Groups*. Cambridge, MA: Harvard University Press.

Truffaut, Francois. 1970. *The Wild Child*. Paris: *Les Films Du Carrosse*. ✦

Chapter 3

Cultural and Historical Constructions of Childhood

Socialization is essential to human development. We develop as we learn the ways of a given society or social group. The language that we speak and how we speak it, the ways we think and feel, and even what pleases and repulses us are largely products of our socialization. Yet, what we learn and when and how we learn it depend on the society into which we are born. Socialization and, therefore, human development are as varied as human societies and their respective cultures are and have been. Although social scientists define the concept of *culture* in a variety of ways, it most generally refers to the way of life developed by a people in adaptation to the environmental and social conditions that they collectively face. Culture consists of conventional understandings that guide peoples' interpretations, actions, and interactions. The process of socialization transmits those understandings from one generation to the next, while at the same time those understandings shape the process of socialization. Moreover, cultures are not static but change as people adapt to changing circumstances. As culture changes, so does the process of socialization. This chapter examines different ways that culture shapes people's conceptions and treatment of children, and historical changes in cultural conceptions of children and in their socialization in Western societies. It thereby documents the remarkable plasticity of human nature and its varied social development.

Socialization in Cross-Cultural Perspective

As noted in the introduction, all societies divide the human life course into stages. They define and treat individuals in those different stages of life differently. Although this is now often called *age grading*, contemporary Western societies place far more emphasis on chronological age than many other societies did and do. People in many past and present societies had and have only a vague notion of their age. Those people often attached or attach some importance to the order in which children are born but ignore birthdays. In many past and present societies, physical size and capability rather than chronological age determine transitions from one stage of life to another. For example, in eighteenth-century North America, a "great boy" of 14 was expected to assume the work of a man, and a sexually mature girl was considered ready for marriage whether she was 14 or 18 (Kett 1977, 13).

Not only are the boundaries of socially defined developmental stages cross-culturally and historically variable but so too are their character and timing. For example, we treat walking as an important developmental milestone that distinguishes dependent "infants" from increasingly independent "toddlers." In contrast, Taria villagers of Okinawa carry infants on their backs for the first two to three years of life so as to prevent them from walking and being underfoot (Broude 1995, 348). To the Taria, allowing children under 2 or 3 independent mobility is uncaring because it invites injury. On the other hand, parents in some societies grant children considerable independence at what many of us would consider too tender an age. Among the Chewong people of the Malay rain forest, for example, children begin the transition from childhood to what the Chewong consider adolescence around 7 years of age. At that age, Chewong children "gradually shift away from parents in order to join a peer group consisting of older children of the same sex. . . . When the transition is fully accomplished, the youngsters spend most of their time together with the peer group sleeping with them in a special corner of the [communal] house." At that point, they are no longer called children but maidens and bachelors (Howell 1988, 160).

Such cross-cultural variation in the character and timing of developmental stages reflects very different expectations—very different norms—about what people of different ages can and should do, learn, and know. For example, Mayan children in Central America start working when they are about 3 years of age and gradually assume more and more responsibility for hauling water, caring for younger children, preparing food, and planting, weeding, and harvesting corn (Small 2001, 25). Many of us in more industrialized societies may consider such heavy labor developmentally inappropriate for young children, but Mayan adults believe it is a natural part of and necessary to children's development. Although we believe that young children should be free from work, we burden them with extensive training and formal instruction that we consider necessary to their development. In many other societies, adults give children virtually no instruction and may even discourage them from asking questions or seeking explanations. They believe children's "natural" curiosity and desire for mastery will lead them to closely watch and mimic adults, learning through trial and error and practice (Lancy 1996; Nicolaisen 1988, 205; Small 2001, 128).

Such variation in the definition, treatment, and training of children reminds us that human development is at least as much a social as a biological or natural process. Socialization varies in relation to the knowledge and skills required to function in a given society or social group. The extensive instruction we give our own children in reading, writing, and mathematics may prepare them for life in our own society but leaves them ill prepared to survive in a primarily agricultural society like the Mayan. Cultural beliefs about the nature of individuals and their maturation also shape how different human societies define and treat their young. Some think of children as balls of clay that must be carefully shaped, while others consider them unripe fruit that naturally ripen (Nicolaisen 1988, 202). Societies that believe children must be carefully shaped, like our own, tend to prolong children's dependency upon adults, while those that believe they naturally ripen tend to grant children more autonomy earlier in life and, in many cases, more responsibilities.

Consideration of cross-cultural and historical variations in conceptions of children and in their socialization helps put contemporary socialization in societies like our own into perspective. The way we raise our children is neither natural nor inevitable. It is one among a variety of ways that produce very different childhoods, children, and, eventually adults. As the anthropologist Clifford Geertz (1973, 45) observes, humans "all begin with the natural equipment to live a thousand kinds of life but end in the end having lived only one." Socialization largely determines the kind of life out of those thousand possibilities that we end up living. It completes our vague and highly plastic biological nature, providing us with our socially and culturally peculiar human natures.

Children in Non-Western Societies

Human infants' relatively long dependency on others for survival shapes how they are cared for in all societies, but those of us who live in more affluent societies can easily forget how fragile their lives can be. Although only four to seven out of every 1,000 newborns die before their first birthdays in more affluent contemporary societies, 200 to 300 did and do die during the first year of life in the past and in many societies still. People who live in societies with such high *infant mortality rates* (the number of infants out of every 1,000 live births who die before their first birthday) know that no matter how well they care for newborns, many will perish. That knowledge often colors how they think about infants and their early development. For example, the Punan Bah of the Bornean rain forest believe that newborns' true souls do not enter them at birth but take refuge in their mothers' breast. They believe that these true souls only enter children when they get their first tooth, around five to eight months of age. Only then are children named, and "only then is the child considered a proper human being" (Nicolaisen 1988, 198).

Like the appearance of the first tooth among the Punan Bah, the acquisition of motor skills such as crawling and walking may signal the transition from one socially defined stage of development to another. Yet, that developmental transition is sometimes purposefully delayed, as it is among the previously discussed Taria villagers of Okinawa, or otherwise socially scheduled. For example, the Piaroa of the Venezuelan jungle constantly carry their infants and never place them on the ground until their parents decide that they can walk, usually around 18 months of age or older. The parents then call all the members of their communal household together to celebrate as they place their child on the ground, and he or she takes his or her first step. After that ceremony, children spend more and more time away from the house, playing with the group of free-roaming small children who populate the village plaza during the day (Overing 1988, 178).

Weaning may also mark an important developmental transition, although its timing varies widely among societies. In many societies, infants and what we would consider young children are almost constantly near their mothers and breastfeed whenever they desire. This often includes sleeping in their mothers' or parents' beds so that they can conveniently nurse and be quickly calmed during the night. People in these societies consider such *co-sleeping* an integral part of infants' and young children's proper care. Mayan mothers, for instance, who co-sleep with their infants, were shocked and highly disapproving when told that North American infants sleep in a different bed and often a different room from their mothers. To them, such sleeping arrangements are a form of child neglect (Small 1998, 113).

The relatively early age at which North American infants are weaned, typically by their first birthday (Broude 1995, 349), would probably also shock mothers in many societies. In those societies, mothers do not discourage young children from nursing until they are three years old or older. For example, !Kung mothers of the Kalahari Desert nurse children until they are three or four. They even take children under that age with them when they gather food, despite the fact that they travel from two to twelve miles on those journeys and carry from 15 to 30 pounds of vegetables back on the return trip. All the while they dig roots, gather nuts, and travel from spot to spot, they carry their infants and young children in slings that rest on their hips so that the children can nurse whenever they please (Broude 1995, 61).

In all known societies, mothers are the primary caretakers of children during infancy, whatever its socially defined duration and character. Yet, in many societies, older sisters and other female kin are also deeply involved in the care of infants. In contrast to !Kung mothers, for example, Jivaro mothers of Ecuador leave infants at home when they go to work in their gardens, often for hours at a time. During these routine absences, an older sister or female cousin cares for the infant (Broude 1995, 177). This is the case in many primarily agricultural societies where mothers spend most of their day in the fields or at markets. Girls as young as six years of age serve as "surrogate mothers" and often spend more waking hours with their younger siblings or cousins than those children's mothers do. In some societies, fathers also help care for infants, especially when the mother is busy, but, in most, fathers rarely or only occasionally interact with babies (Broude 1995, 135).

Whatever its defining event and timing, the end of what different societies consider infancy often brings an abrupt change in children's treatment and experiences. In Indonesia, for example, Javanese fathers carry infants only occasionally when the mother is busy, but after children begin walking, these fathers regularly feed, bathe, play with, and supervise their children and often cuddle them until they fall asleep at night (Broude 1995, 136). In other societies, the end of infancy brings an abrupt end to earlier indulgence. For example, among the Tarong of the Philippines, adults immediately respond to infants' cries and go to great lengths to keep them happy. Yet, when children are weaned at around two years of age, they are "abruptly deprived" of not only their mother's breasts but also her lap. From that point forward, their cries provoke stern scolding rather than solicitous attempts to relieve or distract them (Broude 1995, 116).

It seems that in all known human societies, greater self-reliance is expected of children who are no longer considered infants. For example, upon weaning at around 3 to 4 years of age, !Kung mothers no longer carry their children with them on gathering expeditions but leave them behind in camp. Although adults are always present in the camp because !Kung adults only need to gather or hunt three days a week, they leave the play of the 4- to 14-year-olds who remain in camp with them largely unsupervised. From the time they are weaned until girls start to gather around 14 years of age and boys begin to hunt after they turn 16, !Kung children spend almost all of their time playing with one another virtually free from adult interference (Small 2001, 21).

Children gain increasing independence with increased age in most societies, but those in many are also subject to increasing demands and responsibilities. !Kung children's lengthy exemption from work is somewhat unusual. Like the previously mentioned Mayan, adults in many societies expect children as young as three to perform important work and to assume ever greater responsibility as they grow. Among the Kpelle of Liberia, for instance, adults start commanding children to "fetch and carry" various things when they are around 3 years of age. By 5 years of age, boys fetch and carry all the firewood for their family's household, and girls the water. Around the age of 6, girls also assume primary responsibility for the care of their 2- to 4-year-old siblings, freeing their mothers for other work (Lancy 1996, 145). From that age on, both girls and boys accompany adults to outlying rice fields where they weed, carry rice stalk bundles, chase birds away from newly planted fields, and help in the cutting and burning of brush (Lancy 1996, 146).

In general, the timing and number of chores assigned to children vary in relation to societies' principal form of subsistence. Children in settled agricultural societies like the Mayan and Kpelle tend to work the hardest. In comparison, children in hunting and gathering societies like the !Kung and in more industrialized societies like our own do little work. However, cultural beliefs about children and their development also independently influence the amount of work expected of children. For example, like the !Kung, the Hadza of northern Tanzania hunt and gather, leaving children behind in the village camp while they do. Yet, unlike the !Kung, Hadza adults regularly give children tasks and chores to do in their absence. Moreover, Hadza children do not always stay in camp playing as do !Kung children but often wander from the camp on gathering expeditions of their own, collecting enough food to feed themselves (Small 2001, 22–23). The recent adoption of farming and animal husbandry by some !Kung also illustrates the influence of culture on the treatment and socialization of children quite apart from the demands of different forms of subsistence. !Kung adults in settled agricultural villages work far more and harder than their hunting and gathering counterparts. Yet, despite the increased demands on their time, they have not put their children to work. Like hunting and gathering !Kung, they also do not expect older girls to assume responsibility for the care of younger children so common in other settled agricultural societies (Draper and Cashdan 1988). Perhaps the agricultural !Kung will eventually change their beliefs about children and appropriate activities for them as they adapt to the demands of their newly adopted form of subsistence. For the time being, however, their conventional understanding that children should be free to play remains more influential than the possible contributions of their children's labor.

The relative importance of different agents and agencies of socialization (see Part II) also varies widely across societies and across stages of life within particular societies. Some of that variation reflects societies' varied allocations of child care responsibilities. In all societies, the family, whatever its form, is centrally important to childhood socialization, especially during children's earliest years. However, the influence of different family members on children's socialization varies widely across societies and during different periods of children's lives. As previously suggested, mothers are influential figures in infants' early socialization in all known human societies. Yet, in many, older sisters who care for younger siblings may play as important a part as mothers in infants' and young children's socialization. Fathers are less commonly involved in the care and socialization of infants but often become important figures in children's, especially boys', lives and socialization when they are older. North American Hopi boys, for example, traditionally stayed at home, helping female relatives with chores, until around the age of 8. They then typically killed their first rabbit and were initiated as hunters. After that initiation, they would accompany their father and grandfathers to the fields and sheep camps, where they learned to plant and harvest crops and to herd (Broude 1995, 136).

The importance of peers, both same aged and older, to children's socialization also varies widely cross-culturally and across developmental stages within societies. Peers obviously play a more important part in children's socialization in societies like the !Kung, where children are left to play largely unsupervised by adults, than in societies where children start to work alongside adults at an early age. Like !Kung children, for example, Mbuti pygmy children between 2 and approximately 14 years of age spend most of their time playing with one another in a designated area of the forest where they live called the *bopi*. The Mbuti abhor aggression and avoid competition and conflict. Children first learn that aggression and competition are not tolerated and how to settle disputes and avoid conflict on the *bopi*. They teach and learn these centrally important lessons of Mbuti social life from one another (Small 2001: 149–150). In other societies, same-sexed, most commonly male, peer groups are centrally important to children's socialization. Among the Cubeo of the Northwest Amazon, for instance, boys between approximately 6 and 16 years of age form an autonomous group that chooses its own leaders who enforce rules and discipline members who violate them. These peer leaders are the principal disciplinarians of boys given that Cubeo adults only rarely punish children of either sex (Broude 1995, 319).

Peers' influence over children's socialization obviously depends upon the opportunities children have to interact with one another apart from adults. Children who begin to work alongside adults at an early age clearly have fewer opportunities to do so than children, like the !Kung and Mbuti, who spend most of their waking hours playing with one another. The opportunities for peer interaction among children who regularly attend school probably fall somewhere between these extremes. Although subject to adult direction and supervision while at school, they are in close contact with many similarly aged peers and are often able to avoid adults' direct interference in their peer interactions on playgrounds, during their trips to and from school, and even in classrooms (see Chapter 7).

There is, of course, no formal schooling in preliterate societies, although schools are being introduced into an increasing number of societies where they were previously unknown. Although lacking formal schooling, some societies do have specially designated teachers, such as a village wizard, who instructs the young in cultural traditions and beliefs. However, as already noted, children in many societies receive little formal instruction. For example, Kpelle children learn not only various techniques of rice farming but also such skilled crafts as weaving fish nets and making traps with little instruction. They learn such skills by watching adults, by working alongside them, and from their own mistakes. Adults only rarely correct their largely self-taught students. Kpelle adults consider it a waste of time and energy to teach children what adults are convinced the young will learn "naturally" (Lancy 1996, 146). When Kpelle children reach puberty, they do attend so-called bush school for three or four years, but even then they receive little formal instruction. Instead, they participate in various ceremonies that reinforce Kpelle beliefs and values with which they are already quite familiar (Lancy 1996, 173–176).

The conclusion of childhood across human societies is as varied as its character. In almost all societies, the onset of puberty signals the end of childhood and the transition into either adulthood or a transitional stage similar to what we call *adolescence*. That transition is gradual in some societies and simply occurs as young people increasingly take on adult tasks and responsibilities. These societies do not explicitly mark this transition with special ceremonies or initiation rites, but simply recognize young people as full-fledged adults when they marry. For example, the Punan Bah of Borneo refer to their offspring from the time they start walking until the first physical signs of puberty as *kolovi*, or children. With the onset of puberty, they are called either *kolovi-oro*, child-women, or *kolovi elei*, child-men. Only when they marry do they become *oro* or *elei*, women and men. Those who do not marry remain, and those who later divorce again become child-women and child-men (Nicolaisen 1988, 201).

In contrast, many societies take special note of young peoples' movement out of childhood with prescribed initiation ceremonies. Girls' first menstruation or menarche commonly signals the end of their childhood in those societies and is the occasion for initiation rites. These rites often include a period of seclusion in a separate dwelling and restrictions on with whom and what the initiate can have contact. During this period of seclusion, a girl may receive instruction from her mother or other adult women in how to conduct herself as a woman (Broude 1995, 184–185). In some societies, these initiation rites conclude with elaborate feasts and celebrations. They sometimes also include the controversial practice of clitoridectomy, the partial or complete removal of the clitoris, sometimes called female circumcision but condemned by many as female genital mutilation. The Kpelle, for example, believe that this procedure "cuts the friskiness" out of the girl, a trait they disapprove of in both adult men and women (Broude 1995, 185).

Many societies also have initiation rites for pubescent boys, although fewer than have such rites for girls. These rites sometimes also include a period of seclusion that may include "bush school," when groups of boys within a certain age range live in the bush and receive instruction in secret knowledge that only men possess (Broude 1995, 201). In many societies, boys' initiation into manhood or a transitional stage like adolescence also includes body modification such as tattooing, scarification, and/or circumcision, the removal of the foreskin of the penis, that serves as visible signs of their changed status.

Initiation rites in many societies signal an abrupt change in status from child to adult man or woman. Upon the completion of their initiation, girls are considered marriageable women and boys self-sufficient, marriageable men. In other societies, pubescent boys and girls spend two to three years either after or before their initiation rites in a transitional stage between childhood and adulthood similar to what we call adolescence. In most of these societies, adolescents do the same work as adults and dress like them, but spend most of their leisure time with similarly aged peers (Schlegel and Barry 1991, 41). In a few societies, adolescent males, and less commonly females, spend almost all of their time with one another, working, playing, and even eating and sleeping together in separate quarters from both children and adults. Although some societies consider adolescence a time for sexual flirtation and courtship, few societies allow young people to choose their own marital partners. Instead, adults arrange marriages so as to build alliances and enhance cooperation between families (Schlegel and Barry 1991, 93).

Even a cursory review like this of human societies' different definitions, treatment, and socialization of children exposes the peculiarities of the definitions, treatment, and socialization of the young in societies like our own. Infants and young children in societies like ours are not in almost constant contact with their mothers as those in many societies are. In our society, infants sleep in separate beds and often separate rooms from their parents and are weaned at a comparatively early age. Few have older sisters or other female kin to care for them when their parents are busy. Both younger and older children in Western European and North American societies have little contact with adults, other than parents, compared to children in many societies who freely roam around villages interacting with a variety of adults daily. They even have comparatively little contact with peers much older or younger than they are, spending much of their time in age-graded daycare facilities, schools, and recreational activities. They receive intensive and extensive formal instruction at school and elsewhere, but have almost no opportunity to observe adults engaged in their daily tasks and to learn informally from them. What they see of the adult world is usually filtered through the distorting lens of television, movies, and other mass media of communication (see Chapter 8). They endure a comparatively lengthy adolescence without a clearly defined or ritually celebrated end.

Those of us who live in affluent, highly industrialized societies may decry certain aspects of contemporary childhood and adolescence, but consider their general contours only natural and right. We believe that children everywhere should be exempted from work and free to play, be thoroughly schooled, and be insulated from adults' concerns and responsibilities until they reach adulthood. What we often fail to appreciate is that this conception of childhood and corresponding treatment of the young are of relatively recent historical origin in our own societies. A brief review of the history of Western childhood reveals how contemporary socialization was historically shaped by varied social and cultural changes in Western history that radically altered and continue to alter childhood around the globe.

The History of Western Childhood

The French social historian Philippe Ariès (1962, 128) caused a bit of a sensation in the early 1960s when he claimed that "in medieval society the idea of childhood did not exist." That claim provoked a great deal of interest in the previously unexplored history of childhood in Western societies, much of it directed at refuting Ariès' bold claim. It is now clear that Ariès overstated his case, but his more general and important point is beyond dispute. In the past, childhood and children's socialization in Western societies were radically different from what they are today. Children were, in Ariès' (1962, 329) words, "absorbed into the world of adults" at a much earlier age than they are today. The socialization of most was more informal than it is today. And, children and youth participated in many activities that are considered developmentally inappropriate for them today.

Yet, contrary to Ariès' claim, people of Medieval Europe did have an idea of childhood, although not perhaps the same as in later centuries (Cunningham 1995, 30). Much was written during those times about so-called ages of man that divided the human life course into something like developmental stages. Although not in perfect agreement about specific stages and their timing, that extensive literature did recognize childhood in some form, usually in two stages. *Infantia*, Latin for infancy, generally lasted from birth to what was considered the "age of reason" at around 7 years of age (Bidon and Lett 1999, 107). There were conflicting ideas about the nature of infants and, therefore, about their proper treatment. These ideas mirrored the fifth-century debate between Pelagius, who argued that infants were born with a clean slate, and St. Augustine, who argued that humans are born with original sin and must be subjected to corporal punishment at an early age to curb their evil tendencies (Cunningham 1995, 29). However, available evidence suggests that in everyday life Pelagius's more positive image of the young child usually prevailed and that children under 7 "generally enjoyed freedom" from strict discipline (Shahar 1990, 102). Those years of relative freedom were followed by *pueritia*, Latin for boyhood (girls were typically ignored in this literature), and usually lasted until age 14. This was considered the time of education, although for most children education did not mean schooling but a gradual initiation into the work of adults. *Adolescentia*, or adolescence, followed and lasted until the mid- to late twenties, the usual age at which most European men of the time married (Stearns 1975, 36).

Then as now (see Chapter 9), children's experience and socialization varied greatly depending on their families' social status and class. Medieval European society was divided into what were considered divinely ordained estates ranging from the lowly peasantry to the exalted nobility or aristocracy. With few exceptions, individuals remained in the inherited estate into which they were born throughout their lives. It shaped their childhood socialization and the adult life for which it prepared them.

Although children of the nobility were born into luxury and distinction, they eventually had to demonstrate the grace and honor befitting their exalted station in life. Mothers, nursemaids, and other female attendants raised young noble children in the nursery and women's quarters of the castle or manor during the first few years of their lives. Girls continued to reside in the women's quarters until marriage, learning social graces, needlework, how to sing and play musical instruments, and how to read and write under the guidance of a governess or private tutor (Shahar 1990, 221–223). In contrast, boys left the women's quarters and their mothers at around 7 to 9 years of age. Noble fathers sent sons designated for the knighthood to the court of another feudal lord when they reached the age of reason. There they became court pages and trained for the knighthood. Although they commonly learned to read and write, most of their training was devoted to horsemanship and military skills like fencing. They generally completed their military training by age 15 and served as squires to knights before being knighted themselves between 17 and 19 years of age. However, some were knighted at 15 and immediately joined battles (Shahar 1990, 210–211).

Noble fathers also permanently turned some of their young sons and daughters over to religious orders through a ritual called *oblation*, or the act of offering. This was commonly the fate of noble boys considered too frail for the knighthood and aristocratic girls not destined for marriage (Shahar 1990, 183–184). When such a child was 6 or 7, her or his father took a public vow to give him or her over to a monastery or convent, often along with a payment of money or real estate. The understanding was that the child would eventually become a monk or nun and spend the rest of his or her life in the monastery or convent. Some of these so-called *oblates* did ask to be released from this obligation when they reached their teens or early 20s, but those requests were almost always denied. Although officially banned by the Church in the fifteenth century, the practice of oblation continued informally for some time later in many parts of Europe (Bidon and Lett 1999, 49–50).

The lives of artisans' and merchants' children, most of whom lived in towns and cities, were much different. In Medieval Europe, skilled crafts, such as weaving, baking, carpentry, and metalworking, were governed by monopolistic guilds that had the legal authority to admit people into the trade and strictly controlled how the craft was practiced (Stearns 1975, 49). Those who wanted to enter a trade had to serve an apprenticeship of a specified length that varied among crafts. Fathers contractually apprenticed their sons to a master artisan, often paying him a fee. Those contracts guaranteed the artisan the boy's services for a specified number of years in return for the boy's training; room, board, and clothing; and moral supervision. The age at which apprenticeships began ranged from 7 to as old as 20, but the most typical age was 11 to 13 (Shahar 1990, 232). After apprenticeship, at around 21 years of age, the aspiring artisan became a journeyman who worked in a master's shop for wages but continued to live in the master's home along with apprentices. Only after some years as journeymen did artisans inherit or accumulate enough savings to buy a shop and themselves become master artisans (Stearns 1975, 49).

Children of artisans played and worked around their father's shop from the beginning of their lives. A single building housed the shop and the family's living quarters. Because artisans housed and fed both apprentices and journeymen, their children grew up around a number of unrelated people of varying ages in a family-like atmosphere (Stearns 1975, 48). Sons of artisans generally apprenticed in their fathers' or another trade. Daughters informally learned how to manage a shop household by helping their mothers, who often also taught their daughters basic arithmetic because artisans' wives commonly sold goods and kept the shop's accounts. Artisans' daughters typically became artisans' wives, often marrying journeymen in their fathers' shops (Stearns 1975, 48). Merchants, a separate estate in Medieval Europe, sometimes also apprenticed their sons but more often started to teach them their own business soon after they achieved the "age of reason" at 7 years of age. By the age of 14, these merchants' sons were actively involved in their fathers' business. For example, at that age, the son of one Italian merchant became "his father's representative in the buying and selling of wine, which he tasted with professional skill before announcing his intention to purchase it" (Bidon and Lett 1999, 83). Little is known about the lives of merchants' daughters, although their socialization probably centered on learning how to manage a household and staff of servants. Beginning in the second half of the twelfth century, many children of artisans and merchants, mostly boys, also briefly attended small parish schools where they learned to read, write, and do simple arithmetic because their fathers considered those skills indispensable to their trade or business (Bidon and Lett 1999, 121).

However, most children were born to peasants, who made up at least 60 percent of the population of Medieval Europe (Stearns 1975, 32). Peasant children were incorporated into adult society at an early age, and, as in most agricultural societies, peasant parents put them to work around the age of 7. Peasant households provided no privacy for adults or children, and people of different ages freely mixed at play as well as at work in peasant villages. When children were around 7 years of age, they began to run errands, look after younger siblings, scare birds off crops, and tend animals such as geese, pigs, and cattle (Shahar 1990, 243). With increasing age, they gradually took on more demanding tasks. In the sixteenth century, for example, the former peasant boy Jean de Brie reported that he was "appointed" to tend the geese when he was 8 years old, then to tend the pigs, and, at around 9 or 10, to lead the horses that pulled the plow (Bidon and Didier 1999, 79). By 14 years of age, most peasant children were doing the same and as much work as adults. Their preparation for their adult roles was direct and gradual without acute transitions or rites of passage (Shahar 1990, 247). Although a few peasant children did learn to read from the local parish priest, most remained illiterate, having little time to acquire such an impractical skill.

According to Ariès (1962, 412), a surge of interest in the education and training of children that began in the later fifteenth century initiated a profound transformation of Western childhood. Both the Renaissance and

Protestant Reformation helped stimulate that interest. The Renaissance revival of classical Greek and Roman thought included ideas about the need to mold children—or boys, more specifically—into good citizens. Many Renaissance writers advised parents to begin the education of their children early, teaching them "their letters soon after weaning" (Cunningham 1995, 43). The most influential of those writers, Erasmus of Rotterdam, likened the young child to soft wax that had to be molded into the desired form before it hardened (Cunningham 1995, 44). Yet, the influence of writers like Erasmus was limited to the literate aristocracy and wealthy merchants. The influence of the Protestant Reformation was more widespread. Unlike Catholics, the new Protestants of the sixteenth and subsequent centuries did not believe infant baptism insured children's salvation until they reached the age of reason. Because they believed that faith alone could save an individual's soul, Protestant parents were anxious to bring their children quickly to that faith. For many, that necessitated breaking the obstinate will of the child born with original sin and sinful desires. It also required early religious instruction so that children would understand the faith that could save their immortal souls. Protestant denominations published numerous catechisms for that purpose, and many Protestant churches established parish schools to teach children as young as 2 or 3 how to read those catechisms along with the Bible (Cunningham 1995, 47–50). Among Protestants, methodical training of the young became a concern of parents of all ranks, from the most exalted nobles to the lowliest peasants.

An even more profound transformation of Western ideas about children and childhood occurred in the eighteenth century. At the beginning of that century, the philosopher John Locke's influential *Some Thoughts Concerning Education* advised that the central task of child rearing was to teach the child to subject his or her will to reason. However, he argued that doing so did not require harsh punishment to break the child's will but methodical education that turned learning into the child's play and recreation (Cunningham 1995, 64–65). In the middle part of the century, Jean-Jacques Rousseau countered Locke's arguments in his widely read story of the fictional boy *Emile*. For Rousseau, explicit instruction detracted from children's natural play and recreation, which were their best teachers. He suggested that, up to the age of 12, children should be as free as possible to learn from nature on their own (Cunningham 1995, 66–68). Toward the end of the eighteenth century, Romantic poets and writers fortified the link between nature and childhood that Rousseau first forged. They depicted children as naturally innocent, imaginative, and virtuous. They implied that children must be protected from the corruption of adult society so as to preserve those precious qualities. For Romantic writers, childhood was less a preparation for adult life than "the spring which should nourish the whole life" (Cunningham 1995, 73).

Taken together, these discordant eighteenth-century ideas left a confusing image of the child upon which subsequent Western conceptions of children and childhood built. Children must be carefully and extensively educated so as to develop their powers of reasoning and strong moral character. Yet, children must be free to play and naturally learn through the exercise of their own creative imaginations. Their future success and happiness depend on the early formation of good habits, yet their natural innocence and virtue are sources of inspiration that must be protected from the crushing demands and corruption of adult society. Childhood was thereby set apart from the rest of life as a privileged time of learning and play, freedom and supervision, and protective dependency. However, it would take a century before most children in Western Europe and North America experienced anything close to this ideal childhood.

The experience of the European children who first arrived on North American shores resembled that of their counterparts in Europe at the time, but with the added rigors of settling a new land. For example, many settlers continued to recognize 7 years of age as the "age of reason," as indicated by the common practice of "breeching" boys when they reached that age. Only then were they dressed in their first pair of breeches rather than the gowns worn by all children before that age (Fass and Mason 2000, 82). In contrast, like more radical Protestants in Europe, the Puritan settlers of New England sternly disciplined young children and schooled them early to read the Bible and other religious literature (Vinovskis 1996, 102). South of New England, many children arrived in the New World as parentless indentured servants, following the well-established European custom of placing poor children with a master who was obliged to provide ordinary sustenance and some training in return for services (Mason 1994, 30).

As the European settlement of North America continued, the lives of North American children came more closely to resemble those of European children at the time. Many, although probably not most, of those who lived in the developing towns and cities received rudimentary instruction in reading, writing, and arithmetic at private academies. Sons of merchants started learning their father's business at an early age, and those of artisans apprenticed for a trade when they reached 10 to 13 years of age. Like their European counterparts, girls informally learned how to manage a household by helping their mothers.

The lives of rural North American children were similar to those of European peasant children with one notable exception. Outside of New England, agricultural settlement did not follow the European village pattern but one of single-family homesteads some distance from one another. The social lives of many rural North American children were consequently more circumscribed than those of their European counterparts. Like their European counterparts, rural North American children started working at an early age, scaring birds from crops, weeding fields, and tending crops, but that work, unlike children's work in rural European villages, seldom brought them into contact with neighbors of varied ages. With the Western expansion of European settlement, homesteads became even farther apart, and rural children's relative social isolation often grew along with their independence. For example, when 9-year-old Marvin Powe was sent to round up some runaway horses, he rode and lived off the land for a week before finding them. His father was only starting to ride out to look for Marvin when he returned home with the horses (West 1992, 36). Although rural children everywhere labored for the communal benefit of their families, the work of many North American children, like

Marvin Powe, taught them to be self-reliant and independent at an early age. Growing up on the Western frontier of North America could be even more confusing for girls, who often did the same work as their brothers—"plowing, planting, harvesting, hunting, herding"—until they reached adolescence (West 1992, 36). Most were then "told, quite literally, to come indoors" and perform the domestic tasks assigned to women (West 1992, 38).

Of course, African American slave children never experienced such independence, not because they were young but because they were born slaves. In the early years of life, they either were carried to the fields where their mothers labored throughout the daylight hours or were left behind in often overcrowded slave nurseries where either young slave girls or elderly slaves cared for them (King 1995, 13–14). Like other rural American children, most began working at a young age, performing domestic duties and other chores around the living quarters or working on so-called trash gangs in the fields alongside pregnant women and the elderly (King 1995, 30). Many were impatient to work in the fields, given that such work often entitled them to additional food allowances (King 1995, 22). Although a few slaveholders did maintain schools for slave children, most thought it ill-advised to educate "Negroes." Hence, few slave children learned to read and write, and the few who did so were often secretly taught by literate slaves or their white masters' children (King 1995, 77).

Much of African American slave children's socialization involved harsh lessons about their place in the brutal hierarchy of American slavery. Many routinely saw their parents beaten or otherwise humiliated, and were often harshly punished themselves. Many were "hired out" to other whites on yearly contracts and separated from their families for a year at a time. Others were permanently separated from parents and siblings because of their own or other family members' sale to new owners. More than a few younger slave children were close companions and friends of their white masters' children, but then were abruptly "put in their proper place" by those friends when they reached 10 to 12 years of age. Perhaps as taxing, they had to learn to hide their deep resentment about such treatment behind a mask of deference and humility (King 1995, 91–114). Unfortunately, the end of slavery in the United States did not put an end to many of these humiliations for African American children. For example, a few years after the end of the Civil War, many of the former Confederate states passed legislation giving former slave owners control over apprenticeships of "Negro" minors and "orphans" on their lands, effectively reestablishing their slavery until they reached 18 to 21 years of age (King 1995, 151).

The westward expansion of the European settlement of North America and the formal end of slavery in the United States were both aspects of a deep transformation of Western societies during the eighteenth, nineteenth, and into the twentieth centuries. After centuries of relative stability, the population of Europe exploded during the eighteenth century (Stearns 1975, 63–65). Immigration to North America was spurred by the lack of economic opportunities for that expanding European population, but that expanding population also created economic opportunities in Europe. Demand for all variety of products grew along with the population. Enterprising merchants and artisans attempted to profit from the growing demand by adopting more efficient techniques of production, and thereby undermined the authority of the craft guilds. Innovative landowners introduced new agricultural methods such as crop rotation, specialized in crops best suited to local conditions, and drove peasants from their lands. By the time the French Revolution of 1789 formally overthrew the old feudal order of Europe, its foundations had already crumbled. The Industrial Revolution that spread from England across Western societies during the nineteenth century swept away what remained of it and profoundly transformed childhood and children's socialization in the process (Stearns 1975, 67–82).

Prior to these changes, economic and personal relationships were intertwined. Peasants owed their lord a proportion of their crops in tribute for the use of the land, and the lord owed his peasants a church and priest, military protection, and relief in times of dire need. Apprentices owed their masters their services, and masters owed their apprentices training and a place at their tables and in their households. And, children owed their parents their labor, and parents owed their children spiritual and material support, including an inheritance or dowry to insure their futures. However, as the market economy expanded, economic relationships were increasingly commercialized and severed from personal ties. Work gradually moved from family households to removed shops and factories where people worked for cash wages rather than personal services and provisions. More and more men, women, and children left their homes daily to work for wages, transforming family homes from sites of work into retreats from it. Many families continued to work together on their farms but increasingly raised crops and livestock for the cash market rather than their own subsistence. Wages often provided a more reliable source of income and lured many young people from farms to mills and factories, in many cases with their families' blessing (Cancian 1987, 16–18).

However, most people, especially among the working and lower classes, continued to believe that children owed their family their labor and its fruits, including wages. Even the son of a Massachusetts mill owner, Baxter Whitney, was put to work in his father's mill in 1823 at the age of 6. He worked there full-time, except for two weeks each summer and winter that he spent in school, until he was 13 and was sent to another firm to help machinists construct looms for his father's mill (Kett 1977, 25). Less affluent parents often had little choice but to send their children to work in mills, mines, and factories, requiring their wages to support the family (Clement 1997, 57). For example, surveys of Belgian families revealed that wages of children under 14 accounted for 22 percent of their families' total income in 1853 and a full 31 percent in 1891 (Cunningham 1995, 89).

Yet, many parents sent their children to labor in mines and factories reluctantly. Industrialization was changing the character of work and, in the eyes of many, for the worse. Although most children had worked hard from an early age before industrialization, that work was often irregular and combined with recreation. For example, rural children often worked from dawn to dusk during planting and harvesting season but much less other times of the year.

Singing, storytelling, and other amusements also periodically interrupted work on farms and in shops. In contrast, industrialized labor was unrelenting, especially in its early years, usually taking up 10 or more hours a day, six days a week, throughout the year. Second, children's introduction to work was no longer gradual but abrupt. After industrialization, one day the working-class child had no job, and the next day, usually around the age of 10, she or he did. Third, children employed in mines and factories no longer worked under the supervision of family members or employers personally obliged to care for them (Cunningham 1995, 88). In the earliest years of industrialization, employers sometimes did hire entire families to work in mills and factories under the father's supervision, but that practice was short-lived (Cancian 1987, 17). They increasingly recruited children individually to work in their mills and factories, often preferring them to adult workers who demanded higher wages than children were willing to accept (Cunningham 1995, 142).

The changed character of children's work under industrial conditions provoked outcries against child labor. Throughout most of the eighteenth century, social commentators worried about the idleness of poor children, often echoing Locke's advice that they should be put to work at the age of 3 with a "bellyful of bread daily" (Cunningham 1995, 138). However, by the end of the century, social reformers were more concerned about the detrimental effects of poor children's industrial labor than about their idleness. Describing children who worked in factories as "our poor little White-Slaves" (Cunningham 1995, 139), these reformers campaigned for legislation to limit and regulate children's paid employment. They achieved some early success in Britain with the passage of the Labor Act of 1819 that banned work in factories by children under 9 and limited children under 14 years old to eight hours of work per day (Cunningham 1995, 140). It would take until the end of the nineteenth century, and even longer in some countries like the United States (which did not pass the Fair Labor Relations Act limiting child labor until 1938) for the reformers to accomplish their ultimate goal of legally prohibiting child labor in manufacturing and mining.

Many of those nineteenth-century social reformers were opposed not so much to children working as to their industrial labors. Under the spell of the Romantic linkage of childhood and nature, they continued to believe that agricultural labor in the fresh country air was healthy for children's developing bodies, minds, and characters. Many of these reformers worried more about the corrupting influences of growing industrial cities on their young inhabitants than about exempting them from work, and committed themselves to saving poor urban children from city streets. For example, in 1853, the New York Children's Aid Society started relocating poor children from the city to rural communities in the Midwest and West, and similar societies in other Eastern cities soon followed their lead. The children traveled westward along with a couple of agents of the society on so-called orphan trains, although aid workers considered just about any unsupervised child on the city streets an orphan and made little effort to locate his or her parents. When the children arrived at their destination, they paraded before community meetings of local adults willing to take one or more of the children into their homes in return for the children's services or labor. The aid societies did take various measures to help insure that the children were well cared for and treated in their new homes, but with mixed results. Many were treated as little more than servants, and some quickly ran away from their new homes and back to the cities from which they had come. Yet, such embarrassments did not deter the reformers. Between 1853 and 1929, the New York society alone "placed out," as the practice was then called, 150,000 city children (Holt 1992). Similarly, between 1869 and 1930, British philanthropic agencies sent around 80,000 children from impoverished urban families to Canada, where they were "placed out" with families in return for their agricultural and domestic services (Rooke and Schnell 1991, 190–191). To the British philanthropists who organized these efforts, the still sparsely populated Canada represented the "happy home of childhood" in comparison to the teeming industrial cities of Britain (Rooke and Schnell 1991, 190).

Nineteenth-century reformers campaigned not only to get children out of factories and cities but also to get them into schools. Most children in Western societies did receive some schooling prior to the nineteenth century, but very little by contemporary standards. Few attended for more than three years, and, during those few years, their attendance was commonly intermittent and irregular. The vast majority of parents had to pay for their children's schooling and saw little need to continue doing so once the children had learned to read and, in some cases, write. The family's well-being also depended on children's labors, so work responsibilities took precedence over school attendance even when the children were enrolled in school (Cunningham 1995, 103).

However, beginning in the second half of the eighteenth century, governments in many Western countries devised plans of universal education to instill a common national identity and patriotism among the population (Cunningham 1995, 121–122). Those plans called for the establishment of a system of primary schools with attendance compulsory for children between specified ages. The results of these early efforts commonly fell far short of their goals. Localities resisted attempts to make them bear the cost of running the schools, and compulsory attendance laws were difficult to enforce and widely ignored (Cunningham 1995, 123). Yet, during the nineteenth century the movement toward universal, compulsory schooling gained strength. One effect of the industrial transformation of the economies of Western societies was that children's futures increasingly came to depend on education and character rather than the inheritance of land or a craft (Cancian 1987, 19). Support for public education consequently grew among middle-class parents who could not afford the expense of sending their children to private academies for a number of years. Many also agreed with reformers that universal schooling could also help counter the supposedly inadequate family life of working- and lower-class children. Working- and lower-class parents who desperately needed the income of their working children resisted compulsory schooling laws but were fighting a losing battle. At the end of the nineteenth century and early in the twentieth century, all Western societies established systems of public schools at which attendance was compulsory from the time children were 5 to 7 years of age until they reached repeatedly increased ages. In Britain, for example, the minimum age for leaving school was set at 10 in 1870, raised to 11 in 1893, then to 12 in 1899, and finally to 14 in 1918 (Hendrick 1997, 63). That same year, all the states in the United States had compulsory schooling laws, and 31 of them required attendance until age 16 (Macleod 1998, 75).

Schooling not only spread throughout Western societies during the nineteenth century but also radically changed. Prior to that time, schools consisted of one or more large, ungraded classrooms with students as young as 3 or 4 and as old as 17 or more. Children started their schooling at widely different ages, so a classroom might have a 6-year-old who could already read and write as well as an illiterate 14-year-old who was just beginning his or her schooling. Under the teacher's guidance, children progressed through increasingly difficult primers and other instructional texts at their own pace and without regard to age. Although age-graded schooling was first proposed in the seventeenth century, that proposal was not fully implemented until 1817 with the establishment of the Prussian school system in what is now Germany (Chudacoff 1989, 31). Other Western countries soon followed Prussia's lead. For example, urban schools in the United States started to adopt age grading in the 1850s, and by the 1880s it was standard practice in urban schools (Clement 1997, 107). Although rural schools still often had only one classroom, even in those schools students were divided into grades according to age and given grade-appropriate instruction. With the adoption of age-graded schooling, children started school at approximately the same age and moved together through grades of progressively more complex instruction on a yearly basis. Age-graded schooling thereby imposed a previously unknown age consciousness on children's education that gradually became the general model for their development. Childhood development was increasingly seen as composed of discrete, age-related stages.

Compulsory schooling also transformed Western children from working contributors to their family's economic well-being into dependent schoolchildren, but not without struggles. As mentioned above, many working-class parents desperately needed their children's labor at home or their wages, and resisted compulsory schooling, as they did legal restrictions on child labor (Cunningham 1995, 158). In America, educational reformers often promoted public education as the best means to Americanize the children of immigrant workers, and immigrant parents often opposed it for exactly that reason (Berrol 1995). During the earliest years of compulsory schooling, truancy from school was rampant among working-class and poor children, often with their parents' knowledge, if not blessing. In England and Wales, for example, "there were nearly 100,000 prosecutions a year for truancy in the 1880s" (Cunningham 1995, 158). Over time, however, working-class parents became convinced, as their middle-class counterparts already had, that the longer their children spent in school, the better their chances for landing a decent job in the future (Nasaw 1985, 46). They also came to recognize that working, either at home or for money, and going to school need not be mutually exclusive (Nasaw 1985, 47).

School, unlike work, "let out at three o'clock, leaving the new working class students with free time in the afternoon" (Nasaw 1985, 117), time often filled by work. Many were expected to do various chores around the home and farm during that time, and urban children could also use that time to earn money. Some worked for local shopkeepers, and others as messengers. Many more were self-employed, taking advantage of the many business opportunities on busy city streets. Some sold shoe shines, while others "peddled whatever they could buy cheaply, fit into their pockets or the canvas bag slung over their shoulders, and sell for a profit," such as chewing gum, matches, and peanuts (Nasaw 1985, 52). Perhaps the most visible of these young street traders were the "newsies," who bought newspapers from publishers after school and sold them for a profit on the streets in the evening to workers heading home from their jobs. The newsies also went to entertainment districts on Saturday nights to sell the early edition of the Sunday papers, sometimes employing devious schemes. For example, late one Saturday night in Chicago, a juvenile protection officer found a crying 7-year-old boy begging passersby to buy his last paper so that he could go home. In the meantime, his 13-year-old brother concealed himself in a doorway with the rest of their supply of newspapers, handing his brother another copy after each successful transaction (Nasaw 1985, 84). Although parents expected such enterprising young street traders to contribute their earnings to the family, it was impossible for parents to know exactly how much they were earning. Unlike children who earned a regular wage, it was easy for these children to keep a little of their earnings for their own use to buy hamburgers, candy, or a ticket to the balcony of a vaudeville theater or a nickelodeon showing the new silent movies (Nasaw 1985, 131).

Social reformers were appalled. They had hoped that, where child labor legislation had failed, compulsory schooling would put an end to working children. Even more worrisome was that the work, and play, of urban children exposed them to what the reformers considered the most corrupting influences of the city. On its streets, they freely mingled with all variety of adults but were largely unsupervised by them. The reformers tried to lure the children off the streets and into recreation centers and playgrounds, but with little success. Most working-class kids preferred the freedom of the streets, not to mention the opportunity to make some money, to the heavy adult supervision of recreation centers and playgrounds (Nasaw 1985, 36). The reformers also adopted various strategies to police street children, only to be thwarted by the children's cooperative evasion of such control (Nasaw 1985, 148–151).

However, where the reformers failed, technological and economic changed prevailed. Trolleys brought more people to downtown shopping and entertainment districts, making the street trades more lucrative and attracting adults to trades that children had long monopolized (Nasaw 1985, 187). Messengers and errand boys fell victim to the telephone (Nasaw 1985, 191), and the newsies, the last of the street traders to go, fell victim to the new practice of home newspaper delivery (Nasaw 1985, 192). To add injury to insult, automobiles started killing and maiming more and more children in the early twentieth century, effectively evicting them from city streets (Zelizer 1985, 33). Compelled to attend school, prevented from working, and driven from the streets and many other public places, children in Western societies became increasingly dependent upon adults and subject to their supervision.

An array of social, cultural, and technological changes, some of which had been building for years, came together at the close of the nineteenth century and the opening of the twentieth that profoundly transformed Western conceptions of children and childhood. Viviana Zelizer (1985, 209) describes the American case, but something similar occurred or soon did occur throughout other Western societies.

> Between the 1870s and 1930s, the value of American children was transformed. The twentieth-century economically useless but emotionally priceless child displaced the nineteenth-century useful child. To be sure, the most dramatic changes took place among the working class.... But the sentimentalization of childhood intensified regardless of class. The new sacred child occupied a special and separate world, regulated by affection and education, not work and profit.

The new sacred child of the twentieth century and beyond was endearingly innocent, dependent, vulnerable, and incompetent. Unlike their counterparts in earlier centuries, such children were considered not so much preadult as nonadult (Fass and Mason 2000, 5), requiring years of special protection and treatment, "a sort of quarantine" (Ariès 1962, 412), before they were ready to join adult society. Their proper place was not the field, factory, or street, but the loving family home, age-graded school, or supervised playground.

Legislation regulating and prohibiting child labor, compulsory schooling laws, and the establishment of juvenile courts (Macleod 1998, 141) institutionalized this new conception of childhood, and the new child science of the twentieth century gave it legitimacy. Children no longer worked around and informally learned from adults. They spent the better part of the day and year in school around peers no more than a year older or younger than they. They no longer committed crimes but youthful indiscretions due to their moral immaturity and allegedly inadequate upbringing. All this had the blessing of child and developmental psychologists, who were gaining increasing acceptance as the final arbiters of developmental truth (Hawes 1997, 63). And, the length of this protected, sequestered, and much studied stage of life continued to grow in the twentieth century. The labor of older and older children was restricted and regulated. The age at which the young were no longer subject to compulsory schooling laws was repeatedly raised, as already noted, and they were strongly encouraged and informally coerced into spending more and more years in school. In the United States, moreover, the legal age of sexual consent for girls increased from an average of a little over 10 years old across the various states in 1885 to over 17 in 1920 (Odem 1995, 20). The ideal childhood of eighteenth-century thought, with all its inconsistencies, had become reality for most children in Western societies and was subsequently exported to other societies.

Continuing Cultural Contrasts: Japan and the United States

Children's experience and socialization in the affluent, highly industrialized societies of North America, Western Europe, and Japan are broadly similar, especially in comparison to those of children in the not so distant past and in less affluent societies today. Ideally at least, childhood is a time of play and education, unhindered by work or other demanding responsibilities. Children are largely segregated from adult society and uninformed about a variety of adults' concerns and activities. They spend years in age-graded schools and remain economically dependent during those years. Most do not start working until they reach their teen years, and then only for limited hours and in a narrow range of jobs. Yet, despite these similarities, there are numerous cultural differences among affluent industrialized societies that influence how children are thought about and socialized.

Contrasts between Japan and the United States are particularly instructive for demonstrating the influence of cultural understandings on children's experience and socialization. Both countries are highly advanced technologically and exceptionally affluent in comparison to most societies, yet are culturally quite distinct. Although the contrast can be overdrawn, Americans tend to place a higher value on personal autonomy and self-reliance than do the Japanese, while the Japanese tend to place a higher value on social relationships and group cooperation than do Americans (Small 1998, 99). That and other differences in cultural values and beliefs influence how children are socialized in the two countries from early in their lives onward.

Infants' and young children's sleeping arrangements provide one telling example of the cultural differences between the two societies. As previously noted, American infants and young children commonly sleep in a separate bed and often in a separate room from their mothers. In contrast, Japanese parents place a newborn's bed directly next to their own bed, on the mother's side. Around their first birthday, Japanese children start sleeping in their parents' bed and usually continue to do so until they are 5 or 6 years of age (Johnson 1993, 111). For the Japanese, such co-sleeping is essential to young children's proper development. Most Japanese believe that infants' and young children's dependency on their mothers is an expression of what they consider one of the strongest human emotions, *amae*, or the desire "to depend and presume upon another's benevolence" (Johnson 1993, 156). They consequently do not believe that young children's dependency must be "handled" and gradually broken, as do many North Americans, but that it must be fostered and developed (Small 1998, 102). The Japanese believe that behavioral problems result when young children fail to learn how to properly express their wish for care and attention (Tobin, Wu, and Davidson 1989, 27). According to the Japanese, co-sleeping helps children learn that centrally important lesson.

Japanese mothers also commonly indulge their young children's wishes so as to foster their healthy expression of *amae* to an extent many North Americans would consider spoiling. However, the Japanese draw a clear distinction between "inside" and "outside" (Johnson 1993, 160), and Japanese parents teach children early on that they should act differently in public, on the outside, than they do at home, on the inside. They start teaching their children at an early age not to cry or otherwise draw attention to themselves, to politely bow to others, to use proper terms of address, and to maintain proper postures in public (Johnson 1993, 119). Western observers are often baffled by how undisciplined and demanding young Japanese toddlers are at home but how well behaved they are in public. To the Japanese, that is just a normal part of their development.

The Japanese often liken children's development to a journey outward from the nuclear family into the world (Tobin, Wu, and Davidson 1989, 58–59). That journey involves learning not only proper public etiquette but an important psychological transition as well. The Japanese believe that children's healthy development requires the transfer of their *amae*, or wish for care and attention, from their parents to social groups (Johnson 1993, 123). In order to do so, they must learn to cooperate and feel part of a social group. In contemporary Japan, preschools are principally responsible for teaching children this vitally important developmental lesson. Over 90 percent of 3- to 5-year-old Japanese children attend one or another kind of preschool (Tobin, Wu, and Davidson 1989 46), where the emphasis is on group activities and participation.

North American observers are often surprised by how little time is devoted to academic preparation in Japanese preschools and are shocked at what they consider their inexcusably high student-teacher ratios, commonly 30 or more students per teacher. However, to the Japanese, too much emphasis on academic preparation and lower student-teacher ratios would detract from preschools' most important purpose of giving children experience being a member of a group (Tobin, Wu, and Davidson 1989, 192). The Japanese believe that young children can (and most Japanese children do) learn to read at home. What they cannot learn at home is how to feel part of a larger group, and higher student-teacher ratios increase their opportunities to do so. Japanese preschool teachers and administrators believe that the lower student-teacher or caretaker ratios in American preschools and daycare centers emphasize teacher-student over student-student interaction, and that American preschool teachers are far too quick to intervene in children's disputes and relations (Tobin, Wu, and Davidson 1989, 37). Japanese preschool teachers seldom intervene in their students' disputes but encourage them to handle their own interpersonal troubles (Tobin, Wu, and Davidson 1989, 23). They seldom lecture or scold their students, and believe that American preschool teachers' more interventionist approach is "a bit too heavy, too adultlike, too severe and controlled for young children" (Tobin, Wu, and Davidson 1989, 53). In contrast, many North American observers find Japanese preschool classrooms chaotic and out of control. That contrast reflects a basic cultural difference between Japanese and North American ideas about the primary purpose of early childhood socialization. While the Japanese stress the importance of children's acquisition of cooperative skills and group identification, North Americans place primary emphasis on their development of independence and self-control.

Japanese and North Americans also have very different ideas about children's subsequent development. For example, a comparative study of middle schools in the United States and Japan found that Japanese and American teachers had very different conceptions of puberty and its effects on their students. The American teachers believed that puberty brought on "raging hormones" that made adolescents "difficult to control and prone to dangerous behavior" (Letendre 2000, 73). In contrast, Japanese teachers never mentioned "raging hormones" and believed that puberty brought a burst of energy that enabled their students to study with a new intensity (Letendre 2000, 74). The classroom practices of American and Japanese middle-school teachers reflect these different cultural understandings. Japanese teachers quickly establish classroom routine and spend little classroom time disciplining students, often ignoring minor disruptions or simply directing students back to their academic task. In contrast, American teachers tend to lay down explicit rules and spend much time enforcing them, what they call "classroom management" (Letendre 2000).

These are only a few of the differences between conceptions of children and their socialization in Japan and the United States. However few, they illustrate just how much cultural understandings shape children's socialization and experience independently of societies' relative affluence and technological development. On the other hand, cultural understandings change as people collectively adapt to changing environmental, economic, and social conditions, as the example of the changing conception and treatment of children in Western history illustrates. Complex combinations of interrelated factors influence how children are thought of and treated in different societies and by different groups within a society. What is clear is that children's lives are as varied as the societies and social groups into which they are born.

* * *

Childhood is as much a socially constructed as a natural stage of life, and child development is as much a social process as one of individual maturation. That realization should make us suspicious of broad generalizations about children and their development based on evidence from a particular society or group of societies. Whenever we read or hear such broad generalizations about what children of different ages think, feel, and can learn, we should always ask, at least to ourselves, which children, when, and where.

References

Ariès, Philippe. 1962. *Centuries of Childhood: A Social History of Family Life*, translated by Robert Baldick. New York: Random House.

Berrol, Selma Cantor. 1995. *Growing Up American: Immigrant Children in America, Then and Now*. New York: Twayne.

Bidon, Alexandre, and Didier Lett. 1999. *Children in the Middle Ages: Fifth–Fifteenth Centuries*. Notre Dame, IN: University of Notre Dame Press.

Broude, Gwen. 1995. *Growing Up: A Cross-Cultural Encyclopedia*. Santa Barbara, CA: ABC-CLIO.

Cancian, Francesca. 1987. *Love in America: Gender and Self-Development*. New York: Cambridge University Press.

Chudacoff, Howard. 1989. *How Old Are You? Age Consciousness in American Culture*. Princeton, NJ: Princeton University Press.

Clement, Priscilla Ferguson. 1997. *Growing Pains: Children in the Industrial Age, 1850–1890*. New York: Twayne.

Cunningham, Hugh. 1995. *Children and Childhood in Western Society Since 1500*. New York: Longman.

Draper, Patricia, and Elizabeth Cashdan. 1988. "Technological Change and Child Behavior Among the !Kung." *Ethnology* 27: 339–365.

Fass, Paula, and Mary Ann Mason. 2000. *Childhood in America*. New York: New York University Press.

Geertz, Clifford. 1973. *The Interpretation of Cultures*. New York: Basis Books.

Hawes, Joseph. 1997. *Children Between the Wars: American Childhood, 1920–1940*. New York: Twayne.

Hendrick, Harry. 1997. *Children, Childhood and English Society, 1880–1990*. New York: Cambridge University Press.

Holt, Marilyn. 1992. *The Orphan Trains: Placing Out in America*. Lincoln: University of Nebraska Press.

Howell, Signe. 1988. "From Child to Human: Chewong Concepts of Self." In Gustave Johoda and I. M. Lewis (eds.) *Acquiring Culture: Cross Cultural Studies in Child Development*, 147–168. London: Croom Helm.

Johnson, Frank. 1993. *Dependency and Japanese Socialization: Psychoanalytic and Anthropological Investigations Into Amae*. New York: New York University Press.

Kett, Joseph. 1977. *Rites of Passage: Adolescence in America 1790 to the Present*. New York: Basic Books.

King, Wilma. 1995. *Stolen Childhood: Slave Youth in Nineteenth-Century America*. Bloomington: Indiana University Press.

Lancy, David. 1996. *Playing on the Motherground*. New York: Guilford Press.

Letendre, Gerald. 2000. *Learning to Be Adolescent: Growing Up in U.S. and Japanese Middle Schools*. New Haven, CT: Yale University Press.

Macleod, David. 1998. *The Age of the Child: Children in America, 1890–1920*. New York: Twayne.

Mason, Mary Ann. 1994. *From Father's Property to Children's Rights*. New York: Columbia University Press.

Nasaw, David. 1985. *Children of the City: At Play and at Work*. New York: Oxford University Press.

Nicolaisen, Ida. 1988. "Concepts and Learning Among the Punan Bah of Sarawak." In Gustave Johoda and I. M. Lewis (eds.) *Acquiring Culture: Cross Cultural Studies in Child Development*, 193–221. London: Croom Helm.

Odem, Mary. 1995. *Delinquent Daughters: Protecting and Policing Adolescent Female Sexuality in the United States, 1885–1920*. Chapel Hill: University of North Carolina Press.

Overing, Joanna. 1988. "Personal Autonomy and the Domestication of the Self in Piaroa Society." In Gustave Jahoda and I. M. Lewis (eds.) *Acquiring Culture: Cross Cultural Studies in Child Development*, 169–192. London: Croom Helm.

Rooke, Patricia, and Rudy Schnell. 1991. "Canada." In Joseph Hawes and N. Ray Hiner (eds.) *Children in Historical and Comparative Perspective*, 179–215. New York: Greenwood Press.

Schlegel, Alice, and Herbert Barry III. 1991. *Adolescence: An Anthropological Inquiry*. New York: Free Press.

Shahar, Shulamith. 1990. *Childhood in the Middle Ages*. New York: Routledge.

Small, Meredith. 1998. *Our Babies Ourselves: How Biology and Culture Shape the Way We Parent*. New York: Doubleday.

———. 2001. *Kids: How Biology and Culture Shape the Way We Raise Our Children*. New York: Doubleday.

Stearns, Peter. 1975. *European Society in Upheaval: Social History Since 1750*, 2nd ed. New York: Macmillan.

Tobin, Joseph, David Wu, and Dana Davidson. 1989. *Preschool in Three Cultures: Japan, China, and the United States*. New Haven, CT: Yale University Press.

Vinovskis, Maris. 1996. "Changing Perspectives and Treatment of Young Children in the United States." In C. Philip Hwang, Michael Lamb, and Irving Sigel (eds.) *Images of Childhood*, 99–112. Mahwah, NJ: Lawrence Erlbaum.

West, Elliott. 1992. "Children of the Plains Frontier." In Elliott West and Paula Petrik (eds.) *Small Worlds: Children and Adolescents in America, 1850–1950*, 26–41. Lawrence: University of Kansas Press.

Zelizer, Viviana. 1985. *Pricing the Priceless Child: The Changing Social Value of Children*. New York: Basic Books. ✦

Chapter 4

Basic Processes and Outcomes of Socialization

Although it is sometimes useful to speak of *the* process of socialization, just as we speak of the process of urbanization or industrialization or globalization, the fact is that each of these terms defines a complex reality. Each points to a major focus of interest and identifies certain large-scale effects. But when we study these phenomena, we quickly become aware that each of these terms encompasses diverse events. *Socialization* is not a unitary phenomenon but rather a term for a variety of processes. The relationships among these specific processes are by no means fully worked out and understood. A unified and comprehensive theory of socialization has yet to be achieved. Nevertheless, we shall try, in this chapter, to identify and discuss the major processes. In so doing, we must approach our topic from several angles of vision, each of which illuminates the topic in a somewhat different way. Our goal here will be to present a general "model" of socialization that is broadly applicable and independent of specific cultures. This model is based primarily on a sociological theory, know as *symbolic interactionism*, whose leading developer was George Herbert Mead, although our model incorporates elements of other theories as well. Mead's student, Herbert Blumer, the sociologist who coined this term, explains,

> The term 'symbolic interaction' refers . . . to the peculiar and distinctive character of interaction as it takes place between human beings. The peculiarity consists in the fact that human beings interpret or 'define' each other's action instead of merely reacting to each other's actions. Their 'response' is not made directly to the actions of one another but instead is based on the meaning which they attach to such actions. Thus, human action is mediated by the use of symbols, by interpretation, or by ascertaining the meaning of one another's interactions. (Blumer 1969, 78–79)

A baby is not born with the ability to engage in interpretation but develops it in the course of socialization by developing a *self* (Blumer 1969, 79–82; Stryker 1981, 5–15.) This chapter will explain how that occurs and why it is important. The following chapters will illustrate how this model applies in specific cultural and situational contexts.

To begin, recall our definition of socialization: the process by which we learn the ways of a given society or social group so that we can adequately participate in it. By unraveling this definition, we can fashion a framework that helps us to locate component processes of socialization. Learning involves developmental change in the organism; it occurs primarily in interaction with others who play important roles in that person's life. Such interaction necessarily entails communication of one kind or another, which is most meaningful in the context of emotionally significant relationships; and such relationships are always shaped by the social groups of which the person is a member. Succinctly, then, we may say that socialization leads to certain outcomes that

- are shaped by social groupings of varying scope

- in emotionally significant contexts

- by means of communication

- through interaction with "significant others,"

- and occur over time.

Society and Socialization

Most commonly, socialization processes have been considered in face-to-face contexts such as families, schools, or peer groups. Indeed, we shall focus on these contexts in Chapters 5 through 8. Yet it is clear that such groupings are units in the larger society—the ongoing society whose general structure we sketched in Chapter 2. Parents not only raise their children to function acceptably in the family but also prepare them to leave the family and function acceptably in other settings. Schools do the same. The values and techniques of peer-group relationships, although less obvious, also have their long-term applications. Families, schools, peer groups, and other agencies of socialization may vary in how attentive they are to socially desired outcomes, how they try to bring about these outcomes, and how effective their chosen procedures are. Furthermore, although families, schools, and other social groupings often express divergent expectations toward those being socialized, they also have some important convergent expectations. From this perspective, then, it is reasonable to say that *society specifies certain desirable outcomes or ranges of outcomes of socialization*. For example, every society, just to maintain itself, expends some of its resources to produce children who will become *law-abiding* adults. Children who do not become law-abiding adults are likely to be judged socialization failures. Another socialization outcome specified by the society is *loyalty*. The society seeks to engender loyalty to itself; its institutions and its groups contribute to this outcome in various ways. When children—or adults—demonstrate achievement of socially desired outcomes, society (or one of its institutions) "gives recognition" in the form of prizes, badges, certificates, diplomas, titles, promotions, and so forth.

The most basic goal is a *motivated commitment to sustain responsive participation in society*. Another way to put this is to say that children should become people who recognize and accept legitimate claims made upon them by others. These claims are multiple and diverse, and they differ according to a person's location in the social structure. Some, however, are general. For example, people should accept and function within the limits of communication and emotional expression that are defined as appropriate in different situations. Thus, they may scream at a football game but not in a supermarket. (A parent whose child screams in a supermarket is likely to feel embarrassed because the child is violating a norm—even though the child may be too young to know the norm—and because bystanders tend to attribute the norm violation to the parent, who is expected to uphold the norm for everybody's benefit by restraining the child.) Another general type of claim may be expressed in this way: People should accept the obligations of their roles. If they take a job, they should do the work and meet its other legitimate requirements. If they enter into a friendship, they should be friendly according to the norms of that particular friendship, whatever they may be.

Even in those special cases where people are later trained for patterned withdrawal from society—for example, nuns or monks who take vows of silence—the pattern of behavior is responsive to certain norms; it is not idiosyncratic withdrawal. Such an outcome falls within the range of socially acceptable results of socialization; although it represents a deviant role, it is not defined as a lack of motivated commitment to sustain responsive participation in society. In contrast, the roles of "junkie" or "crackhead"—a drug addict dependent on heroin or crack cocaine—are examples of "dropping out" of society, even though these addicts do interact with suppliers to obtain their drugs. By definition, these behaviors represent failures from the perspective in which we are viewing socialization.

The difference between the role of the monk who takes vows of silence and that of the junkie can be understood more fully by stating another expected outcome. As has been pointed out by sociologist Alex Inkeles (1968) and social psychologist M. Brewster Smith (1968), society expects the development of some kind of *competence*. Different societies require different kinds of competence, and any one society requires different kinds of competence for its diverse social roles. Nevertheless, it seems possible to formulate certain general requirements that transcend this diversity. Inkeles does so in the following way:

> Every individual must learn to be reasonably responsive to the patterns of social order and to the personal needs and requirements of the other individuals with whom he is in contact. In other words, he must be basically socially conforming. He must have the ability to orient himself in space and time and have sufficient command of the rudimentary physical requirements of his setting so as not to destroy himself or be an undue burden on others. (Inkeles 1968, 87–88)

He goes on to say that a society, or any particular status within it, requires a set of mental and physical skills, some kind of knowledge and information, certain ways of thinking about the world, some values that guide action, and a conception of oneself that organizes how one relates to authority, to intimates and peers, and to the larger community (Inkeles 1968, 87–88).

Applying this conception to our example, we may say that our society recognizes—as do many others—certain kinds of "religious competence" and allows the development of institutions in which that competence may be practiced, even when that practice takes the form of withdrawal from verbal communication in order to engage in meditation. In contrast, drug addiction is defined by our society as willful destruction of a person's social competence and is therefore not generally accepted as a legitimate outcome of socialization in this society.

Now it is necessary here to introduce certain modifications of what has just been said. We have argued that many groups in a society have convergent expectations; that is, in any given society, family, school, church, and youth group, for example, may press toward the same general outcomes. Because there is such convergence, we are justified in saying that society specifies certain outcomes. But two important modifications need to be stated. First, the fact that various institutions in a society tend to be mutually supportive in what they expect does not mean that they are entirely so. There is conflict as well as support among institutions. Parents often do not approve of what the school does, and vice versa. The peer group may encourage activities on which the authorities frown. Accordingly, socialization is not a smooth process. The child is subjected to conflicting as well as mutually supportive expectations. As a result, almost every child experiences some inner conflict in trying to sort out conflicting expectations directed to him or her.

Second, in arguing that society seeks to generate a motivated commitment to sustain participation and certain general forms of competence, we ignored certain phenomena that also are among the processes of socialization. Earlier we spoke of "dropping out" as a failure of socialization. What needs to be added here is that whereas some socialization failures may be attributable to particular socializing agents, other failures may be due to society's own contradictory organization. Thus, a society may expect all children to learn certain things but may arrange its institutions in such a way that some are prevented from learning what they are expected to learn. In the United States, for example, one of the goals of the elementary school is to teach children of diverse backgrounds how to get along with others. But many institutional arrangements have segregated whites from blacks and from Latinos in their schooling, so that there is a systematically fostered limiting of competence in this social skill. To take another example: As long ago as 1960, there was a "rediscovery" of hunger and malnutrition in the United States. More than 40 years later, these conditions persist. Political and economic institutions do not deliver food to all who need it. Nutritional deficiencies almost certainly impair mental ability and thus prevent children from learning things they are expected to learn (Balderston 1981; Birch and Gussow 1970; Black 2000; Pike and Brown 1975; Pollitt 1979; Scrimshaw and Gordon 1968; Wolfe, Burkman, and Streng 2000). This again is an example of how the pattern of institutions can generate failures in socialization. More generally, although every society expects various types of minimal competence and seeks to foster more than minimal competence in those activities it most values, no society succeeds in eliciting even minimal levels among all its children, in part because the institutional pattern interferes.

These, then, are the general goals of socialization: *loyalty* to the society, *law-abidingness*, a motivated *commitment* to sustain responsive participation in society, and forms of *competence* that the society accepts as appropriate. These goals are generic; they are universally applicable. Of course, when we become more specific, we find that the same kinds of commitment and competence are not expected of all members of society. The artist and the career soldier differ not only in their kinds of competence but also in the kinds of commitment to social participation expected of them. The soldier will participate in a set of relationships governed by rigid rules of obedience to command. The artist will participate in a set of relationships governed by efforts to attract an audience that will appreciate the uniqueness of his or her vision and skill. Society expects the socialization process to enable every new member eventually to find some appropriate adult status(es) within some legitimate set(s) of relationships. As we noted in Chapter 2, each status entails a role. To that, we can now add that a role (such as the occupational role of soldier or artist) involves a particular type of commitment to social participation and particular types of competence.

While socialization is expected to result in the fulfilling of various specialized roles, it must also, as Inkeles points out (1968), make it possible for persons to participate in a variety of ways with others whose statuses and roles are quite different from their own. The late Robert Hutchins, an educator and social reformer, used to deride a certain engineering school that maintained a Department of Engineering English because, as he put it, "nobody else speaks Engineering English" (Hutchins 1953, 37). Whatever the merit of his derisiveness, the point he was making was that socialization can sometimes result in such an intense commitment to a particular form of social participation as to hamper social participation across role boundaries. A similar point had been made earlier by noted social critic and economist Thorstein Veblen, who spoke of people who develop a "trained incapacity" to function outside their narrow specialty (Veblen 1914, 347).

Every society provides a variety of statuses and roles. Usually it also has more or less explicit rules governing access to at least certain statuses and roles. The social class into which a child is born, for example, may decisively determine those open to that child in later life. As early as 1944, W. Lloyd Warner and his colleagues showed that the type of education young American children receive is determined to a large extent by their social class (Warner, Havighurst, and Loeb 1944). Their conclusions have been borne out by much subsequent investigation down to our own day, as we shall document in following chapters. Ethnic group membership and religion have often been— and in some places still are—decisive determinants of the kinds of social participation that will be allowed and the kinds of competence that children will be able to acquire. In the United States and other societies established primarily by WASPs, children from dark-skinned minorities were long socialized toward less valued statuses and roles, often toward those that sociologist Everett Hughes (1981) characterized as the "dirty work" of the society. In recent years, this trend has moderated somewhat as a result of such occurrences as the civil rights movement and affirmative action programs. It is still the case, however, that children born into more favored segments of society are socialized toward more favored statuses and roles. American society idealizes equality of opportunity, but obviously that does not mean that middle-class boys have an equal opportunity to become day laborers or middle-class girls an equal opportunity to become hotel chambermaids. We may conclude that society has criteria for distinguishing among children, often based on the status attributes of the families into which they are born, and procedures for directing different groups of children into different sequences of experiences that eventuate in different socialization outcomes.

Thus, we see that people—through their institutions—organize society in such a way as to develop in their children both a general commitment to participation in society and a general competence for doing so, and also a variety of commitments and competencies that are considered relevant to particular statuses and roles. And, to the degree that different groups in society have different opportunities, positions, and values, they may also have different measures of competence and different methods of child rearing for developing this competence.

Emotionally Significant Relationships

Where does socialization begin? We have given one answer to this question by saying that society specifies desired outcomes that are to be accomplished by its agencies—its families, schools, churches, youth groups, mass media, and other institutions. From this perspective, socialization begins with the specification of the range of outcomes toward which all newborns will be directed.

But the newborn, of course, knows nothing of this. If we look at the question from this perspective, it requires a different answer. Socialization begins with *personal attachment*, which is the development of an emotional bond with the primary caregiver (Collin 1996, 7) and which may also develop in stable relationships with secondary caregivers. Born active but helpless, vocal but without speech, with only the potentiality to become fully social, and needing care, infants begin to be socialized by being cared for by one or more persons who are committed to caring for them. At birth, children evoke sentiments of pride, love, apprehension, tenderness, responsibility, hope, and so forth in those who receive them as new members of the group. It is essential that such care be given with a consistency that results in a child's secure attachment to the caregivers. The scholar who first studied the importance of the child's secure attachment to his or her caregivers (Bowlby 1958, 1969) believed that ideally the primary caregiver should always be the child's mother. Research in more recent years has come to the conclusion that a father can be the primary caregiver or that such care can be distributed among several caregivers (Bradley 1998; Collin 1996, 169–70). Toddlers (11 to 27 months old) in day care can form an attachment to stable caregivers who have taken care of the child for at least 10 months (Collin 1996, 185). The essential activities of early caregiving include holding and touching, feeding the child, changing diapers, and responding to cries.

From the perspective of the individual child starting out in life, the caregiver-child relationship is where socialization begins. What happens in this relationship that initiates socialization? Many different things.

This is the infant's first relationship with another person. It is therefore the first significant encounter with what it means to be human. Being cared for is one's first experience of social life. As such, and coming before a child can evaluate it, the relationship with the caregiver is virtually all the social life an infant has and therefore presents his or her first expectation of the social world. The infant whose caregiver spends much time with her or him, singing, playing, and feeding, will have a different expectation of social life than the infant whose caregiver provides only minimal and cursory care.

Not less important, in this first attachment the child has the rudimentary beginnings of a sense of self. One fundamental fact of the caregiver-child relationship is that the adult has far more power than the infant. But this is not to say that the infant is necessarily entirely powerless. If its cries of discomfort succeed with some consistency in evoking caregiver response that allays the discomfort, then, we have reason to believe, the infant is launched on a path of experiencing itself as effective. On the other hand, when the infant's cries do not bring a satisfying response, or do so only inconsistently, its sense of powerlessness is intensified.

Ideally, a child has a dependable caregiver, with the result that the child develops a sense of trust and security (Erikson 1963). When the child becomes a toddler (ages 1 to 3), the excitement of walking, combined with a sense of security, prompt the child to explore her or his environment. But she or he still needs the caregiver as a secure base. There is thus an alternation of *attachment behavior*, such as reaching to be picked up, hugging, cuddling, and clinging, and *exploring behavior*, such as walking, climbing, running, jumping, and inspecting everything in sight (Lieberman 1993, 8). Another expression of this alternation is described this way:

> The toddler loves to run off again and again, only to squeal in delight on being pursued and scooped up by the mother. This game is of great symbolic importance for the junior toddler. It reassures him that mobility need not mean alienation or abandonment, and that the mother will not leave him to his own (fledgling) devices but will *want* to retrieve him again and again. For a worn-out parent, this game may seem like an endless tease. For the toddler, it is a crucial reassurance that independence and togetherness can go hand in hand. (Lieberman 1993, 15; italics in original)

In sum, by being cared for, by evoking response and being responded to, the infant obtains its first sense of self, first sense of another person, and first experience of a social relationship. In this relationship, the infant develops its first expectations and thus its first sense of social order. A rudimentary temporal order emerges from such experiences as the interval between crying and being responded to, the interval between feedings, and the alternation of sleeping and

wakefulness. In being cared for, the infant has its first experiences of those sentiments that Charles Horton Cooley identified decades ago as the hallmark of human nature, sentiments such as empathy and love (Cooley 1909).

The child's attachment to the earliest caregiving figure is the first of many
emotionally significant relationships that the child will form in the course of
her or his life with *significant others*—the people who will have an impact on
the child's socialization. It will be followed by various attachments to a diversity of significant others, who may include other adult figures, siblings,
agemates and older children in neighborhood and school, relatives, teachers,
friends and "enemies," fictional figures from movies and television, and persons portrayed in books. A child will form a somewhat different kind of relationship with each of these people; and because each has a different status in
society and a different role in relation to the child, each will make a different
kind of contribution to the child's socialization. These differences will give
rise to problems for the child from an early age, with the conflict between parents and agemates typically being one focus of stress. Four-year-olds encouraged by playmates to cross the street in pursuit of adventure may experience
distress before they follow the suggestion or only after their parents have discovered that they have done so. In either case, they are experiencing an early
form of the conflict of norms and expectations that impinge on them from socializing agents who occupy different statuses.

Communication

Now we face a paradox. Society presses toward certain outcomes, yet socialization begins (most commonly, in North American and other Western societies) in a two-person (or three-person) relationship of mother (or mother
and father) giving care to an infant who cannot speak or think or even understand instruction. How can an infant traverse the path from this beginning to
that of a participating member of society? How can he or she be set upon this
path?

The relevant facts here are that speechless newborns can hear and feel. Recent research has discovered that hearing begins even before birth. In the
twentieth week of gestation, the fetus attends to noises in the mother's body,
including her heartbeat. Starting in the sixth month, the fetus becomes acquainted with the mother's voice and with the intonations and rhythms of the
language she speaks. As a team of linguistics scholars reports, "Already
equipped with some experience of what language sounds like, the newborn
comes into the world prepared to pay special attention to human speech, and
specifically, to [its] mother's voice. These earliest intrauterine experiences
prime the newborn for linguistic input and can therefore be viewed as playing
an important role in the overall process of language development" (Karmiloff
and Karmiloff-Smith 2001, 1–2, 10–14, 43–44). These intrauterine experiences
are so influential that the 4-day-old newborn prefers its mother's voice to another female voice and prefers to listen to the sounds of the language it heard
in the womb than to those of another language, although, of course, it does not
understand the meanings of those sounds (Karmiloff and Karimiloff-Smith
2001, 44–46; Haslett and Samter 1997, 23). Intrauterine experience thus pre-

pares the newborn for the acquisition of language, one of the basic processes of socialization.

While parents and other caregivers generally speak to children as soon as they are born, children don't speak their first words usually until some time between 9 and 12 months of age. But during all this time, they are also involved in *nonverbal communication* with their caregivers. The main channels of nonverbal communication are (1) eye gaze, (2) facial expressions, and (3) gestures. Eye gaze is a way of showing attention. Infants become able to establish eye contact around the age of six weeks, and when they direct a gaze to a caregiver, that generally elicits responsive eye contact from the caregiver. The importance of this continues beyond infancy, according to linguistic scholars who point to the way it contributes to socialization:

> In summary, eye gaze is an important way for infants to gain attention and maintain joint regard. Coordinated eye gaze and joint attention between mother and infant foster secure attachment and effective interaction; caretakers appear to regulate eye gaze behavior with infants so as to maintain optimal stimulation for the infant. Gaze behavior is also associated with social competence and self-regulation among preschoolers. (Haslett and Samter 1997, 41–42)

Facial expressions are expressions of emotions. One widely accepted view today is that anger and fear are "prewired," that is, these emotions and the facial movements that express them are innate in the nervous system and are universal, not culturally variable. Other emotions and their expression, however, develop through the infant's contact with caregivers, who are, of course, participants in particular cultures. Around 3 months of age, infants can distinguish positive from negative emotional expressions in others. They begin to imitate facial expressions of caregivers, and between 3 and 6 months they become particularly responsive to others who present smiling faces. During this first year of life, infants are also learning *display rules*, the social norms governing emotional expression. By the second year, according to one study, infants are already beginning to show self-regulation of their own negative emotional expression, dampening it through such expressions as compressed lips, knit brows, and lip biting (Haslett and Samter 1997, 26–32).

Research on gestures is not yet highly developed, but a couple of points can be made here. An early gesture is reaching. Babies reach for something that they want. Later, around 12 to 14 months, pointing appears. Pointing is especially likely to elicit a verbal response from caregivers (Haslett and Samter 1997, 43–49).

These three forms of nonverbal communication are often intermingled in interactions between infants and caregivers that result in coordinated behavior. This occurs in *preverbal routines* such as feeding, bathing, and bedtime and in games such as peekaboo. With increasing experience in these routines and games, the infant is increasingly able to coordinate with the caregiver with ever greater accuracy. Further, increasingly the infant is able to initiate communication of its intentions to others (Haslett and Samter 1997, 49–55, 103–

105; Nelson 1996, 97). The joint attention and activity of infant and caregiver contributes significantly to attachment and also to the infant's readiness for the more complex coordination with others that is accomplished through language.

Symbols, Language, and Interaction

When infants are born, they can basically feel two conditions, comfort and discomfort. When they feel discomfort, they cry. A mother or other caregiver hears the cry, *interprets* it as a sign of discomfort, and *responds* with activities that she hopes will restore the infant to comfort. She will evaluate, or interpret, her own effort as successful when the child ceases to cry. Her initial efforts may not be "on target" because she may incorrectly interpret the source of the discomfort and the actions that will be effective in assuaging it. She may assume the child is hungry, only to find that it does not nurse. Further trial and error will lead to a "correct interpretation"—one that leads the child to stop crying.

The situation we have just described, along with the preverbal joint-action routines, are the prototypes of interaction from which more complex forms evolve and through which the infant will develop into a person who can function in society. When a child cries, the noise is not simply a noise to the mother or caregiver. The noise is significant to her on two bases. First, she accepts the noise as having a legitimate claim on her attention, because of her relationship to the child. The noise will not go unnoticed as might the noise of an airplane passing overhead, because *for her* it signifies or *symbolizes her* attachment and responsibility to the child. It does so independently of how she chooses to respond to the cry. But the second meaning of the cry is a responsive or *interactive* meaning. She may decide that the cry should be interpreted as meaning she should attend to the infant right away. Alternatively, she may decide to interpret it as one that allows her to wait until a more convenient moment to respond. Or she may decide not to respond immediately, with the express goal of teaching the child to tolerate more discomfort. Whatever her particular response, she engages in an imaginative process—which may take no longer than an instant—in which she represents to herself what the child is probably feeling and what should be done about it. Her overt response to the child's cry occurs only after the process of inner representation.

The capacity to interpret communications from others and to represent to oneself what others may think, feel, and do is fundamental to all of social life. Newborns do not have this capacity, and this is what they must develop. At the outset, they experience discomfort but do not know how it can be assuaged. Crying is involuntary; it is not a communication *to the infant*, even though it is to the caregiver. But in time, as cries succeed in bringing caregiver and comfort, they begin to be more under the infant's voluntary control There is evidence that by the last half of the first year of life, infants have established memory for such repeated sequences of events, although no one can yet say when infants begin to have mental representations of them (Nelson 1996, 154–157). Nevertheless, the child becomes increasingly able to anticipate the mother's or other caregiver's appearance. By the time the child becomes able to stand in a crib, he or she is able to look toward the door through which the caregiver will come and to greet her entry by rocking on her or his feet, reaching out, and changing vocalization. The child has developed some expectations that are responsive to the caregiver's expectations. In this way, the child has made a further advance on the way to becoming socialized. The child begins to learn how to function in society by learning how to function in the relationship with his or her primary caregiver(s).

With the gradual acquisition of language, socialization accelerates and becomes qualitatively changed. The child gradually acquires the capacity to transform something in its own mind (a mental representation) into a message to another person (a linguistic representation), a fundamental capacity in becoming a socialized person, but not an easy task as each struggles to understand the other (Nelson 1996, 121). Recall our account of caregiver-infant interaction. When the infant cries, the caregiver interprets this as a sign of need. But she must discover for herself whether the infant is hungry, wet, cold, has caught its foot in the slats of the crib, or is in some other state of discomfort. The infant's cry is an interpretable symbol to its caregiver but only imperfectly so; and it is not at all a symbol to the infant. As infants acquire the ability to use common gestures and language, they are acquiring the ability to symbolize— to use a representation of an intention or of an object. In place of nonspecific cries, they are able to point or tug or name their wishes to another person. When children are able to present to themselves the same symbol for an object that they present to others, they have taken a large step toward regulating their own behavior and simultaneously a large step toward participating responsively with others. A qualitative change of great importance has thus taken place when, instead of nonspecific cries, children can designate their wishes with words that communicate specifically "bottle," "wet," "pick me up," and so on. They now have at their disposal specific symbols whose meaning *they know* and that they know their caregivers know. They are entering into a world of shared symbols. Their capacity for social interaction is thus expanding enormously as they master an expanding array of shared symbols. In this process, they are gaining the capacity to move beyond the caregiver-child relationship into a larger world of shared symbols.

Language plays a significant part in organizing a social order and in the child's socialization into that order. Language is, among its other functions, a system for classifying objects and events in ways that are socially significant. For example, if a child sits on a table, he or she may be told, "That's not a chair." The table surface lends itself to sitting, just as does a chair; but despite their physical similarities in this respect, they are socially defined as completely different objects, and this difference is embodied in a verbal classification that organizes behavior in relation to those objects. The way in which things and events are verbally classified defines their social nature, and these classifications become a fundamental part of our way of thinking and acting. Our very perception is shaped by our language categories. In time, the child will not even see the table as offering the possibility for sitting, because his or her knowledge of it as being within the category *table* will preclude the possibility.

Categorization of social reality takes more complex forms. A common example in our society is our tendency to characterize many situations in "either-

or" terms. The child may encounter this at the dinner table in the form of "Either eat your vegetables or go without dessert." Another situation of similar form is "Practice the piano (do your homework, clean up your room) or you can't watch TV." Desired activities are thus incorporated in an "either-or" way of thinking that makes them contingent on the performance of some undesired activity—"or else."

Language and Memory

One further indication of the way in which language shapes experience is of particular interest. Sigmund Freud, who developed the theory of human behavior known as psychoanalysis, called attention to "the peculiar amnesia which veils from most people (not from all) the first years of their childhood, usually the first six or eight years" (Freud 1938, 581). He was impressed with the fact that childhood experiences are often vivid and that they include love, jealousy, and other passions. Yet despite the intensity, memories of these early experiences in later years are fragmentary at best. Following up on Freud's observations but dissatisfied with his explanation of this massive failure of memory, Ernest G. Schachtel proposed the following explanation: Memory organizes past experiences in the service of present needs, fears, and interests. Adult memory is organized into categories that are shaped by society. These categories are not suitable to reproduce the intense experiences of childhood because they are shaped by the biases, emphases, and taboos of adult culture. Adult memory is essentially conventionalized, and therefore early childhood experience—in which everything seems new, fresh, and exciting—is incompatible, hence forgotten. In fact, Schachtel argues, many people remember not their experiences but the words for telling of their experiences:

> There are people who experience a party, a visit to the movies, a play, a concert, a trip in the very words in which they are going to tell their friends about it, in fact, quite often they anticipate such experiences in these words. The experience is predigested . . . even before they have tasted of it. . . . [T]hey have seen, heard, felt nothing but the phrase with which later they will report to their friends the 'exciting time' they have had. (Schachtel 1959, 287–289)

More recent thinking agrees that the organization of memory is linked to language acquisition but finds that when children of 2 to 3 have acquired enough language, their memories begin to work in ways similar to those of older children and adults, although they do not become interested in talking about past experiences until about age 4 (Nelson 1996, 159–165, 177). A child's memory is shaped by the conversations it has with parents and other caregivers at home and in preschool who talk over things that have happened, thus supplying language categories. "By the end of the pre-school period children's memory has become socialized through discourse practices at home and school" (Nelson 1996, 181).

Conversation

Although society provides linguistic categories for organizing our thoughts and ideas, conversations themselves may have a problematic aspect for the participants because much of what is said assumes many things left unsaid. Social interaction depends upon interpretive procedures that help the person "make sense of" or "understand" what is going on, including, importantly, understanding other people's intentions. Such interpretive procedures evidently are learned fairly early in the course of socialization. It has been suggested that social games such as "peekaboo" and "pattycake" help prepare the way for developing such interpretive understanding as does pretend play with toys and other objects (Nelson 1996, 320–321). When a child becomes able to answer the telephone and a caller asks, "Is your daddy there?" the child comes to understand that the child not only is being asked a question but also is expected to call daddy to the phone. Nor is it a question when the mother says, "How many times have I told you to close that door?" Nor is the nursery school teacher just making announcements when she says, "It's nap time," or, "It's clean-up time now" (Ervin-Tripp 1977). In all these instances, the child is expected to interpret the language, understand the context, and then act appropriately. Each sentence spoken carries a wider range of meaning than is actually stated, and conversational language must be continually interpreted by the participants.

Gregory Bateson and his coworkers (1956) introduced the concept of *modality*. All spoken communication involves something said and a modality in which it is said—words are said seriously, jokingly, commandingly, questioningly, and so on. Very young children are sometimes unable to interpret the modality being used. For example, they may not understand that parents are commanding, not asking. Certain kinds of playful comments made by older children or adults may not be understood as playful by the very young child, who may burst into tears. When this happens, the older children or adults may engage in a detailed explanation of what was intended. In the course of socialization, most children develop the ability to interpret modality most of the time. Still, there are times when anyone may be uncertain and may ask, "Are you serious?" or "Are you kidding?" Adequate socialization makes such occasions infrequent. We are able to recognize the modality by the combination of words spoken, tone of voice, and the social context in which the words are spoken But even when we understand the modality, we still must continually interpret the words (Haley 1959, 357–374).

Language Mastery

Language acquisition is a major component process of socialization, while *language facility* is the expected outcome of this process. The meaning of language facility in early childhood and in later adulthood for middle-class people in Western societies has been summarized in these words by a developmental psychologist who has studied children's language over many years:

We know, both from common observation and scholarly research, that typically by about 4 years of age most children have mastered basic structures of sentence grammar, have acquired a vocabulary of a few thousand words, speak sufficiently articulately to be understood by strangers, and have mastered some basic pragmatic structures such as how to ask questions and how to address adults and peers. But there is much more to be learned. The most important outcome of language acquisition in childhood is mastery of language at a level sufficient to serve the varied cognitive and communicative representational functions possible for adult language users. These functions include telling stories, making plans, reading novels, gossiping, studying history, reading the newspaper, following written instructions, and formulating formal and informal arguments. (Nelson 1996, 123)

The Significance of Significant Others

With our discussion of emotional attachments and of communication as background, we are now in a position to identify some additional processes that make significant others significant to the child and help the child develop from the primarily biological organism he or she is at birth into a social being as well.

When we say that the task of socialization is to enable the child to learn to participate in society, we refer to a complex type of adaptation that cannot be understood as a kind of mechanical conformity. As our brief sketch of human biological nature in Chapter 2 makes clear, human socialized behavior is not analogous to the behavior of the trained rat running a maze and receiving rewards for making what the experimenter considers correct turns in a correct sequence. Socialization is not simply a process of making correct motions prescribed by trainers. "Running in a rat race" or "jumping through a hoop" like a trained dog are, when applied to humans, terms for caricaturing certain distortions of socialization.

As suggested by our discussion of learning language rules, the essence of socialization is the person's *internal regulation* or *self-regulation* of his or her own behavior in ways that are adequate to the interpersonal situations and to the larger social order in which he or she participates. This capability develops as a result of interaction with significant others.

Significant others present themselves to the child in two essential ways:

- by what they do

- by what they say (and how they say it).

Doing and saying are, of course, organized in terms of roles. Thus a mother at home presents herself to her child by feeding, changing diapers, offering toys, addressing the child with words of endearment, and, perhaps, carrying a briefcase and driving the child to a daycare center. The father may do many of the same activities as the mother, but likely will also be taller, have a deeper voice, talk with different inflections and a different vocabulary, more often watch football, and be brusquer in his handling of the child. An older brother may run and shout, throw a ball, have his own toys, use a still different vocabulary, and be subject to the authority of the parents. These are examples of doing and saying that become significant to the young, developing child.

As infants become aware of the activities going on around them, they become interested in these activities; and because these are the activities of people to whom infants are attached, they want to do what those around them do and, indeed, to be as they are. For example, not long after a mother begins giving her child nonliquid food, the child wishes to feed her as he or she is being fed. The child tries to take the spoon from her and feed her. As the range of observation expands, the child tries other activities that seem interesting: turning light switches on and off, opening the refrigerator, and the like. And while the child's significant others are engaged in such activities, they are also engaged in saying things—naming the objects that they handle ("Drink your milk"), describing what they are doing ("Here's your doll"), and playing word games ("Where's your nose? Show me your nose"). Children begin to repeat the words they hear and to carry out the actions they see others carry out. In short, they perceive their significant others as *role models*, sources of the patterns of behavior and conduct on which they pattern themselves. It is through interaction with these role models that children develop the ability to regulate their own behavior.

Development of the Self

The basic fact that the child's regulation of its own behavior develops from interaction with role models has been noted by numerous interpreters but explained variously by them. A particularly insightful explanation was developed in the first third of the twentieth century by George Herbert Mead, a prominent figure in American sociology who continues to be influential three-quarters of a century after his death, and we follow here in his footsteps as we also elaborate his views and incorporate later developments of the theory. For Mead, the principal outcome of socialization that makes self-regulation possible is the development of the *self* (Mead 1934). The self, in his view, is the capacity to represent to oneself what one wishes to communicate to others. The newborn does not have a self and will not begin to develop one for several months. Language plays a crucial part in the development of the self. This is why, from Mead's point of view, the child's development from simply crying to being able to use socially shared symbols such as "I want bottle" or "Go outside" (for "I want to go outside") is such a significant transformation. Only after acquiring the beginnings of language can a child self-consciously and purposively represent to itself that which it wishes to represent to others. A preverbal child who is being fed something it does not like can spit out the food or tightly close its lips in refusal. In this very specific and very limited situation, the child may be said to "have a mind of its own" and have a way of communicating it to someone else. But there are not many social situations in which it can know its own mind without having words to represent the mental content. It has to know its own mind before it can tell someone else what it wants, and beyond the elementary situation just described, it can only know its own mind by having words that both represent what is in its mind and can be used to represent that content to someone else. This, for Mead, is what it means to have a self—to be able to represent to oneself what one wishes to represent to others. The child who can do this is on its way to becoming a fully social being, that is, on its way to being simultaneously self-regulating and socially responsive.

According to Mead's analysis, the self is both a structure and a process. It consists of two parts or phases, which Mead called the "I" and the "Me." The "I," which is a feature of the human being as biological organism, is the self as an *acting subject*. Spitting is the "I" acting, but this particular action does not have much of a place in the child's future. It will be succeeded by the child engaging in such actions as walking, talking, running, jumping, laughing, hugging, drawing, writing, singing, riding, dancing, imagining, thinking, believing, and many more. The "I" is also the part of the self that enables us to be aware of who we are. The teenage girl who is told, "You are just like your mother," may answer angrily, "I am not my mother. *I am me.*" She is insisting that she knows herself, which is a form of acting toward oneself. And she has taken that mental representation of herself and expressed it in a statement to another person. She has first acted toward herself (knowing) before she acted toward the other person (speaking). The "Me" is the self as *the object of one's own actions*; it is also the accumulation of attitudes toward the person expressed by diverse others that are taken over by the person, mixed with one's own thoughts about those attitudes, and also mixed with one's own experiences and one's reaction to them. The teenage girl in the example is both the knower ("I") and the object of her knowing, that which is known ("Me"). The following sketch illustrates the self process.

A mother tells her daughter, Susan, "You have brown hair." The daughter's having brown hair is part of the mother's attitudes about her daughter, that is, it is part of the mother's ideas about her and something she believes Susan should know. When Susan hears it, it becomes part of her "Me." It may take a while before Susan can make this information part of her usable knowledge about herself, but before long she will be able to say to someone else, "I have brown hair." When she can do this, Susan has become an acting subject toward herself (as well as toward the person she addresses.) Her "I" recognizes something about herself, something originally put into words by her mother. This capacity to be aware of oneself, to act toward oneself, is called *reflexivity*. It is essential for self-regulation. During Susan's early childhood, her mother will comb her hair. At a later period, Susan will look in the mirror and decide, "I've got to comb my hair before going out." That is a reflexive action (she acts toward herself), and it is also part of an interaction because the hair combing is done in anticipation of being with other people who will see her. In Mead's terms (which sociologists still use today), Susie has "taken the role of the others" whom she anticipates seeing, and their attitudes (as she understands them) become part of her "Me." As an "I," she regulated her own action by first responding to the inner representation of people (perhaps only passersby) who will see her and then by combing her hair.

How did Susan become able to take the role of the others? Mead had an explanation focusing first on language and symbols. "Combed hair" and "uncombed hair" are symbols for states of appearance that Susan now shares with others. Shared symbols are known as *significant symbols*. The following vignette captures a significant symbol in the process of formation:

> David, 28 months, has bitten his baby brother. His mother scolds him: "I told you not to do that, David. I am very angry at you ... you can't bite. It's a no-no." David looks at her very seriously, nods his head from side to side, and says "no-no." His mother repeats no-no, now in a softer tone, and helps him get back to play. In the following days, David is seen making pretend biting movements while nodding his head and saying to himself "no-no." (Lieberman 1993, 21–22)

He is working on—struggling—to make "no-no" have the same meaning for himself as it has for his mother.

Play Stage and Game Stage

But there is more to role-taking than language and symbols. In addition, Mead also recognized the importance of the child's observation of others' activities. He postulated that children, following a stage in which they mimic without comprehending, go through two stages of observation toward the development of self. In the first, or *play stage*, children take the roles of single, particular others. They play at being the others who are significant to them. They want to push the stroller, push the broom, carry the umbrella, put on the hat, and do all the other things they see their parents do, including saying what their parents say. The story is told of the 4-year-old boy playing "daddy" who put on his hat and coat, said goodbye, and walked out the front door, only to return a few minutes later because he did not know what to do next. He had taken as much of his father's work role as he could see and hear—the ritualized morning departure. What is noteworthy in this illustration (as in all play) is that the child is now able to govern his own behavior to a certain extent. When he first heard adults say "bye-bye" to him, he did nothing because the sound had no meaning to him. Nor did it mean anything when he first learned to repeat the sound. Now when he says good-bye, he directs himself to walk out the door.

In the play stage, children play at many roles that offer interesting models, not only taking the role of a parent but also playing "cops and robbers," letter carrier, babysitter, race car driver, and so on. During this stage, they progress from taking one role to taking two alternating roles in sequence. Thus, they may say things to themselves that their mothers have said to them, then reply in their own roles of children. Thus, a child playing alone can take these alternating roles. With a playmate, each can take one of the roles; after a time, they can switch roles—"Now you be the babysitter and I'll be the child."

With further development, the child enters the *game stage*. The importance of this lies in the fact that games involve an organization of roles, and the child has to take the roles of everyone else in the game. In Mead's famous example of the baseball game, the child

> must have the responses of each position involved in his own position. He must know what everyone else is going to do in order to carry out his own

play. He has to take all of these roles. They do not all have to be present in his consciousness at the same time, but at some moments he has to have three or four individuals present in his own attitude, such as the one who is going to throw the ball, the one who is going to catch it, and so on. These responses must be, in some degree, present in his own makeup. In the game, then, there is a set of responses of such others so organized that the attitude of one calls out the appropriate attitude of the other." (Mead 1934, 151)

Mead then summarizes the general importance of this example by saying that the self is not completely developed until the individual has a working awareness of any group of which he is a member, a general awareness of how the group functions. Mead refers to this as *taking the role of the generalized other* (Mead 1934, 155). Being able to throw, catch, and bat a ball are necessary but not sufficient to play baseball. A child cannot play the game until being able to comprehend that these physical activities are incorporated in an organized set of roles—pitcher, batter, fielder, and the like. The child must have this organization "in his head,"—as part of his self—so that he can engage in the cooperative activities of the game. The ability to understand the organization of roles that is required to play in a baseball game is an ability that will be required in all social participation in later childhood and adulthood. Organized social activity, whether a baseball game or anything else, requires that all the participants have sufficiently developed selves so that each of them can act appropriately (Mead 1934, 155).

Thus, once children have developed selves, they can act cooperatively with others. They may imaginatively take the position of others and know what is expected of them in their various roles as pitcher on a baseball team, passenger on a bus, clown in a school play, "good and polite child" visiting grandmother, caretaker of younger sister, and best friend to another child. The explanation of such role-taking is a subject of some disagreement among contemporary sociologists. Some would emphasize that performing a role is explainable as learned conformity. The baseball pitcher, in this explanation, learns the rules of baseball and what the pitcher is supposed to do in relation to the batter, the catcher, and the other players. The pitcher does his or her part according to the rules. Other sociologists emphasize that carrying out a role is a creative and interpretive activity. As Ralph Turner, one of the leading advocates of this view, puts it, much role-taking should be regarded as role-*making* because it involves "devising a performance on the basis of the imputed other-role" (Turner 1962, 22–23). The pitcher is not merely pitching according to a set of rules. In addition, he or she imputes a role to each batter—this one swings at every pitched ball, that one waits for a pitch to his liking, and so on—and decides how to try to pitch to each one. If the bases are loaded and there are two outs, the pitcher will devise one kind of role performance if the next batter is a good hitter and another type of role performance if the next batter is not a good hitter. This view of role performance as role-making, as continually developing as the situation changes, is based on Mead's notion of the "I" as active rather than simply conforming. In Mead's words,

The "I" is the response of the organism to the attitudes of others . . . this response of the "I" is something that is more or less uncertain. . . . The "I" gives the sense of freedom, of initiative. The situation is there for us to act in a self-conscious fashion. We are aware of ourselves, and of what the situation is, but exactly how we will act never gets into experience until after the action takes place. (Mead 1934, 176–178)

For young children, the opportunity to experience role-taking and role-making occurs especially in family relationships but is also evident in their relationships with toys (Ball 1967). Children commonly impute identities to their stuffed dolls and toys. They give them parts to play, converse with them, and act toward them. These toys may be given roles of surrogate companions; they may be sources of comfort and security or targets of love, hostility, sympathy, and other sentiments. The children, in their relationship with their toys, explore their own feelings and play with self-images of power, age status, and gender roles. Even computers—as Sherry Turkle demonstrates—are given "life," are considered to have minds of their own, and become objects of interaction (Turkle 1984). The children are thus acting and devising performances on the basis of the roles they impute to others. They are "role-making." Toys and games in this sense facilitate the process by which children engage in imaginative behavior and prepare for subsequent roles and relationships.

In taking the roles of others, children come to learn that sometimes they can "manage the impression" that they are making (Goffman 1959, 208–237). Thus, they may prepare a performance, practice what they will say, put on the right clothes, and act with the right demeanor. Sometimes they may know what others expect but, for whatever reason, choose to act otherwise. Sometimes, because of a miscalculation or slip-up, they are embarrassed or ashamed and seek to cover up or "save face." Such miscalculations reflect inaccurate role-taking. As Sheldon Stryker explains,

Role-taking is the process of anticipating the responses of others with whom one is involved in social interaction. Making use of symbolic cues . . . one organizes a definition of others' attitudes, orientations, and future responses which is then validated, invalidated, or reshaped in ongoing interaction. . . . Accuracy in role-taking is based at least in part on common experience which creates a fund of common symbols; but accuracy in role-taking is variable. (Stryker 1980, 52–53)

Mead's explanation of the development of the self, shaped by language acquisition and role-taking, remains one of the basic building blocks in our understanding of how humans function in society. In certain respects it is unexcelled to this day, 75 years after his death. But there are some gaps, some issues he did not cover. For example, Mead does not distinguish among different kinds of utterance. His approach does not touch on the difference between a parent saying, "Here's your doll" and "Don't do that!" The latter utterance is important in ways the former is not, even though both are statements made by the same role model and both help the child to categorize the world in linguistic terms. The latter statement is made *authoritatively*. It is more than a simple categorization. It is a statement of a *rule*, and it carries with it the suggestion of a *sanction*.

Role models who can present themselves to the child with authority to state rules and to enforce them with positive and negative sanctions play a particularly decisive part in the development of the child's self. An admired uncle who pilots a plane may catch the child's imagination more than his or her father who works at a nine-to-five desk job. But the father, as the model who wields the more effective authority over the child's life, is likely to have greater influence in shaping the child's social participation, at least during childhood. He, along with the mother, makes the child aware of limits to acceptable behavior. In short, the child has impulses and attempts actions that are unacceptable to those who have effective authority to interpret his or her behavior in the light of norms and values and to offer rewards and impose penalties to encourage appropriate conduct. (Effective authority does not rest only with adults. When children play with their peers, they come under a system of norms and sanctions that define forms of acceptable and unacceptable behavior such as "playing fair" and "cheating.") The self is established, then, not only on the basis of taking the role of the other but also through the process of internalizing the values and norms that are effectively presented by authoritative role models. In one sense, socialization can be summed up by saying that what was once outside the individual comes to be inside the individual. Society comes to exist within the individual as well as outside of him or her. This is the developmental change that makes all the difference. As we discussed in Chapter 1, while Mead was developing this basic understanding in the 1920s, the noted Russian psychologist Lev Vygotsky was developing a very similar view, but Americans did not become acquainted with his work until several decades after Mead's influence was established in sociology (Vygotsky 1978, 1986; Nelson 1996, 18–19). While some developmental psychologists are influenced by Mead, they tend to be more immersed in Vygotsky's work, while sociologists are more attentive to Mead.

Time and Outcomes of Socialization

The most general outcome of socialization is a person capable of participating in society. It is important to emphasize that *participating* does not necessarily mean "conforming" or "fitting in." To participate in society means to be able to take action that has social relevance. Thus, a bank robber can be described as partially socialized because he or she knows that money is valued, knows what social establishment keeps a supply in a fairly accessible place, probably has acquired some skill in using a product of society's technology—a gun—and can put all this together in a socially relevant act, a bank robbery. His or her socialization is, however, deviant from the majority's in ways that lead the robber to take actions that threaten the social order. He or she disregards the socially important distinction between legitimate and illegitimate procedures for obtaining money. This disregard represents something awry in his or her socialization, which can be considered unsuccessful. Society's desired goal of law-abidingness, discussed early in this chapter, has not been attained in this case. This may be considered a failure of socialization.

We run into problems, however, if we try to specify what "completely successful" socialization would be. We can't say that it involves conformity with all major values and norms because most people deviate sometime or another in their adherence to one or another major value or norm. Further, and perhaps even more important, certain kinds of nonadherence to usual patterns are deliberate and creative. Nonadherents may be effective in bringing about social changes so that an act that was deviant or illegitimate at one time is not at another. People may join together to organize social movements with the explicit goal of rejecting some prevailing values and norms and replacing them with others that they regard as preferable, and they may succeed in persuading many others that they, too, should reevaluate those values and norms being challenged. Many different kinds of factors bring about social change, and one of them is people who question and find fault with some existing value or norm and successfully challenge it.

While we cannot give a definition of "complete" socialization (even though we can sometimes recognize cases of seriously incomplete socialization), we can say more about the outcomes of socialization. The functioning person—whether bank robber, workaholic, creative artist, revolutionary, innovative thinker, or "ordinary guy"—has an inner organization that has been produced, in part, by a socialization that makes it possible to take the particular kinds of actions that link him or her to the society. We want now to present the main concepts of that inner organization.

More About the Self

The self is the most general outcome of socialization. Without it we would not be fully human. By enabling us to take the role of the other, the self makes it possible for us to interact with people unlike ourselves—those of different sex, of different ages, of different social stations, of different societies, or even, in our imaginations, of earlier time or in fantastic futures. The self enables us to experience shared humanity even when the other person is socially very different.

The self is, then, a structure that gives the person the capacity to function and participate in society by distinguishing different relationships and responding with appropriate differences. For example, within the space of an hour a 6-year-old child completes a school day, plays with other children on the way home, then enters his or her home. In that brief time, the child has switched from the role of pupil to the role of playmate to the role of son or daughter. In enacting its own role, the child takes the role of a series of others in succession—teacher, playmates, and mother or other caregiver. These social accomplishments are possible because the child already has a self, which gives it the capacity to take the roles of others in context, grasping the social situation and expressing role-appropriate behavior and sentiments—deference to the teacher, friendliness to playmates, and affection to the mother. The development of self enables the child to become self-regulating and thereby capable of coordinating his or her activities with others.

The activities of the self are complex and numerous. For example, in almost all adult interaction, a person seeks to control the impression that he or she makes on others. The person endeavors to act in ways that are appropriate to the situation and that convey a particular impression (Goffman 1959; 1967b). This kind of *self-management in social interaction* develops slowly among children over the course of socialization, and we allow them much more leeway in expressing feelings of fear, pain, delight, self-congratulation, and other emotions. Norman Denzin pointed out some time ago, "The young child violates nearly all rules of deference and demeanor. They make claims for self-respect in statements like 'Mommy, look at me. Aren't I pretty?'" (Denzin 1977, 72). Adults ordinarily refrain from such open demands for appreciation; the norm is to wait until someone else expresses it voluntarily. As children grow older, the leeway they are allowed is gradually withdrawn, but along the way their presentation of self can remain uncertain. As Gary Alan Fine notes, "Central to the process of growing up is learning ways of displaying one's social self in public. Adults fear that children will say the wrong thing in public" (Fine 1981, 51). The ability to manage the impression one wishes to make is one of the capacities of the self.

Another activity of the self that Erving Goffman studied is *the self's use of rules* in social interaction. Goffman noted that "the person in our urban secular world is allotted a kind of sacredness that is displayed and confirmed by symbolic acts" (Goffman 1967a, 47). By this, Goffman means that persons are entitled to a certain amount of respect, which is shown by approaching them according to rules. One should keep a certain physical distance from others, for example. Interactions are begun with a ritual greeting—"Hi" or "Hello" or "What's happening?" or some such—and they are terminated with a ritual of departure—"So long" or "Goodbye" or "Have a nice day." A child of 18 months or 2 years who wants the attention of someone may tug on the clothing or body of the person; the child does not yet know the proper *access rituals*. William Corsaro, building on Goffman's work, undertook to study when and how children develop the ability to use access rituals in approaching others. Over a period of several months, he studied two groups of nursery school children, one 2 to 3 years of age, the other 3 to 4, with about 25 children in each group. His observations focused on how children join other children in activity, their "access strategies." He noted that three of the strategies were very adult-like: requests for access ("Can I play?"), questioning participants ("What ya doing?"); and greeting ("Hi"). But these were not the most frequently used. Most common were nonverbal strategies, such as silently coming alongside children playing and starting to do what they are doing. Thus, nursery-school-age children are beginning to develop the social and communicative skills that characterize adult self- and social-regulation, but the skills are not yet very widespread among the children of this age group (Corsaro 1979).

Self-Concept, Identity, Self-Esteem, and Self-Efficacy

We have noted that the self is both a structure and a process and that it has two parts or phases, the "I" and the "me." As a process, the phases interact with each other whenever a person acts in a situation. Consider as an example the situation of a pupil in class who does not understand something the teacher has just said. If, say, that pupil's parents (who are *significant others* for the child) have always told her that she asks too many questions, their judgment is part of her "me"; she was that kind of an object to her significant others and is also now that kind of an object to herself. In the classroom situation, she has a quick inner dialogue in which the "I" is aware of the "me" as a too frequent questioner. The pupil's silent action in the situation may therefore take the form of "I don't understand what the teacher is saying, but let it pass. I'm not going to ask for an explanation." This is, of course, only one possibility. Another pupil may have as part of the "me" the attitude that asking questions is an appropriate part of the pupil role, plus the additional attitude based on previous experience in this class that this teacher criticizes pupils who interrupt with questions before the presentation is completed. Taking the role of the teacher, the pupil anticipates that the teacher will criticize him for interrupting. The teacher's attitude is already incorporated in the pupil's "me." The pupil's "I" is aware of it and decides to wait until after class to ask the question. The "me" says, "Don't interrupt; you'll be criticized." The "I" is aware of this constraining attitude incorporated from a significant other (the teacher) and decides to wait until after the class to ask the question.

The "I" and the "me" are not separate little things inside a person's head; they are two phases of the process of *self-awareness*. We have simply tried, in the above examples, to present in slow motion what is in fact usually a very rapid reflexive activity in which an initiating phase and a constraining phase of an imminent act combine to shape the action that is actually taken. Once the child's self has started to develop, the reflexive activity goes on frequently, though we cannot say whether it goes on every minute of the day. But a changing stream of interactions leads to a stream of evaluations that become part of the "me." A child's mother sends him off to school with a hug, a nonverbal symbol that he understands means she loves him, and he feels good about himself. On the way to school, he encounters a child who doesn't like him and calls him a name, some derogatory term, and he briefly feels bad about himself. At school the teacher tells him he made too many mistakes on his arithmetic test, but she is glad to see that his handwriting is improving—mixed information and a mixed evaluation. At recess he joins his friends in a race to see who can run around the schoolyard the fastest, and he wins. Again, he feels good about himself, but on a different basis from his mother's morning hug: his view of himself now includes "fast runner." The child's daily activities involve him in many interactions that result in a more or less mixed bag of evaluations, which the child is aware of *and which the child himself or herself evaluates.* If the child who called the boy the bad name is one he cares about, he may feel bad about himself for some time; if he is indifferent, the name-caller is not a significant other for him and the remark is quickly forgotten with no enduring effect.

The reflexive activity of the self is ongoing and transient; every moment of it passes. But out of this activity arises a structure that is more stable and enduring. This product is the *self-concept* (Gecas 1982). Morris Rosenberg defines *self-concept* as "the totality of the individual's thoughts and feelings having reference to himself as an object" (Rosenberg 1979, 7). He states that the content of the self-concept includes a person's beliefs about his or her (1) physical characteristics, (2) dispositions, and (3) identities. Physical characteristics of the self-concept include beliefs about how one looks, whether one feels one is too tall or too short or the right height, and any other such beliefs about one's appearance. Dispositions in the self-concept include beliefs about one's personality, abilities, and, generally, one's "tendencies"—sports-loving, chocolate-loving, ambitious, religious, or whatever. Identities are the groups, statuses, and categories to which a child is recognized as belonging. The newborn baby belongs to a family, a sex and age category, a race, and a religion, thus starting out with a set of *socially ascribed identities* (Rosenberg 1979, 9–17). As social experience continues, children develop additional identities that are *achieved identities*, such as best reader in the first grade, tough kid on the playground, beginner at piano lessons, best friend to Melissa, and fan of the New York Yankees. These are identities that are achieved by the child's actions and experiences.

Note that identities are components of the self-concept. While the self-concept is more stable and enduring than any particular occasion of reflexive activity, this does not mean it remains constant. Both ascribed and achieved identities can change, resulting in a change in self-concept. Erik Erikson, a noted scholar of human development, captured this when he wrote of "the discontinuity between the demands made in a given milieu on a little boy and those made on a 'big boy' who, in turn, may well wonder why he was first made to believe that to be little is admirable, only to be forced to exchange, this effortless status for the special obligations of one who is 'big now'" (Erikson 1980, 122). Of course, the reverse may happen. A child may announce that he is a big boy now, while his parents still consider him a little boy. Thus, when achieved identities are at issue, establishment of an identity involves two processes: (1) claiming an identity for oneself, and (2) being assigned an identity by others. Sociologist Gregory Stone proposed, "One's identity is established when others *place* him as a social object by assigning him the same words of identity that he appropriates for himself or *announces*. It is in the coincidence of placements and announcements that identity becomes a meaning of the self" (Stone 1962, 93; italics in original).

Sociologist Lee Rainwater has further refined Stone's analysis. Noting that a person may sometimes announce an identity that he does not really believe is his, Rainwater proposes the concept of *valid identity*:

A valid identity is one in which the individual finds congruence between who he feels he is, who he announces himself to be, and where he feels his society places him. As individuals seek to build identities valid in terms of their own needs, they use the resources—the values, norms, and social techniques—which their culture makes available to them. Each individual tries on identities that emerge from the cultural material available to him and tests them by making appropriate announcements. If these announcements meet with success, he will maintain his identity until it is no longer validated by others or no longer congruent with his inner promptings. (Rainwater 1970, 375)

Thus, when a girl who sees herself as a performer is chosen to play a starring role in a class play, she, at least temporarily, has the actress identity of her self-concept validated.

The self-concept consists not only in one's knowledge and beliefs about who one is but also in one's evaluations of oneself. The basic evaluative judgments that a person makes about herself or himself establishes the level of *self-esteem*. Self-esteem is the product of social interaction. The child who goes to school more poorly dressed than any other is likely to experience a lowering of self-esteem as a result of comparing self to others. The child who shows a talent valued by others is likely to experience increased self-esteem. As these examples suggest, a person's level of self-esteem can change as a result of changes in social participation and social interaction. If, say, the poorly dressed child discovers and is recognized as having an ability that the other children value, for example in sports, its manifestation may well result in their favorable evaluation, which may then result in increased self-esteem, perhaps sufficient to overcome entirely the poor self-esteem experienced because of inferior dress.

One of the bases of self-esteem is *self-efficacy*, which can be defined as a person's assessment of his or her effectiveness, competence, and causal agency, that is, his or her beliefs about being able to shape situations (Gecas 1989, 292, 300; Gecas 2003, 370). As Gecas writes,

> Within the constraints imposed by biology, history, social structure, good and bad fortune, and other factors we may or may not be aware of, we try to control the direction of our lives by exerting our will, pursuing our goals, and affecting our circumstances. While we are indeed products of social and physical forces, we are also causal agents in the construction of our environments and ourselves. (Gecas 2003, 369)

When a person's actions cause something to happen, that person is likely to feel effective, competent, and like someone who can cause things to happen. Self-efficacy first develops in interactions with early caregivers and other significant others. These earliest significant others foster this capacity when they provide an environment for the child that is stimulating, challenging, and responsive to the child's efforts (Gecas 1989, 300). One of the authors of this book once had a student come up after class and report that whenever her brother's 3-year-old son said something, his father would comment, "That's dumb." She wanted to know if the father's repeated practice would harm the child. The reader can surely guess the gist of the answer to her question: That father was not helping his son develop self-efficacy or self-esteem. He was not providing an environment that enabled the child to feel competent and effective.

One reason a change in self-concept is almost never total is because, as already noted, a person has many identities at once, reflecting her or his various social memberships and roles. Sociologist Sheldon Stryker, following up Mead's idea that the complete self is made up of multiple identities ("elementary selves" was Mead's term), has suggested that these identities necessarily are organized in a *salience hierarchy*. *Salience* refers to how prominent an identity is, how likely it is to be the governing identity in a situation, and in how many situations it is considered important (Stryker 1980, 60–61).

We can illustrate this conception in the following way: Consider three families with children in school. All three belong to a church. The children in all three engage in some athletic activity. In one family, being a good Christian is the most important goal, and the children are socialized to that identity in many ways. The family says grace before meals, and the children attend a Bible class two or three times a week. Although expected to do reasonably well in school, the children's role as students is not emphasized, and being academically superior is not as important as being a good Christian. The children participate in recreational sports, but a sports identity is not stressed. In another family, sports participation is central; the children compete in athletic contests. Their religious and academic identities are less salient than their identities as athletes. And in the third, commitment to the student role is more important than to religious or athletic roles, and the children's identities as good students in science or language or social studies are more salient than the religious or athletic identities. The most salient identity is the one that the person feels is more important than others, and it is operative for more times over a wider range of situations than less salient ones.

Sentiments and Emotions

The concept of self, as we have presented it, derives largely from the work of George Herbert Mead, who emphasized that the self is cognitive in nature. In Mead's view, the self is what makes us distinctively human, and the key aspect of that is the ability to know ourselves and act toward ourselves as objects. Although Mead did say a little about emotions, knowing—not feeling—was his central focus.

Mead's perspective has to be supplemented with that of Charles Horton Cooley, his contemporary in the early part of the twentieth century. Where Mead insisted on the importance of our ability to *symbolize* as the human capacity that makes possible reflexivity and taking the role of the other, Cooley stressed the importance of our ability to *sympathize*, by which he meant to understand what another person is feeling. (Since *sympathy* in recent times has come to mean feeling compassion for someone who is troubled or suffering, the term *empathy* is used today in the broader sense that Cooley intended. We will use empathy to express his meaning.) Cooley believed that human nature consists of sentiments and that empathy is the most basic, because it enters into all the others. Sentiments such as love, ambition, resentment, envy, patriotism, hero worship, "school spirit," and what Cooley called the "feeling of social right and wrong" all include empathy because they all include understanding what others are feeling. Cooley wrote, "Human nature in this sense is justly regarded as a comparatively permanent element in society. Always and everywhere men seek honor and dread ridicule, defer to public opinion, cherish their goods and their children, and admire courage, generosity, and success. It is always safe to assume that people are and have been human" (Cooley 1909, 27).

From our present perspective, almost 100 years after Cooley wrote, and with much intervening experience and research, we know that the situation is more complex than he described it. Some people will brave ridicule rather than dread it; not all defer to public opinion, nor do all cherish their children. But certain of his fundamental observations are durable: Such sentiments as honor and ridicule, courage and generosity, are distinctively human and possible in all human societies and thus are not limited to certain cultures, although they receive varying emphasis and are expressed differently in different cultures.

The capacity to create and communicate complex meanings—cognitive and emotional—which we find among human beings everywhere is without equal elsewhere in the animal kingdom. Similarly, the wide range of human sentiment is not found in other species. The mental operations of animals may be quite complex, but there is no evidence that they have selves (Hauser 2000).

It was Cooley's significant insight that the sentiments that he saw as the core of human nature were not inherited. Rather, human nature develops in *primary groups,*

> those simple face-to-face groups that are somewhat alike in all societies, groups of the family, the playground, and the neighborhood. In the essential similarity of these is to be found the basis, in experience, for similar ideas and sentiments in the human mind. In these everywhere, human nature comes into existence. Man does not have it at birth, he cannot acquire it except through fellowship, and it decays in isolation. (Cooley 1909, 30)

Although Cooley's insight (based in part on observation of his own children) perhaps outran the evidence then available to support it, several lines of more recent evidence tend to support and amplify his view. In various ways, they indicate that human nature is a product of involvement with other human beings.

There has been considerable debate about whether emotions are primarily biological in origin or whether they are formed and shaped in social relationships (Scheff 1983). At one time, psychologists would have argued for the biological and sociologists for the social, but the two fields no longer divide in this way. Sociologists such as Thomas J. Scheff and Steven L. Gordon, citing data on the newborn and very young, recognize a biological source of social expression (Scheff 1983; Gordon 1981), and psychologists such as Carol Zander Malatesta and Jeanette N. Haviland stress that early emotions are transformed by socialization (1985). The arguments on emotions and sentiments are complex, and several formulations have been offered. Drawing on various analyses, we present here what seems to us a reasonable view.

The evidence seems to indicate that humans are born with a few basic emotions—anger, fear, sadness, and happiness. These not only become socialized but also become differentiated into a much wider variety of sentiments. Discussing the transformation of emotion, Malatesta and Haviland write,

Emotion finds expression in physiology, feeling states, and motor behavior. In the course of development, any or all of these aspects may undergo transformation to varying degrees. In unsocialized human beings, such as infants, affect expression is a whole body experience, presumably involving all aspects. Later, under the impact of environmental contingencies, as well as of self-directed modulation and the development of symbolic function, favored modes of expression develop. Socialization may be directed at training in one or all of these channels. (Malatesta and Haviland 1985, 103–113)

In infancy, the key socializing factor is mother-infant (or other caregiver-infant) interaction, particularly the mother's face-to-face play with the infant (Malatesta and Haviland 1985, 103–113; Beckwith 1986). At later ages, the tone and content of utterances become more important. Preschoolers, having gained some mastery of the symbols of language, have learned a vocabulary for emotional states and emotional expressions. In the course of childhood, children also learn *feeling rules*, that is, what emotions are expected or acceptable in what situations and how to display or refrain from displaying emotions (Hochschild 1979). One of the important outcomes of socialization is that people have to learn to manage their feelings.

The term *feelings* or *affective state* includes both emotions and sentiments, but sentiments are more numerous and specifically social than are emotions. Sociologist Steven Gordon (1981) defines a sentiment as "a socially constructed pattern of sensations, expressive gestures, and cultural meanings organized around a relationship to a social object." He goes on to point out that most of a culture's vocabulary of named affective states are sentiments rather than emotions. Sentiments develop around social attachments, such as parental love, romantic love, friendship, and loyalty. He illustrates the point with these examples:

Grief, sorrow, and nostalgia reflect social losses. Compassion and pity are sentiments based on empathy, whereas jealousy and envy reflect notions of possession. Moral sentiments that we feel when judging others include indignation, resentment, and contempt, but also gratitude and pride. Our reactions to how others judge us include shame, guilt, and embarrassment. Patriotism and religious reverence are sentiments for social institutions. Humor, impatience, and enthusiasm are relatively transient sentiments, but are learned socially and are expressed within more enduring relationships to which they contribute meaning. (Gordon 1981: 566)

The work of both sociologists and psychologists is thus further developing Cooley's important insights into the socialization of sentiments.

Values and the Self

In Chapter 2, we discussed the concept of values. We gave as examples "freedom" and "equality," and we indicated that values are not always consistent with each other. Our discussion at that point treated values as a part of society. Freedom and equality are values in American society. More precisely, they are values in the culture of American society. This way of stating the matter is correct as far as it goes, but it is limited. It leaves something out. It is now necessary to take the discussion a step further. Individuals appropriate values that become part of the self. People involved in socializing children—adults and other children—act according to values that are part of themselves, and in their interactions they implicitly (not always consciously) communicate one or another value to others. We can construct a vignette, based on scattered observations, that illustrates this important point.

Imagine a group of boys playing baseball, and one boy becomes unhappy about the way some other players are acting and says he is leaving. Others, who want the game to continue, then say, "Come on, don't be a quitter. Stay in the game." These boys are not aware that they are acting in a socializing capacity, but they are, and they probably cannot translate their words into the abstract statement that they are trying to transmit a value, but that's what they are trying to do. They want the unhappy boy to change himself so that the value of sticking things out becomes a strong enough part of his self that it becomes central to the way he regulates his actions in the immediate situation, as well as thereafter. Don't let momentary unhappiness disrupt commitment to the group game. Sticking things out—commitment or dependability—is the value the other boys are promoting.

They promote the value by holding out the threat of assigning the one boy a negative identity—labeling him a quitter. If he is sure of himself and has strong self-esteem, he will be able to resist accepting this label as a valid identity. He may be able to fortify himself by remembering a bit of long-established lore in children's culture: "Sticks and stones may break my bones, but names will never hurt me." If his self-esteem is shaky, however, the threat of such a label may lead him to change his decision to leave the game. He would then be rewarded by avoiding a negative identity and by living up to the value of commitment or dependability that the group is promoting.

As this example indicates, children have values that arise out of their interactions among each other, and these are often different from (and sometimes opposed to) values promulgated by adults. (For a clear illustration of this contrast, see Fine 1987, 59–102. Fine uses the term "moral socialization" rather than "values socialization." The two terms are close in meaning if not exactly identical.) But adults begin to communicate values before children are old enough to form group values of their own. In Chapter 9, we will present a study of how the value of *individualism* is variously interpreted and variously transmitted by parents and by teachers to preschool children of different social class levels.

Incipient Adult Roles

In childhood, children are assigned children's roles, but at the same time they are being prepared for adult roles. By the time a child passes from the age grade of child to the age grade of adolescent, a considerable amount of such preparation has already taken place. In Chapter 11, we shall examine preparation for adult gender roles. Here, we shall briefly look at preparation for three other adult roles: citizen, worker, and consumer.

The role of *citizen* connects the person with the political system and government of the society. As noted earlier in this chapter, every society seeks to foster loyalty, including loyalty to the prevailing system of government. The institutions of a democratic society require "a citizenry with particular habits of mind and particular commitments. These habits of mind and commitments constitute the political culture that students must be educated to value and sustain" (Fullinwider 1996, 16). The study of this aspect of socialization has come to be known as *political socialization*. In one American study, Sandra K. Schwartz found that some political socialization has taken place by the time a child is 5 years old. In her sample of 79 nursery school children, most not yet 5 years old, she found the beginnings of awareness of political symbols and governmental authority. The children were shown a picture containing nine flags, including the American and the Liberian (which resembles the American flag). Asked which flag they liked best, 60 percent chose the American, 19 percent the Liberian, and 20 percent a different flag. Eighty-three percent knew which was the American flag. With regard to agents of government authority, some of the children had heard of the president, but they were more familiar with the policeman. About half of them mentioned that he directs traffic, about a third identified him as enforcing laws, and about a third mentioned his role in helping lost children (Schwartz 1975). In kindergarten and elementary school years, according to several studies, children have a very positive image of the president. The authors of a California study suggest that this image has its origin in religious sensitivities. The most common reply of kindergarten children to the question "Who does the most to run the country?" was God or Jesus. The authors go on to say that "an early religious orientation predisposes children to have more positive feelings toward the president and other civil authorities" (Moore, Lare, and Wagner 1985, 44).

A number of studies have found that during the elementary-school years, children have a very idealized view of political authority (e.g., Greenstein 1969, 45). However, children from segments of society that suffer from discrimination or economic deprivation are less likely to believe that political leaders are so benevolent. In the above-mentioned California study, kindergarten children were asked, "If you were playing in front of your house, and a policeman stopped to talk to you, what do you think he would say?" Almost one-quarter of the non-Anglo children, mostly Mexican, gave a remark that was threatening, compared to only 7 percent of the Anglos (Moore, Lare, and Wagner 1985, 72–73). A study of black inner-city children showed that by the fourth grade, they had developed "a marked degree of malevolence and distrust toward political leaders" (Green 1972, 183). A study in the Appalachian region of eastern Kentucky, a poor rural area, found that children "are dramatically less favorably inclined toward political objects than are their counterparts in other portions of the nation" (Jaros, Hirsch, and Fleron 1972, 209). As these studies suggest, the attitudes of children to political and law enforcement personnel may stem partly from direct experience or possibly from parental/familial teaching. We are not aware of more recent focused studies such as these, but there is more current evidence regarding certain general points.

Education for citizenship has generally avoided controversial issues and focused on teaching children certain formal and ideal aspects of the political organization of society. But this approach is itself controversial because critics believe that it leaves out important modern issues such as human rights education, peace education, multicultural education, environmental education, and global education (Ichilov 1998, 269). However, with the growth in recent years of the Children's Rights Movement and the interest of many socially interested groups, schools today are somewhat more likely to touch on such issues than in the past (Boyden 1997; Ichilov 2003, 650–651).

Although loyalty is a social expectation, and schools are the institution charged with the major responsibility for generating loyalty and the competencies of citizenship, a review of several studies in the United States and other countries concludes, "Overall, then, it seems that the contents associated with citizenship education represent a patchwork more than a coherent idea of how to integrate different concerns into a comprehensive civics curriculum . . . citizenship education is an eclectic and fragmented endeavor" (Ichilov 2003, 651, 659).

As we noted early in this chapter, socialization is intended to lead to various kinds of competence. Most children are expected to eventually acquire the role of *worker*, that is, to become capable of doing some kind of economically useful work in their society. School experience contributes indirectly since it involves responding to requirements of teacher authority, accepting classroom routines, and completing homework assignments. The most intensive direct study of socialization of American children for the adult worker role was done by two sociologists a little more than 25 years ago (Goldstein and Oldham 1979). Their study covered 900 children in the first, third, fifth, and seventh grades in five New Jersey communities with different social characteristics—from working class to upper middle class. Their study examined (1) relevant beliefs and perceptions, (2) values, (3) attitudes and feelings, and (4) work experiences.

This study found that about 80 percent of first graders and 89 percent of fifth graders had some understanding of the concept of work and its relation to money. Occupational stereotyping was also fairly definite even in the first grade. Asked their reactions to "typically male" and "typically female" occupations, 74 percent of the boys and 29 percent of the girls said they would feel positively about being a construction worker; 79 percent of the girls and 24 percent of the boys said they would feel positively about being a nurse. Children have fairly realistic ideas about occupational income differentials, though not about income levels. Thus, even first graders know that bankers and doctors earn more than teachers and secretaries. Awareness of income differentials increases during the elementary years until it becomes quite accurate.

Interestingly, many children in the study ascribed negative feelings about work to the general population, although they tended to be quite positive about their own chores. The researchers believe that this contrast may reflect the fact that children perceive negative adult attitudes and that in time they, too, will come to have less positive feelings toward work.

Children are also aware of social class differences. Even first graders are aware of prestige differences among people—usually explaining such differences on the basis of the importance of the role to the community or on the fact that some people work harder. As children get older, wealth, fame, and power are recognized as the basis for prestige differences.

Children's own work experiences increase with age. "Childwork" (paid work done by children outside the household or for their own family) was done by 13 percent of first graders, 39 percent of third graders, and 75 percent of seventh graders. Neighbors are usually the first employers; yard work, babysitting, and newspaper delivery are the most common types of work In addition, children do chores at home, which are usually sex-typed. Three times as many girls as boys reported doing dishes; four times as many boys as girls reported taking out the trash.

A more recent study in Norway of 10- to 12-year-olds found that children of mothers in full-time employment did more housework than children whose mothers worked part-time. They also found that girls were more likely than boys to help in food preparation, washing dishes, and cleaning (Solberg 1997).

The American researchers summarize their study with these generalizations:

> The process of occupational socialization during childhood has been shown to be developmental in nature, and to follow an age-related pattern. . . . In other words, while work itself in the formal sense may be largely a phenomenon of adolescence and adulthood, preparations to assume one's place in the world of work and growth into an occupational self-identity begin far earlier than that. (Goldstein and Oldham 1979, 17)

We have not been able to find a more recent study of American elementary school–age children's occupational socialization, so we do not know whether children today have significantly different work experiences than those of 30 years ago.

Socialization to work has gone on for centuries in all societies; survival requires that the young be prepared to work. Probably only in fairly recent times, however, with the rise of a broadly based market economy offering a wide array of goods for sale and with more free time, do we find socialization for an adult *consumer* role. Studies of this process mostly begin no earlier than the last quarter of the twentieth century. One early research team defines *consumer socialization* as "the gradual development of a broad range of attitudes, knowledge, and skills which are related to consumption, e.g., attitudes toward television commercials, knowledge of the purpose of commercials, knowledge of brands and products, and skills, such as how to most effectively allocate discretionary monies" (Ward, Wackman, and Wartella 1977, 18). Children develop information-processing skills—skills in selecting, evaluating, and using information relevant to purchasing.

Children are introduced to the consumer role within their families, by accompanying parents to supermarkets and other stores, by participating in and listening to family communications, and by watching television. They receive a great deal of information about products and brands of merchandise available in their society through TV commercials (Seiter 1993). By kindergarten age, 60 percent of children (in samples studied in Boston and Minneapolis–St.

Paul) ask their parents for soft drinks by brand name; this reaches 84 percent by sixth grade. As many as 93 percent of kindergartners ask for cereal by brand name. Understanding of the selling purpose of commercials increases with age, as does the judgment that advertising is not always truthful. Although few mothers engage in purposive consumer training, children's requests for products often initiate interactions with a parent, and in this way families may mediate the impact of television advertising on the children.

There are considerable differences in judgment about the significance of advertising directed to children. Consider the contrast in the following two comments. A professor of marketing writes,

> At early ages, children use advertising as their 'window to the world' of toys, candy, food products, restaurants, and such. . . . Children's worlds expand once they enter elementary school. Here children find a vast pool of peers who can serve as a sounding board for what toys are 'cool,' what candy is really 'neat,' and what brand of clothes is 'cheesy.' Advertising still serves as an information source, but now children have a set of their own experiences and peer experiences to serve as a basis for comparison. Through this set of experiences they learn that commercials sometimes exaggerate, that advertisers are not always truthful, and that they need to access a variety of information sources to find out what they should buy. (John 1999, 21)

While this statement regards the consumer role in a taken-for-granted way and sees the socialization issue as one of a child's increasing sophistication about advertising, a professor of education sees the child's consumer role very differently—as a role that has been disproportionately expanded by the activities of business corporations, to the detriment of children and the society. He sees American society as one in which "kids don't count for much except as consumers," and he further states,

> Kids, especially those under fourteen years old, have become a hot item for corporations because marketeers recognize that young people 'will directly spend an estimated $20 billions this year [1998] and they will influence another $200 billions.' . . . The debate about children's loss of innocence signifies more than society's changing attitude toward young people; it also points to the rise of a corporate culture that reasserts the primacy of individualism and competitiveness and that calls for young people to surrender their capacity to become citizens in the fullest sense—possessed of the widest range of citizen skills and rights—for a market-based notion of identity, one that suggests relinquishing their roles as critical subjects for the passive role of consuming subjects. . . .
>
> As consumer culture replaces public culture and as the language of the market becomes a substitute for the language of democracy, consumerism appears to be the only kind of citizenship being offered to children. (Giroux 1999, 23–24)

In this view, the consumer role for children (and adults) has become so emphasized in contemporary American society that other meaningful and socially necessary roles, especially that of the democratic citizen, have been diminished. We will have more to say on this topic in Chapter 8.

Truncated Childhood, Premature Adulthood

In Chapter 1, we pointed out that childhood is a cultural construction and that societies differ in their practices of age grading. As we also noted, age grading in American and other Western societies has changed over time to include increasing restrictions on the amounts and kinds of work that young children are allowed to do. Preadolescent children are still allowed to earn money by doing occasional yard work or babysitting or a limited number of other activities, work that is regarded as not harmful to health and helpful to their socialization. Other young people may do light work after school, be it in legitimate apprenticeship programs or by helping out in the family business. But work that is dangerous or that takes up the time that preadolescent children are legally expected to be in school is *child labor*, socially proscribed and legally prohibited for those under 18. There are no exact figures of how many children are engaged in illegal child labor, but the number in the United States is estimated at more than 2 million. They work in mines, sawmills, the garment industry, gas stations, and elsewhere (Levine 2003, 4–5).

The International Labor Organization, in Geneva, Switzerland, estimates that at least 120 million children between the ages of 5 and 14 work full-time in developing countries (Forastieri 2002, 9). In 1992, the ILO began an international program to eliminate child labor, but "[a]t the intergovernmental level, child labor has been part of a politically charged debate on human rights, labor standards, ethics, and international trade. In spite of these new trends, little information is available concerning the actual conditions under which these children work" (Forastieri 2002, 2). Another problem, sociologist Loretta Bass (2004, 9–10) points out, is that many children do not have birth certificates or even know their age, which makes it difficult to enforce child labor laws even if there were the will to do so. Child labor is regarded as a necessity for survival in these countries (Bass 2004), as it once was for many—and still is for some—in the United States and elsewhere in the Western world. By Western standards, which lengthen childhood and which the ILO tries to extend to other countries, childhood in the developing countries is truncated, and adulthood comes early. Socialization to work in these countries is not preparation for a later adult role. It is early induction into an adult role.

Another path to a truncated childhood and early adulthood is traveled by children who leave home to live on the streets. An interview and observational study carried out in Toronto, Los Angeles, Miami, and Tampa revealed that these children "present themselves as victims of misunderstanding, neglect, or violence" (Visano 1990, 146). They were in conflict with parents who they felt misunderstood them. They found school boring. They perceive the supposedly nurturing institutions of family and school as non-nurturing and punitive, and so they escape to the streets. "They learn to rely on their wits to structure and to seize upon any opportunity to fend for themselves the best they can. Survival requires them to be constantly on the prowl and ready to score by rolling a drunk, boosting, smashing and grabbing anything of value, or simply panhandling" (Visano 1990, 150). Other street kids become their influential socializers. Eventually, perhaps after a year, disillusionment with street life leads some to disengage and either return to their families or make contact with youth-serving agencies. Living on the street and fending for oneself in socially disapproved ways while still in the age category of childhood are to truncate one's childhood and to adopt a pseudo-adult independence. As the study reports, some find the identity of independent pseudo-adult unsustainable, and they move to regain a childhood identity.

A third way in which childhood (as understood in modern Western countries) is cut short is by forcing or convincing children to join armies and fight in wars. In many countries, civil wars and armed rebellions are currently ongoing or have recently been concluded. In many of them, children have been forced by adults to participate as armed soldiers or in related hazardous duty such as laying mines or spying. While international law defines a *child soldier* as anyone under 18 (Singer 2005, 7), children as young as 7 are known to have engaged in combat. In a civil war fought between 1991 and 2001 in Sierra Leone, a country in West Africa, 80 percent of the fighters in the rebel Revolutionary United Front were between the ages of 7 and 14. Many of them had been kidnapped to participate (Singer 2005, 15). In Afghanistan, surveys found that approximately 30 percent of all Afghan children had engaged in military activities at some point in their childhood (Singer 2005, 25). This figure was reported in a publication entitled *Child Soldiers Newsletter* (Singer 2005, 225, n. 57). Child soldiers are found in conflicts in Central and South America, Europe, the Middle East, Asia, and Africa (Bass 2004, 147–178; Singer 2005, 16–34). According to some studies, in 55 countries as many as 30 percent of child soldiers are girls. In 27 of these countries, they were abducted; and in 34 of them, they were in combat (Singer 2005, 31–32). For child soldiers, adulthood begins at an early age.

From a modern Western perspective, child soldiering is a form of child abuse that can have possible damaging developmental effects. As one observer writes,

> Childhood is meant to be a period of development that involves interaction with family and establishment of interpersonal networks that enhance children's understanding of their social surroundings and how to act within them. The use of violence during this stage can become a central element of a child's sense of self and even carry over into adulthood, long after any of the original motivations or contexts behind that behavior have disappeared. While the scarring is not necessarily permanent, it certainly creates difficulties both for the children and their interface with society. (Singer 2005, 123–124)

A Stock of Social Knowledge

In summarizing the principal outcomes of socialization, we have thus far focused on the inner structures that are created through socialization—a self and its components (identities, self-awareness, self-knowledge, self-concept, self-management, self-esteem, and self-efficacy), and incipient adult roles. In discussing these structures we have alluded to such aspects of social life as rules, symbols, attitudes, feelings, communication, and information. These are, so to speak, the materials or resources that the socialized person must make use of in functioning, no matter what particular pattern he or she develops. In concluding this chapter, it is useful here to make explicit the fact that these materials or resources are part of a large stock of social knowledge, as sociologist Alfred Schutz pointed out, that the socialized person begins to acquire soon after birth and continues to acquire throughout the life course (Schutz 1967, 80–81). The social world is made up of an immense number of social objects—work, politics, money, family, God, material goods, knowledge, pleasures, transportation, fashion, discipline, crime, education, sports, and armed combat—and the list could be greatly extended. Each of these social objects can be further divided and specified in different ways. The socialized person inevitably acquires some kind of knowledge about some of these social objects, more about some than about others, including how to think and feel about the object; what to do about it, if anything; what are preferred or approved actions with regard to each; and what actions are disapproved. Such a stock of knowledge—limited or extensive or in-between—is an outcome of socialization required by every socialized person who participates in the society.

References

Balderston, Judith B., et al. 1981. *Malnourished Children of the Rural Poor*. Boston: Auburn House.

Ball, Donald. 1967. "Toward a Sociology of Toys." *Sociological Quarterly* 8 (Autumn): 447–458.

Bass, Loretta E. 2004. *Child Labor in Sub-Saharan Africa*. Boulder, CO: Lynne Rienner.

Bateson, Gregory, Don Jackson, Jay Haley, and John Weakland. 1956. "Toward a Theory of Schizophrenia." *Behavioral Science* 1: 251–264.

Beckwith, Leila. 1986. "Parent-Infant Interaction and Infants' Social-Emotional Development." In Allen W. Gottfried and Catherine Caldwell Brown (eds.) *Play Interactions*, 279–292. Lexington, MA: Lexington Books.

Birch, Herbert, M. D., and Joan Dye Gussow. 1970. *Disadvantaged Children: Health, Nutrition, and School Failure*. New York: Harcourt Brace/Grune & Stratton.

Black, Susan. 2000. "Nutrition and Learning." *American School Board Journal* 187 (2): 49–51.

Blumer, Herbert. 1969. *Symbolic Interactionism*. Englewood Cliffs, NJ: Prentice Hall.

Bowlby, John. 1958. "The Nature of the Child's Ties to His Mother." *International Journal of Psychoanalysis* 34: 1–23.

——. 1969. *Attachment*. New York: Basic Books.

Boyden, Jo. 1997. "Postscript, Childhood and the Policy Makers: A Comparative Perspective on the Globalization of Childhood." In Alison James and Alan Prout (eds.) *Constructing and Reconstructing Childhood*, 216–229. London: Falmer Press.

Bradley, Robert H. 1998. "In Defense of Parental Investment." *Journal of Marriage and the Family* 60 (August): 791–795.

Collin, Virginia L. 1996. *Human Attachment*. Philadelphia: Temple University Press.

Cooley, Charles Horton. 1909. *Social Organization*. New York: Scribner.

Corsaro, William A. 1979. "We're Friends, Right? Children's Use of Access Rituals in a Nursery School." *Language in Society* 8: 315–336.

Denzin, Norman. 1977. *Childhood Socialization*. San Francisco: Jossey-Bass.

Erikson, Erik.1963. *Childhood and Society*, 2nd ed. New York: W. W. Norton.

——. 1980. *Identity and the Life Cycle*. New York: W. W. Norton.

Ervin-Tripp, Susan. 1977. "Wait for Me, Roller Skate." In Susan Ervin-Tripp and Claudia Mitchell-Kernan (eds.) *Child Discourse*. New York: Academic Press.

Fine, Gary Alan. 1981. "Friends, Impression Management, and Preadolescent Behavior." In Steven R. Asher and John M. Gottman (eds.) *Development of Children's Friendships*. Cambridge: Cambridge University Press.

——. 1987. *With the Boys: Little League Baseball and Preadolescent Culture*. Chicago: University of Chicago Press.

Forastieri, Valentina. 2002. *Children at Work*, 2nd ed. Geneva, Switzerland: International Labor Office.

Freud, Sigmund. 1938. "Three Contributions to the Theory of Sex." In A. A. Brill (ed.) *The Basic Writings of Sigmund Freud*. New York: Modern Library.

Fullinwider, Robert K. 1996. "Multicultural Education: Concepts, Policies, and Controversies." In Robert K. Fullinwider (ed.) *Public Education in a Multicultural Society*, 3–22. Cambridge, U.K. and New York: Cambridge University Press.

Gecas, Viktor. 1982. "The Self-Concept." In Ralph Turner and James F. Short (eds.) *Annual Review of Sociology*, Vol. 8: 1–31. Palo Alto, CA: Annual Reviews, Inc.

——. 1989. "The Social Psychology of Self-Efficacy." In W. Richard Scott and Judith Blake (eds.) *Annual Review of Sociology*, Vol. 15: 291–316. Palo Alto, CA: Annual Reviews.

——. 2003. "Self-Agency and the Life Course." In Jeylan T. Mortimer and Michael Shanahan (eds.) *Handbook of the Life Course*, 369–388. New York: Kluwer Academic/ Plenum Publishers.

Giroux, Henry. 1999. *The Mouse That Roared*. Lanham, MD: Rowman & Littlefield.

Goffman, Erving. 1959. *The Presentation of Self in Everyday Life*. Garden City, NY: Doubleday Anchor.

——. 1967a. "The Nature of Deference and Demeanor." In Erving Goffman, *Interaction Ritual*. Garden City, NY: Doubleday Anchor.

——. 1967b. "On Facework." In Erving Goffman, *Interaction Ritual*. Garden City, NY: Doubleday Anchor.

Goldstein, Bernard, and Jack Oldham. 1979. *Children and Work: A Study of Socialization*. New Brunswick, NJ: Transaction.

Gordon, Steven L. 1981. "The Sociology of Sentiments and Emotion." In Morris Rosenberg and Ralph H. Turner (eds.) *Social Psychology*, 562–592. New York: Basic Books.

Green, Eugene. 1972. "The Political Socialization of Black Inner-City Children." In Anthony M. Orum (ed.) *The Seeds of Politics*. Englewood Cliffs, NJ: Prentice-Hall.

Greenstein, Fred I. 1969. *Children and Politics*, Rev. ed. New Haven, CT: Yale University Press.

Haley, Jay. 1959. "The Family of the Schizophrenic: A Model System." *Journal of Nervous and Mental Disease* 129: 357–374.

Haslett, Beth Bonniwell, and Wendy Samter. 1997. *Children Communicating. The First 5 Years*. Mahwah, NJ and London: Lawrence Erlbaum.

Hauser, Marc D. 2000. *Wild Minds: What Animals Really Think*. New York: Henry Holt.

Hochschild, Arlie Russell. 1979. "Emotion Work, Feeling Rules, and Social Structure." *American Journal of Sociology* 85(3): 551–575.

Hughes, Everett C. 1981. *Men and Their Work*. Westport, CT: Greenwood Press.

Hutchins, Robert Maynard. 1953. *The Conflict in Education in a Democratic Society*. New York: Harper & Brothers.

Ichilov, Orit. 1998. "Conclusion: The Challenge of Citizenship Education in a Changing World." In Orit Ichilov (ed.) *Citizenship and Citizenship Education in a Changing World*, 267–273. London, UK and Portland, OR: Woburn Press.

——. 2003. "Education and Democratic Citizenship in a Changing World." In David O. Sears, Leonie Huddy, and Robert Jervis (eds.) *Oxford Handbook of Political Psychology*, 637–669. New York: Oxford University Press.

Inkeles, Alex. 1968. "Society, Social Structure, and Child Socialization." In John A. Clausen (ed.) *Socialization and Society*, 73–129. Boston: Little, Brown.

Jaros, Dean, Herbert Hirsch, and Frederick J. Fleron Jr. 1972. "The Malevolent Leader: Political Socialization in an American Sub-Culture." In Anthony M. Orum (ed.) *The Seeds of Politics*. Englewood Cliffs, NJ: Prentice-Hall.

John, Deborah Roeder. 1999. "Through the Eyes of a Child: Children's Knowledge and Understanding of Advertising." In M. Carole Macklin and Les Carlson (eds.) *Advertising to Children: Concepts and Controversies*, 3–26. Thousand Oaks, CA: Sage Publications.

Karmiloff, Kyra, and Annette Karmiloff-Smith. 2001. *Pathways to Language: From Fetus to Adolescent*. Cambridge, MA: Harvard University Press.

Levine, Marvin J. 2003. *Children for Hire*. Westport, CT: Praeger.

Lieberman, Alicia. 1993. *The Emotional Life of the Toddler*. New York: Free Press.

Malatesta, Carol Zander, and Jeanette N. Haviland. 1985. "Signals, Symbols, and Socialization: The Modification of Emotional Expression in Human Development." In Michael Lewis and Carolyn Saarni (eds.) *The Socialization of Emotions*, 89–116. New York: Plenum.

Mead, George Herbert. 1934. *Mind, Self, and Society*, edited and with an Introduction by Charles W. Morris. Chicago: University of Chicago Press.

Moore, Stanley W., James Lare, and Kenneth A. Wagner. 1985. *The Child's Political World*. New York: Praeger.

Nelson, Katherine. 1996. *Language in Cognitive Development: Emergence of the Mediated Mind*. Cambridge, UK, and New York: Cambridge University Press.

Pike, Ruth L., and Myrtle L. Brown. 1975. *Nutrition: An Integrated Approach*, 2nd ed. New York: Wiley.

Pollitt, Ernesto. 1979. *Poverty and Malnutrition in Latin America: Early Childhood Intervention Programs*. New York: Praeger.

Rainwater, Lee. 1970. *Behind Ghetto Walls*. Chicago: Aldine.

Rosenberg, Morris. 1979. *Conceiving the Self*. New York: Basic Books.

Schachtel, Ernest G. 1959. *Metamorphosis*. New York: Basic Books.

Scheff, Thomas J. 1983. "Toward Integration in the Social Psychology of Emotions." *Annual Review of Sociology* 9: 333–354. Palo Alto, CA; Annual Reviews.

Schutz, Alfred. 1967. *The Phenomenology of the Social World*, translated by George Walsh and Frederick Lehnert. Evanston, IL: Northwestern University Press.

Schwartz, Sandra Kenyon. 1975. "Preschoolers and Politics." In David C. Schwartz and Sandra Kenyon Schwartz (eds.) *New Directions in Political Socialization*. New York: Free Press.

Scrimshaw, Nevin, and J. E. Gordon (eds.). 1968. *Malnutrition, Learning and Behavior*. Cambridge, MA: MIT Press.

Seiter, Ellen. 1993. *Sold Separately: Children and Parents in Consumer Culture*. New Brunswick, NJ: Rutgers University Press.

Singer, P. W. 2005. *Children at War*. New York: Pantheon Books.

Smith, M. Brewster. 1968. "Competence and Socialization." In John A. Clausen (ed.) *Socialization and Society*, 270–320. Boston: Little, Brown.

Solberg, Anne. 1997. "Negotiating Childhood: Changing Constructions of Age for Norwegian Children." In Alison James and Alan Prout (eds.) *Constructing and Reconstructing Childhood*, 125–144. London: Falmer Press.

Stone, Gregory. 1962. "Appearance and the Self." In Arnold Rose (ed.) *Human Behavior and Social Processes*, 86–118. Boston: Houghton Mifflin.

Stryker, Sheldon. 1980. *Symbolic Interactionism*. Menlo Park, CA: Benjamin/Cummings.

———. 1981. "Symbolic Interactionism: Themes and Variations." In Morris Rosenberg and Ralph H. Turner (eds.) *Social Psychology: Sociological Perspectives*, 3–29. New York: Basic Books.

Turkle, Sherry. 1984. *The Second Self: Computers and the Human Spirit*. New York: Simon & Schuster.

Turner, Ralph. 1962. "Role-Taking: Process versus Conformity." In Arnold M. Rose (ed.) *Human Behavior and Social Processes: An Interactionist Approach*, 20–40. Boston: Houghton Mifflin.

Veblen, Thorstein. 1914. *The Instinct of Workmanship and the State of the Industrial Arts*. New York: The Macmillan Company.

Visano, Livy. 1990. "The Socialization of Street Children." In Patricia A. Adler and Peter Adler (eds.), Nancy Mandell (guest editor), *Sociological Studies of Child Development*, Vol. 3: 139–161. Greenwich, CT: JAI Press.

Vygotsky, Lev. 1978. *Mind in Society: The Development of Higher Psychological Processes*. Cambridge, MA: Harvard University Press.

———. 1986. *Thought and Language*. Cambridge, MA: MIT Press.

Ward, Scott, Daniel B. Wackman, and Ellen Wartella. 1977. *How Children Learn to Buy*. Beverly Hills, CA: Sage.

Warner, W. Lloyd, Robert J. Havighurst, and Martin B. Loeb. 1944. *Who Shall Be Educated?* New York: Harper & Brothers.

Wolfe, Pat, Mary Ann Burkman, and Katharina Streng. 2000. "The Science of Nutrition." *Educational Leadership* 57: 54–59. ✦

PART II
Agencies of Socialization

Introduction

Socialization occurs in many *settings* and in interaction with many people, organized into *groupings* of various kinds. While some of these settings are private, others are semi-public or public—recall our vignette in Chapter 1 reporting an observation of a mother and child in a bank. Socialization has been studied in carpools in which parents take turns driving children from several families to and from school (Adler and Adler 1984), on playgrounds (Lever 1978; Thorne 1993), in Little League baseball games (Fine 1987), and in many other situations. One public setting ripe for study is the interaction of parents and children in supermarkets. One can observe young children modeling themselves on their parents by picking items from shelves without parental direction. The parent's response to the child's efforts—whether approval, acceptance, annoyance, or anger—completes the interaction and defines a socialization situation. These are but a few examples of the multiplicity of socialization settings.

The groupings in which children are socialized are generally referred to as *agencies of socialization*. The word *agency* has two overlapping meanings. One meaning is "a representative." This meaning is familiar in several contexts. For example, a travel agency is a representative of airlines and hotels for people making travel arrangements. An insurance agency represents insurance companies to people who want to buy insurance. Agencies of socialization represent society as a whole. Families and schools are society's representatives and have legal obligations in socializing children. While they have considerable leeway in how they operate, they are nonetheless subject to some limits. Parents who abuse or neglect a child are subject to action by law enforcement agencies, which enforce some of society's legal rules. State laws in the various states, and provincial laws in Canada, prescribe goals and standards for schools. For example, the New Jersey State Constitution specifies that every school must provide children with a "thorough and efficient" education. Throughout the United States in the late twentieth and early twenty-first centuries, there is much public discussion of "failing schools," with claims that some schools are not meeting their legal obligations. The reasons are much disputed, but in some cases a state's Department of Education has taken control of a school district from the local authorities who are judged to have failed in their job.

The second meaning of the word *agency* is "action." Peer groups and the mass media of communication do not have legal responsibilities for socializing children, but they do act in ways that have socializing consequences, as, of course, do families and schools. The concept of agency as action applies not only to groups and organizations but also to individuals. One of the central issues in sociology is designated by the phrase "agency versus structure." This issue asks to what degree individuals are constrained, determined, or influenced in their actions by their positions in the social structure, and to what degree they are free to ignore or act contrary to the pressures put on them in these positions. Some now outmoded theories one-sidedly stressed such influence and described socialization as a one-way process: Society prescribes, and the individual conforms.

The *interactionist theory of socialization* that we have presented in Chapter 4 presents a more complex view. The influence of structure is, to be sure, necessarily a part of the theory. Society does require certain kinds and degrees of conformity in order to function, and children in certain social positions are to some degree systematically socialized differently from children in other social positions. *But a central concept of the interactionist theory of socialization is that socialization produces a self, and the self enables a person to take individual action as well as anchoring the person in the social structure.* The capacity for individual agency begins even when the self is in an early stage of development. Developmental psychologists (e.g., Lewis and Feinman 1991, 123) have an expression, "the terrible twos," referring to the fact that around age 2 a child learns to say "no" and may say no repeatedly to whatever parents ask or demand, thereby driving them to distraction. Resistance to social demands and expectations takes many forms during childhood and adulthood, and varies in extent among individuals. Socialization is not a process that stamps out a uniform, conforming product. Some years ago, philosopher-historian Isaiah Berlin called attention to a saying of eighteenth-century philosopher Immanuel Kant: "Out of timber so crooked as that from which man is made nothing entirely straight can be built" (Berlin 1998, xi). While this saying can undoubtedly be interpreted in more than one way, we can understand it here as a vivid metaphor that captures a basic idea of contemporary sociology and psychology: Children are so variable in endowment, temperament, experience, and inclination that socialization cannot turn them into standardized look-alike units. They all have their own quirks. *They act in individual ways, while agencies of socialization act to shape the children's actions into socially acceptable and socially desirable patterns. Individuation and socialization proceed concurrently.*

The various socialization agencies each have their own more or less distinctive functions in preparing children for social life. These functions are sometimes contradictory. But it is also the case that they may reinforce each other's efforts. Common *cultural images of the child* affect many agencies. Thus, when "getting along with others" was a dominant goal in socialization, as was true in the 1940s and 1950s in the United States, family, school, church, voluntary associations, and even informal peer groups worked toward this end (Riesman, Glazer, and Denny 1950). During the 1960s, socialization concerns changed in some degree. The (former) Soviet Union had launched *Sputnik*, the world's first space satellite, in 1957, and Americans in many walks of life became apprehensive that the United States was falling behind in science, with the possible consequence that its bitter rival would become militarily dominant. The result was a new emphasis on academic competence. Families and schools tended to share the increased emphasis on academic achievement.

During the 1970s there was again something of a shift in socialization emphasis. Although academic competence remained important in families, in schools, and elsewhere—and still is important—it was not the focus of intense concentration that it had been earlier. (The United States not only launched its own space satellites but also sent men to the moon and brought them back in 1969.) No other single concern quite replaced it, yet the changes in society yielded new emphases. One significant contender for the new dominant concern was that of revising or repealing old stereotypes, particularly gender role stereotypes. Until the 1970s, socialization took place within a framework that led fairly clearly to different socialization paths for boys and for girls. Increasingly in North America and Europe, more slowly in some other parts of the world, these stereotypes began to be revised. At one point AT&T, then the dominant telephone company in the United States, published photographs of women climbing telephone poles to make repairs and of men working as telephone operators sitting at switchboards. Whereas each of these occupations was formerly restricted to the other sex, now both were open to both sexes.

This is but one illustration of a wide movement to change traditional expectations and therefore socialization expectations that had been sex-specific. This is not to say that everyone concerned with socialization agreed with the changes. The point is, rather, that the question of whether boys and girls should be confined to traditional sex-specific experiences was now emerging near the center of attention for all persons who were in any way concerned with socialization. This question followed upon, and to some extent competed with, an earlier concern with revising minority group stereotypes, one that gathered momentum when in 1954 the U.S. Supreme Court outlawed intentional segregation of blacks and whites in schools. An organized civil rights movement and an organized women's movement, respectively, were influential in bringing about these significant social changes.

Also competing for increased attention in the late 1970s and early 1980s were people with disabilities, including children who were hearing-impaired or had physical, developmental, or other disabilities. In part this was a result of an increased interest in people with disabilities—1981 was the United Nations–designated International Year of the Disabled—and in part a result of a general movement for the rights of children. Children with disabilities, it was affirmed, should by right, insofar as possible, have the same opportunities as other children—to a good early education, to any public facilities, to entertainment and sporting activities, and later, without discrimination, to higher education and jobs. It was also affirmed that normal children without such major disabilities should recognize the human dignity and rights of those with disabilities and should not stigmatize or discriminate against them.

The 1980s also brought slowly increasing awareness that North American families were becoming increasingly varied in structure and that not all children came from families with a breadwinner father and a stay-at-home mother. Two-parent families were increasingly two-job or two-career families.

Several types of single-parent families—divorced, separated, never-married—were increasingly numerous and gained increased public awareness.

The 1990s saw a new emphasis on multiculturalism. From the earliest days of American society beginning with the Pilgrim landing in 1620, there had been an unspoken assumption that the United States was a white, Christian (primarily Protestant) country, although the Constitution adopted in 1787 prohibited an official religion and despite the fact that there were religious minorities as well as blacks living in the country. They were later joined by large numbers of Latinos and Asians. Even Catholics, whose numbers became larger than those of any single Protestant denomination, were often treated with suspicion. When John F. Kennedy, the second Catholic to run for president of the United States and the first to be elected, was running in 1960, he felt obliged to address a meeting of Protestant ministers and to reassure them that he would not take orders from the Pope if he were elected president. By the 1990s, cultural and religious diversity were more widely accepted. Whereas schools formerly celebrated only Christmas, by the 1990s December holiday celebrations in many schools also included the Jewish festival of Hanukkah and the recently created African American festival, Kwanzaa. Despite resistance in some quarters, cultural diversity is increasingly recognized and accepted. The institutional environment has changed. The Southern Poverty Law Center, an Alabama organization dedicated to opposing ethnic and religious hatred and bigotry, developed in the 1990s an educational program called "Teaching Tolerance," which is widely disseminated in public schools throughout the country. In Canada, multiculturalism has long been government policy and, since the early 1970s, is overseen by a cabinet minister, the Secretary of State for Multiculturalism.

Another concern of the 1990s (continuing into the 2000s) was what appeared to be a rising wave of children's violence. A number of communities around the country experienced episodes of children bringing guns to school—elementary school as well as high school—and shooting dead other children and teachers. Although there were probably no more than a dozen such incidents, they were unprecedented and aroused widespread concern. Some schools developed programs to teach children how to resolve conflicts without allowing their anger to explode into violent assault on others.

Finally, the 1990s and the first years of the twenty-first century show a renewed concern with children's academic performance in elementary schools. Specifically, this concern now takes the form of insuring that children master basic skills of reading and arithmetic. There is a new focus across the United States and Canada on standardized testing to determine whether children have reached the required standards. Critics of the emphasis on testing allege that it influences teachers to "teach to the test," a narrow focus that diminishes children's opportunities to let their curiosity guide them to explore topics of interest and to develop their creative, expressive abilities. Another emerging issue in this period is how the schools and other institutions should deal with the growing public awareness of homosexual partnerships and homosexuality more generally. This issue is part of a more general, ongoing issue of how to socialize children to sexuality, one that is very contentious in the United States.

In sum, if we look back over the last 50 years or so, we can recognize several shifts of attention and concern in socialization beliefs and practices, from getting along with others to an emphasis on academic competence to still newer emphases on revising certain minority and gender stereotypes, adapting to new types of family, and accepting and integrating multiculturalism and diversity. The earlier concerns are not discarded; they are edged away from the center of attention and worked into newer patterns.

Before proceeding to our discussion of particular agencies, it is important to make clear that some socialization outcomes are consciously sought by the agency of socialization, whereas others are unintended. Socialization always takes place in overlapping time frames. For example, when a parent tells a child to take his or her feet off the furniture, the parent is most likely thinking of keeping the furniture clean and unscratched. The parent may or may not be thinking at that moment about developing in the child "respect for property," "respect for authority," "neatness," "self-restraint in positioning one's body," or any other of a number of long-term objectives that might be considered socially desirable. But even though the parent may not have these latter objectives in mind, they may nonetheless be among the consequences of the interactions whose goal is simply to save the furniture. We are, then, alluding to an important distinction between *purpose* and *function* (Merton [1949] 1968). A purpose is a goal that a person or group wants to accomplish; it is an *end in view*. A function is a consequence, or effect, of action and interaction. Purposes and functions may sometimes coincide; thus, knowledge of arithmetic is one of the goals, or purposes, that the elementary school endeavors to attain. It is also a function, that is, a consequence of good teaching. Poor teaching can result in a *dysfunction*, a lack of arithmetic knowledge and skill, despite the teacher's sincere good purpose. Good intentions sometimes result in good consequences, but not always—whether in teaching, parenting, or any other human activity. If purposes and functions never coincided, socialization would probably be impossible. Nevertheless, it is important to bear in mind that socialization agencies have functions that are not necessarily among their purposes.

One reason why functions and purposes do not entirely coincide is that although the family, school, and others are agencies of society, they also "have a life of their own." When we say that society—through law, custom, and public opinion—delegates certain socialization functions to specific agencies such as families and schools, we are not describing a process that is the same as an army captain directing a subordinate to carry out an assigned task. Agencies of socialization necessarily have more leeway in how they achieve the goals assigned to them than does the captain's aide. Agencies of socialization are accountable to the society only within rather broad limits. A school that does not include arithmetic in its curriculum will be examined by a state agency or criticized by parents, and it will be pressured to meet at least a minimum standard. But a great deal of what goes on in schools, in families, or in other agencies of socialization is not scrutinized, not subject to sanctions by society.

It is therefore not entirely useful—but useful up to a point—to think of agencies of socialization as carrying out society's mandates. Such agencies are not like machines processing a raw material into a predetermined product. Not only do socialization agencies develop purposes of their own (such as successful survival, popularity, prestige, expansion, and growth) but the persons in those agencies (the agents—individual parents, individual teachers, and principals) also develop *their* own purposes (such as popularity or prestige). One result is that different agencies and agents sometimes work at cross-purposes. It is a safe assumption that every child will, at some point, experience inner conflict arising from conflicting demands or expectations of different agents. Teacher and parent, parent and playmate, coach and teacher, teacher and playmate, teacher and television, playmate one and playmate two—each of these pairs of agents is likely to generate conflicting expectations at some point in almost every child's life. The child has the task of resolving the conflict in some way or other. The child is in society, and society is in the child, but society does not speak with a single voice.

The concept of "agency of socialization" needs, then, to be understood in this somewhat complex way. Any such agency generates processes, purposes, and functions of varying import. Some of these mesh together into a prevailing cultural focus, while others generate conflict and pose dilemmas for children trying to find their way in society.

With this understanding of the complex relationship between agencies of socialization and society, we turn now to an examination of some of the most important agencies in our society.

References

Adler, Patricia, and Peter Adler. 1984. "The Carpool: A Socializing Adjunct to the Educational Experience." *Sociology of Education* 57 (October): 200–210.

Berlin, Isaiah. 1998. *The Crooked Timber of Humanity,* edited by Henry Hardy. Princeton, NJ: Princeton University Press.

Fine, Gary Alan. 1987. *With the Boys: Little League Baseball and Preadolescent Culture.* Chicago: University of Chicago Press.

Lever, Janet. 1978. "Sex Differences in the Complexity of Children's Play." *American Sociological Review* 43 (August): 471–482.

Lewis, Michael, and Saul Feinman (eds). 1991. *Social Influences and Socialization in Infancy.* New York: Plenum Press.

Merton, Robert K. [1949] 1968. *Social Theory and Social Structure.* Glencoe, IL: Free Press.

Riesman, David, with Nathan Glazer and Reuel Denny. 1950. *The Lonely Crowd: A Study of the Changing American Character.* New Haven, CT: Yale University Press.

Thorne, Barrie. 1993. *Gender Play: Girls and Boys in School.* New Brunswick, NJ: Rutgers University Press. ✦

Chapter 5

Families

M ost children begin life in some kind of family. At one time, sociologists wrote about "the family" because there was an assumption that a family is a group consisting of a man and woman married to each other for life and procreating their own biological children. Further, the husband/father was the breadwinner and the wife/mother was the homemaker who also had primary responsibility for raising the children. This type of group is technically called a *nuclear family* and is commonly referred to as "the traditional family," although there is much dispute about how far back that tradition goes. While it was always known that some children lived in other kinds of households, these were regarded as relatively minor deviations from the prevailing norm.

Today, there is wide recognition (although not universal acceptance) that the composition (the membership) of families has changed greatly and now is diverse. For example, in 1970, 40 percent of U.S. households consisted of nuclear families, but in 1990 only 26 percent were. (Taylor 1997, 68). By 2002 this percentage had declined further to 23.6 percent (United States Bureau of the Census 2002). In 1960, 75 percent of children lived in nuclear families (Taylor 1997, 68). Available census figures show that in 2002, 69 percent of children lived in two-parent families, but this figure also includes children in step-families and children who were adopted, as well as biological children of two parents (Fields 2003). In 1970, 12 percent of children lived in single-parent households; this increased to 27 percent in 1993 (Taylor 1997, 68) and it remains at about that figure (Fields 2003, Table 1). Some studies estimate that 40 percent of American children born to married parents will experience a parental divorce before the age of 18 (Amato and Booth 1997, 10; Martin, Emery, and Peris 2004, 283). In addition to these changes in composition, the nuclear family has significantly changed in that many mothers now have paying jobs in the labor market, a practice that was much less common before 1970. In 2002, 62.4 percent of children living with two parents had both parents in the labor force (Fields 2003, Table 4). Full-time homemakers are now a minority. There are children living with one parent and one or two grandparents. There are children living with one parent who has a cohabiting partner, who may be of the same sex or the other sex. There are other household compositions, too numerous to present in detail in the present work.

There are, then, many kinds of families, and although some people believe there should be only one kind of family, the "traditional" kind, such a definition no longer describes the situation that actually exists. Many sociologists

131

would probably accept this definition of a *family*: *"a collection of individuals who have a commitment to the general wellbeing of one another and who label themselves a 'family'"* (Landesman, Jaccard, and Gunderson 1991, 66). This definition has its problems—for example, infants don't have commitments or a concept of family, but they are nonetheless certainly members—but no definition of families as they exist today can cover every possible aspect. This definition covers all persons who are mentally and emotionally capable of commitments. The key feature is that it departs from legal and religious bases for definition and rests on function and self-definition. This accords with two trends in American and some other societies: (1) increasing freedom of choice in living arrangements, and (2) recognition of increasing diversity in how people live. Some laws have changed in accord with this new reality, and some religious denominations also accept it, while some do not.

Socialization begins in families. We will begin with some brief comparisons of families in different cultures. Then we will cover some points that apply to children in American society regardless of what type of family they are in. Our discussion will then be organized on the basis of different types of family composition. It will also include some points on socialization in different age periods (infancy, early childhood). While socialization varies by family composition and by age of the child, it also varies by social class and by ethnic group membership. These latter aspects of variation will be discussed in Chapters 9 and 10.

Socialization refers to the overall process by which children become participating members of society. The activities of parents that contribute to this outcome are sometimes referred to as *parenting, caregiving,* or *child rearing.* These terms are essentially synonymous.

Some Cross-Cultural Comparisons

Researchers have done many comparative studies of parenting in different societies. These indicate some of the ways in which parenting is carried out differently, and we present here a few examples. We must add the cautionary note that there is *also considerable difference among parents within a particular society.* All of the studies are small-scale, that is, they are based on relatively small numbers of cases. This means that their results can only be suggestive, not definitive. But that is how research into new topics usually begins. Knowledge builds slowly as studies accumulate. We do not always have large-scale studies that might be able to establish differences with greater certainty. In any case, differences between societies are never absolute; that is, it never happens that all the people in one society do things one way and all the people in another society do things totally differently. We are always dealing with trends or tendencies, not absolute differences.

A study of interaction between mothers and their 5-month-old infants in the United States, France, and Japan, based on 24 middle-class mother-infant dyads each in New York City, Paris, and Tokyo, found some similarities as well as some differences. For example, all the mothers engage in tactile kinesthetic play, that is, touch and movement play with their infants. There was no difference among them in this type of activity. However, for another activity, object stimulation, that is, trying to get their infant to focus on something in the immediate environment, the difference was significant. American mothers engaged in this activity considerably more often than the French or Japanese mothers. American mothers were also more likely than French or Japanese to speak to their infants with a special tone of voice known technically as *infant register* and colloquially as *motherese* or *parentese*, while French and Japanese mothers spoke to their infants in conventional adult tones (Bornstein, Tal, and Tamis-LeMonda 1991).

A study in Montreal, in the Province of Quebec, Canada, compared aspects of infant socialization among native Québecois and two immigrant groups, Vietnamese and Haitian. The infants were seen at three ages—3 1/2 months, 6 months, and 9 months. The study looked at three aspects: (1) social and physical environment, (2) mothers' beliefs about infant development, and (3) mother-infant interaction. We have room here to mention only a few highlights from the study. The Haitian and Vietnamese infants receive more social stimulation than Québecois in a familiar context because they sleep in their parents' bedrooms and there is usually a relative other than immediate family living in the small apartment. The Québecois, on the other hand, are more surrounded by toys; the mothers consider it important that the infants play by themselves and have practical learning experiences from that play. Haitian mothers consider it important to play with their infants at their request and respond quickly to them, but they are not intent on introducing stimulating activities at an early age. The Québecois mothers, on the other hand, introduce activities early with the intention of stimulating cognitive development. Vietnamese mothers are more directing and restraining than the other two groups when the infants were 9 months old (Pomerleau, Malcuit, and Sabatier 1991).

Another study looked at cultural variations in relationships between toddlers (12- to 24-month-olds) and their families in four very different communities: a peasant town in Guatemala, a poor tribal community in India, a middle-class urban community in Turkey, and a middle-class urban community in the United States. The Guatemalan and Indian children generally had contact with a wider array of people than did the Turkish and American children. Whereas Turkish and American middle-class children live with parents and siblings and often have their own room, the Guatemalan and Indian children live in compounds with relatives nearby who take an active part in caregiving. American and Turkish middle-class mothers consider it part of their role to play with their children. Some of the Guatemalan mothers "laughed with embarrassment at the idea of playing with their children" because that role belongs to other children and to grandparents (Rogoff et al. 1991, 177). Another striking difference among these communities was the variation in children's opportunities to observe adult economic activity. Guatemalan toddlers could observe their mothers' home-based sewing and weaving. The Indian children could see their mothers work in the fields or accompany them to daily paid labor outside the home. The Turkish and American middle-class toddlers did not have comparable situations; their learning about adult economic activity comes more slowly and later in life. In this respect, they have a more prolonged childhood.

In a small-scale study comparing mothers' interactions with 3-year-old children in a Pennsylvania town and in Cambridge, England, the researchers found that there was considerable talk about the rules of the house in both places. The English mothers, however, focused on appropriate meal-time behavior and politeness, whereas the social-rule talk by American mothers focused more on noisiness and wild behavior. In efforts to correct behavior, English mothers were more likely to invoke a general norm whereas American mothers focused on individual responsibility. For example, an English mother whose children are on a table says, "Tables aren't for walking on." An American mother whose child has knocked herself while rushing around says, "That's because you weren't watching what you were doing" (Dunn and Brown 1991, 161, 163).

These few examples of cross-cultural studies illustrate several important points: (1) Although there are differences within cultures, nonetheless there are also differences among cultures in how parents define their socialization tasks; (2) socialization begins from children's birth, in their infancy; and (3) socialization differences appear in several ways—in how much stimulation parents think is important in infancy, in how parents speak and respond to infants, in how strongly parents emphasize individual responsibility in children, in the extent to which parents routinely share child rearing with others, and in how early children are introduced to realities of the adult world. When considered in combination, these variations make clear that it can be a dangerous oversimplification to think there is such a thing as "the child." Parents in different societies have different beliefs about what a child is and how to deal with their child, and those various beliefs tend to reflect their society's shared perceptions and norms in their several societies.

Families in the Community

The family into which a child is born *places the child in the community and in society.* This means that newborns begin their social life by acquiring the status their families have, and they will retain this status certainly through the first few years of their lives, very probably until they reach adulthood, and only somewhat less probably as they move through adulthood. This long-understood process, *status inheritance*, has been recognized as one of the most important mechanisms of socialization in families. Summarizing several research studies, Norella Putney and Vern Bengtson (Putney and Bengtson 2002, 170–171) explain that the family's socioeconomic location—including income, wealth, and quality of residence and neighborhood—affects the children's progress in education, perceptions, and expectations of what is possible, and the goals to which they might aspire. It affects parents' ability to invest in their children's education. Not only do parents' statuses influence the attitudes and aspirations that they attempt to transmit to their children, but also the residence neighborhood helps determine the children's world of potential peers, who exert their own influences, as we discuss in Chapter 7. The importance of status inheritance is discussed in further detail in Chapter 9.

The child's family-given status is an important determinant of the way others respond to him or her. Children of ministers are expected to be better behaved than children whose parents are not clergy. Children of working-class parents, especially boys, are generally expected to be tough. Children of low-income parents are sometimes thought to be less intelligent than children of middle-class parents, and so teachers may expect them to do less well in school than children of middle-class parents. This is a negative stereotype that adds further disadvantage to poor children because some teachers may make less effort to have the children learn at the high standard of which they are possibly capable. A favorable stereotype can also lead to burdens for some children. Since Asian American children as a category have been academically successful disproportionately to their numbers in the population, teachers and others are sometimes surprised to find some who are average or below average in academic ability and performance. These children may experience social discomfort for not being able to live up to the stereotype.

These are examples of expectations that are held about children whose families are in particular occupational, social class, or ethnic statuses. Some children may act in ways that largely conform to such expectations, while others may not. Either way, the child usually has to deal with the expectations. An example from the British film, *Billy Elliott*, released in 2001, is illustrative. This film focused on a young working-class boy who, on his way to a boxing lesson at a neighborhood center, sees a ballet class in progress and develops an immediate desire to become a ballet dancer. Much of the film is devoted to his struggles with his coal-miner father and brother, as well as others in his neighborhood, to defy their expectations and realize his nonstandard ambition. He is supported only by a ballet teacher who believes he has talent. Among other things, the film illustrates in a dramatic way how a child can experience inner conflict because of conflicting expectations from different socialization agents.

The family's status in the community affects not only the way others respond to the child and the kind of formal education he or she is likely to receive; it also mediates for the child the culture available in the larger society (Handel 1972, 125–130). Any family participates directly in a limited number of subcultures and networks (some based on social-class position, some based on ethnic group membership or on religion, and possibly others based on kinship, occupations, or personal interests such as sports or music or Bible study). These are versions of the larger society that are made most directly available to the child through example, teaching, and taken-for-granted daily activity. At the same time, any family is likely to be aware of at least portions of other subcultures that may serve as objects of emulation or derogatory comment. In these ways, the families into which children are born present them with selective versions of the larger society, with the result that children may become impressed early on with the importance of religious devotion, or baseball, or school achievement, or ethnic loyalty, or making money, or sexual intercourse as a primary focus of attention, depending upon the emphasis of the subculture(s) in which their families participate.

In recent years, some research attention has been being directed to ways in which parents' personal social networks may influence socialization. A *personal social network* consists of "those people outside the household who engage in activities and exchanges of an affective and/or material nature with members of the immediate family" (Cochran and Brassard 1979; cited in Cochran and Niego 1995, 396). Neighbors, friends, and relatives can be included in such networks, and they can be supportive of parents with babysitting, child-rearing advice, help with errands, providing information about schools and teachers, taking children on outings, teaching children how to do a task, and other ways. They can also act in stressful ways, such as criticizing a parent's handling of a child or introducing perspectives that the parents oppose. When children participate in face-to-face interaction with adults known to their parents, whether or not parents are present at the moment, the network can influence the children. When such adults are responsive to children, their actions can foster the child's trust in adults and therefore in the wider social world beyond the family that the child is engaged in exploring. As researchers observe,

> Time together is also likely to include the exchange of ideas and feelings that are a part of everyday conversation. With practice and encouragement, a child gains confidence and skill in expressing his or her own beliefs, as well as in listening to the views of others. Adults will encourage children to behave appropriately and follow instructions (talking quietly in museums and libraries, not wandering off in a park) to ensure that standards are met. . . . Adult network members . . . through such 'ordinary' activities as gardening or a visit to the park, may enhance the social and emotional wellbeing of children. (Cochran and Niego 1995, 405–406)

In sum, a family is not simply a passive transmitter of a subculture to children but plays an active part in screening in and screening out elements of available subcultures (Hess and Handel [1974] 1995, 14–15). This is accomplished (1) by means of *activities*, for example going to church, celebrating holidays, visiting friends, and watching baseball games on television; and (2) through *comment and comparison*, such as evaluating such activities and the people who do or do not participate in them, and evaluating the groups and subcultures of which these activities are a part. Families that go to church regularly are accepting that part of the culture, while families that do not are either indifferent or antagonistic to it. Visiting friends expresses acceptable ways of interacting with friends— whether that involves playing cards, discussing current events or sports, serving drinks, or whatever. Such activities are the parts of the culture that parents make visible to their children. From time to time, parents and older siblings may have occasion to comment, whether favorably or unfavorably, on how some neighbors or somebody else does things, and such implied comparisons also help children define their culture and define themselves.

Families as Groups of Interacting Persons

Back in 1926 Ernest W. Burgess, a colleague of Mead's at the University of Chicago and a leading sociologist of the family, published a brief article—"The Family as a Unity of Interacting Personalities"—whose title became famous for its originality in approaching the family as a group of interacting members, rather than in the prevailing fashion as a cultural or legal institution (Burgess

1926). By "unity," he did not mean "harmony." Unity consists in the interaction, including conflict, among the family members. Burgess did many studies of marriage and divorce, but no studies of families that included children.

Some families may consist of only two people, a mother and child, a father and child, or a grandparent and child. A two-person unit is called a *dyad*. Most families contain three or more people. A unit of three or more people is called a *group*. The terms *dyad* and *group* apply not only to families but to others types of association as well, but our discussion here refers only to families. In both dyads and groups the members have emotional ties to each other. In the preceding chapter, we discussed the development of emotional attachments between infant and parents. In the course of time, those attachments become more complex and become woven into a pattern of daily interaction among the family members. Every family develops its own pattern of emotions, activities, and interactions—its own family world (Hess and Handel [1959] 1995).

In their concept of *family worlds*, developed in a study based on interviews with both parents and all the children between ages 6 and 18 in 33 two-parent families, Hess and Handel observe that two conditions characterize such families. Each member is connected to all the others, but each is also separate from one another.

> Every family gives shape to these conditions in its own way. Its life may show greater emphasis on the one or the other; yet both are constitutive of family life. The infant is born from the womb into the limits of his own skin, with individual properties of sensitivity and activity. He possesses an irreducible psychobiological individuality that no amount or kind of intense socialization can abolish. His parents, too, remain individual persons no matter how deep their love, how passionate their desire for one another" (Hess and Handel 1959 [1995], 4); (note that in the language convention of the time, the masculine pronoun was customarily used to represent the combination of male and female.)

Instead of assuming that socialization is a one-directional process, with both parents always consistent with each other, Hess and Handel offer a concept of *mutual regulation* in which children and parents are interactive. Each child as well as each parent contributes to the pattern of mutual regulation. Before the concept of "agency" gained currency, this study in effect argued for and demonstrated children's agency, while also showing that parents have a preponderant power over their children. Along with each family's uniqueness, there are, of course, categories of similarity and difference among families, which we discuss here and in Chapters 9 and 10.

Since children's first social relationships are family relationships, it is in this group that they acquire their first experience of being treated as persons in their own right. They receive care for their dependency and attention for their sociability. The kind of care and attention that they receive during their first and second years of life, according to Erik Erikson, strongly affects their resolution of the issues of trust versus mistrust and autonomy versus shame and doubt. Does a child come to trust or suspect those around him or her? Does the child come to feel doubtful or confident in her or his actions? The basis is laid in these first years for establishing later ties with people outside the family (Erikson 1950). Erikson was a psychoanalyst who treated children and who considered childhood cross-culturally, as he had had some exposure to American Indian societies through his association with anthropologists who studied them.

At the outset, newborns are presumably unaware that they are separate and distinct persons. As time goes on, they become aware, first, that they and their mothers (or other caregiving persons) are separate, and then that there are other members of the household—father, and perhaps siblings. Children learn that others have wishes, interests, and ways of their own and that it is advantageous to adapt to them. Others do not invariably appreciate children and their needs and wishes. Indeed, the appreciation may vary according to how responsive the child is. Living in a household shared with others, children learn that they must share the resources of the household—the space, the furnishings and other objects, and the time and attention of parents and siblings. They learn the ways in which their cooperation is sought and the ways in which they may compete for what they want when it conflicts with what other family members want. In interacting with their children, parents may be more or less expressive of their feelings, more or less authoritative, more or less protective. The parent, in dressing a young child, may demand or plead for cooperation; when disciplining the child, a parent may be angry or matter of fact. Siblings may be more or less jealous, more or less interested in accepting a brother or sister as playmate and companion.

Through these various kinds of interaction with family members—such as being cared for, resisting, being disciplined, showing affection, and being accepted as a companion and playmate—the child develops initial capacities for establishing relationships with others. These capacities will find later expression and further development in relationships with nonfamily playmates, coworkers, authority figures, friends, and, ultimately, perhaps, a spouse and children.

The family into which the son or daughter is born is the child's first *reference group*. A reference group is any group, whether a person belongs to it or observes it at a distance, whose values, norms, and practices a person adopts and is influenced by in evaluating his or her own behavior. The child develops consciousness of its membership in a family and, as its experience in the family continues, the family's ways come to seem "normal." The child identifies with the family as a group; the family group becomes part of the child's self. (Thus, a reference group is a particular kind of generalized other, which we discussed in Chapter 4.) *The pattern of interaction among family members becomes a model for the child.* The child's socialization is affected not only by having a hardworking or an alcoholic father, a loving or an indifferent mother, or a helpful or distant older sibling. It is affected also by whether the family interaction is characteristically relaxed and good-natured or tense and guarded; whether it emphasizes or minimizes the distance between parents and children or between males and females; and whether it is typically cooperative or competitive. Thus, a young child who knows only a protective and mutually supportive mother and father relationship will likely first approach other families with the trust built into its self-image.

Parents and children may communicate with each other in many situations in the course of a day, and all of them may contribute to the children's socialization. One setting of some importance is the family dinnertime, when parents are usually home from work and children from school and after-school activities. Although in recent years there has probably been some decline in the number of families whose members all gather together for dinner, because of varying schedules, for those that still do the dinner hour is a socialization setting. More than four decades ago, scholars identified some of the ways in which it is important: (1) Through family table talk, the family's culture is transmitted. (2) Family members talk about their experiences, and these are discussed, commented on, and evaluated. Family idea patterns and values are expressed, and their application to specific situations is illustrated. (3) Parents sometimes use the occasion as an instructional situation. (4) Family table talk can contribute to stimulating or to discouraging children's expressions of their interests. (5) "The family is an audience for individual performances, chiefly conversational. Through these performances family members reveal their abilities to, and try them out on, each other. . . . This table audience, both in the responses which it gives to, and in those it withholds from, its individual members carries the greatest weight in the molding of personal traits" (Bossard and Boll 1966, 137–144).

A recent study of dinner table talk adds further to our understanding of its importance: "To become competent conversationalists, children have to learn how to choose and introduce topics for talk, respond appropriately, tell a story, or develop an argument" (Blum-Kulka 1997, 3). For American middle-class parents, the dinner table is also an important setting for the teaching of politeness (Blum-Kulka 1997, 181).

This discussion of table talk enlarges our understanding of language acquisition as an important aspect of socialization. In Chapter 4, we discussed language acquisition as a process of learning words, understanding them as significant symbols so meanings can be shared with others, and, further, learning to put those words together in sentences that others can understand. Now we see that language socialization goes still further. It involves learning how to use language in social contexts. Further, we see how parental language use contributes to shaping children's possible acquisition of the parents' values, norms, and practices. The family dinner table has long been an important setting for this to occur.

Family Composition and Interaction

In continuing this discussion of family interaction as an influence on child socialization, it is necessary to consider different parental configurations. In the space available, it is not possible to discuss every possible family arrangement. We concentrate on some major patterns for which we have some information.

Two-Parent First-Marriage Families

A family headed by a husband and wife in a first marriage remains a widely accepted cultural ideal in the United States, although an increasing number of people reject it and another large number who subscribed to the ideal abandoned it in disappointment and divorced. In the last decades of the twentieth century, a major historical change occurred in this type of family. Previously, a wife who worked at a paying job was likely to give up the job when she became a mother. Now, that is less likely. Seventy-five percent of the mothers of young children, and even more than 50 percent of mothers of infants, have jobs for pay. Despite this great change, the great bulk of parenting is still done by mothers. According to some accounts, fathers' participation in the tasks of parenting and child rearing has increased only slightly. Further, some studies show that fathers regard their participation in parenting work as discretionary; that is, they decide whether or not they want to do it (Arendell 1997, 19–21). One consequence of this pattern is that children

> are being prepared to assume more or less conventional gender roles, including future parental ones. In addition to having gender differences modeled by their parents and acquiring gendered identities through interaction and family socialization, children participate in a culture organized along gender lines. This environment perpetuates an ideology that espouses gender differences, including women's 'innate' capacity for nurturing and caregiving.... Parents attempting to rear less gender-differentiated children must contend with these cultural pressures. (Arendell 1997, 21–22)

Gender socialization, a topic we discuss more fully in Chapter 11, is certainly an important process and outcome of socialization in the family, but it is not the only important aspect of family socialization. The way *parental authority* is exercised is another significant dimension. A study of two-parent families published more than 40 years ago presented a set of three types that continues to offer some illumination (Gans [1962] 1982). There is no reason to believe that this set of types is out of date, even though it may not cover all possible cases. The first type is called the *adult-centered family.* This type of family is run by adults for adults. In this type of family, the wishes of the children are clearly subordinate to the wishes of the parents. When the children are with adults, they must act as adults want them to act: to play quietly in a corner or to show themselves off to other adults in ways that reflect well on the parents. But once the children are with their peers, they have considerable freedom to act as they wish as long as they do not get into trouble. Parents in these families are not very self-conscious or purposive in their child rearing. They "are not concerned with *developing* their children, that is, with raising them in accordance with a pre-determined goal or target which they are expected to achieve. [They] have no clear image of the future social status, occupational level, or life style that they want their children to reach. And even when they do, they do not know how to build it into the child-rearing process" (Gans 1962 [1982], 54, 59–60; italics in original). Sociologist Herbert Gans, who formulated this typology, found the adult-centered family among working-class Italian Americans in Boston. In a later study, Jack Weller found this type of family among the poor Anglo-Saxon mountain people of Appalachia (Weller 1965).

The second type is called the *child-centered family*, in which parents subordinate their own pleasures to the demands and happiness of their children. In this type of family, unlike the adult-centered family, children are planned and serve as their parents' most easily shared interest. Family companionship is important; parents spend time playing with their children, and give up some adult pleasures for them. They want their children to have a happier childhood than they had. Each child adds to the shared enjoyment and family unity, at least while the children are young. Some high-school–educated lower-middle-class and some immigrant families are of this type. Sometimes, although the parents are not necessarily permissive, the children dominate their parents unmercifully.

In a more recent study of two-parent families, Scott Coltrane also identifies a child-centered type of family. He writes,

> Couples were child-centered in that they placed a high value on their children's well-being, defined parenting as an important and serious undertaking and organized most of their non-employed hours around their children. Talking to most of the parents I got the feeling that their children were their number one priority. For instance, one father described how his social life revolved around his children, commenting 'they are the central driving force in my life.' (Coltrane 1996, 62)

This characterization is very close to Gans's, although their studies were conducted almost 40 years apart.

The third type in this set is the *adult-directed family*. Parents are generally college-educated and know what they want for their children much more clearly than do parents in the child-centered type. Emphasis is placed on individual growth. Children are taught to strive for self-development in accordance with their own individuality, and parents exert considerable pressure on their children to do well in school (Gans 1962 [1982]). Two recent studies by Chin (2000) and Lareau (2003) provide additional description and analysis of this type of family, although neither author adopts Gans's type label. We shall say more about these two studies in Chapter 9.

This set of types provides a useful introduction to differences among two-parent families. However, it does not cover two issues that have captured research attention in recent years. One is the issue of the role of fathers in families. The other is the issue of the consequences of mothers working in the paid labor force. We touched on these briefly at the beginning of this section, but we now want to explore them in more depth.

What are the traditional parental gender roles that sociologist Terry Arendell (1997) deplores in the quotation from her work cited a few paragraphs above? She notes the entrenched cultural belief that mothers are believed to have an "innate" capacity for nurturing and caregiving. What about fathers? She reports studies that show they do much less parenting than mothers and feel that they have the right to decide how much they will do. Another sociologist, David Popenoe (1996), who is a strong believer in the importance of fathers in socializing children, believes that fathers play a more important and distinctive role in socializing children than critics of fathers believe. Unlike Arendell and several other feminist sociologists who believe that mother and father roles can be made gender neutral (interchangeable) in socialization, he believes fathers play a different, *complementary* (not complimentary) role to that of mothers. He believes the differences are innate, although he also believes that men can learn to be more nurturing than they are.

The first contribution that a father makes, according to Popenoe as well as others who make the same point, is that an available father is a role model for both sons and daughters. A boy learns from his father how to be a man, which Popenoe believes a boy can't learn from his mother. He learns about "male responsibility and achievement . . . how to be suitably assertive and independent, and how to relate acceptably to the opposite sex." Daughters learn how to relate to men. "They learn to appreciate their own femininity from the one male who is most special in their lives, again assuming that they love and respect their fathers. . . . In addition, daughters learn from their fathers much that will be of value in their work and professional lives, especially the skills they need for coping in a still male-dominated world. They learn about assertiveness, independence, and achievement. Girls with supportive fathers are, in general, more successful in their careers" (Popenoe 1996, 142–143).

Popenoe argues that fathers emphasize play more than caretaking, and that play is important in children's development, although he agrees that they should be more active in caretaking also. He says that fathers' play with their children is physically stimulating and exciting and often requires children to test their physical and mental skills. Mothers' play, in contrast, takes place more at the child's level, and is not as challenging. Fathers stress competition, risk-taking, initiative, and independence, whereas mothers emphasize security and personal safety. In discipline, too, fathers and mothers are said to have complementary styles. Fathers are firm, whereas mothers will bargain more. Mothers are more aware of children's differing moods and differing contexts, and will adjust discipline accordingly. In sum, Popenoe concludes that, while there can be considerable overlap in gender characteristics in parenting, "gender-differentiated parenting undoubtedly is related to something fundamental in the human condition" (Popenoe 1996, 143–147).

A number of sociologists and psychologists have conducted studies in which they find a new pattern of fatherhood developing in American society. Kathleen Gerson, for example, is more optimistic than Terry Arendell, believing that more men are developing a shared parenting outlook, although she agrees with Arendell, and disagrees with Popenoe, that differences between female and male caretaking behavior are not innate but are the result of society's construction of gender roles. *Social construction* here refers to (1) society maintaining norms that define what is expected of mothers and of fathers, and (2) employers organizing work in ways that limit fathering—for example, not giving men paid leave when their baby is born, or later, for example, paid leave to see their child perform in a school play during work hours. Such arrangements are time-honored, but that does not mean that they are innate in female and male biology. They may be hard to change, but they can change. More social supports for involved fatherhood would result in more men taking on active caretaking roles (Gerson 1997). Despite their considerable differences in the way they analyze many aspects of family relationships, Gerson, like Popenoe, believes that fathers are important in raising children, and she is critical of the media of mass communication and of some social scientists because they "have supported and even helped create the view that a father's low level of involvement does no harm" (Gerson 1993, 188).

Scott Coltrane studied couples that engage in shared parenting. In these couples, both fathers and mothers reported that the men's involvement in nurturing their children had changed them greatly. He concludes, "My findings suggest that when domestic activities are shared equally, 'maternal thinking' develops in fathers as well as mothers, and the social meaning of gender begins to change. . . . What it means to 'mother,' or to be a 'real man,' is not fixed in stone, but slowly shifts as new patterns of household labor are negotiated in countless families" (Coltrane 1996, 83). From this statement we see that Coltrane shares with Arendell and Gerson the view that differences between men and women in caretaking behavior are not innate, contrary to Popenoe's view. The concept of *negotiation* is an important one in understanding interaction in many contexts. In the present context, it means that parents are not routinely enacting culturally prescribed gender roles as though they were reading from a script but are working out their own pattern—talking to each other about who should do what and reaching agreements rather than depending on prevailing norms that "that's a woman's job; men aren't supposed to do that." And it implies that any parents could do that if they decided to. Culture provides role guidelines, but in an open society people do not have to be prisoners of culture. They can innovate and thus create new patterns of activity. If others also hear about, read about, talk about, and adopt the new patterns, the culture itself changes.

Pressure on men to become more actively involved in raising their children largely developed from the women's movement that began to gather momentum in the 1960s. Although this movement splintered into different fractions, including at least one that believes that there are important innate differences between males and females, the dominant view seems to be that apart from menstruation, pregnancy, and breastfeeding, women and men are more similar than different, and the similarity increases as more people accept this view and drop their insistence on difference. That has, in fact, happened to some extent, one result being that women for some time have been moving into jobs that people once believed only men could do. If women can do things that people once believed only men could do—such as driving trucks, fighting fires, and serving as corporate executives—then it follows that men can perhaps do things, such as nurture babies and children, that people once believed only women could do. Diane Ehrensaft, who studied couples who engage in shared parenting, reports that a survey carried out by the women's magazine *Ladies' Home Journal* in 1985 found that 84.2 percent of its readers believe that men are just as good with children as women. From her own study, she concludes that more men are engaging in shared parenting with their wives but that it is not "simply a one-generation transformation. Things are drastically different, yet something of the old still remains. The male-female personality differences that make parenting a lopsided affair will fade with each new generation, but will take at least one or two to really disappear" (Ehrensaft 1987, 251, 258).

A second pressure on men comes from the fact that *mothers* are now doing many of those more open jobs. As noted above, more than 50 percent of mothers of infants and 75 percent of mothers of young children are working for pay (Arendell 1997, 19–21). Families with both a husband and wife working are referred to as *dual-earner* or *two-job families*. When both are working not only for current income but also with a goal to advance in knowledge, skill, and responsibility as well as earnings, they are known as *dual-career* families. This increase in maternal employment has come about not only because many women, as well as men, now aspire to careers but also because many couples find that a husband's income is not sufficient to maintain a standard of living that the parents consider adequate. This new type of family organization that has developed over the last 35 or 40 years has prompted controversy and research regarding the consequences for young children.

One review of research by psychologists concludes, "Research conducted across many domains of development, from infancy through young adulthood ... all converge on the conclusion that maternal employment per se is not detrimental to children's development" (Gottfried, Gottfried, and Killian 1999, 16). One important reason they give is that "fathers are more involved and engaged in activities with their children, and more involved in child care when mother [the] is employed, and this involvement increases as mothers' work hours increase from infancy through adolescence" (Gottfried, Gottfried, and Killian 1999, 22–23). Another study compared fathers in single-earner and dual-earner families and found that those in dual-earner families were much more active with their first-born children than were fathers in single-earner families (Crouter and McHale 1993, 190). Clearly, these conclusions regarding fathers' involvement diverge sharply from sociologists' research, which does not find as great an increase.

Other psychologists disagree about harm. One review of several fairly recent studies concluded that when the mother works full-time outside the home during her child's infancy, the child at 1 year old is more likely to have an insecure attachment to the mother. This seems to be particularly true for boys. One limitation of these studies is that they do not examine the quality of the alternate care, so it is possible that some of the negative effects might be due to poor-quality substitute care rather than to the mother's absence at work (Chase-Lansdale, Michael, and Desai 1991, 38–39). However, another study finds that insecure mother-infant attachments are more likely in dual-earner families in which the marriage is in trouble, so that dual-earner families with a harmonious marriage would not necessarily lead to this result (Crouter and McHale 1993, 196).

Dual-earner families often put their infants and young children into daycare settings. One issue that this has raised is whether putting them in daycare generates insecure maternal attachment. What is the effect on the child's sense of security? A review of research on this issue concludes that "the evidence is insufficiently clear to warrant any confident conclusions about the effects of infant day care" (Thompson 1991, 21). Reasons for this uncertainty stem from other variables, particularly family influences on the child, the child's own temperament and characteristics, and the quality of the daycare.

A more general question asks about all possible effects on children of a mother's employment. One team of authors has reviewed a great deal of research, mostly on middle-class families, and concluded, "It is impossible, given existing findings, to say that children consistently and unambiguously benefit from, or are harmed by, maternal employment" (Zaslow, Rabinovich, and Suwalsky 1991, 237). This is because the consequences of a mother's employment for the child are believed to depend on a number of other factors, which are supported by only fragmentary evidence. The main factors are as follows:

1. *Sex of the child.* Girls seem to benefit more than boys from mother's employment. Girls gain a broadened view of gender roles and develop high personal aspirations. Boys experience a negative parent-child relationship as well as some decrease in cognitive development (Zaslow, Rabinovich, and Suwalsky 1991, 243–245).

2. *Maternal role satisfaction.* Some research suggests that "when a mother is satisfied with her employment role, whether she is employed or a homemaker, her children show more optimal development, whereas dissatisfaction with employment role is associated with negative outcomes" (Zaslow, Rabinovich, and Suwalsky 1991, 258–262).

3. *Paternal endorsement of mother' employment.* Some research suggests that when fathers support the mother's paid employment, children are more content than when the fathers don't (Zaslow, Rabinovich and Suwalsky 1991, 264).

Another recent study agrees substantially with this report but offers some additional findings as well. This study of families of third- and fourth-grade children compared employed mothers and mothers who are full-time homemakers. It identifies three types of parental control (1) *authoritarian,* in which parents demand obedience and do not hesitate to spank children; (2) *authoritative,* which grants a participation role in family decision making to third- and fourth-grade children; and (3) *permissive,* which involves few rules for children. Full-time homemakers were more likely than full-time employed mothers to use an authoritarian style of control, and their children tended to have less adequate social skills and to be less well liked by peers. The study also found that the employed mothers' lesser use of authoritarian discipline contributed to their children performing better on achievement tests in school (Hoffman and Youngblade 1999, 286–288).

The studies just discussed look at the consequences for children of mothers' employment entirely in terms of the family situation. A study by sociologists Toby L. Parcel and Elizabeth G. Menaghan takes a step back for a wider view and looks at how parents' jobs affect their home environment and certain early socialization outcomes. They studied 781 children between the ages of 3 and 6 whose mothers were employed. Their study presents a great number of complicated research results that are not easily summarized. But some of their central conclusions, in simplified form, can be approached by first stating what they thought they might find. They hypothesized that (1) certain aspects of parents' jobs (full-time or part-time; complexity of the work; amount of pay) (2) together with certain parental characteristics (mother's amount of schooling; mother's level of self-esteem) (3) would influence their children's home environment (particularly maternal warmth and cognitive stimulation). This chain of factors would then (4) influence certain outcomes in their children, specifically later abilities in reading and arithmetic and behavior problems. What they find is that all of this possible chain of influence does not work itself out directly but is further influenced by other factors such as having an additional child or a marriage breaking up. Their basic conclusion is that "there is no simple answer to questions concerning the benefits or dangers of maternal employment. Much depends on the quality of that employment, the demands of partners' occupations, and the demands of other children. It is clear that both mothers' and fathers' work may be more or less helpful to children depending on other resources on which parents may draw and other responsibilities they must shoulder" (Parcel and Menaghan 1994, 159).

Scott Coltrane reports on research that shows that both employed mothers and their children benefit when the fathers take an active part in caring for their children. The women regard the household division of labor as more fair, and they are not as depressed as women whose husbands do not take an active part. Preschool children whose fathers do 40 percent or more of the within-home child care benefit significantly: they show more cognitive competence, more empathy, more self-direction, and less gender stereotyping than preschool children whose fathers do not take such an active part in their care (Coltrane 2004, 234).

In "the traditional family," mothers were usually home when children came home from school. In 1990, 75 percent of mothers of school-age children were employed, most of them full-time and many of them either working overtime or working more than one job to make ends meet. They are not home when children complete their school day. According to one estimate, 3.5 million school-age children spend some time after school unsupervised by either an adult or an older child (Belle 1999, ix, 2). This situation has led to concern about the consequences. A recent study looked at a variety of after-school arrangements, supervised and unsupervised, of 53 children of full-time employed mothers. Some children had structured activities, such as going to a sports program or a lesson, doing homework, and taking care of their younger siblings. Some were on their own. Of the latter, some could structure their own activities, while others did little but watch television to counter boredom, loneliness, or fear. Whatever the arrangement, children faced challenges. One was "finding meaning in the way they spend after-school time. All of the children in this study needed to come to terms with their parents' absence during the after-school hours and sometimes on into the evening and on weekends,

Some had to explain to themselves their own heavy responsibilities, including sibling care. Others needed to make sense of their isolation or lack of freedom" (Belle 1999, 110). The author also notes, "One of the most crucial challenges to children in the after-school hours is moment-to-moment self-regulation. . . . Children need to comply with appropriate rules and guidelines for behavior, avoid undue risks, and complete required tasks, often without adult assistance or prodding. This proves a particularly difficult challenge for some" (Belle 1999, 101). These after-school challenges provide vivid examples of children's ongoing efforts to develop a self.

The overall trend that includes mothers working and that requires both mothers and fathers to work long hours has been characterized as

> the encroachment of industrial time on family time. As work consumes time, parents spend less time with children. The lack of sensitive, responsive, consistent care from overworked parents or substitute providers can lead to decreased cognitive and social skills . . . and promote personal attachment insecurity that encourages uncooperative and problematic behavior in children. . . . These developments, in collusion with financial problems generated by stagnant wages, help pave the way for . . . harsh outcomes for children. (Glass and Estes 1997, 282)

Stepfamilies

There is a high frequency of divorce in the United States, but there is also a high frequency of remarriage, resulting in stepfamilies. In fact, the fastest growing type of family in the United States is the stepfamily, and 17 percent of all families headed by a couple with children under age 18 are stepfamilies (Hetherington 1999, 137). While there has been considerable research on stepfamilies, very little of it deals with socialization of children. One observation that has been made is that children face a difficulty of adjusting from the family culture in which they have been raised to a new family culture that may bring new values, new rules, and new family routines (Furstenberg and Cherlin 1991, 83–84). Among the few relevant findings are that stepfathers tend to be more authoritarian, more permissive, or more inconsistent than biological fathers, and that such parenting leads to poor outcomes for children, such as poor school grades (Pasley, Ihinger-Tallman, and Lofquist 1994, 8; see also Hetherington 1999, 148). Also, in the early years of a remarriage, children of the mother often tend to resist the stepfather's efforts at closeness and attempts to exercise authority (Bray, Berger, and Boethel 1994, 73). At the same time, mothers' ability to oversee their children's activities is diminished, and conflict with them rises, as communication breaks down. This *remarriage transition*, as it is called, eventually passes and the family is "restabilized." This works out better if the remarriage occurred before the children are adolescent. If the children have entered adolescence, problems are greater (Hetherington 1999, 146). Research on stepmothers provides no information on how they try to socialize the children of their new marriage. One scholar points out that "it is easy to lose sight of the fact that there is as much diversity among stepfamilies as there is among families of first marriage." And he concludes,

"Overall . . . the daily character of stepfamily life does not appear to differ greatly from the perception of life of members in first-married households" (Furstenberg 1987, 49, 51). None of these studies examines socialization closely.

A recent review of studies of children in stepfamilies reveals that most of them focus on the issue of "positive" versus "negative" outcomes. The reviewers cite a study based on nationally representative samples in the United States and in Britain that found that approximately 20 percent of stepchildren are at risk for negative outcomes and that this percentage is somewhat higher than for children living with both biological parents. On the other hand, after discussing several other studies, the authors also state, "It would be difficult to accurately predict which children resided in stepfamilies and which resided in first-marriage families on the basis of behavioral outcomes (e.g., academic achievement, aggression, anxiety, depression, delinquent acts)" (Pasley and Moorfield 2004, 322–323). Risk of negative outcomes can be reduced by parenting that involves warmth, consistent monitoring of children, firm but responsive control, low degree of coerciveness, and expectations for mature behavior (Pasley and Moorefield 2004, 322).

Some scholars who have studied stepfamilies note that stepsiblings and half-siblings may influence each other, but they report that no research has been done on this topic (Ganong and Coleman 1994, 100–108). The more recent review cited in the preceding paragraph makes no mention at all of stepsibling and half-sibling relationships. In the last section of the present chapter, we discuss sibling relationships in intact families. The points discussed there may be applicable, with modifications, to stepfamilies, but we do not know in what ways.

Single Mothers

While there are some families that consist of single fathers and their young children, the vast majority of single-parent families (90 percent) are headed by mothers (Guttmann 1993, 82–83). An early study identified one key feature of socialization in these families: Children grow up a little faster in them—in the sense of being assigned and taking responsibility—than in two-parent families, particularly if the mothers work full-time in the paid labor force. Four- and 5-year-olds are sometimes expected to make their own beds, 8-year-olds may vacuum floors and clean up the kitchen, and 10-year-olds may cook. Parents may require a teenager to look after a younger child. "The result is that children in single-parent households often become surprisingly self-reliant and adult in their manner. Single parents sometimes describe one of their children as 'nine going on forty-nine'. Their children are young, yes, but they appear mature" (Weiss 1979, 79–82).

Whether one considers growing up faster to be desirable or undesirable depends on one's point of view regarding childhood. A more recent study, based on several large samples, presents data and arguments that growing up with a single parent increases the risk for undesirable outcomes, when compared to growing up with two biological parents. The authors do acknowledge, however, that many children raised by single mothers do quite well.

Thus, such comparisons are not absolute differences. A key concept for understanding such comparisons is *risk*, which can be illustrated by one of the comparisons the authors present: 87 percent of children who grow up with two biological parents receive a high school diploma by age 20, compared with only 68 percent of those who grow up with only one biological parent (whether a single mother or with one biological parent and one stepparent). Thus some children in the first category become dropouts, and two-thirds of children in the second category graduate, but the 19 percent difference expresses the concept that children in the second category are *at greater risk* of not completing high school (McLanahan and Sandefur 1994, 9). The authors found other risks, as well. When children who have grown up with a single parent reach their late teens and early twenties, they are more likely to have trouble finding a job; they are more likely to be idle (McLanahan and Sandefur 1994, 48–49). Growing up in a single-parent family increases a girl's risk of becoming a teenage mother and a boy's risk of becoming a teenage father (McLanahan and Sandefur 1994, 51–56). They found that children of widowed mothers are at slightly less risk of negative outcomes than children of divorced or never-married mothers. Also, boys born to never-married mothers do worse than boys who live with divorced or separated mothers (McLanahan and Sandefur 1994, 64–78).

The authors of this study find three major factors that help explain why children of one-parent families have a greater risk of doing poorly in life than children of two-parent families. (1) One-parent families tend to have much lower income than two-parent families. In 1992, the U.S. Census Bureau reported that about 45 percent of single-mother families were living below the official poverty line, compared to only 8.4 percent of two-parent families (McLanahan and Sandefur 1994, 23). By 1996, 50.3 percent of families headed by single mothers were living below the poverty line compared to 10 percent of two-parent families. The median income of two-parent families with children under age 18 was $50,000, while that of single-mother families was below $18,000 (McLanahan and Teitler 1999, 92). Not only can parents with more money send their children to better schools and pay for extracurricular activities and summer camps, but also, the authors point out, their "family income may affect the kind of neighborhood a child lives in. Children who live in middle-class neighborhoods where most children graduate from high school and go to college are likely to pick up the message that staying in school is essential and that 'hanging out' or 'dropping out' is not acceptable behavior in the community" (McLanahan and Sandefur 1994, 94). (2) In order to grow up securely and develop their abilities, children need parents who are willing and able to spend time with them helping with homework, reading, and listening to them talk about how their day went in school, and, not least, parents who monitor and supervise their social activities outside school. Children in single-parent families spend less time with parents than those in two-parent families (McLanahan and Sandefur 1994, 95–104). (3) Children raised in one-parent families face a number of disadvantages in terms of access to community resources. They are more likely to live in disadvantaged neighborhoods, more likely to associate with peers who have negative attitudes toward school, and more likely to change residences frequently (McLanahan and Sandefur 1994, 132).

While single-parent families are structurally alike—that is, one parent is absent—they differ in the process by which that structure was produced. The largest number result from divorce (33 percent). Next are widowed (29 percent), followed by married with husband absent (21 percent), and mother never married (17 percent) (Guttmann 1993, 83). While some research ignores the differences among these categories and focuses on single mothers overall, other studies have focused on divorced mothers. An extensive review of this research concludes that there are three main possible reasons why children of *divorced single mothers* are negatively affected: (1) *Family structure.* One parent is absent, and that absence deprives children of an important source of support, guidance, and role model. (2) *Family process.* Conflict between the parents before and after the divorce produces great stress on children. Parents become less effective as parents, and they inevitably drag the children into their conflicts. (3) *Economic disadvantage.* The mother and her children experience a sharp decline in living standards. They may have to move to a poorer neighborhood with less well-financed schools. The single mother often has to cut back on what she can give her children. The children experience themselves as poorer than they were and may be perceived as poor by others, leading to some social stigma and an increased risk of what is known as "acting out," that is, expressing anger in anti-social or self-destructive activities. The author concludes that all three explanations have some validity, but the strongest research evidence supports the family process explanation. Prolonged conflict between parents damages children's social functioning (Guttmann 1993, 200–201). The economic disadvantage explanation clearly does not apply to all, since one-half of all children growing up with single mothers do not live in poverty. (Weinraub and Gringlas 1995, 66). A subsequent review of studies comes to pretty much the same conclusions as this analysis, with two additional points that "the stress of divorce tends to disrupt the quality of parenting from the custodial parent" and "living in a single-parent household often undermines the quality of relations with noncustodial parents" (Amato 2004, 275–276).

"Acting out" is sometimes also called *externalizing behavior problems* and includes being disobedient, aggressive, demanding, and lacking in self-control. The category *internalizing behavior problems* includes depression, anxiety, and low self-esteem. Studies of young children in the United States and in Britain found that young children from divorced parents were more likely to manifest externalizing behavior problems than children in married-parent families, and these differences persisted into adolescence. No consistent differences of internalized behavior problems were found between children of married parents as compared with those of divorced parents (Martin, Emery and Peris 2004, 284).

Teenage Mothers

Nineteen percent of first births in the United States are to teenage mothers, of whom 80 percent are unmarried (Mauldon 2003, 41–42). The teenage pregnancy rate in the United States is far higher than in any other industrialized country. Of the approximately 1 million teenage pregnancies each year in the United States, only 13 percent are intended. Seventy-two percent of these mothers aged 15 to 19 are not married when they give birth. Less than half of them marry in the next 10 years. Most of the biological fathers do not provide consistent financial support (Maynard 1997, 1–5). There are some ethnic variations: Among African Americans, 90 percent are single. Among Hispanic Americans, the percentage ranges from 42 percent to 55 percent, and among whites it is 54 percent (Weinraub and Gringlas 1995, 74–76).

Many teenage mothers live with their families of origin, where they may obtain information about parenting from their own mothers, as well as financial support and child care support. Even so, they are disadvantaged in several ways that affect their socialization responsibilities. They are likely to live in impoverished neighborhoods, to have gone to poor schools, and to have had low educational aspirations and experienced school failure. Teenage parents have been found to have especially unrealistic expectations for their children. Because they are still struggling with the challenges presented by their changes of status, role, and identity from pleasure-seeking teenager to mother with responsibilities, they often have difficulty maintaining a well-regulated emotional and intellectual environment for their child. Compared to more adult mothers, they provide less stimulation and are less responsive to their child. Their discipline of their children tends to be more restrictive (Weinraub and Gringlas 1995, 74–76; Brooks-Gunn and Chase-Lansdale 1995, 129; Maynard 1997, 13). When the children reach adolescence, they are more likely than children of mothers who gave birth in their 20s to repeat a grade in school and to be rated unfavorably by teachers (Moore, Morrison, and Greene 1997, 171). Children born to mothers age 18 or younger were two and a half times more likely than children born to mothers age 20 or 21 to be victims of child abuse by the age of 5 (Goerge and Lee 1997, 210).

A study in which 50 teenage mothers were observed for three years in a high-school program for teen parents provides some evidence that such programs can increase parenting skills and help to reduce the risk of unfavorable outcomes for their children. The observer notes that the mothers developed a highly competitive culture. They competed with each other in four major ways: (1) providing material possessions to their children, (2) bragging about the physical and cognitive development of their children, (3) increasing their knowledge of parenting, and (4) providing better quality care in comparison with other parents. They worked to prove their competence as parents in an effort to counter the widely held view that they shouldn't be having children. In their talk, they tried to prove that they are not only better parents than other teens but also better than mothers who delayed having children until their 20s and 30s. Although they spent exorbitant sums on lavish gifts for their children, using credit cards or money from their parents or boyfriends, the author concludes that the program helped these mothers to develop a goal of being a good parent and pushed them toward a mainstream model of child rearing (Higginson 1998). Another scholar of teenage motherhood, although not presenting research results, observes, "Academic programs serving young mothers offer many examples of resilient and determined participants earning diplomas and going on to community college or even four year universities" (Mauldon 2003, 49).

Siblings

Parents are not the only members of families who socialize children. Any family that consists of more than one parent and one child sharing a household is a group. For ease of communication we have discussed such groups as though they consisted of two parents and one child, but many of those families (as well as single-parent families) include at least two children who are siblings (i.e., they have at least one parent in common). Interaction between or among siblings constitutes part of the socialization process. A study by Douglas B. Downey and Dennis J. Condrin (2004) illustrates one important socialization result of sibling relationships. Examining data from more than 20,000 6-year-old children near the end of their kindergarten year, and from their teachers, the authors found that children with siblings were judged by teachers to have better social skills than those with none. The children with siblings, whether one or more and whether brothers or sisters, were better able to form and maintain friendships, get along with children who are different, comfort or help other children, and express feelings and opinions in a positive way. They also show more self-control. Overall, the authors find that siblings are resources for each other (Downey and Condrin 2004, 335, 345–347).

The study just described is based on a large-scale survey. It presents findings on some important socialization outcomes of sibling interaction, but it provides no information on sibling interaction itself. A study by Gerald Handel (1986, 1994) identifies some of the ways that interaction among siblings and their parents is significant. He identified four issues that they have to deal with:

1. *Equity.* In this context *equity*, which comes from the same Latin root as *equal*, refers to the issue of being treated fairly. Children are sensitive to what they consider unfair or unequal treatment by parents. A child may complain that parents allow a sibling to get away with things for which he or she is punished. Children often feel they have to retaliate in order to maintain equity in a sibling relationship. Thus, a 12-year-old boy says of his sister, "If she wouldn't tease me, I wouldn't tease her" (Handel 1994, 509). Such interactions can be understood as part of children's effort to develop and maintain a value of fairness and to communicate to others (siblings and parents) that their own self is entitled to be protected by that value.

2. *Maturity.* The fact that children in a family are of different ages can create an issue for both the older and the younger. A younger child may indeed be allowed to "get away with" something that is not tolerated in an older child. And an older child may be allowed a privilege that is not granted a younger child, who may consider it an instance of inequitable treatment. Thus, both are learning about age-graded norms. The difference in maturity can work in a different way. An older child may share knowledge with a younger one. Thus, a 12-year-old girl, asked who she

goes to with a problem, replies, "My sister. She usually gives me good advice. We talk over problems. I've helped her, too, like persuading Mother to let her stay out later" (Handel 1994, 512).

3. *Loyalty.* Parents usually expect their children to be loyal to the family and to each other. Sometimes children try to form an alliance against their parents, which doesn't always succeed. For example, 12-year-old Caroline expresses her exasperation with her 6-year-old sister: "My mother is more often on Cynthia's side because both of us [Caroline and 10-year-old brother] are against Cynthia and Cynthia is such an innocent angel. If you ask her to promise not to tell my mother and father something, she promises and then she tells" (Handel 1994, 516). Such interactions socialize children to the tasks of forming relationships and to knowledge of the ways in which they can proceed in unintended directions.

4. *Individuality.* At the same time that siblings are trying to form bonds with each other they are also trying to establish their own individuality. A widespread complaint of one child about a sibling to a parent—"He (or she) borrows my things without asking"—is an effort to set limits to what the sibling can claim as a right on the basis of family loyalty. Each child tries to establish an area of privacy so as to establish some control over the claims that siblings and parents can make on the basis of loyalty. Privacy is perhaps an outer manifestation of a child's effort at *self-demarcation*, an effort to claim an individuated self. Self-demarcation is illustrated by an 11-year-old boy who was asked, "How are you different from the other people in the family?" He replied "I make so much noise. Nobody else hardly does. I think I like more fiction books. I like geography; only my Mom does. She likes Russian geography" (Handel 1994, 518; see also Bank and Kahn 1997, 52).

Children negotiate these issues, sometimes working them out by themselves, sometimes with parental participation or intervention. These interactions contribute to their understanding of how to deal with others and can influence their self-evaluation, as well as, obviously, their evaluation of their siblings. We can hypothesize that how these issues are dealt with contributes to long-term relationships between siblings—whether they are friendly or distant in later years.

Grandparents in the Twenty-First Century

All of the types of family composition that we have discussed are two-generation, parent-child families. Here we wish to take note of a prediction that grandparents may well play a larger role in the socialization of children as the twenty-first century proceeds than they have in the twentieth century. Sociologist Vern Bengtson notes that over 4 million children already live in a grandparent's household because the parents cannot care for them, often because of such factors as imprisonment, drug addiction, mental illness, and parental violence (Bengtson 2001, 7). He predicts a substantial increase in grandparents' participation for a combination of reasons. One key factor is increased human longevity. Longer life means that more children than ever before will have grandparents. He cites a study by Peter Uhlenberg, reporting that, of children born in 1900, only 21 percent had a living grandparent when they reached age 30, whereas 76 percent of children born in 2000 are predicted to have a living grandparent when they reach that age (Uhlenberg 1996; cited in Bengtson 2001, 6). Obviously, if this prediction is correct, even more than 76 percent will have living grandparents when they are young children. The increased "supply" of grandparents, combined with continuing high levels of divorce, single motherhood, two-job and two-career families, in addition to the factors mentioned above, implies that parental roles in socialization *may* decrease somewhat and grandparental roles may increase (Bengtson 2001, 13–14). For now, this is a hypothesis, not a research result. It is put forward during a period when there is widespread recognition that a great deal of change is happening in family composition and in relationships among family members and that increased longevity may be significant in shaping some of that change.

* * *

Families are complex groups. They create worlds of their own, but those worlds are not separate from the outer world. Within each family world, children influence their parents as well as being influenced by them, although the greater degree of influence is usually from parents to children. Siblings influence each other. Parents' jobs influence their parenting styles. Parenting is also influenced by the parents' social status and ethnic group membership, as we shall discuss in Chapters 9 and 10.

References

Amato, Paul. 2004. "Divorce in Social and Historical Context." In Marilyn Coleman and Lawrence H. Ganong (eds.) *Handbook of Contemporary Families*, 265–281. Thousand Oaks, CA: Sage.

Amato, Paul, and Alan Booth. 1997. *A Generation at Risk*. Cambridge, MA: Harvard University Press.

Arendell, Terry. 1997. "A Social Constructionist Approach to Parenting." In Terry Arendell (ed.) *Contemporary Parenting*, 1–44. Thousand Oaks: Sage.

Bank, Stephen P., and Michael D. Kahn. 1997. *The Sibling Bond*. New York: Basic Books.

Belle, Deborah. 1999. *The After-School Lives of Children*. Mahwah, NJ: Lawrence Erlbaum.

Bengtson, Vern. 2001. "Beyond the Nuclear Family: The Increasing Importance of Multigenerational Bonds." *Journal of Marriage and Family* 60(1): 1–16.

Blum-Kulka, Shoshana. 1997. *Dinner Talk: Cultural Patterns of Sociability and Socialization in Family Discourse*. Mahwah, NJ: Lawrence Erlbaum.

Bornstein, Marc H., Joseph Tal, and Catherine Tamis-LeMonda. 1991. "Parenting in Cross-Cultural Perspective: The United States, France, and Japan." In Marc H. Bornstein (ed.) *Cultural Approaches to Parenting*, 69–90. Hillsdale, NJ: Lawrence Erlbaum Associates.

Bossard, James H. S., and Eleanor Stoker Boll. 1966. *The Sociology of Child Development*, 4th ed. New York: Harper & Row.

Bray, James H., Sandra H. Berger, and Carol L. Boethel. 1994. "Role Integration and Marital Adjustment in Stepfather Families." In Kay Pasley and Marilyn Ihinger-Tallman (eds.) *Stepparenting*, 69–80. Westport, CT: Greenwood Press.

Brooks-Gunn, Jeanne, and P. Lindsay Chase-Lansdale. 1995. "Adolescent Parenthood." In Marc H. Bornstein (ed.) *Handbook of Parenting*. Vol. 3, *Status and Social Conditions of Parenting*, 113–149. Mahwah, NJ: Lawrence Erlbaum.

Burgess, Ernest W. 1926. "The Family as a Unity of Interacting Personalitites." *The Family* 7: 3–9.

Chase-Lansdale, P. Lindsay, Robert T. Michael, and Sonalde Desai. 1991. "Maternal Employment During Infancy: An Analysis of Children of the National Longitudinal Survey of Youth (NLSY)." In Jacqueline V. Lerner and Nancy L. Galambos (eds). *Employed Mothers and Children*, 37–61. New York: Garland.

Chin, Tiffani. 2000. " 'Sixth Grade Madness': Parental Emotion Work in the Private High School Application Process." *Journal of Contemporary Ethnography* 29 (2): 124–163.

Cochran, M., and J. Brassard. 1979. "Child Development and Personal Social Networks." *Child Development* 50: 609–615.

Cochran, Moncrieff, and Starr Niego. 1995. "Parenting and Social Networks." In Marc H. Bornstein (ed.) *Handbook of Parenting*, Vol. 3, *Status and Social Conditions of Parenting*, 393–418. Mahwah, NJ: Lawrence Erlbaum.

Coltrane, Scott. 1996. *Family Man: Fatherhood, Housework, and Gender Equity*. New York: Oxford University Press.

——. 2004. "Fathering: Paradoxes, Contradictions, and Dilemmas." In Marilyn Coleman and Lawrence H. Ganong (eds.) *Handbook of Contemporary Families*, 224–243. Thousand Oaks, CA: Sage.

Crouter, Ann C., and Susan McHale. 1993. "The Long Arm of the Job: Influences of Parental Work on Childrearing." In Tom Luster and Lynn Okagaki (eds.) *Parenting. An Ecological Perspective*, 170–202. Hillsdale, NJ: Lawrence Erlbaum.

Downey, Douglas B., and Dennis J. Condrin. 2004. "Playing Well With Others in Kindergarten: The Benefit of Siblings at Home." *Journal of Marriage and Family* 66 (May): 333–350.

Dunn, Judy, and Jane Brown. 1991. "Becoming American or English? Talking About the Social World in England and the United States." In Marc H. Bornstein (ed.) *Cultural Approaches to Parenting*, 155–172. Hillsdale, NJ: Lawrence Earlbaum.

Ehrensaft, Diane. 1987. *Parenting Together*. New York: The Free Press.

Erikson, Erik. 1950. *Childhood and Society*. New York: W. W. Norton.

Fields, Jason. 2003. "Children's Living Arrangements and Characteristics: March, 2002." In the U.S. Bureau of the Census, *Current Population Reports*, P 20-547. Washington, DC: Bureau of the Census, June 2003. *http://www.census.gov/mainwww/cprs.html.*

Furstenberg, Frank F., Jr. 1987. "The New Extended Family: The Experience of Parents and Children after Remarriage." In Kay Pasley and Marilyn Ihinger-Tallman (eds.) *Remarriage and Stepparenting*, 42–61. New York: Guilford Press.

Furstenberg, Frank, Jr., and Andrew Cherlin. 1991. *Divided Families*. Cambridge, MA: Harvard University Press.

Ganong, Lawrence H., and Marilyn Coleman. 1994. *Remarried Family Relationships*. Thousand Oaks, CA: Sage.

Gans, Herbert. [1962] 1982. *The Urban Villagers: Group and Class in the Life of Italian-Americans*. New York: Free Press.

Gerson, Kathleen. 1993. *No Man's Land: Men's Changing Commitments to Family and Work*. New York: Basic Books.

——. 1997. "The Social Construction of Fatherhood." In Terry Arendell (ed.) *Contemporary Parenting*, 119–153. Thousand Oaks, CA: Sage.

Glass, Jennifer, and Sarah Beth Estes. 1997. "Employment and Child Care." In Terry Arendell (ed.) *Contemporary Parenting*, 254–288. Thousand Oaks, CA: Sage.

Goerge, Robert M., and Bong Joo Lee. 1997. "Abuse and Neglect of the Children." In Rebecca A. Maynard (ed.) *Kids Having Kids*, 205–230. Washington, DC: Urban Institute Press.

Gottfried, Adele E., Allen W. Gottfried, Coleen Killian. 1999. "Maternal and Dual-Earner Employment: Family Environment, Adaptation, and the Environmental Impingement Perspective." In Michael E. Lamb (ed.) *Parenting and Child Development in "Nontraditional" Families*, 15–37. Mahwah, NJ: Lawrence Erlbaum.

Guttmann, Joseph. 1993. *Divorce in Psychosocial Perspective*. Hillsdale, NJ: Lawrence Erlbaum.

Handel, Gerald. 1972. *The Psychosocial Interior of the Family*, 2nd ed. Chicago: Aldine.

——. 1986. "Beyond Sibling Rivalry: An Empirically Grounded Theory of Sibling Relationships." In Patricia A. Adler and Peter Adler (eds.) *Sociological Studies of Child Development*, Vol. 1, 105–122. Greenwich, CT: JAI Press.

——. 1994. "Central Issues in the Construction of Sibling Relationships." In Gerald Handel and Gail Whitchurch (eds.) *The Psychosocial Interior of the Family*, 4th ed., 493–523. New York: Aldine de Gruyter.

Hess, Robert D., and Gerald Handel. 1995. *Family Worlds*. Lanham, MD: University Press of America. (Reissue of 1974 edition published by University of Chicago Press. First edition published in 1959 by University of Chicago Press.)

Hetherington, E. Mavis, 1999. "Stepfamilies." In Michael E. Lamb (ed.) *Parenting and Child Development in "Nontraditional" Families*, 137–159. Mahwah, NJ: Lawrence Erlbaum.

Higginson, Joanna Gregson. 1998. "Competitive Parenting: The Culture of Teen Mothers." *Journal of Marriage and Family* 60(1): 135–149.

Hoffman, Lois, and Lise M. Youngblade. 1999. *Mothers at Work: Effects on Children's Well-being*. Cambridge, U.K.: Cambridge University Press.

Landesman, Sharon, James Jaccard, and Virginia Gunderson. 1991. "The Family Environment." In Michael Lewis and Saul Feinman (eds.) *Social Influences and Socialization in Infancy*, 63–96. New York: Plenum Press.

Lareau, Annette. 2003. *Unequal Childhoods*. Berkeley: University of California Press.

Lever, Janet. 1978. "Sex Differences in the Complexity of Children's Play and Games." *American Sociological Review* 43: 471–483.

Martin, Michele T., Robert E. Emery, Tara S. Peris. 2004. "Single-Parent Families: Risks, Resilience, and Change." In Marilyn Coleman and Lawrence H. Ganong (eds.) *Handbook of Contemporary Families*, 282–301. Thousand Oaks, CA: Sage.

Mauldon, Jane. 2003. "Families Started by Teenagers." In Mary Ann Mason, Arlene Skolnick, and Stephen D. Sugarman (eds.) *All Our Families*, 2nd ed., 40–65. New York: Oxford University Press.

Maynard, Rebecca A. 1997. "The Study, the Context, and the Findings in Brief." In Rebecca A. Maynard (ed.) *Kids Having Kids: Economic Costs and Social Consequences of Teen Pregnancy*, 1–21. Washington, DC: The Urban Institute Press.

McLanahan, Sara, and Gary Sandefur. 1994. *Growing Up With a Single Parent*. Cambridge, MA: Harvard University Press.

McLanahan, Sara, and Julien Teitler. 1999. "The Consequences of Father Absence." In Michael E. Lamb (ed.) *Parenting and Child Development in "Nontraditional" Families*, 83–102. Mahwah, NJ: Lawrence Erlbaum.

Moore, Kristin Anderson, Donna Ruane Morrison, Angela Dungee Greene. 1997. "Effects on the Children Born to Adolescent Mothers." In Rebecca A. Maynard (ed.) *Kids Having Kids*, 145–173. Washington, DC: The Urban Institute Press.

Parcel, Toby L., and Elizabeth G. Menaghan. 1994. *Parents' Jobs and Children's Lives*. Hawthorne, New York: Aldine de Gruyter.

Pasley, Kay, Marilyn Ihinger-Tallman, and Amy Lofquist. 1994. "Remarriage and Stepfamilies: Making Progress in Understanding." In Kay Pasley and Marilyn Ihinger-Tallman (eds.) *Stepparenting*, 1–14. Westport, CT: Greenwood Press.

Pasley, Kay, and Brad S. Moorefield. 2004. "Stepfamilies: Changes and Challenges." In Marilyn Coleman and Lawrence H. Ganong (eds.) *Handbook of Contemporary Families*, 317–330. Thousand Oaks, CA: Sage.

Pomerleau, Andree, Gerard Malcuit, and Colette Sabatier. 1991. "Child-Rearing Practices and Parental Beliefs in Three Cultural Groups of Montreal: Québecois, Vietnamese, Haitian." In Marc H. Bornstein (ed.) *Cultural Approaches to Parenting*, 45–68. Hillsdale, NJ: Lawrence Erlbaum.

Popenoe, David. 1996. *Life Without Father*. New York: Free Press.

Putney, Norella M., and Vern L. Bengtson. 2002. "Socialization and the Family Revisited." In Richard Settersten, Jr. and Timothy J. Owens (eds.) *New Frontiers in Socialization*, 165–194. Oxford, UK: JAI/Elsevier Science.

Riesman, David, with Glazer, Nathan, and Denney, Reuel. 1950. *The Lonely Crowd: A Study of the Changing American Character*. New Haven, CT: Yale University Press.

Rogoff, Barbara, Jayanthi Mistry, Artin Goncu, and Christine Mosier. 1991. "Cultural Variation in the Role Relations of Toddlers and Their Families." In Marc H. Bornstein (ed.) *Cultural Approaches to Parenting*, 173–183. Hillsdale, NJ: Lawrence Erlbaum.

Taylor, Ronald L. 1997. "Who's Parenting? Trends and Patterns." In Terry Arendell (ed.) *Contemporary Parenting*, 68–91. Thousand Oaks, CA: Sage.

Thompson, Ross A. 1991. "Infant Day Care: Concerns, Controversies, Choices." In Jacqueline V. Lerner and Nancy Galambos (eds.) *Employed Mothers and Their Children*, 9–36. New York: Garland.

Thorne, Barrie. 1993. *Gender Play*. New Brunswick, NJ: Rutgers University Press.

Uhlenberg, Peter. 1996. "Mutual Attraction: Demography and Life-Course Analysis." *Gerontologist* 36: 226–229.

United States Bureau of the Census. 2002. Table 66, "Households, Families, Subfamilies, and Married Couples: 1980–2002"; and Table 74, "Family Households With Own Children Under Age 18 by Type of Family, 1990 to 2002." In *Current Population Reports* P20-547, and earlier reports. Washington, DC: Bureau of the Census *http://www.census.gov/main/www/cprs.html*.

Weinraub, Marsha, and Marcy B. Gringlas. 1995. "Single Parenthood." In Marc H. Bornstein (ed.) *Handbook of Parenting*, Vol. 3, *Status and Social Conditions of Parenting*, 65–87. Mahwah, NJ: Lawrence H. Erlbaum Associates.

Weiss, Robert S. 1979. *Going It Alone: Family Life and Social Situation of the Single Parent*. New York: Basic Books.

Weller, Jack E. 1965. *Yesterday's People: Life in Contemporary Appalachia*. Lexington: University of Kentucky Press.

Zaslow, Martha J., Beth A. Rabinovich, and Joan T. D. Suwalsky. 1991. "From Maternal Employment to Child Outcomes: Preexisting Group Differences and Moderating Variables." In Jacqueline V. Lerner and Nancy L. Galambos (eds.) *Employed Mothers and Their Children*, 237–282. New York: Garland. ✦

Chapter 6

Schools

A modern society requires a literate population in order to function. According to one estimate, more than 90 percent of children in the world spend at least some time in school, and this spread of mass education is correlated with nations' efforts to become part of a modern, global economy (Meyer, Kamens, and Benavot 1992, 1–2, 11–12, 19–20, 153). When the United States was founded as a country in 1789, most of the population lived by farming, and most children learned what they needed to know by working on the farm alongside their parents. Some might also go to school for a year or two, possibly learning to read and do some elementary arithmetic, but many did not. A small number of wealthy people sent their children to private schools. Forty or fifty years later, as urban centers were growing, literacy became more important, and the concept of free public schooling available for all children gained increasing acceptance. Standards of schooling, represented by number of years of attendance at school, gradually increased (Brint 1998, 172). In the early years of the twentieth century, when school organization in the United States consisted of eight years of grammar school (also called primary school) and four years of high school (also called secondary school), graduation from the eighth grade was the norm for the majority of the population. Eventually graduation from high school became established as the standard minimum that all children should meet, although even today not all do.

Schooling is subject to many cross-pressures. Schools fail to educate adequately a substantial number of students, and many of them drop out before graduating from high school. At the same time, there is increasing pressure for students to gain some kind of post-secondary education, whether from a four-year college, two-year college, or specialized vocational school. During this same period, there has been an increasing belief that children need some kind of organized instruction even before they enter public school, and the last half of the twentieth century saw the growth of what is known as *nursery school* or *preschool* for children in the age range of 3 to 5. This development is not unique to the United States but is found in many industrialized countries. Attendance at preschool is not usually compulsory, as is attendance at primary school (which can be public, religious, or secular private), but parents increasingly view it as an important socialization experience for their children. Educators and public policy analysts believe that preschool is particularly desirable for children who come from homes that are unable to prepare children adequately for public school. Because of its growing importance, we begin our discussion

159

of the school as an agency of socialization with the preschool. Discussion of preschools requires us also to give some attention to daycare, which takes several forms, none of which are defined as schools but which nonetheless have socialization consequences. We then proceed to a discussion of public schools under three major headings: school and society, the classroom as an organization, and the interaction between family and school. Our attention will be restricted to public schools. The link of schools with peer groups will be referred to in the next chapter.

Preschools and Daycare Centers

We begin by noting a distinction between two kinds of institutions for caring for children of preschool age. *Daycare* originated in the late nineteenth century as a service for working-class mothers who were obliged by economic necessity to work in paying jobs; a child usually stayed in daycare for a full day. *Preschool* (also called *nursery school*) originated as a service to upper-middle-class and upper-class mothers who did not work at paying jobs. Children usually went to them for a half day. Changes in the family since the 1970s—particularly increases in divorce, single mothers, and two-job and dual-career families—have led to an increase in full-day nursery schools. The preschool offers somewhat more formal instruction as part of its program than does daycare, but the distinction between the two types of institution is not rigid, and there are many blends (Tobin, Wu, and Davidson 1989, 168–174).

The growing utilization of daycare and preschool contributes to a trend of introducing the child at younger and younger ages to influences of formal organizations outside the family. A few generations ago, until the age of 6 a child stayed at home with parents; was introduced to relatives, neighbors, and neighborhood children; might be taken to church and on parental shopping trips; but was not usually placed in any kind of formal organization. The introduction of kindergarten as part of public school around 1900 brought the age down to 5. Nursery schools introduce such influences at ages 4 and 3. Daycare centers increasingly accept infants and toddlers.

What are these influences? Briefly, these are the requirements of fitting into a larger organization and cultural requirements as conveyed through the authority of teachers and the pressures and pleasures of peer-group membership. A cross-cultural study of preschools in China, Japan, and the United States reveals some goals common to all three countries as well as some interesting differences. Before discussing these, it will be helpful to describe how the study was conducted. The authors found one preschool each in Beijing, Tokyo, and Honolulu that agreed to let them not only observe but also videotape the activities among the children and between children and teachers. The authors followed this up by showing all three videotapes to audiences of parents, teachers, and principals in all three schools, as well as to similar audiences from other schools in the three countries. They conducted audience discussions and administered questionnaires to over 200 audience members in each country (for a total of more than 700). They thus obtained "insider" and "outsider" interpretations and evaluations, which allowed them to reach their conclusions (Tobin, Wu, and Davidson 1989).

The study's findings are complex and nuanced, and in the space available here we can only indicate a few of the highlights. The authors found agreement in all three countries that a major purpose of nursery school is to help children become more independent and self-reliant, meaning children should be able to dress, feed, and control themselves. Also, in all three countries parents and preschool staff agreed that an important task of the school is to counteract "spoiling" that the child might receive at home. However, there were distinct cultural differences in what was meant by *spoiling*. China has a government policy requiring most parents to restrict themselves to having only one child, in order to limit population growth. (China has 1.2 billion people already. One out of every five people in the world is Chinese. However, very recently it has changed its policy so that a family with one daughter is allowed to try to have another child.) The Chinese are concerned about what they call the "4-2-1 syndrome": four grandparents and two parents lavishing all their attention on one child. (That concern is not likely to disappear soon, despite the new policy.) Reluctance to discipline and a willingness to overindulge the child are the dangers that the school needs to counter. In Japan, educators believe that the selfishness or unruliness of a spoiled child comes not from overindulgence but from insufficient love and attention at home. The American view is that spoiling results from parents who are too busy to give the child proper love and attention but buy the child off with material things (Tobin, Wu, and Davidson 1989).

Some other cultural differences are noteworthy. The Japanese emphasize equality, and they downplay individual differences among preschool children. They believe that effort and character are more important than inborn ability. A major goal is to develop in children a sense of group membership and skills in group participation. Because they want children to be responsive to group norms, teachers tend not to control disruptive behavior by acting authoritatively. Instead, they look to other children in the class to exert pressure to curb the disruptive child. Chinese and American viewers of the Japanese video thought the Japanese preschool room was too uncontrolled, but the Japanese believe their procedures are the correct ones. The Chinese preschool also has the goal of developing a strong group identity, but it is much more tightly controlled than the Japanese. All the children do the same thing at the same time, including all going to the bathroom at the same time. Americans and Japanese who viewed the Chinese video both considered the Chinese preschool to be too rigid and too highly regimented. Teachers directed children's play, in contrast to the Japanese school where children were allowed more spontaneity. In contrast to these two versions of groupism, the American preschool emphasized the individuality of each child, in keeping with the American value, individualism. The children are free to make many choices in activity. However, teachers do set limits. The children have to clean up and put away toys at the end of a play period, and teachers do exercise authority with a child who is seen as difficult.

Societies differ not only in their cultural beliefs about children but also in basic philosophy as to whose responsibility daycare and preschool should be. In the United States and in the United Kingdom, nonparental daycare is considered a private responsibility. Individual families have to find and pay for day care if they want it (Lamb and Sternberg 1992, 8–9). In Sweden, by contrast, the national government has overall responsibilty for preschool and other forms of daycare, while the schools and centers themselves are run by the municipalities (Lamb and Sternberg 1992; Hwang and Bromberg 1992). Child care is considered a right that all families can use, if they wish, and many well-to-do families send their children to municipal daycare centers (Hwang and Bromberg 1992, 45–46). About 85 percent of children of a single working parent are in municipal daycare, as are about 67 percent of those with two working or studying parents (Hwang and Bromberg 1992, 51). In Canada, the federal government encourages daycare, but child-care policy is a provincial rather than a national responsibility, and practices vary considerably across the country. The Province of Quebec is most supportive, viewing daycare as a public responsibility and offering large subsidies. The other provinces set minimum regulations and have mixtures of privately arranged daycare and licensed regulated daycare, some public and some for-profit (Baker 2001).

In Italy, the Catholic Church controlled almost all preschools until the last third of the twentieth century. Laws passed in the 1970s established government-organized nurseries known as *asile nido* for children younger than 3 and nursery schools known as *scuola materne* for children ages 3 to 5 (Corsaro and Emiliani 1992, 90 ff.). The former are open 9 hours a day, five days a week, while the latter are open 8–10 hours a day, five days a week, and a half day on Saturday (Corsaro and Emiliani 1992, 95, 104). While the national goal is to have these available equally all over the country, building and staffing them have progressed unevenly. Some regions lag behind others in availability. The south of Italy, the poorest section of the country, is particularly underserved (Corsaro and Emiliani 1992, 113).

Head Start

Although the American political system treats day care and nursery school access as an individual family matter, not a public responsibility, there is one important exception. During the 1960s, as part of President Lyndon Johnson's War Against Poverty, the federal government adopted a preschool program for poor children ages 3 to 5 called *Head Start*. It continues to operate, now under the Department of Health and Human Services. Because poor children begin school with less preparation than middle-class children, this federally funded program seeks to help poor children by providing instruction and nutritious meals and a variety of health services. The federal government gives grants of federal funds to local public and private nonprofit agencies, although not enough money is provided to enable all eligible children to enroll. Twenty percent of the costs must be supplied by the local community. Parent involvement is a key aspect of the program, which operates in all 50 states, the District of Columbia, Puerto Rico, and the U.S. territories. In addition, there is now an American Indian Head Start Program and a Migrant Head Start Program for children of migrant farm workers. In 1994 the program was supplemented with Early Head Start to offer education and health benefits to poor families with children younger than 3 (U.S. Department of Health and Human Services 2001).

Early evaluations of Head Start programs concluded that children did not benefit much from them, but these conclusions have been reexamined and judged faulty. Later, more careful independent evaluations found considerable benefits. Sociologists Doris R. Entwisle, Karl L. Alexander, and Linda Steffel Olson have reviewed this research. It shows that children who attended preschool Head Start programs had better math achievement through grade five than "controls" (children of comparable background who did not attend Head Start). In the seventh grade, only 14.6 percent of Head Start children were in Special Education classes compared to 34.9 percent of the controls, and only 19.9 percent had been held back a grade, compared to 34.9 percent of the control group. Long-term follow-ups showed that Head Start children were more likely to maintain responsive participation in society: they were more likely to be in high school, in the military, or employed, whereas the controls were less likely to be employed and more likely to be school drop-outs, in prison, or on public assistance (Entwisle, Alexander, and Olson 1997, 17–20).

The Head Start children gained eight IQ points in first grade. These gains gradually faded in two or three years, but Entwisle, Alexander, and Olson believe that these short-lived gains could help explain the long-term gains cited above. They emphasize that the first two years of school are a critical period because children's internal and external worlds are undergoing change at the same time. The children experience a new form of social organization—a classroom with desks, blackboards, clocks, bells, and a roomful of others competing for approval from a new authority figure. Memory, general learning capacity, and speed of cognitive processing all increase between the ages of 5 and 8 (Entwisle, Alexander, and Olson 1997, 8–9). The authors offer a number of hypotheses to explain why the short-lived IQ gains might have had long-range effects: (1) The temporarily higher IQs might have influenced teacher perceptions so they perceived the Head Start children as smart and well adjusted to school demands. These perceptions "could have triggered a more positive cycle of achievement and expectations that helped the child do better in later grades, long after the initial IQ benefits had faded." (2) First grade teachers may have found children with Head Start experience easier to teach. (3) Parents may have become more favorably impressed with their children's abilities, and, presumably, their increased enthusiasm stimulated their children to work harder or more effectively. (4) The children themselves may have gained a new self-awareness of their increased ability (Entwisle, Alexander, and Olson 1997, 18). Although not in a position to choose among these or other possible explanations, these authors affirm the long-range positive effects of children's participation in Head Start.

Daycare Centers

A large number of American children are placed in daycare rather than in nursery schools. There has been a long-running debate as to whether children are helped or harmed by this experience. Questions remained unresolved partly because studies did not always distinguish (1) lengths of time (number of years and hours per week) children were in daycare, (2) quality of the daycare, and (3) type of daycare setting (home care or daycare center).

A study of more than 1,000 children, followed from birth until age 4½, in 10 American cities, conducted by the National Institute of Child Health and Human Development (NICHD), provides some answers that are more solidly grounded than those of earlier studies. One key is quality of child care. High-quality child care, judged by observers, was identified by a number of criteria, including the caregivers speaking positively and showing positive physical contact with a child, expressing positive emotion, stimulating the child's cognitive and social development, and showing sensitivity to the children. Children who attended high-quality daycare scored higher at age 4½ on tests of pre-academic skills and on language than those who attended lower-quality daycare, regardless of how many hours they were in daycare or what type of daycare. Children who had experience in daycare centers showed better language development and memory development than children whose entire experience was in home care. On the negative side, quantity also had an effect: Children who averaged 30 hours or more per week showed more behavior problems than children who averaged less than 10 hours a week. The study reaches the general conclusion that "early child care is associated with both developmental risks and developmental benefits for children's functioning prior to school entry. . . . The risk is that more hours in child care across the first 4 and 1/2 years of life is related to elevated levels of problem behavior at 4 and 1/2 years. The benefit is that higher-quality child care, quality that improves over time, and more experience in centers predicts better performance on measures of cognitive and linguistic functioning" (NICHD Early Child Care Research Network 2002, 156–157). Results such as these have wide implications: 81 percent of the children entering kindergarten in 1998–1999 had child care experience prior to beginning school. This research, however, does not tell us what percentage of these spent any time in day care centers and what percentage had all their day care in home care, which tends to be more prevalent because it is less costly (NICHD Early Child Care Research Network 2002, 134).

In evaluating the outcomes of children's daycare experience, the large-scale study just described concludes that cognitive outcomes, as measured by tests, are favorable for children who attended high-quality daycare. But the study also concludes that more time spent in daycare is associated with more behavior problems at age 4½. Although a full explanation of this unfavorable outcome is not available, some understanding may be gained from observational studies carried out by Robin L. Leavitt and Martha Bauman Power (Leavitt 1991, 1995; Leavitt and Power 1997). They joined with 22 students whom they supervised in observing 14 different kinds of daycare programs over a period of seven years (Leavitt and Power 1997, 40). Their work focuses not on cognitive development but on emotional socialization, including how children are socialized to regulate and interpret their own bodies. A basic finding of their research is that child-care workers are overworked, underpaid, and not adequately trained (Leavitt and Power 1997, 40, n. 1). One caregiver may be responsible for from eight to sixteen children, many of whom may be in the daycare center for as long as 10 hours (Leavitt 1991, 94–95; 1995, 6). The result of this work situation is that the caregivers show insufficient empathy for the children in their care. They organize the children's day into tightly scheduled routines. Managing the children takes precedence over attending to a child's expression of needs that may disrupt the schedule or require individualized attention (Leavitt 1995, 7). Leavitt writes, "Insofar as children's expressions of their physical and emotional needs and inclinations are subordinate to the adult-imposed schedule, they are 'silenced.' Indeed, a degree of violence can be seen in the physical management of children when the adults tie them to their chairs or use force" (Leavitt 1991, 103). While some caregivers did show flexibility and empathy, that was not the norm.

An important aspect of caregiving in daycare centers involves dealing with children's bodies—"diaper changing, toileting, nose wiping, feeding, washing, dressing" (Leavitt and Power 1997, 44). Children have to learn *body rules*, that is, to manage their bodies according to rules that caregivers announce and enforce, such as "walk, don't run; walk slowly; walk quietly; keep your hands in your lap/to yourself; keep your feet on the ground; sit cross-legged; stay behind the line; move only when I call your name; raise your hand; use the toilet; don't wet/soil your pants; don't spit" (Leavitt and Powerr 1997, 49). These rules require children to control impulses. The children sometimes look for ways to evade these rules and resist complying with them, though such efforts are not often successful (Leavitt and Power 1997, 57–60.) To recall our earlier mention of children's agency in Chapter 1, the children here are exercising agency, not simply being formed by the structure in which they are embedded. That said, daycare staff are engaged in what has been called "civilizing children's bodies," and the authors of this study believe that their observations show that this is not being done with sufficient consideration for children's needs and feelings (Leavitt and Power 1997).

The caregivers establish an emotional climate in which children's efforts to communicate with them are ignored or dismissed. These young children are expected to control their emotions. This expectation includes a norm of not crying, even though crying is a primary form of communication for infants and toddlers. A crying child may be told to smile. Generally, the caregivers seem primarily interested in the children's surface behaviors, not in their actual feelings. The authors suggest that this emotional distancing comes about because of the nature and circumstances of the caregivers' work: responsibility for many babies and toddlers, drudgery of changing diapers and feeding, isolation from adult society, and inadequate personal and institutional resources. But a consequence, Leavitt notes, is that "[t]o the extent children's emotions, and their selves, are not given meaning through recognition and response, caregivers facilitate each child's loss of self" (Leavitt 1995, 15). The studies reported by Leavitt and Power may help us understand why day care experiences increase the risk of behavioral problems at age 4½.

School and Society

Public schools are established by governmental authority. In strongly centralized countries like France, schooling is controlled and administered by the national government. In the United States, the Constitution restricts the powers of the national government and leaves most educational requirements to the states. (A notable exception is a federal law passed in 2001—the No Child Left Behind Act—requiring that states that wish to continue receiving federal money must require that standardized tests be administered to every third-grade child and every eighth-grade child. Most states comply because they want the money, although a small number are suing to overturn the law.) Each of the 50 states regulates schooling within the state, but each of them also delegates much authority to local school boards. The situation in Canada is similar, where provinces have responsibility for education. There is, consequently, much variation among the states and provinces and within each of them. Nevertheless, there are some things that can be said with generality, despite the variation.

Since schools are created by governments, whose top decision-making officials are elected, they are political creations. This fact is often obscured because it seems remote from the day-to-day business of schooling. What politicians are doing in their state capitals doesn't seem to have much connection with teaching reading or arithmetic. It is also obscured by the fact that most people believe that schools should not be politicized in the narrow sense of politics, that is, being pressured by the political party in power at any given time. No teachers, principals, or other school employees should have to prove that they voted for the party in power or should have to work for it in the next election in order to get or keep a job. Nor should teachers be pressured or allowed to teach the views of only one political party. These are the kinds of things that are meant when people say that politics should be kept out of the schools. Ordinarily, politics in this sense are kept out of public schools. This is the norm, although, like all norms, it is sometimes violated. (A particularly flagrant example of political corruption of a school system and its effects on education is described in a detailed case study by Anyon [1997].)

But there is a larger meaning to politics, and in its larger meaning it is always a factor in schooling and, ultimately, in socialization. In a democratic society, *politics* is *the process of making decisions in a governmental unit* (nation, state, province, city, town, county) among *competing interests.* People in a community have different interests and tend to vote for officials who they believe will best represent their interests. That applies, as well, to local school boards who, in many communities, have the authority to require people to pay taxes to pay for the schools. (Taxes are usually based on property values.) Parents with young children often want the schools to be well financed so they can offer high-quality educational programs. The parents may be willing to pay more in taxes to achieve this goal. People with no children or whose children are already adult often (not always) have less interest in the quality of the schools and are more interested in having lower taxes. Businesses usually try to pay as little tax as possible. Elections for members to the school board are often decided by which candidates of these particular competing interests receive the most votes. A school board elected to cut taxes and reduce school costs that decides that it has to cut out, say, its art program because of reduced funds, may in this way be denying opportunity to pupils with artistic talent who will not get the instruction that would develop that talent.

Also, some school districts have a larger *tax base* (i.e., are wealthier) than others. Pupils in a school district that has money for one computer for every 17 students are less likely to become as proficient as those in a school district that has money to buy one computer for every four students. For example, in 1997–1998, only 10 percent of elementary schools and 29 percent of middle schools had one computer for every four students; only 24 percent of elementary schools and 35 percent of middle schools had high-speed access to the Internet somewhere in the school (Becker 2000, 49, Table 1). Change in computer access has, however, been rapid. A survey by the National Center for Educational Statistics reports that by 2003, virtually 100 percent of all U.S. public schools had at least one computer with Internet access (National Center for Educational Statistics 2005, Table 1). This survey also shows a narrowing of the gap between schools with high minority and low minority populations. In 1998, there was one computer for every 17 students in schools with more than 50 percent minority students, compared with one for every 10 or 12 students in schools with less than that minority percentage. By 2003 this had narrowed to one for every five students in high minority schools, compared to one for every four students in schools with less than 50 percent minority students (National Center for Educational Statistics 2003, Table 7).

The recently increased equality of computer and Internet access across types of school populations does not eliminate other inequalities that have existed for generations, many of which continue. Wealthier districts can afford to hire more teachers than poor ones and can keep class sizes smaller, giving each child more attention (Wenglinsky 2001). They have more money for school libraries, equipment, special programs, and other resources that enhance educational quality. (In large cities in the United States and some Canadian provinces, school boards often do not have school taxing authority because the state or provincial legislature keeps that power for itself. The same kinds of issues are contested in the legislatures as in local school boards.) *Politics involves raising and spending money for public purposes, including schools, and money influences student opportunity, and therefore politics influences schools and individual opportunity for learning.*

Equal educational opportunity for all children is a popular ideal in American society (Gutmann 1988, 128; Katznelson and Weir 1985, 207–208). The concept of equal educational opportunity is considerably more complicated than appears on the surface (Gutmann 1988, 127–171). But one of the basic facts about schooling in the United States (as in other countries) is that opportunities for learning are unequal. The quality of education available to some students is better than the quality available to other students. This *inequality of opportunity* is not random The inequality has a pattern. Generally, children from poor families and working-class families receive inferior schooling compared to those from middle-class and wealthy families. Generally in the United States, because larger proportions of African American and Hispanic families than whites are poor, children from these ethnic backgrounds tend to receive inferior schooling compared to children from white, non-Hispanic families, although families from these ethnic groups who have become middle class generally fare better than working-class and lower-class members of these groups. There are two broad reasons for this pattern: (1) The schools treat children unequally, and (2) children from these categories come from families less able to help them with schooling. We have already discussed part of the first reason: Schools with less money cannot give their pupils everything that schools with more money can give. We will add to this discussion in the remainder of this section and in the section on the classroom. We will discuss the second reason in the section on family interaction with schools.

Inequality of opportunity in schooling is not inadvertent but, from one point of view, serves one of the purposes of schooling. According to educational sociologist Steven Brint, schooling in contemporary societies has three purposes: (1) transmission of school knowledge, (2) socialization, and (3) sorting people for higher- and lower-level jobs (Brint 1998, 100). This distinction is useful in calling attention to the fact that schooling involves more than teaching reading, arithmetic, history, and other subjects. However, once we gain this broader awareness, we should recognize that what is transmitted in school knowledge and how it is transmitted are aspects of socialization. As we shall discuss shortly, school knowledge is not one single thing but varies considerably among different kinds of schools. The kind of school knowledge children acquire is part of their socialization into society. And the sorting of people into higher- and lower-level jobs derives from the kind of socialization that children receive in schools.

Returning now to Brint's distinction, in democratic society the third purpose should be achieved by offering every child an equal opportunity to compete on equal terms. But we have already noted that discrepancies in wealth among school districts put lower-income pupils at a disadvantage. Their schools tend to have less well paid, less qualified teachers, as well as fewer funds for the materials and equipment. Thus, the differences in school financing are a major factor in sorting, which begins in the early grades.

A second factor occurs within schools. This is the practice known as *tracking*. A track is a course of study at a certain level of difficulty. Pupils are assigned to a track according to their supposed level of ability, a practice also known as *ability grouping*. Thus, even in the first grade children considered more able are assigned to a higher track than those considered of less ability. But ability is often not evaluated carefully, and there is often a disposition to judge African American and Hispanic, but not Asian, students as having lesser ability so that they are disproportionately assigned to lower tracks. Their educational disadvantage cumulates through the years, since having less demanding and less challenging work in the earliest years keeps them from handling more difficult tasks at each successive grade level.

Two main sociological theories have been proposed to explain educational inequality or educational stratification. One is called functionalism. *Functionalism* postulates that the institutions of society fit together in a relatively smooth way to meet society's needs. According to this idea, society needs people with varying degrees and types of education to fill jobs that vary in their skill requirements. Not every job requires the maximum education possible, and therefore people who are going to fill jobs with lesser requirements will not need the highest level or highest quality education. According to this theory, the society functions smoothly because the inequality in the educational institution matches up nicely with the inequality of job demands in the work institutions. The major difficulty—and it is a very serious difficulty—with the functionalist theory of educational stratification is that it offers no explanation of why certain categories of people (working class, poor, certain minorities) should almost always be the recipients of the lesser education (Collins 1977).

The other theory is known as *conflict theory*. According to this theory, as explained by Randall Collins (1977, 125), society is made up of diverse status groups competing for advantage in the form of wealth, power, and prestige. Each of these status groups is composed of families and friends, linked to each other by religion, or ethnicity, or educational level—people who share a sense of status equality based on participation in a common culture. A shared culture consists of combinations of such elements as social manners, style of language use, tastes in clothing and décor, ritual observances, usual topics of conversation, opinions and values, and preferences in sports, media, and arts. Individuals gain their fundamental sense of identity from participating in such groups, and they contrast their own group with others that make them feel uncomfortable. Members of any such group may distinguish themselves from others by giving themselves some kind of moral superiority which can take various forms—"taste," "breeding," "respectability," "plain folks," or "good fellows." These are some categories that status groups use to feel they are more honorable or more worthy than others.

Collins goes on to argue, "The main activity of schools is to teach particular status cultures both in and outside the classroom. . . . The public school system in the U.S. was founded under the impetus of WASP elites with the purpose of teaching respect for Protestant and middle-class standards of cultural and religious propriety, especially in the face of Catholic working-class immigrants from Europe. . . . The content of public school education has consisted especially of middle-class, WASP culture." (Collins 1977, 126–127). (*WASP* is an acronym for White Anglo-Saxon Protestant, referring primarily to people whose ancestors came from England, Scotland, Wales, Northern Ireland, the Netherlands, and the Scandinavian countries. *Elites* are people of the highest status category among all categories or the highest status within any particular category.) Control of the schools generally, Collins argues, is in the hands of representatives of the business community. This elite status group sets educational requirements that connect schooling and later employment. New members who share the elite culture can be selected for elite positions through schooling. Schooling is also used "to hire lower and middle employees who have acquired a general respect for the elite values and styles" (Collins 1977, 127). Collins's analysis of conflict theory can be understood as in agreement with Brint's point that schooling has a function of sorting people into different status levels.

But inequality is, ironically, coproduced to some extent by the poor parents of poor children. Taxing authorities and classroom authorities often operate in ways that disadvantage poor children but parents sometimes contribute, unknowingly, to their children's receiving inferior education. We shall discuss this issue in the section on family-school interaction.

The Classroom as an Organization

A school classroom is an organization, as is any human association that has continuity. It has certain characteristics or structural qualities that shape socialization. Ordinarily, students spend about 1,000 hours per year in a classroom and will spend approximately 7,000 hours in school between kindergarten and the end of sixth grade (Jackson 1968, 5). (Since the length of the average school day has changed little over several decades, these time estimates are likely valid as current approximations.) The organizational characteristics of the classroom contribute to making those hours consequential for children's participation in society.

Authority

Children beginning school come into contact with a new source of authority, the teacher. The teacher's authority has at least two main aspects. One is control of the classroom. As one author states, "One of the teacher's main functions is to control pupils' social behavior by rewarding appropriate acts and punishing misbehavior" (Bossert 1979, 11). Children are taught rules of behavior beginning in kindergarten (if they have not already learned them in nursery school). In an observational study of kindergarten that has become a classic, Harry L. Gracey noted that children entering kindergarten already know how to get along with others in their families and play groups. The job of kindergarten is to teach them the student role. To accomplish this, "The teachers expended most of their efforts, for the first half of the year at least, in training the children to follow the routines which the teachers created. The children were, in a very real sense, *drilled* in tasks and activities created by the teachers for their own purposes and beginning and ending quite arbitrarily (from the child's point of view) at the command of the teacher" (Gracey 2001, 97; italics in original). One teacher was quoted as saying that she hated September because of the need to conduct this repetitive activity, but by January the pupils know how to comply with what is expected of them.

Nevertheless, authority is not established once and for all in kindergarten. Anthropologist R. Timothy Sieber, in a study of first graders, gives a number of examples of teachers' efforts to bring children into compliance with the student role: "Bobby, we can do without smart alecks in this class! Now sit up straight"; "Let me see all your faces! I don't see Lois's face because she's not listening"; "Hey, you at the back table! I want you looking up here!"; "Jeremy, you should be watching, not talking with Hannah!"; "I'm waiting until everyone's quiet and ready . . . I'm waiting . . . I'm waiting" (Sieber 1981). These quotations are good illustrations also of how children are induced to sustain responsive participation in society, which we discussed briefly in Chapter 4.

The other main aspect of authority is organizing and presenting what is taught. Teachers have to gain and keep children's interest. Two professors of education note a contemporary complication: "Many urban schools now have multi-ethnic groups and children with special needs in their classrooms. Many teachers have not been prepared in any way to deal with these differences." They go on to note more generally that what we see as standard fare in elementary schools are teachers who are responsible for ten or more subject areas. Somehow the subjects need to be organized and managed with a group of 23 to 26 children. Teachers wrestle with how to group students for different activities; they must decide what to teach and what to drop; and they must decide how much time to spend on one area versus another. Pressure for mastery of the three Rs limits the amount of time spent on other parts of the curriculum. (Lieberman and Miller 1992, 22–23)

Class Size

A classroom has many more people in it (often more than 30) than the household in which a child lives. Since most of what children do is done in the presence of others, they have to learn to cope with a somewhat formalized multi-person situation. The structural characteristic here is the asymmetry of 30 or so pupils being supervised by and wanting the attention of one teacher. This results in what has been called a *hidden curriculum*. This term has gained favor as a way of calling attention to the informal and unofficial matters that are taught, matters that may or may not be noticed by those who have responsibility for teaching the official curriculum. Major elements of this hidden curriculum are (1) learning to wait one's turn, which means not only waiting to satisfy one's wishes to speak or perform but also often abandoning those wishes if the activity moves on to something else; and (2) learning to ignore and not be distracted by those around one. As one observer of classroom functioning states,

> If students are to face the demands of classroom life with equanimity they must learn to be patient. This means that they must be able to disengage, at least temporarily, their feelings from their actions. It also means . . . that they must be able to re-engage feelings and actions when conditions are appropriate. In other words, students must wait patiently for their turn to come, but when it does they must still be capable of zestful participation. They must accept the fact of not being called on during a group discussion, but they must continue to volunteer. . . . In most classrooms, powerful social sanctions are in operation to force the students to maintain an attitude of patience. If he impulsively steps out of line, his classmates are likely to complain about his being selfish or 'pushy.' If he shifts over into a state of overt withdrawal, his teacher is apt to call him back to active participation. (Jackson 1968, 18)

The hidden curriculum thus involves two related but distinguishable aspects of socialization: (1) Learning to be patient is an aspect of *self-regulation*, which is one of the principal expected outcomes of socialization. Since learning to be patient develops through interaction with others (teacher and classmates), it provides a good example of how the self is a social product. (2) The above quotation identifies another aspect, which is *emotional socialization*. While it may be regarded as also part of self-regulation, it deserves separate mention. The child is being socialized to engage and re-engage emotions or feelings in step with changes in classroom activity.

Evaluation

Sociologists Karl Alexander and Doris Entwisle, who have studied children in the early years of schooling, point out that there has been little previous study of children's significant life-course change from "home child" to "schoolchild" (Alexander and Entwisle 1988, 1). They note some of the ways the beginning of school is important:

> The beginning school transition, like other major transitions, implies that the self is redefined. The person's role set is revised in a major way by some nonfamilial authority. . . . Children add a whole new role set when they begin school and must construct a new definition of self. They are now producers, not just consumers, and their handiwork is reviewed by teachers, principals and other school personnel as well as by a new set of peers."(Alexander and Entwisle 1988, 97–98)

Since pupils differ in the rate and quality of their learning and in the various kinds of social facility that are encouraged in the classroom (for example, promptness, cooperativeness, and cheerfulness), their progress toward desired goals is evaluated. Although the teacher is the main source of evaluation, children also evaluate themselves. For example, they know when they can't spell a word or solve a problem. Even in kindergarten, children may evaluate each other with such epithets as "stupid," "dummy," and "dumb-dumb" (Gouldner 1978, 58). In the grades, the class as a whole may be asked to evaluate a student's work "as when the teacher asks, 'Who can correct Billy?' or 'How many believe that Shirley read that poem with a lot of expression?' " (Jackson 1968, 20). The classroom environment is one in which children are being evaluated in a variety of ways—by teacher comments, self-judgments, classmates' judgments, report cards, marks and comments (and perhaps gold stars, red stars, or blue stars) on exercises and papers, classroom displays of the "best" papers, and requests that a child bring a parent in for a conference. Inevitably, the classroom environment often becomes highly competitive (Bossert 1979, 71–72).

This ongoing and multifaceted process of evaluation contributes to socialization in three main ways.

1. The first is that *the evaluations become processed into the child's developing self*. Children learn certain of society's values and norms, and in this way their selves are transformed. They learn to be neat, prompt, able to follow instructions, and so forth—or they learn that they are not very good at being neat, or prompt or at following instructions. They learn to think of themselves as being good in math or not so good in math, good or not so good in reading, and so on. These evaluations of children's achievements in skills, subject matters, and social performances thus gradually accrue to their emerging selves. Children thus come to know themselves as particular kinds of social beings, ones who may aspire to certain kinds of future opportunities but not to others. Alexander and Entwisle state, "There is good reason to think that how children make the transition to full-time schooling will have implications both profound and long-last-

ing—whether the children are black or white" (Alexander and Entwisle 1988, 3).

2. While their selves are thus evolving, *children are also acquiring an academic reputation that affects the way teachers treat them.* Numerous studies point to the advantage teachers offer those students whom they perceive, for whatever reasons, to have greater ability. One study finds that good readers are allowed to make mistakes without being interrupted and corrected, while poor readers are not; another finds that teachers wait longer for answers from good than from poor students; and still another finds that teachers are more likely to praise a good performance from a high-expectation child than from a low-expectation child (Karweit 1981; Boocock 1978).

3. Still another way in which evaluation affects socialization is that children, while acquiring a reputation among teachers, are also building up a semi-public "cumulative record." The quality of this record (and reputation) serves as a ticket of admission (or refusal) for later opportunities. At any given point during the formation of this reputation and record, their quality affects children's progression to the next step—for example, whether they will be put into a slow, fast, or average section, whether they have done well enough in lower grades to be admitted to college preparatory classes in high school, and whether they have done well enough in high school to be admitted to a college (and, if so, to what kind of college and with what likelihood of a scholarship, and the like). In short, the school classroom functions as a system of selection for sequences of interlocking opportunities leading to particular kinds of adult roles (Parsons 1959).

Moral Climate

According to one group of educators who conducted a detailed study of classrooms, a great deal of what goes on in schools has moral implications. They argue that

> like doctoring, teaching is also a form of *treatment*, a way of trying to make people better than they are, which means that it is always legitimate to ask questions about how well or how poorly the teacher's students are being treated. And to raise questions about how one person treats another, no matter what the relationship, is to enter the domain of moral judgments.... This means that teachers are in a position to be kind or cruel, fair or unfair, considerate or inconsiderate, domineering or cooperative, as their fancy or their moral temperament suits them.... They are also in a position to embarrass publicly or shield from embarrassment those students who exhibit weaknesses.... Classrooms, then are *morally charged environments.*... (Jackson, Boostrom, and Hansen 1993, 173; italics in original)

Research projects conducted in various cities have, for many years, shown that poor children are often demeaned by teachers. African American and Hispanic poor children are particularly likely to receive such treatment, from black teachers as well as white. A study in St. Louis revealed one set of practices. In a kindergarten in a virtually all-black school with an all-black faculty, the teacher made permanent seating assignments on the eighth day of school. The author notes,

> Within a few days, only a certain group of children were continually being called on to lead the class in the Pledge of Allegiance, read the weather calendar each day, come to the front for 'show and tell' periods, take messages to the office, count the number of children present in the class, pass out materials for class projects, be in charge of equipment on the playground, and lead the class to the bathroom, library, or on a school tour. This one group of children, who were always physically close to the teacher and had a high degree of verbal interaction with her, she placed at Table 1. (Rist 1973, 85–86)

The author goes on to note that these children were all dressed in clean clothes. The children at Tables 2 and 3 were more poorly dressed, in some cases dirty. This teacher had access to parental preregistration forms and to a list of children from families receiving welfare payments. Her practices express her lower opinion of poor children.

A New York City study found that teachers defined African American students as inadequate. Their expectations for the students were low, and the goals they set for the students were low, compared to expectations from middle-class children (Leacock 1969, 205). The likely result of these lower levels of expectation is a reduction in the children's levels of aspiration, levels of accomplishment, and probably even levels of intelligence.

These practices are degrading in quiet ways. But verbal abuse is not unknown. During the 1990s a professor of education spent a year in an "ultimately unsuccessful effort to improve a cluster of schools in Newark, New Jersey," where she saw "the anguish and anger of students and teachers—and the systematic abuse of children by some school staff—all of whom are caught in the tangle of a failing school system and unrealized school reform." In her report of her study, she seeks "to reveal ways in which poverty and racial isolation have often trivialized efforts in this city to teach, to learn, and to bring about change" (Anyon 1997, xiv). While her report presents a detailed and complex account of how political, economic, and social factors led to a profound deterioration in Newark schools—a process similar to that in most of America's big cities as the middle class mostly moved to the suburbs—we focus here on how all this plays out in the classroom in the form of verbal abuse. In one elementary school, whose pupil population was 71 percent black and 27 percent Hispanic, she heard one black male teacher tell a girl that her breath "smelled like dog shit," and her clothes "smelled like stale dust." Some other comments that she overheard and found not atypical are as follows:

> "You're disgusting; you remind me of children I would see in a jail or something." (*Black teacher to her class of first graders.*)

> "Shut up and push those pencils. Push those pencils—you borderline people." (*Black teacher to his class of black and Hispanic sixth graders.*)

"If I had a gun, I'd kill you. You're all hoodlums." (*White fifth-grade teacher.*)

"Why are you so stupid! I'm going to throw you in the garbage." (*White basic skills teacher to a black boy.*)

"Don't you have *any* attention span? You have the attention span of cheerios!" (*White principal trying to quiet a class of fourth graders.*) (Anyon 1997, 29–30)

She interviewed 25 black students. This brief exchange with a 9-year-old boy suggests something of the demoralizing consequences of such abuse:

Anyon: "Tell me about your teacher."
Boy: "He says we're animals. Hooligans. He said we should be in a zoo. I feel bad when he say that. I get kinda sad."
Anyon: "So what do you do?"
Boy: "I put my head down." (Anyon 1997, 32)

These teacher evaluations of students go beyond criticism of specific performances. They demean the very selves of the children to whom they are directed. They accuse the children of defects that are deeper than inadequacies of specific task performance. Such accusations of comprehensive personal failure cannot but undermine self-esteem and self-efficacy. They undermine the ostensible purpose of the school as an agency of socialization. While some children may have other sources of self-esteem that enable them to be resilient enough to not be depressed and defeated by such teachers, there is a strong chance that the boy who is sad and puts his head down is more typical of children who receive such abuse from teachers.

Family-School Interaction

While schools have independent power to influence children, their ability to do so is conditioned by the kinds of families that the children come from. Schools are organized on the assumption that parents have prepared children for school and continue to support children's school efforts. Preparation takes many forms. For example, learning to read involves, among other things, being able to follow a story. Children who have been read to or told stories from an early age usually learn to read more quickly and with more understanding than children who have not had that experience. Middle-class children are more likely to have had such preparation than working-class or lower-class children (Handel 1999, 15). In general, middle-class parents have a fuller understanding of how their activity can help their children. The significance of parental involvement and its complex interplay with the school can be illustrated with summaries of two important studies that deal with this issue.

Anthropologist John Ogbu sought to understand why so many children in "Burgherside," a low-income neighborhood of Stockton, California, in which 92 percent of the elementary school population consists of blacks and Mexican Americans, failed in school. Like some other researchers before him, he found that teachers expect low-income children to fail. He found that Burgherside parents have high educational aspirations for their children and that the children also have these aspirations. But he found, in addition, something that had not often before been reported as a central finding by an observer sympathetic to low-income children:

> **Burgherside children lack a serious attitude toward their school work.... Burghersiders do not fail in school because, although they try, they cannot do the work.... Rather, Burghersiders fail because they do not even try to do the work. They are not serious about their school work and therefore make no serious effort to try to succeed in school.** (Ogbu 1974, 97; boldface in original)

In pursuing this, Ogbu found that the children were acquiring the belief that schooling was no use because it would not open up the opportunities that good school performance ought to.

> In general, Burgherside parents appear to be teaching their children two contradictory attitudes toward education. On the one hand, they emphasize the need for more education: *You are not going to grow up to be like me. Get your education.* On the other hand, they teach their children both verbally and through their own lives that it is not easy for Burghersiders who have "made it" in school to "make it" in society. They believe that for one of them to get a good job he must be "twice as qualified" as a Taxpayer competing for the same job. A Burghersider who merely has the same qualifications as a Taxpayer has no chance of success in a competition with a Taxpayer. That is why, Burghersiders say, they become discouraged and give up, saying, *Oh, I know I will never make it.* (Ogbu 1974, 98; italics in original)

(Taxpayers are whites living in another neighborhood who not only pay taxes but also are publicly acknowledged as and consider themselves to be Taxpayers. They consider themselves the bearers of mainstream culture and also the bearers of the costs of running the city. Although Burghersiders pay taxes, they are often publicly described and treated as non-taxpayers.)

An important element in Ogbu's analysis is his distinction between subordinate and immigrant minorities. *Subordinate minorities* are those that were incorporated into the United States against their will—American Indians, blacks, and Mexican Americans of the Southwest included by conquest after the Mexican-American War. *Immigrant minorities* are those that came to the country looking for religious, political, or economic betterment. Members of these two types of minority perceive American society differently. Reduced effort in school by children of subordinate minorities is a mode of adaptation to a longtime limited opportunity for social rewards. By not working hard, the children reduce their anxiety about whether working hard will pay off. They are convinced it won't, so they don't.

This type of adaptation has further consequences. Blacks and Mexican Americans developed the belief that they couldn't "make it" in society. Whites developed the belief that these minorities were "inferior." Both sets of beliefs become the basis for behavior in the school. Black and Mexican American children in Stockton maintain the pattern of school failure adaptation by such practices as frequent absence from school and not taking schoolwork seriously. Teachers, who mostly come from the "Taxpayers," often regard the Burgherside children's problems as psychological, while the Burgherside parents more often see the problems as matters of instruction and educational guidance.

Under these circumstances, according to Ogbu's analysis, remedial programs that are entirely focused on the children in their school setting cannot succeed. Compensatory educational programs that were tried in Stockton were, he believes, naïve in trying in eight months to change attitudes and behavior patterns that had been developed and transmitted over several generations. Burgherside parents and school children perceive schooling in terms of its "payoff" in later employment opportunities. From this viewpoint, equal educational opportunity has to mean not merely equally favorable learning conditions in the school but also equal access to later rewards according to educational achievement.

The school, the parents and children of subordinate minorities, and the political and economic authorities of Stockton have become involved in a mutually reinforcing set of self-fulfilling prophecies. (1) White employers believe African American and Mexican American workers are inferior and, for this reason, discriminate against them in employment even when they have the requisite educational qualifications (Ogbu documented cases of such discrimination); (2) parents, knowing of such discrimination directly or indirectly, discourage their children from expecting occupational success; (3) children learn from their parents and others not to expect much economic reward even for good educational qualifications and so do not try to do well in school; and (4) teachers see the poor performance of subordinate minority children, and this confirms their already existing belief in these children's inferiority, a belief they share with other "taxpayers," including prospective employers. Each category of person in this cycle has an expectation or "prophecy" about some other category of person and acts in such a way as to bring about the result that is anticipated.

Active parental discouragement of their children's commitment to schoolwork, growing out of the parents' sense of long-term discouragement, is one type of family-school interaction. The situation in Stockton has become more complex over the years with remedial programs and the increasing entry of immigrant Asians, but the black children have continued to lag behind others, and family perspectives continued to play a part (Ogbu 1991). Although we do not know of other studies that report the same parental pattern as Ogbu found, the kind of minority situation that he described in Stockton is not unique, and it is likely that other families elsewhere relate to schooling as the Burghersiders did.

A more recent study by sociologist Annette Lareau (2000) reveals important distinctions in the way working-class and middle-class parents relate to schools. Lareau studied first- and second-grade classes in two elementary schools in the San Francisco Bay area. She observed in classrooms and interviewed parents, teachers, and principals. The pupil population of one school, which she calls Colton, comes primarily from working-class families; fathers have occupations such as carpenter and janitor. Most parents are either high-school graduates or high-school dropouts. Slightly more than half the pupils are white, one-third are Hispanic, and the rest are black or Vietnamese immigrants. The pupil population of the other school, called Prescott, comes primarily from upper-middle-class and middle-class families; the parents, who are mostly college graduates or with advanced degrees, have occupations such as lawyer, doctor, engineer, and corporate manager. More than 90 percent of the pupils are white; the rest are black or of Asian descent. Almost 25 percent of the mothers, aunts, and grandmothers are former teachers (Lareau 2000, 16, 25).

The first question Lareau addressed was whether the teachers in the two schools made different kinds of requests to parents. She found that teachers in both schools wanted help from parents in the form of three "Rs": They wanted parents to *read* to their children, to *reinforce* the classroom material, and to *respond* to teacher requests for assistance. While parents in both schools read to their children, there were significant differences in the way parents in the two schools defined their relationship to the school, and these differences resulted in different educational experiences for their children. The working-class parents defined family and school as separate domains. The parents had the responsibility to prepare children for school; it was the teachers' responsibility to educate the children. Parents regarded the teachers as professionals with expertise; they often felt unable to help their children with homework, and were concerned that if they tried, they would do something wrong. Lareau observes that the Colton parents regard school as they do work; it takes place during specified hours away from home. In contrast, there was much more interconnection between the Prescott parents and the school. Upper-middle-class parents bring work home, and, similarly, they consider education to be something that goes on at all hours, not just during the defined school day. Unlike working-class mothers, the upper-middle-class mothers felt free to walk into their children's classrooms at any time to see what was going on. This sense of ease was facilitated by the fact that almost every mother worked as a volunteer in the classroom for an hour every other week. Only one Colton mother was observed to volunteer. Only 60 percent of Colton parents came to a parent-teacher conference compared to 100 percent of the Prescott parents. Only 35 percent of Colton parents came to a school open house compared to 96 percent of the Prescott parents.

In contrast to Colton mothers, Prescott mothers defined themselves as playing an active part in their children's education. Colton mothers did not interact much with each other, while Prescott mothers did. One result was that Prescott mothers had much more information about what went on in school. They knew the reputations of different teachers, and they were not shy about asking the principal to assign their child to a teacher they wanted or not assign the child to a teacher they didn't want. In addition, Prescott parents played an active role by taking such actions as asking that their child be placed in a certain program such as a gifted program or a speech therapy program, asking the teacher to send home a duplicate set of textbooks to work with at home, asking for additional information to confirm the accuracy of the teacher's judgment, complaining to the teacher about the classroom program, complaining to the principal about the teacher's performance, having their child's academic standing evaluated independently by a psychologist, having their child tutored during the school year and the summer, and rejecting the school's recommendation that their child repeat a grade. Prescott parents' educational and occupational status was equal or superior to that of teachers, and they were not as deferential to them as the Colton parents. In fact, Lareau says that Prescott teachers had a fourth "R" for parents: They wanted parents to *respect* the teacher's advice and actions, and not do things the teacher considered unhelpful.

What are the educational consequences of these two different styles of parental relationship to the school? How can the difference be explained? While, overall, Colton parents were less involved with their children's schooling than Prescott parents, Colton parents with high-achieving children were more likely to attend school events, read to their children, ask teachers to suggest educational activities to do at home, and review their children's school papers than Colton parents whose children were not doing well. In contrast, the Prescott parents most involved with the school were those whose children were not performing well and were at the bottom of the class. "Rather than simply accepting the generic education handed out by the school, the parents sought to alter the school experience, increase the efficiency of home activities, and go beyond the school by hiring professional educators" (Lareau 2000, 129). The result was that "Prescott low-achievers often had customized educational experiences which operated twelve months a year and were tailored to their specific needs. Colton parents had difficulty pinpointing the nature of their children's educational problems, understanding the dialogues at school, and making certain that their children completed school work at home" (Lareau 2000, 139). While parental intervention could help improve children's school performance, upper-middle-class children were also under more pressure and stress than the working-class children. Children who had to repeat first grade generated less trauma in working-class families than in upper-middle-class families who were more intensely involved.

The basic explanation that Lareau proposes for the different ways in which working-class and upper-middle-class parents relate to their children's elementary schools is a difference in class cultures. While she notes that teachers attribute the difference to a difference in values and parental concern, Lareau argues that that is not an adequate explanation. Rather, she places the emphasis on differences in *cultural capital*. By this she means cultural resources that differ between the two classes. Specifically she identifies the following differences in cultural capital: (1) upper-middle-class parents felt *competent* to help their children in school, and this is partly due to their higher education. Working-class parents sometimes had difficulty understanding the "big words" that teachers used and felt confused. (2) Because the Prescott parents had a college education and at least equal and often higher social status than the teachers, they felt *confident* in dealing with teachers. Colton parents looked up to educated people and felt a gulf between themselves and teachers. (3) Upper-middle-class parents' higher *income and material resources* made it easier for them to connect to the school. Almost all Prescott parents had paid house cleaners and two cars, so transportation to school was not a problem, as it sometimes was for Colton parents. (4) The fact that upper-middle-class parents *work at home as well as at their work site* corresponds to the ideas teachers have about education. Parents who work at home on evenings and weekends provide role models for their children. Working-class parents do not share this concept of work. For them, work is separate from home life, and similarly they regard school as separate from home life. (5) The final difference contrasted social networks:

> Finally, *networks*, themselves linked to social class position, provide parents with different amounts of general information about schooling. Upper-middle class parents had teachers, resource specialists, principals, counselors, and special education teachers among their aunts, uncles, sisters-in-law, grandparents, friends, and neighbors. By contrast, working-class parents had gas station attendants, carpenters, convenience store salespersons, janitors, factory workers and policemen among their relatives and neighbors. A few working-class parents did have relatives who were upwardly mobile and attended college, but often these relatives were geographically removed as well as socially distant and were not a frequent or reliable source of insight and information. (Lareau 2000, 172–173)

One final point of Lareau's analysis should be noted. Cultural capital is only a potential until it is *activated*. Not all upper-middle-class parents use the cultural capital that is in their possession. Further, some working-class parents are motivated and able to transcend their limited cultural capital. Thus, class position does not automatically translate into a particular kind of socialization. It creates probabilities that certain kinds of experiences may occur, but those probabilities come into existence only when parents take the actions that their resources make possible.

* * *

In the modern world, schools are essential to children's socialization. They introduce children to impersonal authority and to participating in large groups in the classroom and on the playground. In many countries, preschool is institutionalized so that all children experience a similar transition from the home. In the United States, preschool and daycare are individual options. High-quality daycare and preschool contribute to children's cognitive development, so that those who have access to it have advantages that others do not. Such early inequality of opportunity persists through the school years. Even so, daycare socializes children to strong control—some would say over control—of their emotions, and children who spend many hours a week in daycare are at greater risk for behavior problems than those who don't.

Schooling socializes different social categories of children to different kinds and levels of future expectations, despite democratic political theory that prescribes equal opportunity for all. Money and other resources are differentially allocated to schools serving different social class levels, resulting in disproportionate schooling disadvantage for African Americans, other minorities, and poor whites. Poor and working-class parents are less knowledgeable than middle-class parents in dealing with teachers and principals and are therefore less able to assist their children gain any help they need.

References

Alexander, Karl, and Doris Entwisle. 1988. *Achievement in the First Two Years of School: Patterns and Processes*. Monographs of the Society for Research in Child Development, Serial no. 218, vol. 53, no. 2.

Anyon, Jean. 1997. *Ghetto Schooling*. New York: Teachers College Press.

Baker, Maureen. 2001. "Families, the State and Family Policies." In Maureen Baker (ed.) *Families: Changing Trends in Canada*, 4th ed., 267–283. Toronto: McGraw-Hill Ryerson.

Becker, Henry Jay. 2000. "Who's Wired and Who's Not: Children's Access to and Use of Computer Technology." *The Future of Children*, 10(2)2: 44–75.

Boocock, Sarane Spence. 1978. "The Social Organization of the Classroom." In Ralph H. Turner, James Coleman, and Renee C. Fox (eds.) *Annual Review of Sociology*, Vol. 4, 1–28. Palo Alto, CA: Annual Reviews.

Bossert, Stephen T. 1979. *Tasks and Social Relationships in Classrooms*. Cambridge, U.K.: Cambridge University Press.

Brint, Steven. 1998. *Schools and Societies*. Thousand Oaks, CA: Pine Forge Press.

Collins, Randall. 1977. "Functional and Conflict Theories of Educational Stratification." In Jerome Karabel and A. H. Halsey (eds.) *Power and Ideology in Education*, 118–136. New York: Oxford University Press.

Corsaro, William A., and Francesca Emiliani. 1992. "Child Care, Early Education, and Children's Peer Culture in Italy." In Michael E. Lamb, Katherine Sternberg, Carl-Philip Hwang, and Anders G. Broberg (eds.) *Child Care in Context*, 81–115. Hillsdale, NJ: Lawrence Erlbaum Associates.

Entwisle, Doris R., Karl L. Alexander, and Linda Steffel Olson. 1997. *Children, Schools, and Inequality*. Boulder, CO: Westview Press.

Goelman, Hillel. 1992. "Day Care in Canada." In Michael E. Lamb, Katherine Sternberg, Carl-Philiip Hwang, and Anders G. Bromberg (eds.) *Child Care in Context*, 223–263. Hillsdale, NJ: Lawrence Erlbaum.

Gouldner, Helen. 1978. *Teachers' Pets, Troublemakers, and Nobodies: Black Children in Elementary School*. Westport, CT: Greenwood Press.

Gracey, Harry. 2001. "Learning the Student Role: Kindergarten as Academic Boot Camp." In Jeanne H. Ballantine and Joan Z. Spade (eds.) *Schools and Society*, 95–100. Belmont, CA: Wadsworth.

Gutmann, Amy. 1988. *Democratic Education*. Princeton, NJ: Princeton University Press.

Handel, Ruth D. 1999. *Building Family Literacy in an Urban Community*. New York: Teachers College Press.

Hwang, C. Philip, and Anders G. Bromberg. 1992. "The Historical and Social Context of Child Care in Sweden." In Carl-Philip Hang and Anders G. Broberg (eds.) *Child Care in Context*, 27–53. Hillsdale, NJ: Lawrence Erlbaum.

Jackson, Philip. 1968. *Life in Classrooms*. New York: Holt, Rinehart, & Winston.

Jackson, Philip, Robert E. Boostrom, and David T. Hansen. 1993. *The Moral Life of Schools*. San Francisco: Jossey-Bass.

Karweit, Nancy. 1981. "Time in School." In Alan C. Kerckhoff and Ronald Corwin (eds.) *Research in Sociology of Education and Socialization*, Vol. 2, 77–110. Greenwich, CT: JAI Press.

Katznelson, Ira and Margaret Weir. 1985. *Schooling for All*. New York: Basic Books.

Lamb, Michael E., and Katherine Sternberg. 1992. "Sociocultural Perspectives on Nonparental Childcare." In Michael E. Lamb, Katherine Sternberg, Carl-Philip Hwang, and Anders G. Bromberg (eds.) *Child Care in Context*, 1–23. Hillsdale, NJ: Lawrence Erlbaum.

Lareau, Annette. 2000. *Home Advantage: Social Class and Parental Intervention in Elementary Education* 2nd ed. Lanham, MD: Rowman & Littlefield.

Leacock, Eleanor Burke. 1969. *Teaching and Learning in City Schools*. New York: Basic Books.

Leavitt, Robin L. 1991. "Power and Resistance in Infant-Toddler Day Care Centers." In Spencer Cahill (ed.) *Sociological Studies of Child Development*, Vol. 4, 91–112. Greenwich, CT: JAI Press.

——. 1995. "The Emotional Culture of Infant-Toddler Day Care." In J. Amos Hatch (ed.) *Qualitative Research in Early Childhood Settings*, 3–21. Westport, CT: Praeger.

Leavitt, Robin L., and Martha Bauman Power. 1997. "Civilizing Bodies: Children in Day Care." In J. Tobin (ed.) *Making a Place for Pleasure in Early Childhood Education*, 39–75. New Haven, CT: Yale University Press.

Lieberman, Ann, and Lynn Miller. 1992. *Teachers—Their World and Their Work*. New York: Teachers College Press.

Meyer, John W., David H. Kamens, and Aaron Benavot. 1992. *School Knowledge for the Masses*. London: Falmer Press.

National Center for Educational Statistics. 2005. *Internet Access in U.S. Public Schools and Classrooms: 1994–2003*. Table 1, "Percent of Public Schools with Internet Access, by School Characteristics, 1994–2003." Table 7, "Ratio of Public School Students to Instructional Computers with Internet Access, by School Characteristics, 1998–2003." *www.NCES.ed.gov* (accessed December 11, 2005).

NICHD Early Child Care Research Network. 2002. "Early Child Care and Children's Development Prior to School Entry: Results From the NICHD Study of Early Child Care." *American Educational Research Journal* 39(1): 133–164.

Ogbu, John U. 1974. *The Next Generation: An Ethnography of Education in an Urban Neighborhood*. New York: Academic Press.

——. 1991. "Low School Performance as an Adaptation: The Case of Blacks in Stockton, California." In Margaret A. Gibson and John U. Ogbu (eds,) *Minority Status and Schooling*. New York: Garland.

Parsons, Talcott. 1959. "The School Class as a Social System: Some of its Functions in American Society." *Harvard Educational Review* 29: 297–318.

Rist, Ray. 1973. *The Urban School: A Factory for Failure*. Cambridge, MA: MIT Press.

Sieber, R. Timothy. 1981. "Socialization Implications of School Discipline or How First Graders Are Taught to 'Listen.'" In R. Timothy Sieber and Andrew J. Gordon (eds.) *Children and Their Organizations*, 18–43. Boston: G. K. Hall.

Tobin, Joseph J., David H. Y. Wu, and Dana H. Davidson. 1989. *Preschool in Three Cultures*. New Haven, CT: Yale University Press.

U.S. Department of Health and Human Services, Administration for Children and Families. 2001. "Head Start Fact Sheet." Washington, DC: U.S. Department of Health and Human Services.

Wenglinsky, Harold. 2001. "How Money Matters: The Effect of School District Spending on Academic Achievement." In Jeanne H. Ballantine and Joan Z. Spade (eds.) *Schools and Society: A Sociological Approach to Education*, 197–203. Belmont, CA: Wadsworth/ Thomson Learning. ✦

Chapter 7

Peer Groups

W hile families and schools are socializing agencies organized primarily by adults, children are also socialized into a world in which adults are peripheral. This children's world is generally designated by the term *peer group*. The term is a bit misleading since it does not designate a single group in which a child participates but rather all those groups made up of children in which any particular child participates. Any given child is likely to belong to more than one peer group, although there may be overlapping membership. Thus, a peer group may consist of the children in one's block or in one's apartment building. Another may consist of playmates at school. A third may be the children in the same Boy Scout or Girl Scout troop, or those who go to the same summer camp or music school. Yet another may be made up of the cousins whom the child may see as a group at periodic intervals. It would therefore be more accurate to speak of children's "peer world," since a child's actual peer groups might differ in significant ways and the child might have different roles within them. For example, adult values might be more prominent in a Girl Scout or Boy Scout troop than in the neighborhood backyard or back alley peer group. We shall use the conventional term, however, and the reader will be able to judge from the context when we are referring to a particular type of peer group and when we are more generally discussing the peer world.

A children's peer group as a socializing agency has certain distinctive characteristics: (1) By definition, it is made up of members who have approximately the same age status or are within a limited age range and who decide whether a particular child is "too young" or "too old" to belong. (2) Within the peer group, members have varying degrees of prestige and power. (3) The peer group is centered about its own concerns. Whereas adult authority figures may instruct the child in traditional norms and values with an awareness that the child must learn to function in adult society, peer groups do not have such a responsibility. (4) Thus, any long-run socializing implications are largely unintentional. Children participating in peer groups do not do so with the aim of preparing themselves for adult society, although peer group experiences have such import. In fact, as sociologist William Corsaro points out, many peer group activities are "a result of children's attempts to make sense of, and to a certain extent to resist, the adult world" (Corsaro 1997, 96).

A child's peer group participation may begin in a very rudimentary way in the park sandbox, in a daycare center, or in a home even before the age of 2. Although egocentricity, expressed in *parallel play* (two or more children side by side, each engaged in solitary play), rather than any form of sustained cooperation, is still the order of the day, this changes after a time (Rubin 1980, 16–19). Parallel play may be followed by the formation of rudimentary pairs and later by a succession of peer groups (Rubin 1980, 93). With increasing age, the peer groups gain in *solidarity* (a feeling of unity that leads to cooperation) and complexity, and they usually increase in size, while the activities and interests on which they focus change with the children's maturation and social development.

Peer groups give children experience in egalitarian types of relationships that are qualitatively different from relationships with authority figures. In peer groups children engage in a process of give-and-take not ordinarily possible in relationships with adults. In the family and in school, children necessarily are subordinate to parents and teachers, however benign that subordination may be. Any activities—physical or verbal—between adults and children are not the same as in relationships between equals, and even if they approach such interactions, these are not likely to be sustained for long periods of time as is the case in peer groups (Hartup 1979).

Peer groups have their own subcultures with their own norms, values, and established patterns of behavior. Children entering a group want the companionship, attention, and goodwill of its members. For having acceptable characteristics and acting in the appropriate or valued manner, the group rewards its members by bestowing attention, approval, or leadership. For being or behaving otherwise, the peer group punishes by disdain, ostracism, or other expressions of disapproval. As in their responses to other socializing agencies, particularly family and school, children come to view themselves as objects from the point of view of the group. That is, they eventually come to see themselves as the other members see them. The group standards become their own, and they are reinforced by the feelings of solidarity and support that children obtain from one another. At the same time, children are likely to feel that, as participating equals, they have a part in setting and establishing the norms.

Equality as value and norm holds for some contexts and not others. A game of tag or hide-and-go-seek may include children of both sexes and span an age range of about 7 to 12; all are equal, and they are likely to experience themselves as such. But when the group is practicing basketball or choosing sides for a baseball or hockey game, the differences in skill associated with age level are likely to become prominent. Age differences of a year or two become significant, and the older child who skates faster or catches a ball more reliably or takes the lead in organizing games can become a role model for the younger one. In the same way that children identify with reference groups and derive their standards of thought and judgment from these groups, so, too, might children identify with *reference individuals*, and derive standards of behavior and values from them (Merton 1968, 302). Younger children see in the older ones models of what they might become *soon* (while still children), and the older ones become aware that they can be a model to younger ones.

A basic contribution that peer groups make is that they help to lessen children's dependence on adults. Children establish new emotional ties and identify with new models. In seeking acceptance and respect from others at their own level—peers and near-peers—they pull away from their parents and other adults and gain enough strength to resist some parental wishes and demands. In later years, ideally, they also gain sufficient strength to become somewhat independent from their peers.

Peer Culture

While children are absorbing adult culture at home and in school, they also—on the street, on the playground, in school corridors, and in backyards—sustain an age-limited subculture of their own. It consists of a range of interests and activities, rules, traditions, distinctive expressions and gestures, and ways of making and breaking peer relationships. The richness of children's subculture is suggested by landmark studies conducted in Britain by Iona and Peter Opie. In one landmark study, they identified many forms of "the lore and language of schoolchildren" such as nonsense rhymes, riddles, tongue twisters, jeers, trick bets, and what they called "codes of oral legislation" such as "losers weepers, finders keepers" (Opie and Opie 1959). These are known mostly to children, circulated largely by them, and passed down from one generation of children to another. The study turned up parallels in the United States and on the European continent, suggesting that at least certain aspects of the peer culture transcend ethnic and national boundaries. In the twenty-first century, the peer culture undoubtedly leaps across national boundaries through the Internet, although we have not found any study that documents this process.

Another of the Opies' studies reports on some 2,500 games played by children ages 6 to 12. While many of these are simply slight regional variants of basic games (none of which requires even such minimal equipment as a ball), children nonetheless sustain a great variety of games that can be roughly classified into 11 different types: chasing, catching, seeking, hunting, racing, dueling, exerting, daring, acting, guessing, and pretending. Excluded from the study were party games, scout games, team games, and any sport that required supervision (Opie and Opie 1969).

This study, carried out over a 10-year period in many parts of Britain, discloses that certain kinds of rules appear repeatedly. There are, for example, rules for starting a game. Two or three children on a street or playground initiate the idea and then, to round up enough to play, they issue a traditional "summons" to others around. In one region, for example, children call out, "All in, all in, a bottle of gin; all out, all out, a bottle of stout" (Opie and Opie 1969, 17). While there is considerable local variation in the particular wording of the call, the practice of some such traditional way of starting a game is widespread. Similarly, there are rules for avoidance of a disliked role. Some games require one child to take a role that sets them apart from all the others. That role is often called "it." In a game such as hide-and-seek, one child has to seek and find all the others who have hidden. Children often try to avoid being the first to be "it." The way to do this is to shout out some particular phrase or make some particular gesture. The last one to do so is the first "it" (Opie and Opie 1969, 18). In the United States, children have a rule to temporarily remove themselves from a game—perhaps to tie a shoelace or to go to the bathroom.

Children may cross their fingers and call, "times" (Knapp and Knapp 1976, 29).

Games and their rules are taught to younger children by older children and may be transmitted this way for decades or even centuries. But games also rise and fall in popularity. At the present time it seems likely, although we do not have extensive research, that street and playground games have declined greatly overall as a result of the wide diffusion of television and of video games. Certainly, North American children some of the time still play some of the games their predecessors did, but it seems likely that the frequency has declined as manufactured forms of popular culture such as video games have become more popular and time-consuming. Perhaps, also, it has been suggested, the kinds of traditional summons to games that Iona and Peter Opie found are being replaced by calls on cell phones, but we do not know at what age children begin to use cell phones for this purpose or whether the procedures that children have long practiced to begin games have disappeared from their peer culture. We shall have more to say about the commercial aspects of popular culture in the following chapter on the media of mass communication.

It has long been customary to refer to peer culture as though it exists in two major forms: adolescent peer culture, which is outside the scope of this book, and childhood peer culture, which precedes it. However, Evaldsson and Corsaro (1998, 380 ff.) call attention to the fact that children's participation in peer culture evolves. Three- and 4-year-olds work out interactional routines that establish their membership in the group. These routine ways of playing prepare them for future changes in their lives. For example, preschool children improvise fantasy play and games including rules about who (which character) can do what. But in the course of play, they can't stick to the rules. Their cognitive skills are not yet up to this task, and they take actions that deviate from the rules. But this activity prepares them for coming stages of peer culture at elementary school age, when their social competence will be greater and they will be able and willing to use rules more consistently and effectively (Evaldsson and Corsaro 1998, 398–399). Strictly speaking, then, observation of children at different ages indicates that they participate not in a peer culture but in a series of gradually evolving peer cultures, although no researcher has yet followed a single group of children throughout childhood to document the changes in a particular group.

Play

In Chapter 4, we discussed a basic principle of human activity: Human beings have to interpret everything in their world in order to function. Language consists of categories that interpret the world and define the objects within it, but, of course, people use the categories that language provides for their own individual interpretive goals. For example, if a young child hits a younger sibling, the parent may say, "This is your sister. Be nice to her." The parent is defining (interpreting) the family relationship for the child and defining a category of behavior that should go with the definition of the relationship. When adults interpret situations for children, they usually are trying to get children to interpret the situations in the same way that the adults do, whether that involves regulating the relationship between siblings, emphasizing the importance of saying a prayer before a meal, insisting on the necessity to take a bath, or any of the dozens of situations in which adults (first parents, then teachers) transmit their interpretations to the children for whom they are responsible.

When children play, they have freedom to create their own interpretations. As the preceding discussion suggests, those interpretations fall broadly into two large categories: (1) interpreting concerns that originate among children, and (2) interpreting concerns that originate from interaction with adults. Our discussion of children's games portrays some interpretations that, in contemporary society, originate among children. (Hundreds of years ago, adults and children played many such games together, but they have long since become part of an adult-free children's culture. Adults today largely have no interest in or knowledge of how to avoid becoming "it.")

One way that children interpret adult creations is to appropriate them for their own use and reinterpret them. This can be illustrated by a study of life histories gathered from a dozen working-class men who grew up in the Yorkville neighborhood of New York City, alongside the East River, and still lived there when they were interviewed. They all talked about their childhood play. One said, "Everybody used to meet in the middle of the street, and it was a lot of fun, then. And in the summer you were sent down to the street, you sat on the stoop, you played games on the stoop . . . four corners, maybe, when you were a kid, or something like that there, hot beans. Then again, there was no traffic, so the street was wide open. It was one massive playground, New York City in them days." In the author's analysis and summary of the interviews, he writes,

> The playground that was New York was created out of the particular conjunction of land, water, people, buildings, and transportation that gave Yorkville its special urban character. Children appropriated the streets and turned them to their own uses. Sewer covers, seen with children's eyes, revealed a versatility unimaginable to their designers. They served as the ring for games of marbles; as goals for hockey played on roller skates; and as bases for stickball, a version of baseball invented in the streets of New York, played with a broom handle for a bat and a rubber ball known as a 'spaldeen.' The distance between sewer covers became a measure of excellence: 'Like in stickball, if you could hit it three sewers, it was great.' (Handel 1984, 35–36)

Streets and sewers, artifacts based on adult ideas for organizing and building cities, become reinterpreted by children as components for their games.

Appropriation and reinterpretation of adult ideas begin at an early age. William Corsaro, who has conducted extensive observational research in preschools in the United States and in Italy, reports an example from an Italian preschool. In the outside play area, he observes three boys carrying a carton in which is a bucket filled with rocks. They march toward him, calling out, "Here comes the bank! Here comes the bank! . . . The bank with money." One of the boys takes down the bucket with rocks and says he will give some money to

Corsaro, and as rocks are taken out there is conversation between them about how much money. Corsaro writes that he was intrigued because "These kids had created a whole new dimension in banking, a bank that makes house calls" (Corsaro 1997, 2).

Young children improvise games that can be understood as efforts to comprehend aspects of the adult world. Life in families entails dealing with the power of parents and other adults and with tensions that arise as children are pressed to conform to parental expectations. "Playing house" provides an opportunity to try on adult family roles or to engage in fantasy resolution of such tensions. A charming example: In a preschool, a girl asks a boy to rejoin her in playing house. He says, "I'll live with you there but I'll work here, and I'm working now," and he continues building with blocks (Read 1976, 347; cited in Rubin 1980, 42). "Playing doctor" helps children to deal with anxieties relating to pain and illness. Most children have experienced some pain and illness, and thus have been on the receiving end of medical attention. Playing the doctor helps a child gain what psychologists call *active mastery* over their fears. The child who is doctor is doing the curing rather than passively enduring the pain of the patient. The game also gives boys and girls an opportunity to gain or reinforce their knowledge of each other's anatomy. Playing "cops and robbers" offers children a chance to be lawbreakers in fantasy, and also law enforcers. Playing Batman or Superman or any mythical omnipotent character gives children temporary transcendance over their normal condition of being less powerful than adults.

The author of a recent essay describes a game she played up to the age of 10. She spent part of each summer visiting her grandmother in a working-class suburb of Boston. Although not Catholic, she went to Mass with the friends she made there. To keep cool on hot August days, she and her friends went inside the church

> to play the confession game. One girl would tell her sins and the others would invent her chastisement. We were fond of the word 'flagellation.' Peggy, who was pale and fat, entertained the fantasy of scourging herself for a mystic bridegroom. I considered converting, so as to be eligible for sainthood.... Marie scornfully rejected any thought of taking the veil. She had already tried smoking and had no intention of practicing any romantic austerities. It was she who first pointed out that there was a cavity between our thighs and that boys would want to put their 'thing' there, and that if we let them 'it would hurt like hell the first time, but you do it for love.' (Thurman 2002, 86)

In this confessional game, the girls are clearly struggling with adult concepts of sin. Further, as social psychologist Zick Rubin notes, "[S]exual concerns are likely to be prominently revealed in groups of nine- to twelve-year-olds" (Rubin 1980, 96). A recent study of preadolescent (ages 9 to 12) peer groups among middle-class and upper-middle-class children finds that girls, from age 9, can show interest in boys without being criticized by other girls, and the more adventurous ones flirt with boys, call them on the telephone, go to parties with them, and begin dating (Adler and Adler 1998, 52).

Although cross-gender interactions such as those just described occur, Gary Fine notes explicitly (Fine 1987) that peer cultures in this age group are gendered, that is, to a great extent, boys and girls maintain separate cultures. Barrie Thorne (1993) made extensive observations of children on school playgrounds and in classrooms, and, while she, too, found gender separation, she also found many kinds of cross-gender interactions. She concludes that it is a great oversimplification to believe that children's play falls into only two conditions: either separate worlds of boys and girls or boys against girls. This topic will be discussed further in our chapter on gender.

Sports

The link between the games of children's peer groups and the world of adults is probably nowhere as evident as in sports. In our culture, sports are not only a major form of leisure activity; they are also held up for children as a means of achieving physical health and of learning leadership skills, loyalty, and other desirable traits, and as valuable training in competitiveness and give-and-take relationships. The value, however, that stands out the most both in sports and in the surrounding world is pride in achievement. As socializers of young children, adults may stress the importance of self-development and fair play, but as children become older and more sophisticated, they tend to give more weight to success and achievement. Adult sport stars themselves serve as models. If these stars perform outstandingly—be it hitting a home run, scoring a touchdown, shooting the winning goal or basket, or winning a tennis match—they dramatically express their delight by shouting, jumping, and waving their arms. The former values of suppressed emotional expression and modesty in achievement have in recent years been replaced by expressiveness and self-congratulations. Children thus have a license to follow this same pattern.

Parents also serve as models in valuing success and achievement. Especially in their behavior as spectators and supporters of the home teams—including the local teams in which their children participate—they readily overlook the questionable calls by the referees or the fouls the referees do not see, as long as they favor the home team. Children are socialized to want to win at almost any cost and to feel badly if they lose.

In a study of children's sports in the public and parochial schools of Battle Creek, Michigan, Harry Webb found that the higher the grade, the greater importance placed on "beating one's opponent" and the less importance placed on "playing the game fairly." He concludes by drawing a parallel with the business world, saying that to insist

> on play's contribution to the development of such 'sweetheart' characteristics as steadfastness, honor, generosity, courage, tolerance, and the rest of the Horatio Alger contingent, is to ignore its structural and value similarities to the economic structure dominating our institutional network, and the substantial contribution that participation in the arena thus makes to committed and effective participation in the wider arena. (Webb 1969, 164)

In short, Webb is saying that the prevailing economic system does not favor such "sweetheart" characteristics and that sports activity is similar to business in its demands to be competitive. Further, he is saying that participation in competitive sports helps prepare participants to compete later in the economic world. That belief in the socializing value of competitive sports is widely held today, more than 35 years after the publication of Webb's paper.

Sociologist Gary Alan Fine carried out observational and interview studies of Little League baseball, played by 9- to 12-year-old boys, in New England and Minnesota. The Little League is a national organization created by adults to teach boys the game and to have them compete in uniformed teams on a regular schedule. Each team has an adult coach, usually a father of one of the players. Parents come out to watch their sons play. Fine's study documents with observations most of the points made in the above two paragraphs. Of particular interest is Fine's conceptualization of the games as situations in which two kinds of moral socialization are going on. One is being conducted by the coaches, and the other by the players among themselves as peers. Coaches have a mental framework—a set of moral concepts—in terms of which they interpret how boys are playing. When the boys do something that the coach believes violates the expected standard, he says something that amounts to a moral evaluation of the deficiency. For example, one of the values that coaches emphasize is the importance of effort, trying hard, or, in Little League lingo, *hustle.* Fine provides an example: "Assistant coach to twelve year old after he is called out trying to stretch a single to a double: 'If you hadn't loafed on the way to first you would have made it' " (Fine 1987, 63). When a team loses a game, the coach invariably considers the loss due to a lack of "hustle."

Other moral values that coaches promote are teamwork and sportsmanship. Fine notes that children of this age—preadolescents, as they are called— are very peer oriented, but even so, coaches consider that the boys' commitment to teamwork is not as strong as it should be. Coaches believe that players may be more focused on personal glory—acting as "prima donnas," the coaches call it, or "hot dogs," as the players say—than in being team players. To the coaches, teamwork is a moral value in which they have to instruct their players (Fine 1987, 71).

When a boy fails in a play (strikes out at bat or misses a catch, for example) or his team loses a game, or he is upset by an umpire's call, he may engage in inappropriate actions and displays of angry emotion. As Fine notes, "The preadolescent may forget that his presentation of self must be based on adult conceptions of the world—a world in which hostility is inappropriate and sanctionable" (Fine 1987, 68). When this happens, a coach may try to calm the boy down without criticizing.

The boys' concerns overlap with those of the adults, but peers exert their own pressures on each other. They criticize each other for what they consider emotionally inappropriate behavior. They value displays of toughness when a player is willing to risk an injury or do something to intimidate an opposing player. They are critical of a boy who loses self-control, loses "his cool." Fine sums up his discussion of the moral efforts of adults and boys:

In examining preadolescent behavior, one is struck with the degree to which preadolescents wish to adopt the adult male sex role; they are attempting—somewhat hesitantly to be sure—to adopt the values of their male leaders. This, of course, doesn't mean that pre-adolescents are mini-adults; adult values are transformed. They are the values of adults with rough edges still attached; the legacy of childhood behavior and the lack of sophistication of preadolescent behavior shape what preadolescents do and what they think is right. Yet the standards they set for themselves and for their adult guardians reflect imperfectly those values set for them by their adults. By the time of preadolescence, boys recognize that being 'men' is an important task for them, and it is a task they accept. (Fine 1987, 102)

Sociologist Sherri Grasmuck (2005) recently published a study of a neighborhood organization in Philadelphia, the Fairmount Sports Association (FSA), that is somewhat similar to, but not affiliated with, the Little League. It sponsors baseball teams for boys in age groups 7 to 9, 10 to 12, and 13 to 15, and it organizes their games played in a field that neighborhood adult volunteers created in a city park, after a struggle with city authorities, in the late 1960s. These were white, ethnic, working-class men with a passion for baseball, who fought to keep African Americans and Latinos out of their neighborhood. By the 1990s there was considerable gentrification in the neighborhood, with an influx of college-educated, middle-class professionals, many of them African American and Latino. Despite considerable tension between old-timers and newcomers, parents from the two groups worked together to keep the FSA going. The number of white ethnic children in the neighborhood had declined, and the old-timers needed minority children to keep the games going, The newcomers wanted their children to participate in these games. Grasmuck observes (2005, 191–194) that racial and class integration, both among the parents and among the children, proceeded surprisingly smoothly, considering the antagonisms of 30 years earlier. While some local and other particular circumstances facilitated this outcome, Grasmuck suggests that her study provides at least "a qualified vote for the constructive potential of sport" (Grasmuck 2005, 194).

In addition to helping socialize working-class and middle-class, and white and minority, children into cooperative team play, which resulted in some interracial friendships that lasted well into late adolescence (Grasmuck 2005, 200), the FSA games had other outcomes worth noting. This study parallels Fine's in two respects: (1) Adult socialization and peer group socialization are both occurring, and they are intertwined; and (2) both adult socialization and peer socialization are centered on defining and understanding what masculinity is. Grasmuck (2005, 198) notes,

This entire community had as its target the socialization of children into the culture of baseball and softball. Yet, despite the weight of adult messages, the children had their own impulses, their own meanings and practices to throw into the pot. Along the way, the culture they created, especially as it pertained to masculinity, mattered to the outcomes and was important to the overall feel of the adult-orchestrated games.

Adult masculinity was expressed in the competing teaching styles of the coaches, most of whom were fathers of boys in the program. Coaches tended to be stereotyped as either "screamers" who yelled at and terrified boys for the slightest mistake or "fuzzies" who were more easygoing. While Grasmuck's observations show this to be an oversimplification, she does conclude (2005, 100–103) that some coaches exhibit what she calls "tough masculinity" and others "tender masculinity." Coaches who teach tough masculinity expect boys to suppress emotions of fear and weakness, and to accept pain or injury without crying. Younger boys often, and older boys sometimes, would cry after making an error. The "tough masculinity" coaches do allow anger, pride, and laughter, considering these to be masculine. Coaches with a "tender masculinity" style are accepting of boys' emotions as well as expressions of pain. They are comfortable with gestures of tenderness between boys and toward them.

Grasmuck finds (2005, 198–199) that much of the boys' interactions can be understood as their efforts to sort out what masculinity is and how they can express it in themselves. They are aggressively competitive with each other to demonstrate best baseball skills, and they monitor each other and discuss relative skills. Every team develops a skill hierarchy among the players, with some being "top dogs" and others "underdogs." This finding is not unfamiliar. What is perhaps Grasmuck's most original finding, from the perspective of the present work, is that in some teams there were players whom she calls "positive emotional workers." These are players with better baseball skills who were able to be supportive of weaker players. They were able to give a pat on the back or a word of encouragement to a player who struck out or made an error. These positive emotional workers were very important in maintaining team strength and resilience. Grasmuck sees their performance as manifesting a nurturing style of masculinity. On teams that did not have any positive emotional workers, the players turned on each other when they were in a tense situation or suffered a setback. The players on these teams had more difficulty coping with such challenges (2005, 149, 199).

In contrast to the adult-organized games of Little League or FSA are the informal games organized by children themselves. In these, the peer group has autonomy and shapes its own rules. Some peer group processes in these situations are described by Edward Devereux in his autobiographical essay on play and backyard baseball:

> . . . [B]ecause there was no official rule book and no adult or even other child designated as rule enforcer, we somehow had to improvise the whole thing; this entailed endless hassles about whether a ball was fair or foul, whether a runner was safe or out, or, more generally, simply about what was fair. We gradually learned to understand the invisible boundary conditions of our relationships to each other. Don't be a poor sport or the other kids won't want you to play with them. Don't push your point so hard that the kid with the only catcher's mitt will quit the game. Pitch a bit more gently to the littler kids so they can have some fun, too; besides, you realize that you must keep them in the game because numbers are important. Learn how to get a game started and somehow keep it going, as long as the fun lasts. (Devereux 1976, 48–49)

Such informal games are probably less common today than formerly, as adult-organized games have gained in popularity. But not every boy participates in organized games, and informal pickup baseball games such as Devereux describes have not disappeared from American children's culture. In her recent ethnographic study of contrasting middle-class and working-class socialization experiences, Annette Lareau (2003, 67, 74) writes of one boy and others in his neighborhood, "Tyrec and other working-class and poor children learn how to be members of informal peer groups. They learn how to manage their own time. They learn how to strategize.... Informal, impromptu outdoor play is common in Tyrec's neighborhood. A group of boys approximately his age, regularly numbering four or five but sometimes reaching as many as ten, play ball games together on the street. . . ." We will present additional aspects of Lareau's study in Chapter 9.

For some children, especially boys living in poverty, sports is often imagined as an avenue to social mobility, as a way to fame, fortune, and a better life. The heroes of the sports world—especially in such television-publicized sports as football, basketball, baseball, and hockey—are honored and acclaimed in the child's as well as the adult's world. The pattern is not only North American. Speaking of soccer in Brazil, which she describes as "an all-consuming commitment bordering on fanaticism," sociologist Janet Lever describes 4- and 5-year-olds starting with small rubber balls mimicking older children. Early teenagers from poor neighborhoods play with intensity and fantasize that scouts of professional teams are studying their play (Lever 1972, 148; see also Lever 1984).

Peer Group Structures and Processes

A social structure is a social relationship that continues over time. Such relationships are maintained through interactions. Interactions can also change relationships. Thus, a marriage today is a structure that is maintained when interactions within it are satisfying or at least acceptable to both partners. If they become unacceptable to one or both, the marriage may dissolve in separation or divorce.

Within peer groups, which have a kind of overall structure, are three more specific kinds of structure—play groups, friendships, and, in later childhood, cliques. These overlap, so it is a bit artificial to distinguish them, but nevertheless such a distinction is useful for analytical purposes.

Play Groups

In our discussion of play, we have alluded to play groups without specifically identifying them as such. As our examples there suggest, a play group is often a loose affiliation of children, consisting of whoever is available to join in the play on the street or playground or wherever. The membership is somewhat fluid. A group can also have a more fixed membership if it consists of children who play together on a fairly regular basis.

Children's first play groups form under adult auspices in daycare centers and preschools or when they are brought together in homes by adult caregivers. Corsaro has observed a number of aspects of play groups of 3- to 5-

year-olds in preschools. One aspect is the *formation of temporary affiliations*. Two or three children may be playing together in a collaborative activity. Because they are focused on their joint activity, they do not want it to be disrupted by another child who may come by and want to join in. They have developed a sense of *sharing* and are thus likely to exclude the newcomer. These groups do not seem to have an enduring character. At another time of day, each child may be in a new group. Children interpret these experiences and develop a general interactional strategy. Corsaro notes,

> Through their experiences in preschool, children come to realize that inter-action with peers is fragile, and acceptance into ongoing activities is often difficult. Therefore, rather than limiting their social contacts to one or two playmates, the children most often develop stable relationships with sev-eral playmates as a way to maximize the probability of successful entry and satisfying peer interaction. (Corsaro 1997, 123–126)

Preschool children also develop ways of *resisting adult power and authority*. When a preschool prohibits bringing toys from home, children nonetheless bring them in a hidden way and show them to playmates. When children are supposed to clean up, they may develop *collaborative strategies* to delay or avoid putting toys and other materials away (Corsaro 1997, 42, 133). Corsaro empha-sizes the independence and creativity of children in constructing collaborative activities such as appropriating and reinterpreting aspects of adult culture and resisting adult authority. British sociologist Allison James presents a similar view in comments that cover an older age range of children. She extends the view by adding that "the true nature of the culture of childhood frequently re-mains hidden from adults because children have managed to disguise the ways in which they have appropriated adult language and artifacts.... Children cre-ate for themselves considerable room for movement within the limits imposed upon them by adult society" (James 1998, 394–395). She provides an extended discussion of ways in which children and adults have different ideas of what foods are good to eat, and she notes that children develop "verbal onslaughts ... against adults and their control of food" in school lunchrooms and elsewhere. She offers this example:

> *Old Mrs. Riley had a fat cow*
> *She milked it, she milked it*
> *She didn't know how.*
> *She pulled its tail instead of its tit.*
> *Poor Mrs. Riley covered in shit.*

> The implied sympathy contained in the last line of this rhyme is not genu-ine, for gales of laughter always accompany the relating of this event. (James 1998, 403)

The study from which this example is cited is included in an anthology that is devoted to exposing and calling into question what the editor calls "the myth of childhood innocence" (Jenkins 1998).

Collaboration in play requires the development of interpersonal skills. Those skills develop in interaction among peers, but there is some evidence that children's relationships with their parents also influence those skills. Studies show that children whose parents are warm and responsive to them are more accepted by their peers, whereas parents who are more demanding and directive and express more negative emotions have children who are less well accepted by peers. (Degree of acceptance implies level of interpersonal skill.) Parental activities such as instructing, advising, and coaching may also contribute to interpersonal skill. Evidence also indicates that when mothers "facilitate preschool-aged children's interactions with peers by giving assistance to 'help them play together' and by monitoring their play activities in a nonintrusive manner, children are rated as more socially competent" (O'Neil and Parke 2000, 202).

Among 5- and 6-year-olds, social competence with peers seems to involve a child's ability to understand emotions of others, and such understanding appears to begin in interaction with parents. Playful interaction with fathers is suggested as one basis, but the process is not fully understood. How parents deal with their children's emotional upsets also affects social competence. A child's *emotional regulatory ability* is shaped by his or her parents. One study, in a larger review, found that "fathers' acceptance and assistance with children's sadness and anger when children were 5 years old was related to children's social competence with peers at 8 years of age" (O'Neil and Parke 2000, 211).

Social psychologist Zick Rubin notes that children can provide certain resources for each other that are different from those adults provide. He identifies three functions of play groups for their participants: (1) *Learning social skills*, which include techniques for establishing and maintaining social interactions and relationships. He calls particular attention to the importance of communicating successfully, which involves "the ability to imagine oneself in the other person's role." He elaborates, "Relationships with peers can make unique contributions to the learning of many other social skills, including techniques of engaging others in activities, of tact, and of dealing with conflict. . . . [I]t is from their interactions with peers that they can best learn how to survive among equals in a wide range of social situations." (2) *Comparing oneself meaningfully to others.* An important process contributing to children's development of individual identity involves comparing oneself to others. Children engage each other in many kinds of comparisons throughout childhood. Early on, two children may stand back to back to see who is taller. One child may challenge another to see who can run faster from one point to another or jump higher. (3) *Gaining security through group belonging.* While a secure attachment to parents is important, belonging to a group of peers helps to develop self-awareness and knowledge of social reality in ways that the relationship to adults cannot (Rubin 1980, 4–6).

When children emerge from their families into their peer world, they emerge with a self-in-formation But emerging into the peer world does not mean leaving their families; relationships with parents continue. A study by Canadian researchers in Sudbury, Ontario, of elementary-school-age children's relationship with parents and with peers finds that "competent parenting is essential for competent friendship. . . . [A] child's relationships with parents and friends do not develop sequentially but in parallel. . . . Thus, while friendships are important, many of the defining functions of friendship (e.g., cooperativeness, helpfulness, intimacy, and trust) are not formed exclusively within this relationship but find their roots within the crucible of parenting" (Bigelow, Tesson, and Lewko 1996, 157–158). As their interaction with peers increases and continues over time, that self-in-formation will gain in complexity because it will be anchored in the peer group as well as in the family, and will also be shaped by interaction with teachers in preschool, kindergarten, and elementary grades. The freedom to be found in play groups makes possible development of aspects of the self that become known to peers but may or may not be hidden from adults. In any peer group, one or two children may emerge as leaders, as sources of ideas for how to play and as influential in getting others to follow.

The age composition of a group can shape the interactions. One of the Yorkville men who recounted his life history tells of his childhood peer group and reveals how it affected his self-concept:

> I grew up with fellows who were two or three years older than me, so if I was like nine, they were twelve, you know . . . and I think this helped me an awful lot growing up, because I didn't really have that babyish thing about me when I was small. I always hung out with fellows three or four years older than me. I was always the youngest one in the crowd. I believe it gave me the smarts—the experience, how to handle different situations, you know. (Handel 2003, 63, 35)

According to Patricia A. Adler and Peter Adler, a wife-husband team of sociologists, the spontaneous free play of children has in recent years been curtailed somewhat by a growing trend of adult organizing of children's after-school activities. Where once children gathered on their own to play in the schoolyard, the neighborhood, or someone's house, for many children the after-school hours are increasingly spent in programs organized by adults in YMCAs, recreation centers, community centers, or private associations. Drawing on others' work as well as their own, they suggest that this has occurred for two main reasons: (1) the increase in dual-career families, resulting in a need for nonparental supervision, combined with adults' goals for children's "edification"; and (2) growing concern about dangers to unsupervised children in public places. This situation has led to "a boom industry" of organized after-school activities, catering particularly, but not exclusively, to the middle class. However, let us point out here, as we noted in Chapter 4, that an estimated 3.5 million children in the United States are unsupervised and on their own after school and thus do not yet participate in the growing trend toward adult-organized activities for them. Of course, conversely, the trend likely affects many more children than those the Adlers studied in one city.

Over a six-year period, the Adler wife-husband team observed, interacted with, and interviewed elementary and junior high school students, mostly white and in public schools. They concluded that these children tend to proceed through a kind of after-school career, with something like a sequence of stages. In their earlier school years, their after-school play is mostly spontaneous and child organized, not yet under adult supervision. Many then go into recreational activities, such as those sponsored by YMCAs; by a private organization such as Kidsport Fun and Fitness Club, a business that offers programs for 8- to 12-year-olds; or school-organized programs such as Program for Afterschool Learning (PAL), for which parents must pay and which offer lessons in arts, crafts, and sports. The authors note, "Although universal participation is initially held as an ideal, this progressively diminishes as competition escalates" (Adler and Adler 1994, 316). Although the organizations have democratic philosophies, adults running the programs tend to push for competition and selection for excellence of performance as children get older, so that many children are progressively sidelined. The authors analyze this sequence as having significant socialization consequences. "[C]hildren learn several important norms and values about the nature of adult society. They discover the importance placed by adults on rules, regulations, and order. Creativity is encouraged, but acknowledged within the boundaries of certain well-defined parameters. Obedience, discipline, sacrifice, seriousness, and focused attention are valued; deviance, dabbling, and self-indulgence are not" (Adler and Adler 1994, 325). The authors conclude that these adult-organized activities represent a junior version of the adult world and that "play has become used as the vehicle for infusing adult work values into children's lives" (Adler and Adler 1994, 326).

Friendships

Peer groups provide settings in which children develop close relationships of their own choosing. Within the larger peer group, by the age of 8 or 9, and occasionally earlier, children often establish special friendships with someone of the same sex, a relationship that Harry Stack Sullivan famously called *chums* (Sullivan 1953, 245). These chum relationships are the first experience of peer intimacy and validate the child's sense of acceptability and worthwhileness. Each child friend reinforces the other's self-esteem by accepting without question the other's role identity. These friendships are opportunities to value someone else as well as to be valued. Such acceptance provides *affirmation* of each child's sense of self. However, a friendship is also subject to *conflict*, which raises doubts about whether the understandings the friends had are still workable. As two scholars note, "Conflicts . . . contribute to the construction of social relationships by illuminating the 'fit' between individuals, that is by demonstrating when the skills, interests, and goals of two individuals mesh and when they don't" (Hartup and Laursen 1993, 49).

The concept of friendship changes meaning from early childhood to later. In nursery school, children use the term *friend* to mean the child they are playing with at the moment, and sometimes the two of them use it to exclude a third child who wants to join in. Similarly, a child who wants to join two playing together may announce that he or she is a friend and therefore should be allowed to join (Corsaro 1985, 122–125, 163–164). Between the ages of 4 and 6, children begin to form the idea that friendship is a distinctive body of knowledge, and they begin to apply their idea in their interactions with playmates (Rizzo 1989, 117–118). (In other words, recalling our discussion in Chapter 4 of acquisition of a stock of knowledge of social objects, friendship is an early social object, part of that growing stock of social knowledge.) Children's idea of friendship comes from a variety of sources: parents, teachers, television characters, older children, and others, all of whom may give children advice on how to behave as a friend, what to do, and what not to do (Rizzo 1989, 114).

According to one scholar, in the early elementary school-age years, ages 6 to 8, *friend* still means partner in play but not just for the moment; rather, it means someone who plays with you with some regularity. A "best friend" is someone who plays with you regularly and shares things freely with you. Around ages 8 and 9, friendship comes to include the idea of helping when in need, including offering companionship when you are lonely. Around age 9, children begin to emphasize the idea of dependability, someone you can rely on, someone you can trust (Youniss 1980, 174–185). A more recent study of friendship among first-grade children in school finds that dependability—or loyalty—appears earlier than age 9; it is part of the concept of friendship as expressed in the interactions of 6-year-old children, although not an aspect they can put into words in an interview (Rizzo 1989, 117). Friendship is also expressed through such actions as helping a friend, sharing things, and showing approval of the friend's schoolwork or action or personal characteristic, suggesting that 6-year-olds operate with a more complex idea of friendship than scholars had previously thought (Rizzo 1989, 50 and *passim*). The author of this study also finds that disputes between friends—as distinguished from disputes between children who are not friends—are usually efforts by the children to have each other live up to the norms of their friendship (Rizzo 1989, 105).

Gary Fine finds from his study of boys in Little League baseball that friendship makes certain distinct contributions to preadolescent children's interactional competence. One is learning how to present oneself (one's self) to others. This activity has come to be referred to as *impression management* (Goffman 1959, 208–237). As children gain in self-awareness and self-control, they become more conscious of how they want others to regard them and more skilled in behaving in ways to attain their goal. It includes developing flexibility so as to be able to present oneself in accordance with the interests and concerns of one's different friends. Friendship relationships provide the opportunities to develop this social skill.

Friends provide each other with what Fine calls "a staging area," that is, a context for acting in ways that other people would find objectionable. The emotional bond allows a friend, for example, to engage in pranks without being criticized by his friend. Friends also support each other as they explore ways of expressing interest in sexuality and in attitudes toward school.

A third contribution is that in friendship, children learn to be sensitive to someone else. In interactional exchanges in which each is "tuned in" to the other, each further develops her or his social self. Each experiences an expansion of self-understanding and an increased knowledge of the complexities and nuances of relating to another person (Fine 1981).

Cliques

In addition to their study of increasing adult supervision of children's play, discussed above, Patricia A. Adler and Peter Adler also carried out over eight years an extensive study of the social life of about 300 middle-class and upper-middle-class preadolescent (third- to sixth-grade) children. A central aspect of their social life, which flowed from school to neighborhood to homes and other locations, was the existence of *cliques*. The authors offer this definition:

> Cliques are . . . friendship circles, whose members tend to identify each other as mutually connected. Yet they are more than that; cliques have a hierarchical structure, being dominated by leaders, and are exclusive in nature, so that not all individuals who desire membership are accepted. They function as bodies of power within grades, incorporating the most popular individuals, offering the most exciting social lives, and commanding the most interest and attention from classmates. (Adler and Adler 1998, 56).

The key to clique organization is popularity. In every grade, some children are more popular than others. The bases of popularity differ by gender. The most popular boys tend to be those who show outstanding athletic ability, who seem tough, and who show sophistication in social and interpersonal skills. Girls' popularity was based on their family's socioeconomic status and their parents' permissiveness. Those from the wealthier families, and whose parents didn't supervise them too closely, tended to be the most popular. Also, physical attractiveness, enhanced by expensive fashionable clothes, contributed to the likelihood of girls' popularity. Also important is precocity:

> Precocity refers to girls' early attainment of adult social characteristics, such as the ability to express themselves verbally, and understanding of the dynamics of intra- and inter-group relationships, skills at convincing others to see things their way and manipulating them into doing what they want, and an interest in more mature social concerns (such as makeup and boys). As with the boys, these social skills are only partly developmental; some girls just seem precocious from their first arrival in kindergarten. (Adler and Adler 1998, 51)

In each grade, the most popular girls and the most popular boys grouped together in separate gender-based cliques. Each clique generally had a leader, who was able to control the group and set norms for the other members to follow. Through various techniques, the group tried to maintain its exclusivity. Some children who wanted to be included (wannabes) tried to copy clique members in behavior, dress, and speech. Next in rank was what the authors call a middle group, and below them were social isolates who sometimes tried to participate in activities with classmates but were rejected and had no real friends. Among the top clique, the wannabes, and the middle group, there was some fluidity of membership as some children lost popularity and others moved up a notch or two (Adler and Adler 1998, 38–114).

Cliques and the peer culture in which they take shape are significant in children's socialization in several ways. First, "Through interacting with their peers, and by judging themselves against the standards and behavior of peer norms, people forge self-conceptions that lie at the core of their being" (Adler and Adler 1998, 207). Second, in their clique strivings, children learn about a structure of society that they will encounter as adults, the distinction between in-groups and out-groups, the socially favored and the less favored. Third, they learn about jockeying for power and status within the larger peer group and within a clique (Adler and Adler 1998, 211).

Bullying

Children can hurt other children. They sometimes do it one against one, and sometimes as a group against one. When one child is repeatedly harassed, taunted, and/or physically attacked by another child or a group of children, the perpetrators are engaged in bullying a victim. According to Norwegian psychologist Dan Olweus, a leading scholar of this form of peer interaction, his studies in Norway reveal that bullying begins as early as the second grade and declines year by year. In grades two through six, an average of 11.6 percent of children were bullied on the way to school or at school, compared to 5.4 percent in grades six through nine. Boys were more often victims than girls. Slightly more than 10 percent of boys and about 4 percent of girls in the elementary grades were identified as bullies. He reports comparable distributions for studies in Sweden and England. He comments that bully-victim problems in elementary school grades were more widespread and severe than had been assumed prior to these studies (Olweus 1993, 15–16). Bullying is about as frequent in rural areas as in big cities, although parents and teachers in cities are somewhat more aware of the problem (Olweus 1993, 23).

Typical victims are more anxious and insecure than children in general. Although they usually have good relationships with their parents—sometimes seen by teachers as overprotected by mothers—the victims see themselves as unattractive failures; they seldom have a single good friend in their class. A few have committed suicide. Bullies tend to be more aggressive not only toward other children but toward adults as well. Olweus considers bullying to be a component of a general antisocial, rule-breaking pattern. Follow-up studies indicate that those who are still engaged in bullying in grades six through nine are more likely than others to be convicted of serious crimes as young adults (Olweus 1993, 31–36). Olweus devotes the second half of his book to programs and procedures to diminish the extent of bullying.

Olweus is considered the "father" of bullying research (Smith, Pepler, and Rigby 2004, xvii). His work stimulated attention to bullying in many countries. Efforts to develop and evaluate intervention strategies, either using his approach or trying out alternatives, were recently reported in a series of chapters for Australia, Belgium, Canada, England, Finland, Germany, Ireland, Spain, Switzerland, and the United States (Smith, Pepler, and Rigby 2004). Each of the strategies in these several countries involves some combination of teacher training, modifying classroom and school climate, involvement of parents, peer courts, individual counseling of victims and/or bullies, and solicitation of broad community support for these and other anti-bullying activities. The intervention efforts require dealing with many complexities. With few exceptions, results across these countries in reducing bullying were modest (Pepler, Smith, and Rigby 2004, 322). Among the researchers, there are debates as to whether bullying results primarily from individual characteristics of bully and victim or from the interaction processes in peer groups. Another debate is whether to address bullying head-on or more indirectly through such procedures as increasing children's understanding of social relationships. Finally, researchers, who are convinced that evidence shows that bullying can have severe long-term negative effects on both the victim and the bully (Rigby, Smith, and Pepler 2004, 1), face some skeptics who "still hold to myths about bullying: 'It is just kids being kids', 'They will grow out of it', and 'It prepares you for life' (even though some bullying results in death through suicide)" (Pepler, Smith, and Rigby 2004, 321). Thus, despite recent cross-national attention to bullying, communities are divided or uncertain as to whether bullying is a problem that calls for adult intervention.

* * *

Peer groups are complex organizations that are essential to children's socialization. Children begin life in the care of adults and subject to adult direction and authority. Adult guidance and authority continue in family and school throughout childhood. But children inevitably enter a world of peers. The participants in that world sustain a culture of their own, influenced by but distinctive from adult culture. The values and norms of children's culture are often in conflict with those absorbed from adults, challenging every child to sort them out, both individually and jointly with peers and with adults. Children organize themselves in complex patterns of play, friendship, and cliques. Every child's self will be shaped by the ways she or he finds a place in that peer world.

References

Adler, Patricia A., and Peter Adler. 1994. "Social Reproduction and the Corporate Other: The Institutionalization of After-School Activities." *The Sociological Quarterly* 35(2): 309–328.

——. 1998. *Peer Power: Preadolescent Culture and Identity.* New Brunswick, NJ: Rutgers University Press.

Bigelow, Brian J., Geoffrey Tesson, and John H. Lewko. 1996. *Learning the Rules: The Anatomy of Children's Relationships.* New York: Guilford Press.

Corsaro, William A. 1985. *Friendship and Peer Culture in the Early Years.* Norwood, NJ: Ablex Publishing Corporation.

——. 1997. *The Sociology of Childhood.* Thousand Oaks, CA: Pine Forge Press.

Devereux, Edward. 1976. "Backyard Versus Little League Baseball: The Impoverishment of Children's Games." In Daniel M. Landers (ed.) *Social Problems in Athletics.* Urbana: University of Illinois Press.

Evaldsson, Ann-Carita, and William A. Corsaro. 1998. "Play and Games in the Peer Cultures of Preschool and Preadolescent Children: An Interpretive Approach." *Childhood* 5(4): 377–402.

Fine, Gary Alan. 1981. "Friends, Impression Management, and Preadolescent Behavior." In Steven R. Asher and John M. Gottman (eds.) *The Development of Children's Friendships*, 29–52. Cambridge, U.K.: Cambridge University Press.

———. 1987. *With the Boys: Little League Baseball and Preadolescent Culture*. Chicago: University of Chicago Press.

Goffman, Erving. 1959. *The Presentation of Self in Everyday Life*. Garden City, NY: Anchor Books.

Grasmuck, Sherri. 2005. *Protecting Home: Class, Race, and Masculinity in Boys' Baseball*. New Brunswick, NJ: Rutgers University Press.

Handel, Gerald. 1984. "A Children's New York: Boys at Play in Yorkville." In Vernon Boggs, Gerald Handel, and Sylvia F. Fava (eds.) *The Apple Sliced: Sociological Studies of New York City*, 33–49. New York: Praeger.

———. 2003. *Making a Life in Yorkville: Experience and Meaning in the Life-Course Narrative of an Urban Working-Class Man*. New York: Aldine de Gruyter.

Hartup, Willard W. 1979. "Peer Relations and the Growth of Social Competence." In Martha W. Kent and Jon E. Rolf (eds.) *Social Competence in Children, Primary Prevention of Psychopathology*, Vol. 3, 150–170. Hanover, NH: University Press of New England.

Hartup, Willard W., and Brett Laursen. 1993. "Conflict and Context in Peer Relations." In Craig H. Hart (ed.) *Children on Playgrounds*, 44–84. Albany: State University of New York Press.

James, Allison. 1998. "Confections, Concoctions, and Conceptions." In Henry Jenkins (ed.) *The Children's Culture Reader*, 394–405. New York: New York University Press.

Jenkins, Henry. 1998. "Introduction: Childhood Innocence and Other Modern Myths." In Henry Jenkins (ed.) *The Children's Culture Reader*, 1–37. New York: New York University Press.

Knapp, Mary, and Herbert Knapp. 1976. *One Potato, Two Potato*. New York: Norton.

Lareau, Annette. 2003. *Unequal Childhoods*. Berkeley: University of California Press.

Lever, Janet. 1972. "Soccer as a Brazilian Way of Life." In Gregory P. Stone (ed.) *Games, Sport, and Power*. New Brunswick, NJ: Transaction Books.

———. 1984. *Soccer Madness*. Chicago: University of Chicago Press.

Merton, Robert K. 1968. *Social Theory and Social Structure*, enlarged ed. New York: Free Press.

Olweus, Dan. 1993. *Bullying at School*. Oxford, UK: Blackwell.

O'Neil, Robin, and Ross D. Parke. 2000. "Family-Peer Relationships: The Role of Emotion Regulation, Cognitive Understanding, and Attentional Processes in Mediating Processes." In Kathryn A. Kerns, Josefina M. Contreras, and Angela M. Neal-Burnett (eds.) *Family and Peers: Linking Two Social Worlds*, 197–225. Westport, CT: Praeger.

Opie, Iona, and Peter Opie. 1959. *The Lore and Language of Schoolchildren*. Oxford: Oxford University Press.

———. 1969. *Children's Games in Street and Playground*. Oxford: Oxford University Press.

Pepler, Debra, Peter K. Smith, and Ken Rigby. 2004. "Looking Back and Looking Forward: Implications for Making Interventions Work Effectively." In Peter K. Smith, Debra Pepler, and Ken Rigby (eds.) *Bullying in Schools*, 307–324. Cambridge: Cambridge University Press.

Read, Katherine H. 1976. *The Nursery School*. Philadelphia: Saunders.

Rigby, Ken, Peter K. Smith, and Debra Pepler. 2004. "Working to Prevent School Bullying: Key Issues." In Peter K. Smith, Debra Pepler, and Ken Rigby (eds.) *Bullying in Schools*, 1–12. Cambridge: Cambridge University Press.

Rizzo, Thomas A. 1989. *Friendship Development Among Children in School*. Norwood, NJ: Ablex Publishing Corporation.

Rubin, Zick. 1980. *Children's Friendships*. Cambridge, MA: Harvard University Press.

Smith, Peter K., Pepler, Debra, and Rigby, Ken, eds. 2004. *Bullying in Schools*. Cambridge: Cambridge University Press.

Sullivan, Harry Stack. 1953. *The Interpersonal Theory of Psychiatry*. New York: W. W. Norton.

Thorne, Barrie. 1993. *Gender Play*. New Brunswick, NJ: Rutgers University Press.

Thurman, Judith. 2002. "Doing It in the Road." *The New Yorker*, June 10, 2002.

Webb, Harry. 1969. "Professionalization of Attitudes Toward Play Among Adolescents." In Gerald S. Kenyon (ed.) *Aspects of Contemporary Sport Sociology*, 120–131. Chicago: The Athletic Institute.

Youniss, James. 1980. *Parents and Peers in Social Development*. Chicago: University of Chicago Press. ✦

Chapter 8

Media of Mass Communication

Society is based on *communication*, defined simply by a team of communication scholars as "how people arrive at shared meanings through the interchange of messages" (Rubin, Rubin, and Piele 1996, 6). Another scholar adds an important elaboration—the concept of *interpretation*. He writes, "Communication involves the interpretation, ordering, exchanging, and sharing of meaning" (Altheide 1995, 57). The exchange of meaningful messages occurs at all levels of social organization. Two friends arranging to meet for lunch, a parent and child talking about school, a shopper buying shoes from a salesperson, a professor teaching a class, a political candidate speaking to an audience of cheering supporters, a government committee discussing proposed laws and regulations—these are but a few illustrations of the wide scope of communication. Virtually everything we do is based on communication.

The most elementary form of communication is a conversation between two people, a unit sociologists call a *dyad*. Communication in dyads, small groups, and large public gatherings has two features common to them: (1) The communicators are in each other's presence, and (2) the media of communication are the human voice, which carries spoken language, and the human body, which utilizes "body language," that is, gestures, posture, and facial expressions whose meanings can be interpreted. For most of the time that humans have been on earth, co-presence has been a requirement in all but a very few kinds of communication situations (such as leaving markings on a trail). The invention of writing introduced new media—clay tablets, papyrus, paper—and made it possible to communicate with people who were not present, but since the only way to make multiple copies of a written text was one at a time by hand, the numbers who could be reached in this way remained fairly small.

The invention of media of mass communication—*mass media*, for short—changed the nature of communication and of society because co-presence was no longer a restrictive condition. The media of mass communication are those media that use an impersonal medium to communicate with large numbers of people who are not in each others' presence or in the presence of the primary communicator. And, indeed, the mass media make it necessary to modify the concept of communication offered above. Because there is little exchange or interchange of messages, communication through a mass medium involves a communicator who sends messages to a very large dispersed audience (masses of people) whose members receive and interpret the messages but generally do not send messages back to the initial communicator.

The invention of the printing press in the fifteenth century made possible the first mass media, print media—books, newspapers, magazines, and, later, comic books. The twentieth century saw the invention of several new kinds of media, beginning in the early 1900s with the moving picture or movie. Then came electrical and electronic media—radio in the 1920s, television in the 1930s (but not introduced into the marketplace until the late 1940s because the requirements of fighting World War II made materials and production facilities unavailable), and the Internet starting in the 1970s but not commercially available until the 1990s. Broadcast television was later supplemented by cable and satellite means of transmission. Other additions were the invention of the video cassette recorder (VCR), which makes it possible to record a TV program on magnetic tape for later viewing, and digital video disc (DVD), both of which allow for recording and distributing movies and television to a mass audience. Also included in the mass media are the means of recording and distributing music to a dispersed audience, the compact disc (CD) being one recent form. The computer, originally an instrument for doing office work (word processing and mathematical calculations), became a mass medium with the development of the Internet.

Since the nineteenth century, some adults have been concerned that the mass media have harmful effects on children. In the 1880s Anthony Comstock, a very prominent and influential crusader against taverns, prostitution, and anything else that he considered vice, wrote a book entitled *Traps for the Young* (Comstock [1883] 1967) which he offered as a comprehensive survey of "Satan's schemes for victimizing children." Two chapters were devoted to "Household Traps." Among the most sinister of these, in his judgment, was the daily newspaper. An example of how the newspapers do their dirty work of corrupting the young is provided in this account:

> These publications are mighty educators, either for good or evil. Sold at a cheap price, from one to five cents each, they are within the reach of all classes. More: they enter the homes—often files of them are preserved— and are especially within the reach of the children, to be read and reread by them. The father looks over his paper in the morning to ascertain the state of the market, to inform himself as to the news of the day. His attention is attracted by the heavy headlines designed to call attention to some disgusting detail of crime. A glance discloses its true character. He turns away in disgust, and thoughtlessly throws down in his library or parlor, within reach of his children, this hateful debauching article, and goes off to business little thinking that what he thus turns from his child will read with avidity. (Comstock [1883] 1967, 13)

Comstock does not tell us whether the home newspaper files were kept by the father in spite of his disgust or whether they were preserved by children who scavenged debauching articles in the parlor after they had been thrown down by the father.

Because electronic media have become so important in contemporary society, concern over the harmful effects of print media has markedly diminished, although it has not entirely disappeared. Children begin watching television long before they can read, and, after they do learn to read, they don't often go to newspapers. Not many commentators today still consider newspapers to be a debaucher of children (and some school curricula include newspapers). Commentators' lack of concern is understandable: Studies of media activities of national samples of American children between the ages of 2 and 18 found that less than 15 percent of children under 10 even glance at a newspaper on any given day (Roberts and Foehr 2004, 99).

In the 1940s and 1950s psychiatrist Fredric Wertham assigned a debauching role to comic books in his book *Seduction of the Innocent* (Wertham 1953). Although Wertham's claim that reading comic books causes juvenile delinquency made him a prominent and popular "expert," historian William W. Savage, Jr. characterizes Wertham's book as "pompous, polemical, biased, and poorly documented" (Savage 1990, 96). Comic books have lost some appeal to children as television viewing and video games have gained, and now adults have little concern about them.

However, from time to time, here and there, a school board or a group of parents presses to have certain books removed from school libraries or public libraries because of a belief that the book will damage children. Sometimes the book is a children's classic, read by children for many decades but reinterpreted today as harmful by these adults. Recently, stories that involve witches or magic are sometimes the target of these efforts because the adults believe, as Anthony Comstock did, that Satan is a genuinely evil force that exists and that witches and magic are tools he uses to corrupt children. Thus, a classic such as *Hansel and Gretel*, in which a boy and girl are captured by a witch before they destroy her, is sometimes a target, as are more recent works such as a series of stories about a boy named Harry Potter who studies witchcraft and has magical powers. On January 1, 2002, the *New York Times* published a picture of a crowd of people watching a bonfire; the caption read, "Christ Community Church in Alamogordo, NM, burned *Harry Potter* books, along with works by Shakespeare, after the Rev. Jack Brock called them 'satanic deception.' At the Vatican, the Roman Catholic Church's most famous exorcist said the Devil was behind young Potter" ("Burning Books" 2002). Another target is books that deal with sexuality, including some that present a family with two gay men or two lesbian women as parents.

Efforts to make such books inaccessible to children occur from time to time, but they do not constitute a large-scale movement, nor do they appear to represent a widespread concern. Rather, most concern has shifted to the nonprint media. For example, in a book entitled *Raising PG Kids in an X-Rated Society*, Tipper Gore (1987), a psychologist and the wife of then senator (and later vice president and presidential candidate) Al Gore, expressed concern over the explicitly sexual lyrics and increasingly dramatic violence communicated in rock-and-roll music via MTV—music television presented by cable—and in phonograph records and albums and CDs. During the presidential campaign of 2000, the Democratic vice presidential candidate, Senator Joseph

Lieberman, stated that if Gore and he were elected, they would exert pressure on the movie, television, and music recording industries to reduce the level of violence in pictures and lyrics.

Although some adults have not only great concerns but also strong beliefs about how and how much television, movies, and CDs influence children, it is not easy to arrive at clear evidence that those concerns and beliefs are well founded. While there are some studies these days on how movies or CDs influence children, over several decades the most research and theorizing have been done on how television does or does not influence children. Television is the medium that has generated the most sustained concern among the public and has attracted the most attention from researchers who have worked hard to try to understand how television affects viewers, including children. For these reasons, we will focus on television in the remainder of this section. Our discussion will try to clarify why the impact of television remains somewhat uncertain despite the great amount of research activity.

The accumulated literature on how television does or does not affect children deals primarily with three main topics, all of which need to be considered: (1) What aspects of television have consequences for children? Stated another way, what are the issues? (2) What research methods produce the information we need to understand the relationship between children and television? And (3) How do children relate to television? What theories explain the relationship?

The Major Issues

The issues that have generated the greatest scholarly effort as well as public concern over several decades are, first, the possible consequences of the sheer activity of watching, and second, the consequences of the content, that is, what is actually shown and heard on the screen.

Viewing as an Activity

Children begin watching TV at a very young age. One recent study, based on telephone interviews with 1,065 parents of children age 6 months to 6 years, reported in the *New York Times*, states that babies as young as 6 months of age are watching television, videos, and DVDs. "On a typical day, the study found, 59 percent of children 6 months to 2 years watch television, and 42 percent watch a videotape or a DVD" (Lewin 2003, 1). A Dutch scholar and her American coauthor citing a Dutch study and an American one claim that children between 4 and 5 months of age "start to develop an interest in television programs" and that observational studies show that the infants like programs with brightly colored fantasy figures such as *Sesame Street* and *Teletubbies*, as well as commercials (Valkenburg and Cantor 2002, 203). According to Professor Aimee Dorr, whose specialties include both communication and education, estimates from several studies suggest that by age 3 or 4 some children may be watching anywhere from 21 to 35 hours a week. She dramatizes the amount of time devoted to watching by stating, "At age 65, average American citizens may have given nine full years of their lives to watching television!"

(Dorr 1986, 102–104). This estimate was made before it was known that babies began watching, and it may be greater now.

When children are watching, there are many other things that they might be doing but are not doing. They may not be building with blocks. They may not be looking at picture books. They certainly are not playing outdoors. School-age children who come home from school and turn on the set also are not playing outside with peers, are not reading books for enjoyment, and are not developing a hobby. In short, the activity of watching may, and in some cases does, displace other possible activities that many scholars of childhood believe would contribute more to the development of personal interests, knowledge, and social and intellectual skills.

How might one study the influence of television viewing on children? One way would be to find a community without television but into which it is to be introduced and study the children in the community before and after. Presumably—assuming there are no intruding influences—any changes would be the result of watching TV. A group of psychologists in British Columbia, Canada—Tannis MacBeth Williams and colleagues—were able to do just that (Williams 1986). They discovered a town that, in 1973, because of its geographical setting, was as yet without television reception but was about to receive it. They called the town *Notel*. Nearby they found two comparable communities; one received only one TV channel—they called it *Unitel*—and one received Canadian and U.S. networks; they called this town *Multitel*. The latter two were to be "control" communities to allow the researchers to take intruding factors into consideration. Only if changes occurred in Notel and not in Unitel and Multitel could they then be said to be due to the effect of TV. They called their research "a natural experiment."

The researchers studied all three towns through observation and through giving various questionnaires and tests to children and adults before TV was introduced to Notel and again two years later. Regarding use of television, their findings were similar to other studies. Children watch three to four hours a day. The authors note the difficulty, however, of getting meaningful precise data, especially for very young children. There is a great difference between "time in the room with the set on" and paying attention to a program. Neither reports by the children themselves nor ones by their parents are very reliable. Children may pop in and out of the TV room, and while watching, may in fact do other things—draw, play games, read comics, do homework, and converse with others.

Williams and her colleagues asked first of all what activities were replaced when the children spent so many hours a week watching TV. The data are limited, but the authors do report that following the introduction of television in Notel, children participated less in sports and in community activities. For children age 12 and under, the mean sports participation score (based on the number and frequency of participation in sports activities) before TV was introduced was 13.45; after TV was available, it was down to 9.62. For Multitel during the same period, the sports participation score actually went up from 5.10 to 7.57. For total community activity, the participation score went down in

Notel from 64.03 to 41.38. This drop was twice as large as for Multitel during the same period.

Television watching has been widely criticized for its detrimental effects on education. The British Columbia researchers addressed this issue by asking: Does watching TV have a positive or negative effect on reading skills and creative thinking? In both cases, in this study, the results were not favorable to television. For reading, the authors explain the lower ability-to-read scores after the introduction of television by the concept of *displacement*. Learning to read, they say, requires practice, but once TV is available, the children spend so much of their time watching television programs that they practice reading less, and thus the reading ability scores go down. Reading has been displaced by television.

Likewise the creative thinking of the children fared worse after the introduction of television. Using a psychological test called the alternative uses task, in which children are asked to think of all the ways particular objects such as a knife, shoe, button, or key can be used, they found that Notel children before they had access to television scored higher than comparable Unitel and Multitel children but, two years later, when they all had television, their scores were essentially the same. The researchers suggest the explanation that television provides children with ready-made ideas and encourages them to be mentally passive. Also, the time spent with television displaces other activities and experiences that require more mental activity and would improve problem-solving ability. However, communication researchers George Comstock (not to be confused with Anthony Comstock!) and Erica Scharrer in a review and technical analysis of this study conclude that "the evidence does not support the hypothesis that viewing diminishes creative capability" (Comstock and Scharrer 1999, 243).

Comstock and Scharrer also examined a number of studies relating television watching to school performance. One issue is whether watching increases children's vocabulary. The studies they cite show contradictory results, and their conclusion indicates the complexity of what seems to be a simple research question:

> First, television viewing does not contribute to general vocabulary except possibly for the viewing of educational programs. Children's entertainment, such as animated cartoons, has no benefit. Second, children of greater mental ability who would have a better command of language are more likely to choose programs with a higher quality of language, so that although educational programming may teach vocabulary, any positive association between viewing and vocabulary is surely partly and possibly wholly explained by the programs chosen by those of superior skill. Third, any effects of overall viewing are limited to jargon, brands, and entertainment figures (and such specialized vocabulary eludes the scope of tests of general vocabulary). Fourth, the absence of observable effects is attributable to the ubiquity of television, which leads to the diffusion of what television presents through social interaction. . . . Television almost certainly has increased the vocabularies of young people, both general and media-specific. However, it is no longer necessary to view television to gain the bene-

fits because these words and phrases will be passed on by people. (Comstock and Scharrer 1999, 229–230)

A few particular studies of the educational program *Sesame Street*, in contrast to Comstock and Scharrer's last sentence, affirm its definite contributions to the educational development of preschool children. One study in the 1980s showed, "Children who viewed *Sesame Street* often between ages 3 and 5 showed more improvement in vocabulary than did infrequent viewers" (Huston and Wright 1996, 54). A study in the 1990s "contained measures of school readiness, letter and number skills, and vocabulary. When performance on these measures at age 5 was analyzed in relation to viewing between ages 2 and 4, *Sesame Street* viewers had higher scores than children who rarely or never viewed" (Huston and Wright 1996, 54).

Comstock and Scharrer also looked at studies that deal with behaviors that can interfere with school performance—such as hyperactivity, reduced perseverance and attention span, and lowered impulse control. They report that, for preschool-age children, "The viewing of educational programming such as *Sesame Street* and *Mr. Rogers' Neighborhood* was consistently associated with more favorable scores on such measures. . . . Content did matter, with violence associated with less favorable scores" (Comstock and Scharrer 1999, 237). Studies of school-age children between the ages of 5 and 9 show pretty much the same results. Viewing educational programming has favorable effects, while violence appears to be a key element in adverse effects (Comstock and Scharrer 1999, 237).

They then looked at studies that examine relationships between amount of viewing and scholastic work and achievement. They conclude that children in the early grades who watch a great deal of television (they are known as *heavy viewers*) displace acquisition of basic skills of reading, writing, and arithmetic. The children don't like to invest mental effort and concentration on reading and can become hostile to book reading, finding it dull and boring. The authors go on to say, "Television promotes a particular way of storytelling. It socializes young viewers to prefer undemanding content. Young viewers come to express the values of television in their use of other media. Viewing not only interferes with and displaces scholastic endeavors but also shapes the motives and directs the preferences of the young toward the trivial and the banal" (Comstock and Scharrer 1999, 245–262).

While this line of argument seems clear in ascribing definite causal influence to television, it becomes less clear when we consider another part of Comstock and Scharrer's analysis. Which children are the heavy viewers? They identify five factors that influence heavy viewing:

1. Lower mental ability (an individual trait).
2. Conflicts with parents or peers (interpersonal relationships).
3. Lower socioeconomic status (a social attribute).
4. High household centrality of television (a household norm).

5. The perception that there is no other activity more necessary or rewarding (a personal value).

After presenting this list, they write, "Our conclusion is that a substantial portion of the negative association between amount of viewing and scholastic performance is attributable to self-selection, with those who for a variety of reasons would perform at a lower level watching greater amounts of television" (Comstock and Scharrer 1999, 260).

Readers may recognize that Comstock and Scharrer have, in effect, presented us with a scholarly version of that old conundrum, "Which comes first, the chicken or the egg?" Does heavy viewing of television cause poor school performance, or do children whose personal and social characteristics lead to poor school performance become heavy viewers? There is evidence that the answer to both parts of the question is "Yes." But what could be done? If violent program content is the main culprit, would limiting violent content reduce heavy viewing and then lead to better school performance? Or would it lead to reduced viewing and something other than improved school performance, perhaps more truancy and hanging out at the mall or on the street? If the problem is not television but the personal and social characteristics that lead both to poor school performance and heavy viewing, who is to intervene and how? Could there be school programs that make school more interesting than television, breaking into the cycle and stimulating greater interest in school despite the disadvantageous characteristics these children bring? Perhaps adults don't have sufficient creativity to tackle this problem. Perhaps they don't have enough incentive to try. Perhaps the social structure does not provide the incentive.

Violent Program Content and Children's Aggression

Perhaps second only to the time-absorbing nature of television watching has been the issue of violent program content and its possible effect on children's behavior. The preceding discussion has already indicated that heavy viewing of violent program content is at the very least associated with poor school performance; according to some analyses, it is a contributing cause. But another major concern has been the question of whether heavy viewing of violent content causes or contributes to anti-social behavior. Does watching violent programs make children behave more aggressively? Does it stimulate them to criminal behavior? Public discussion, research, and theorizing on this issue have been going on for more than 50 years. Between 1952 and 1996, the Congress of the United States held 28 hearings on television violence (Comstock and Scharrer 1999, 265–266). This averages out to a hearing almost every 18 months. Between 1963 and 1990 there were, according to one count, 217 separate research studies on the question of the relationship between television violence and anti-social behavior, although some of these deal with adults, not children (Comstock and Scharrer 1999, 274). During the 1990s, there were reports on this issue from three prestigious organizations, the Center for Disease Control, the National Academy of Sciences, and the American

Psychological Association; all concluded that the mass media contribute to aggressive attitudes and behavior (Gunter and McAleer 1997, 93).

The earliest studies of the relationship between television violence and children's behavior were laboratory experiments in the 1960s. As we discussed in Chapter 1, laboratory experiments in social science have both advantages and drawbacks. There is no kind of study that is "perfect." Nevertheless, the Canadian study by Williams and her colleagues (Williams 1986) looms large in importance because it was "a natural experiment," carried out not in a laboratory but in the real world. They sought to study this question of aggression by observing children's behavior during free play and by obtaining teacher and peer ratings of aggression for both Notel and the control communities before and after television was introduced into Notel. The authors acknowledge certain limitations in carrying out their research—especially the small number of children observed and the fact that the same children could not be studied directly two years later—but their results, they say, were clear and significant. The aggressive behavior of children in Notel increased significantly following the introduction of TV. The children produced many more physical acts of aggression and verbal aggressive remarks two years after getting TV than they had before, while for the control communities the changes in physical and verbal aggression were slight. The authors who conducted this part of the research conclude,

> ... [T]here was a significant increase in the aggressive behavior of Notel children following the inception of television in the community. The increase occurred for both physical and verbal aggressive behavior; it occurred for both boys and girls; it occurred at more than one age level; it occurred for children who were initially low in aggressive behavior as well as those who were initially high in aggressive behavior; and it occurred for the same children studied longitudinally and same-age children compared cross-sectionally. (Joy, Kimball, and Zabrack 1986, 334)

The study by Williams and her colleagues is unique. No other such "natural experiment" has been reported. The conclusions of that study, which was done in the 1970s, have stood up well. In 2001, the leading author, now writing under the name Tannis M. MacBeth, writes, "Our research findings have been carefully reviewed and widely cited. Almost all of these responses have been positive and have concurred with our interpretations. More recent research has tended to support rather than contradict our findings and conclusions" (MacBeth 2001, 196–213). Other studies addressed to the issue of how viewing television violence affects aggressive behavior have had to rely on other methods. We draw on summary overviews of a variety of work to present a few illustrations.

As previously mentioned, the earliest studies in the 1960s were laboratory experiments with nursery-school children. Some children were shown a short film in which an adult character repeatedly hits a large, inflatable plastic doll, commonly called a Bobo doll, that rebounds to an upright position after being hit. The children were then put in a playroom with many toys, including a

Bobo doll. Other children who hadn't seen the film were also put in the play-room. Those who had seen the film acted more aggressively toward the Bobo doll than those who had not seen the film (Dorr 1986, 72–73; Gunter and McAleer 1997, 107; Comstock and Scharrer 1999, 274). However, one reviewer of this experiment argues that an experimenter who shows a violent film to children may be communicating to them that the experimenter does not mind violence. Hence, it is incorrect for researchers to interpret the children's aggression simply as a response to the film, without taking into account the social situation that the experimenter has created and in which the children act (Felson 1996, 105–106).

In the 1970s and 1980s another type of study, known as a *panel study*, was introduced. Dorr provides an explanation of this type of study:

> In panel studies, the television viewing patterns and aggressive behavior of the same group of children (a panel) are measured at two or more points in time. The question, then, is whether variations in children's aggressive behaviors are related to variations in their viewing of aggressive programs. The answer comes from two types of analyses. In one, the relationship between viewing and behavior data from the same point in time is examined to determine if children who watch more aggressive television are also more aggressive. These are termed *concurrent effects*. In the other type of analysis, behavior at one point in time is related to viewing at another earlier point in time to determine if children who watch more aggressive television then become more aggressive. These are termed *lagged effects*. (Dorr 1986, 75; italics added)

One panel study began with 875 third-grade boys and girls and managed to contact 427 of them 10 years later at age 19. The amount of violent television programs each watched was determined by asking for their three or four favorite programs; the researchers then scored these programs for violent content. To arrive at a score for aggressive behavior, the children were asked questions such as "Who is always getting into trouble?" and "Who says mean things?" Children were then assigned a score depending on how often they were named in answer to such questions. The results of the study were mixed. For girls, the study found neither concurrent effects nor lagged effects at both the earlier and later ages, that is, no connection between amount of violent programs viewed and aggressive behavior. For boys, there was a concurrent effect in the third grade but not at age 19. That is, viewing and aggressive behavior are related at age 8 or 9 but not at age 19. That is, there is a concurrent effect at the early age but not at the later. But the viewing of violent content in the third grade was related to aggressiveness at age 19—a lagged effect. It is this kind of lagged effect that critics of TV violence are most concerned about (Dorr 1986, 76).

Mixed results are not uncommon in studies of this issue. So also are disagreements about what particular studies show. For example, Comstock and Scharer disagree with Dorr in interpreting the results of the panel study just described. They believe the study shows that males and females are affected equally by the programs (Comstock and Scharrer 1999, 294). Yet, when all is said and done, if viewing television violence makes some difference in amount of aggressive behavior, how much difference does it make? In the language of research, What is the size of the effect? Based on their review of many different studies, Comstock and Scharrer state,

> Our conclusion is that the size of effect for the most measured and most common type of antisocial behavior, interpersonal aggression, is modest but far from minute—between 4 and 10 percent of the variation in scores. We estimate ... that the effect size for the most serious acts is smaller than for interpersonal aggression. . . . Our [overall] conclusion, then, is that size of the effect is moderate to small in magnitude but socially substantial. (Comstock and Scharrer 1999, 298)

Curiously, although they devote considerable effort to evaluating measurements of effects, they do not explain what they mean by "socially substantial." A claim that a moderate or small effect is socially substantial calls for some explanation, but they do not provide one.

The Power of Advertising

Despite the existence of a small number of so-called public television stations that are supported by a modest amount of federal government funds and donations from viewers, foundations, and some corporations (Comstock and Paik 1991, 309–310), television in the United States is primarily a business that obtains its money from the sale of advertising time. Advertising agencies prepare commercial messages ("commercials") on behalf of their clients and buy from a TV network or station the right to show a commercial at a particular time period when a particular program is showing. The great majority of programs are preceded, interrupted by, and finished off with commercials. According to one estimate in late 1979, 2–11-year-old light viewers of television saw about 5,000 commercials a year, and heavy viewers 33,000, with the average child seeing 20,000. A decade later, the average was estimated at 40,000, primarily due to a shift from 60-second to 30-second and shorter commercials (Comstock and Paik 1991, 188). A decade after that, the estimate remains 40,000 (Kunkel 2001, 375–394). One of the earliest studies of how television was becoming integrated into American culture reported that children's "involvement with commercials is as deep and intense as it is with programs" (Glick and Levy 1962, 206). Young children enjoy commercials, especially if they are funny (Signorielli 1990, 102).

One issue that sometimes arises is whether children actually watch the commercials. The invention of the remote control device has made possible both zipping and zapping. *Zipping* occurs when a viewer, watching a program recorded on a VCR, fast-forwards through the commercial. *Zapping*, on the other hand, occurs when a viewer changes channels when the commercials appear or eliminates the commercials, manually or using a special device, when the program is taped for later viewing. There is not much information on how much zipping or zapping children do. Indirect evidence that children do watch commercials comes from research indicating that they ask their parents for products widely advertised on children's programs such as toys, cereals, candy and snacks, and fast-food restaurants (Signorielli 1990, 102). Children ask their parents for these products, and they learn about them from TV commercials.

The great number of commercials that children see has led some adults to be concerned, even anxious, about the power of all this advertising to shape the minds of children. Between 1968 and 1992 an organization called Action for Children's Television (ACT) fought against what it considered the over-commercialization of children's television by mobilizing parental pressure on television producers and on various government agencies (Seiter 1993, 97–98). Television networks and stations, as well as advertisers and advertising agencies, resisted these efforts. But even after ACT disbanded, its concerns remain alive.

Comstock and Paik identify five "points of contention" regarding commercials on children's television programs:

1a. Because very young viewers can't distinguish commercials from programs, and because they do not understand that a commercial is trying to sell them something, advertisers are acting unfairly and deceptively toward children.

1b. The response to this criticism is that even very young children can tell the difference between commercial and program, even though they cannot define what advertising is. Also, the message can't hurt children because they can't buy anything; they have to get their parents to spend the money.

2a. Children can be harmed by feeling deprived if they can't have an advertised product. They can also be harmed by feeling angry or frustrated if some toy that they get does not perform as the commercial promised. Sugared foods, highly advertised, can harm them.

2b. The response is that parents decide on foods and that putting a product in the best light is in the nature of advertising.

3a. Because parents may disapprove of a product the child requests, the commercials can stimulate child-parent conflict or lead to a parent giving in to the child just to avoid the conflict.

3b. The response has been twofold: The conflict isn't serious, and requests can be used as teaching situations.

4a. Relying on advertising to support programming makes for poor quality programming because the goal is to get the largest audience possible, not to provide the best educational content. Therefore, in order to hold attention, such techniques as animation, swift scene changes, loud music, and violence are used; these do not contribute to children's intellectual and emotional development.

4b. The answer has been that programming for children is popular; they are getting what they want.

5a. Many programs feature particular toys, and this turns the program itself into a commercial.

5b. The counterarguments are that the practice of marketing toys in con-
junction with television characters and personalities has a long history
going back to Mickey Mouse and Donald Duck, and the programs don't
have persuasive messages to stimulate purchase. (Comstock and Paik
1991, 191–194)

Comstock and Paik (1991, 194–225) then undertake to examine studies that
bear on the first three of these points of contention to see which way the evidence
falls. From their detailed examination we select what seem to us the highlights
and present them in the same order as the points of contention.

1. Very young children can tell the difference between commercials and
   programs from the stylistic differences between the two types of content, but they don't have any understanding of what the differences
   mean. That is, they do not understand that commercials are trying to sell
   them something. By around the age of 8, children do understand that
   commercials are trying to sell them something. The authors then note
   that since young children don't understand what advertising is for, the
   advertising that they see can be considered deceptive.

2. On the issue of self-esteem, they can cite only one study. In that study the
   researcher showed one group of children a commercial in which a child
   builds a tall, complex tower with blocks, and another group of children a
   commercial in which the tower was more modest. When both groups of
   children were then given blocks to play with, those who saw the bigger
   tower showed more anger and frustration. The authors believe this illustrates their contention that commercials can lower self-esteem when
   they portray accomplishments that the viewer cannot achieve.

3. Their conclusions on the third area of contention are that only a rough
   estimate can be made of the frequency of children's purchase requests.
   Further, the degree of conflict and disappointment that occurs when requests are denied also is difficult to gauge precisely (Comstock and Paik
   1991, 215, 217).

The reach of advertising to children has lengthened with the development
of what are called *program-length commercials*. In these productions, the distinction between commercial and program is almost obliterated because the program incorporates toys or characters that are also the products being sold in the
commercials. The entire production amounts to a sales pitch. An example is a
syndicated program called *G. I. Joe*, which one study showed was seen in 110
markets and could be seen in 87 percent of American homes (Comstock and Paik
1991, 230–232). (A television market is a geographical area in which the homes
can receive the signal from a particular TV station.)

Much of the criticism of TV advertising to children as well as at least some
of the research on the topic have been based on an implicit assumption that advertising is bad. More specifically, the assumption is that advertising manipu-
lates children to want things they don't need or shouldn't have, and it
influences them to be materialistic. After reviewing several studies of this

kind, Signiorielli adds, "Exposure to commercials can also have a number of unintended consequences, such as increased parent-child conflict, increased unhappiness, and increased materialism" (Signiorielli 1990, 110). This approach is countered by two different kinds of approach. One is that advertising is not as influential as sometimes supposed. Advertising can be mediated by how parents and children talk to each other; parents can and often do refuse to buy a requested product that they consider unsuitable. There are also other sources of information than the ads—for example, the opinions of peers. Gunter and McAleer note that even if a child tries a product once, it will not be bought again if it does not prove satisfactory. They also note that there are many heavily advertised products that fail to catch on (Gunter and McAleer 1997, 148).

The other counter approach is sharply different. It steps back from the ads and looks at the wider culture of which advertising is a part. A clear example is provided by Ellen Seiter, a professor of telecommunications. She writes that it is a middle-class delusion, one propagated by some "child experts," to believe that children can be shielded from consumption. Their interest in television and toys will remain strong, despite what parents do. She is critical of scholars—mostly men—who blame women and children for interest in consumer goods and shopping, while they are oblivious to their own consumption tastes and activities. Everybody in a modern society, she argues, depends on commodity consumption—clothing, furniture, music, toys, and all the rest—not only for survival but also for *participation in society, for inclusion.* Although consumers don't control what is available for them to choose from, in choosing what to buy they do exercise some creativity and express their taste. The things people choose to buy have social meanings by which they are linked to others. Further, "The deliberate, chosen meanings in most people's lives come more often from what they consume than from what they produce" (Seiter 1993, 3–4).

In her subsequent development of her argument, Seiter makes a number of interconnected points. First, our modern society is a consumer society in which buying and selling are basic features. Second, advertising is an integral part of a consumer society, a society in which what we consume is part of our identity. Third, our relationships to other people are partly based on our consumption patterns. Fourth, children's television and children's toys are largely manifestations—often exaggerated manifestations—of adult culture. Fifth, while the growth of the toy industry in the second half of the twentieth century is partly due to advertising directed to children, it is also due to the fact that mothers have become so busy that they needed new ways to keep children entertained.

While regarding television, advertising, toys and other consumer products as necessary aspects of contemporary social reality, Seiter (1993, 7–8) makes a further interesting point, namely, that they contribute importantly to children's ability to form social relationships. She asserts that most children are away from home before they begin school, either at a babysitter's or in a daycare center or preschool, away from parents and with children their own age. In these settings—on such occasions as sitting together at a snack table or a show-and-tell session—they admire each other's T-shirts and lunch boxes that feature TV and film characters. They talk eagerly about the popular toys that they have—Barbie dolls, Ninja Turtles, Batman, and other admired favorites. Most children, she says, know the same commercials, television programs, movies, and music.

These consumer products become a resource for developing interactional skills and relationships, for forming social ties to others.

> Consumer culture provides children with a shared repository of images, characters, plots, and themes; it provides the basis for small talk and play, and it does this on a national, even global scale. Outside the house, children can bank on finding that nearly every other child they meet will know some of the same things—and probably *have* many of the same things—that they do. Thus very young children are now sufficiently immersed in consumer culture to be able to strike up a conversation with one another about a character imprinted on a T-shirt or a toy in hand.... Mass market commodities are woven into the social fabric of children's lives; they are seen on sleepovers, at show-and-tell in school, on the block or in the apartment building, on the T-shirt. (Seiter 1993, 7–8)

Finally,

> Young children have good reasons for liking television and wanting toys, and mothers have good reasons for providing them. Children's interest in consumer culture involves much more than greed, hedonism, or passivity; it involves the desire for community and for a utopian freedom from adult authority, seriousness, and goal directedness. As a mass culture, toys and television give children a medium of communication.... (Seiter 1993, 50)

In brief, far from regarding advertising as harmful to children, Seiter views it as generating attachments to toys. These attachments, in turn, become a basis for children communicating with other children, thereby fostering social skills and a sense of membership in a community. Further, she adds the point that children's involvement in consumer culture is also based on a desire to escape adult authority and adult socialization pressures to be serious and self-disciplined. We may note that this is paradoxical, that while, in the short run, children's consumer culture provides an escape from these pressures, at the same time it is facilitating a long-run participation in a consumer culture that is created by adults and in which the children will participate even more fully when they become adults.

The preceding paragraphs describe an ongoing debate about *the nature of advertising and its influence on children.* From the discussion we can identify three main points of view that can be concisely summarized as follows: (1) Advertising is influential and has bad effects on children (Signiorielli). (2) Advertising is not so influential, and therefore not so bad, because other social relationships and experiences modify its effects (Gunter and McAleer). And (3) advertising is a good influence on children because it integrates them into the consumer culture in which they are inevitably going to spend their lives and provides them resources for developing social skills (Seiter). In a historical study of the rise of the children's clothing industry in the mid-twentieth-century, sociologist Daniel Thomas Cook agrees with Seiter (Cook 2004, 5, 151), but he frames the issue not as a debate about the nature of advertising but as a debate about *the nature of the child* (Cook 2004, 148–149). He identifies two basic positions: (1) Some adults, including some scholars, view children as vulnerable, impressionable, and needing protection from parents and other adults. They are hostile to what they consider corporate influence and exploitation of children. (2) Others see children as having considerable autonomy and ability to make their own choices and decisions—having "agency" is the contemporary expression. Adults who emphasize children's agency are not much concerned about corporate exploitation of children. Cook observes that those who work in and profit from industries that sell to children are among those who hold this view (Cook 2004, 149). But he also insists that we cannot understand recent and contemporary children and childhood without considering their necessary involvement in consumer culture (Cook 2004, 151).

Gender and Racial Stereotyping

A *stereotype* is an unrealistic generalization about a category of people. It disregards all the variation among the people in the category and focuses on one or a few supposed major characteristics that are attributed to all the members of the category. Most stereotypes are unfavorable toward the category, although a few are favorable. Either way, they provide simplified and distorted views of categories of people. One widespread form of stereotyping is ethnic jokes, which are constructed on the supposed attributes of Irishmen, Englishmen, Frenchmen, Poles, Jews, Swedes, Italians, and African Americans. At one time, such jokes were a staple of popular entertainment, but they have come to be seen as demeaning and, although they continue to circulate privately, they are now less acceptable in public entertainment.

Stereotypes can be communicated not only in words but also in visual portrayals. Although gender and racial stereotyping on television have generated occasional protest, they have not been issues of widespread public concern to the same extent as violent programming and advertising directed to children. But sociologists and other students of the mass media have paid attention to ways in which television has contributed to stereotyping and thereby to a distorted picture of society.

A study of children's television by F. Earle Barcus (1983) discovered imbalances in portrayals that amount to a kind of stereotyping. He studied 50 hours of children's programming. He found a total of 1,107 characters identifiable by sex. Of these, 78 percent were male, and 22 percent female. Since the proportions of males and females in society is close to 50–50, the overrepresentation of males in this sample of programming implies that males are more important or more interesting or both. The imbalance amounts to a stereotype, which was intensified by other imbalances. For example, 88 percent of the heroes in these programs were male. Females were less often shown as employed than were males. Gender stereotypes clearly showed up in other aspects of character portrayal: Female characters tended to be kinder, warmer, and more unselfish than male characters. The males were more active, independent, and violent. The males also were portrayed as more apt to seek fame, wealth, and thrills, as well as to be motivated by hatred (Barcus 1983). A later study (Thompson and Zerbinos 1995) that also focused on gender stereotyping examined 175 episodes of 41 different cartoons shown in the early 1990s and compared the findings to those of similar studies in the 1970s. Although the authors found some lessening of stereotyping, male characters continued to be more active, talkative, and prominent than female characters. They conclude that gender stereotyping continued only somewhat diminished compared to 20 years earlier.

Although some studies focus on children's programming, others focus on programming in general since children also watch programs that are not produced for a child audience. Those programs also tend to portray males and females in stereotyped ways. The question is, what is the effect of such portrayals on child viewers? Psychologists Robert Liebert and Joyce Sprafkin appraise the results of one such study of sixth through tenth graders by stating that

> television depicts the most commonly held cultural stereotypes or 'mainstream views.' Those who are already likely to hold the mainstream view will not be influenced much by television. For them, TV shows are just repeating 'what they already know' about people. On the other hand, individuals who would not otherwise hold the mainstream view but watch a lot of television will be influenced over time, in the direction of moving toward the mainstream. (Liebert and Sprafkin 1988, 193)

It turns out that in this study, most boys as well as poor girls and girls with lower IQs hold mainstream views derived from the influence of parents and peers, so that they would have stereotyped views of gender no matter how much or how little television they watch. Brighter girls and those from more advantaged homes receive less mainstream views from their mothers and other women. Therefore, they will have fewer stereotyped views of gender unless they are heavy viewers of shows that present these stereotypes.

Toy advertising on children's television is also quite stereotyped. Ads directed to girls tend to show girls playing with dolls, often in a girl's bedroom. Their clothing and hairstyles, as well as the room furnishings, are traditionally feminine. Commercials for boys' toys show much more activity. A boy playing with an action figure is likely to be shown impersonating the character. Ellen Seiter observes, "Boys *become* their toys in play; girls take care of their toys" (Seiter 1993, 128–131). Another media scholar notes differences in the formal features of ads. Those for boys are more likely to have loud, powerful, dramatic music, while the music in ads directed to girls is more likely to be cute and sweet. In ads directed to boys, the narrator or voice-over is likely to be male and often uses a loud, dominant, aggressive voice, while the announcer in ads to girls is likely to be female and to use a voice that is happy and cheerful or sweet and tender (Kline 1993, 244). These formal features contribute to perpetuating established notions of gender difference and gender distinctiveness: Boys are lively and tough, and girls are placid and gentle.

In addition to gender stereotyping, commercials on children's television programs also engage in racial stereotyping. The stereotyping can be fairly subtle. Seiter observes that white children in commercials are often seen in home settings but black children are not. Black children are often included in commercials along with whites, but they are placed less favorably. She illustrates the point with a description of a commercial in which a white boy and girl and an African American boy pop up behind a white piano being played by a bear. The children push into the spotlight while eating cookies, but the African American boy is partly hidden from view by the piano or is pushed out of the frame by the other two. Seiter describes other commercials that use other formal features that similarly give less prominence to the African American than to the white children (Seiter 1993, 136). However, there are important exceptions to this treatment. Black children are used in commercials to show that a product is "cool," the latest thing. Black children are prominently featured in ads for sports products and music, drawing on a stereotype that they all have natural talents in these areas. Commenting on the commercials of a major toy manufacturer, Seiter notes that "African American and white girls on Mattel commercials are frequently portrayed as close, intimate friends—embodiments of interracial friendship as a utopian ideal." Without further elaboration she then states, "There is far more integration and interracial friendship on children's commercials than there is on most prime time television or, for that matter, in most of the classics of children's literature" (Seiter 1993, 138–139). Thus, although Seiter is critical of gender and racial stereotyping in children's commercials, her observation about interracial friendships implies that such portrayals counteract stereotyping by showing the children as full equals.

Generally, television programs and commercials adhere to established norms in society. Widely accepted cultural stereotypes regarding race, ethnicity, and gender are reproduced in programs and commercials. But individual programs and advertisers sometimes push beyond the stereotypes and take a step or two toward revising or undermining them. For example, although interracial friendships exist, they are not commonplace. Portraying them in a commercial is a step toward making them seem more everyday, more normal, rather than something that calls attention to itself.

Research Methods in Television Studies

As we discussed in Chapter 1, in order to understand anything it is necessary to obtain information about it and to understand the connections among different pieces of information. Research methods are ways of obtaining information, and theories help in understanding connections among different pieces of information. Methods and theories are closely interrelated, as we shall try to explain. Although we discussed theories and research methods in the study of children and childhood more generally in Chapter 1, and everything we discuss in this book involves research and theory, we provide a more focused discussion of research methods and theories in the study of television's influence on children here because of television's prominence in modern societies and the prolonged debate about the impact of television on children. Moreover, there has been and continues to be great controversy about public policy, as the many congressional hearings suggest. People want to know if, and how, television may harm children and what, if anything, government should do about it. But there is also controversy about what are the appropriate research methods and theories to answer these questions. There is no clear path to an answer. The following discussion of methods and theories is intended to cast more light on, although not resolve, the controversial issues we have discussed above.

Experiments

As we discussed in Chapter 1, an experiment attempts to isolate the effect of one factor, such as watching a violent film, on some other factor of interest, such as subsequent violent behavior, from all other factors that might confound or disguise the effect. It does so by exposing one group to the isolated factor but not a matched control group, and then assessing any subsequent difference between the two groups on the factor of interest. For example, in the Bobo doll experiment discussed earlier in this chapter and Chapter 1, one group of children watched the film of an adult repeatedly hitting the doll, while another group did not. The difference in subsequent aggression displayed by the two groups of children in the playroom suggested that watching an aggressive film increases aggressive behavior.

Yet, as discussed in Chapter 1, the issue of *external validity* clouds the interpretation of the results of this and other experiments in the social sciences. That is, it is impossible to know whether the results of carefully controlled and, therefore, artificial experiments are generalizable to everyday social life. As Comstock and Scharrer (1999, 278) observe, "The challenges to external validity or generalizability to everyday life . . . are serious. . . . [T]he laboratory departs from the everyday in the brevity of the television exposure, the absence of the possibility of retaliation, and the exclusion of competing and countervailing communications." Many children watch hours of different kinds of television programming in a week and often talk with parents and peers about what they watch. Moreover, their own aggressive behavior provokes negative sanctions from adults and retaliation from the targets of their aggression. In everyday social life, unlike in the laboratory, the influence of watching a violent television program is not "isolated" from other confounding influences, and understanding the complete interplay of these influences is necessary in order to assess how and the degree to which watching particular kinds of programming influence children's subsequent behavior.

As we discussed in Chapter 1, and Comstock and Scharrer (1999, 278) observe, field experiments would seem to provide a solution to the problem of external validity but are extremely difficult to conduct. Comstock and Scharrer (1999, 278) explain that field experiments "contrive to produce in naturalistic surroundings the factors on which causal inference in experimentation depend—the manipulation of experience and comparability among treatment and control groups. Unfortunately, these conditions are hard to achieve outside the laboratory." In fact, although they cite a few examples of field experiments involving teenagers and adults, they do not cite any with children.

Surveys

In Chapter 1 we noted that surveys usually ask a large number of people individually to answer forced-choice questions either during an interview, sometimes conducted over the telephone, or on a questionnaire that they fill out themselves. Surveys are routinely used by advertisers to learn about responses to advertising, including whether viewers of a TV commercial more often ask for or buy the advertised product than nonviewers. For studies investigating the relationship between viewing violent programs and aggressive behavior, panel studies using surveys are often used because they try to uncover how much influence viewing violent programming at one point in time has on later behavior.

Content Analysis

Content analysis is a widely used method in communication research that we did not discuss in Chapter 1. Content analysis is designed to examine the characteristics of a communication. The researcher creates categories that are then used to classify parts of a communication. Probably the most frequent use of content analysis in studies of children and television has been to identify violent acts in programs. All kinds of programs watched by children have been examined for their violent content. Violent acts are identified and then counted. A controversial aspect of this use of content analysis has been researchers' use of the category *violence* to include a wide variety of different kinds of communication such as a cartoon character assaulting another, a shootout between human actors in a crime movie, and a news presentation of scenes from an ongoing war (Liebert and Sprafkin 1988, 86–88, 116–118). Studies often combine this kind of content analysis and survey. For example, a researcher might ask children to name their favorite programs and how often they watch. The survey may also ask children about some behavior, such as how often they get into fights. The researcher then does a content analysis of the programs named in order to count the violent acts in each. The next step is to see whether heavy viewers of programs with more violent acts get into more fights.

Audience Interpretive Response

A major objection to content analysis is that the researcher makes up the categories used to characterize the content of communications according to her or his own judgment. Viewers are not consulted, and no consideration is given to the possibility that viewers' interpretations of content may differ significantly from those of the researcher. There are clearly reasons to suspect that children's interpretation of television content may differ from that of an adult researcher.

In recent years a few researchers have shifted attention away from the analysis of the content of television programs and other communications to audiences' responses to and interpretations of television programs and movies. These researchers commonly use unstructured or conversational interviews or focus groups, like those we discussed in Chapter 1, to get viewers to talk about their responses to programs in their own words. Although still relatively rare, a few studies have used this research method to investigate children's responses to and interpretations of television programs (e.g., Buckingham 1993; Moores 1993). In one such study, for example, the sociologist Laura Fingerson (1999) interviewed a number of 9- to 13-year-old girls both individually and in focus groups about their reactions to then popular family situation comedies. Her findings demonstrate that these girls did not uncritically view these programs but evaluated the realism of them, comparing them to their own family experiences; they critically assessed the programs' messages in terms of their own values. They also used these programs as a source of topics in their own peer interactions, collaboratively constructing shared interpretations of what they had individually watched (Fingerson 1999, 412). This study, and others like it, suggest that we cannot fully understand how the content of television programs influences children without knowing how children themselves, both individually and collectively in their peer groups, interpret what they watch.

Theories of the Relationship Between Children and Television

The earliest studies of the relationship between television and children were done when television was just beginning to be introduced into American society. Television sets were not part of everybody's environment, as they are today. Researchers could assume that watching a television program was a distinctive experience, separate from other experiences. Some people had television, but many others did not. If children who watched a program were compared with children who didn't, and the viewers behaved differently from the nonviewers, then researchers drew the conclusion that viewing the program caused the different behavior in the viewers. Usually, however, the researchers did not study viewing of actual programs. They assumed that a satisfactory equivalent was achieved by bringing children into an experimental laboratory and showing a brief film on a TV set. The results were treated as though the children had watched an actual program.

These early studies were based on a then influential psychological theory known as *behaviorism*. In its simplest form this theory explains human behavior in terms of two basic concepts, *stimulus* and *response*. Human beings, like other animals, are assumed to act on the basis of receiving a stimulus and then responding to it. The stimulus causes the response. Watching a short film with violent action was the stimulus; hitting the Bobo doll in the playroom afterward was the response. Thus, underlying the theory of behaviorism is the concept of *causality*, which is shorthand for *cause and effect*. In this theoretical conception a television program causes behavior in the viewer. The behavior is the effect.

Even in the early days of such research, this concept was challenged by one of the founders of communication studies and his colleagues:

> In a sense the term 'effect' is misleading because it suggests that television 'does something' to children. The connotation is that television is the actor,

the children are acted upon. Children are thus made to seem relatively inert; television, relatively active. Children are sitting victims; television bites them. Nothing can be further from the fact. It is the children who are most active in this relationship. It is they who use television, rather than television that uses them. (Schramm, Lyle, and Parker 1961, 1; cited in Dorr 1986, 23)

Ever since, researchers have struggled with the concept of effect. We saw the difficulty with the concept in our discussion of heavy viewing and poor school performance. Does heavy viewing cause poor school performance, or is heavy viewing the chosen escape of children who do not do well in school? Which is cause, and which is effect?

Because the cause-effect framework is so basic in the natural sciences, and because it also continues to be influential in many areas of the social sciences (as well as in much of our everyday thinking), it is not easy to break out of this way of thinking. However, a number of theories about the relationship between children and television are built on a very different concept, the concept of *interpretation*. These approaches start from the premise that human beings necessarily act on the basis of interpreting the objects and events they encounter. From this point of departure, a television program or a commercial is not a stimulus that directly elicits a response. It is an object—a complex communication—that must be interpreted in order to be understood. A number of different theories that build on the concept of interpretation have been proposed. These are also known as *constructivist* approaches. Dorr presents a brief explanation of the underlying assumptions:

> The constructivist perspective affirms that an individual selects and interprets the raw materials of experience to produce his or her understanding of what that experience is. Physical reality is not denied; there are objects, people, animals, sounds, words, and events everywhere in life. But what is attended to and what is dismissed, what is considered important and what unimportant, how elements are organized into categories and hierarchies, and what meaning is attached to any physical reality are all determined by the individual. The active work that must be done in order to make sense of experience, this social construction of reality . . . ultimately transforms even physical reality into different realities for different people. (Dorr 1986, 21)

Sociologists would agree with most of this statement but would insist that it does not do justice to the expression "social construction of reality." Meaning is not only determined by the individual; it is also constructed in many forms of social interaction. For example, while individuals differ in their sense of humor, deciding whether something is funny is not always an individual interpretation but arises in a group. A child who tells a joke to which others respond, "That's not funny," may still believe it is, but will find it harder to maintain that belief. Individual interpretations of what's funny do not stand up easily to contrary group interpretations. Groups construct interpretations of what is funny. (As we noted above, ethnic jokes were once a staple of public entertainment. In an era when multiculturalism has become a value, public telling of ethnic jokes is mostly interpreted as offensive.)

There are several constructivist approaches. We have called them *theories*, although strictly speaking they are not theories but theoretical approaches. A theory is a set of closely worked out interdependent propositions. There is as yet no such theory of how children relate to television. But there are ways of thinking about it, efforts to advance toward a theory, and these are the best we have to work with at the present time.

Uses and Gratifications

The first theory to get away from the concept of effect is known as the *uses and gratifications approach*. Instead of assuming that television does something to people, including children, Jay Blumler and Elihu Katz assumed that viewers use television to obtain gratification (Blumler and Katz 1974). Their research focused on how people use television and what gratifications they obtain from viewing different kinds of programs. Uses and gratifications research is mostly based on interviews or on written essays. Children are asked why they watch or are asked to write an essay relating to television programs. Such studies are mostly done with school-age children, since preschool children are harder to interview and cannot write. A review of several studies has identified several different uses that children make of television and several different kinds of gratification that they get from watching. In summary, these are (1) to fill time; (2) to learn; (3) for companionship—in fantasy, with the television characters, and also with fellow viewers, whether family or friends; (4) as a source of conversation material; (5) to escape problems or boredom; (6) for arousal—of curiosity, excitement, amusement; (7) to improve a bad mood; and (8) for reassurance and comfort (Gunter and McAleer 1997, 17–28). Clearly, children are using television in a variety of ways. Any particular child may be seeking different gratifications from different programs or on different viewing occasions. The child has to interpret the occasion and the program.

Cultivation Theory

Cultivation theory, or cultivation analysis as it is also called, was originated by George Gerbner, a professor of communication, and carried further by his colleagues and students. This approach does not try to assess the impact of individual TV programs, neither in the short term nor in the long term. In other words, it does not pay attention to issues of either *concurrent effects* or *lagged effects*. Rather, it conceives of all of television programming as having a consistency and commonality that are more significant than the differences among programs. Notwithstanding the variety of programs, cultivation theory argues that television programming as a whole generates a version of reality. The more time people watch television, the more they come to believe the real world is like the world depicted on television. Cultivation theory focuses on *cumulative effects*. In the words of two proponents of this theory,

> Cultivation is about the implications of stable, repetitive, pervasive and virtually inescapable patterns of images and ideologies that television (especially dramatic, fictional entertainment) provides . . . cultivation research

approaches television as a *system* of messages—a system whose elements are not invariant or uniform, but complementary, organic, and coherent—and inquires into the functions and consequences of those messages as a system, overall, *in toto* for its audiences. The focus of cultivation analysis is on the correlates and consequences of cumulative exposure to *television in general* over long periods of time. (Shanahan and Morgan 1999, 5; italics in original)

Cultivation theorists hold that television programming, especially network drama, supports and dramatizes the conventional values, beliefs, and behavior of society, and what is portrayed above all is *power*. Much of the action in network drama deals with "how to manage and maintain the social order." From this perspective, TV violence can be understood as "the key to the rule of power." It is the cheapest and quickest dramatic demonstration of who can and who cannot get away with what against whom. An early study found that about one-third of male major characters, but few women, were concerned with violations and enforcement of rules of society. It also found that, compared to light viewers, heavy viewers believe society is more dangerous. The heavy viewers have a greater sense of danger and mistrust (Gerbner and Gross 1980, 152–153).

Semiotics

Semiotics is the study of *sign systems*. Human beings function with a variety of sign systems. For example, the alphabet is a sign system. A child learning the alphabet learns that the letter *b* is a sign for the sound "buh." Letters combine into more complex signs, words. Traffic lights are a sign system. Red is a sign for stop, and green for go. Brands of merchandise constitute a sign system. Among automobiles, a Mercedes is a sign of wealth, while a Chevrolet is a sign of more modest economic status. Clothing is a sign system. In the days when movie studios produced a large number of cowboy movies called *westerns* a child viewer soon learned the sign system and could immediately tell the good guys from the bad guys because the good guys wore white hats and the bad guys wore black hats. When children are dressed for church, they are clothed in "their Sunday best," which is a sign of solemnity, in contrast to everyday clothes, which are a sign of routine activity. Sign systems are sometimes referred to as *codes*, and the person who is able to use a system is said to *decode* it. Verbal language is a code. "Cracking the verbal code is a major intellectual concern of infants and children, occupying large amounts of time and energy" (Hodge and Tripp 1986, 78). A child learning to read is learning to decode letters and words. But reading is more than decoding. Once the child can read words, she or he has to proceed to understand the meaning of the sentences, paragraphs, and stories.

Robert Hodge and David Tripp, two Australian media researchers, believe that to understand the relationship between children and television, it is necessary to take a semiotic approach. They argue that television programs produce complex sets of signs on two different tracks, a video track and an audio track. In any one program, these combine into what they call "a vast meaning-potential complex, an interrelated set of verbal and visual meanings. But this potential is only abstract until there is someone to realize it. Interpretation is an intensely active process" (Hodge and Tripp 1986, 7).

As children begin watching—and listening to—television they begin to decode the variety of sounds and images that come from the TV set. What they can decode depends upon their level of mental development. As their mental development proceeds, their skill at decoding increases. "The hours of what many parents think is 'wasted time' that go into the normal child's viewing development can be seen . . . to build up a kind of cultural knowledge" (Hodge and Tripp 1986, 52). In time, children become able to distinguish differences in what Hodge and Tripp call *modality*, that is, the degree of reality of a message. Hodge and Tripp illustrate the concept in this way. They note that human communication occurs in more than one code at a time. Thus, the statement "It's a monster" is weakened in modality when accompanied by laughter but is modally strengthened if that statement is accompanied by a scream. They also point out that tone of voice can affect modality and this is why the sound track of a film can affect the modality of the image.

The authors provide an illustration of a child's interpretation of modality in an interview with a 6-year-old boy:

INTERVIEWER: What about if somebody gets killed on television?

GEORGE: Um. . . . They're not really killed.

INTERVIEWER: They're not really killed on television?

GEORGE: They're just pretend bullets and they just pretend they're killed and they get all dead on purposely.

INTERVIEWER: I see . . . and what happens in life when somebody gets killed?

GEORGE: Um . . . they die. (Hodge and Tripp 1986, 112)

Hodge and Tripp write that George and the other 6-year-olds they interviewed recognized (decoded) the processes of media production, acting, and the use of tomato sauce to represent blood. They write also of an interview in which 9-year-old girls speak of seeing a television program after which they pulled the head off a doll and stabbed a teddy bear. The girls tell this with smiles and laughter, and the authors conclude that "we need to take account of the modality of the action: stabbing, kissing, or beheading Teddy or dolls, rather than people. These children are quite clear about the difference between cruelty to people, and cruelty to dolls" (Hodge and Tripp 1986, 115). Thus, discussions of the influence of television or other media must always consider interpretation and modality.

Computers, the Internet, and Video Games

The latest media to become integral parts of our cultural world stem from new information technology, centering especially on the computer and video games. These developments also have been in constant flux with new technical advances and capabilities appearing in rapid succession. The consequences of this new information technology for socialization are wide and varied, some of which are fairly clear, others of which remain to be adequately understood. From the perspective of a child who has a computer in his or her own room at home and whose parent wants to discipline the child for some reason, the computer is simply one more device that provides the child with increased autonomy. This perspective is captured by communications scholar Joshua Meyrowitz when he writes, "At one time, parents had the ability to discipline a child by sending the child to his or her room—a form of 'excommunication' from social interaction. Such an action, however, takes on a whole new meaning today if the child's room is linked to the outside world through television, radio, telephone, and computer" (Meyrowitz 1985, 256).

Consumer electronic technology thus seems to have forced a modification of possible parental discipline by giving children resources that enable them to maintain more control over their social situation than was previously possible. Parents have to think up other disciplinary strategies to achieve their socialization goals.

Access to Computers

The increase in computer use in homes and schools has been rapid. However, computers are not yet universal in American and Canadian children's rooms, or even in their homes or schools. According to a survey in the year 2000 of 15-year-olds among member countries of the Organization for Economic Cooperation and Development (OECD), approximately 80 percent in the United States had access to a computer at home, with 69 percent having access to the Internet. In Canada, Sweden, and Australia, the computer access figure was even higher. In schools, the computer access rate was approximately 75 percent (OECD 2002; cited in Statistics Canada 2002).

However, research also reveals that there is a wide disparity by income in the ownership of home computers. A 1998 survey in the United States found that 91 percent of children in families with incomes of more than $75,000 a year had computers in their homes compared to only 22 percent of children in families with income under $20,000. African American and Hispanic children are less likely than other children to have access to a home computer and to the Internet. These differences by income and ethnicity have come to be called *the digital divide*, to indicate the large gap between the potential educational and socialization experiences of the different groups. Differences in access based on children's age and gender are minimal (Becker 2000). One writer on technology trends states that, in contrast to those who believe the digital divide is a temporary problem, it is actually widening. While poorer families begin to acquire computers, children in better-off families leap ahead by acquiring better technology, faster access, and more services. This accelerating technology advance increases motivation, knowledge, and skill, leading to a "fluency gap" (Tapscott 1998, 11).

In schools, too, access to computers is not equally distributed, although such access is becoming more available from year to year. Where funds have been short, the well-to-do schools were more likely to have access to the latest computer equipment. Schools do play some role in reducing the digital divide. The OECD report (2002) notes that although 15-year-olds in single-parent families were 40 percent less likely than those in two-parent families to use computers at home, they were equally likely to use them at school.

For those children with computers in the home, use of them begins early. According to one study in 2000, preschool children ages 2 to 5 averaged 27 minutes per day, while school-aged children age 6 to 11 averaged 49 minutes per day (Shields and Behrman 2000, 6). Some zealous parents buy laptops for babies under a year old, hoping that early contact with the screen and keyboard will speed their cognitive development, disregarding experts' advice that it won't (Lewin 2005). According to a newspaper report (Kershaw 2006) about parents obtaining email addresses for their newborn babies so they can have a store of waiting messages from relatives and family friends in an inbox when they learn to read, a child younger than 2 knows that the word *mouse* refers to two different objects, an animal that likes cheese and fears cats, and a device that moves things on a computer screen. Vocabulary pertaining to computers is now, for some, a prekindergarten vocabulary.

Implications for Socialization

When home computers first came into prominence, many critics and researchers expressed concerns about their influence on children, concerns not very different from those expressed when movies, comic books, radio, and television were first introduced. Some pointed out benefits of the new media while others stressed dangers and risks, despite the fact that research on consequences of computer use for children is not yet very extensive (Kinder 1999, 10).

The Internet, which became commercially available in late 1993, added dramatically to the possible uses of the computer and the implications for socialization. At this point, however, there is not yet much research on its consequences for children (Kinder 1999, 10; Turow 2002). The issues raised are essentially the same as those raised over earlier means of mass communication. Ellen Wartella, Dean of the School of Communication at the University of Texas, and Nancy Jennings present a general review of initial reactions to and subsequent research following the introduction of movies, radio, television, and, now, computers and the Internet. They write,

> Debates surrounding the introduction of earlier media have highlighted the novel attributes of each technology, but the promises and concerns have been fundamentally similar. In general, proponents of media innovation argue that the new technology benefits children by opening up new worlds to them, while opponents argue that new media might be used to substitute for real life in learning ethical principles, undermining children's morality and causing them to engage in illicit sexual and criminal behavior. Research on children and media has followed a recurrent pattern, reflecting the shifting focus of public concerns. In each case, initial studies have tended to examine which demographic groups of children were gaining access most quickly, how much time they spent with the new technology, and their preferences for different genres or types of use. Then as the technology became

more pervasive, research has tended to shift toward a greater emphasis on how the content of media exposure may be affecting children. In fact, the overwhelming similarity in research studies from epoch to epoch—across movies, radio, and television—is quite striking. (Wartella and Jennings 2000, 32)

They go on to observe, "Current debates surrounding the emergence of computer technology and new media echo the promises and concerns of the past" (Wartella and Jennings 2000, 35).

Marcia Kinder, a professor of critical studies of film and popular culture, also sees the concerns about the new media as the same as those about earlier media. However, she sees the issue in somewhat different terms. She perceives a major conflict between "those who see children primarily as passive victims being contaminated by an increasingly corrupt culture and those who perceive them as active players grappling with the inevitable processes of social and historical change" (Kinder 2000, 1; see also Buckingham 2000; Heins 2001).

Communication Professor Joseph Turow foresees new issues introduced by the Internet, and especially the World Wide Web, in addition to the familiar ones introduced by the earlier media. He acknowledges that almost no research has been done on this, and he proposes what he calls an "information-boundaries perspective on families and the Internet." Because the Internet is interactive, and because each family member can have independent access, there is decreased parental control of information that children can receive and also information that children can send out, for example giving identifying information in order to receive a free gift from some marketer. He and a colleague conducted telephone interviews with a national random sample of 1,001 parents of children 8 to 17 and 304 children aged 10 to 17. They found that children are much more likely than parents to say it is OK to give sensitive personal and family information to a commercial website in exchange for a free gift. The Internet introduces a new basis for family conflict: 41 percent of the parents and 36 percent of the children report family tensions over children's release of information to the Web (Turow 2002, 224). This is a first glimpse of how the Internet is changing the socialization environment in families. Further changes are in store, as Turow notes: "The notion of a discrete 'Web' in the home is also likely to blur as interactive digital television, radio, and print materials become common via broadband technologies. Along with these new developments will come a wide variety of target marketing activities aimed at youngsters as well as parents and entire families" (Turow 2002, 228).

Video Games

Video games, played both on computers and on stand-alone game platforms, have become very popular. They were introduced commercially when a video arcade opened in 1971 with one coin-operated game (Wolf 2001, 1). Since 1983, when a major producer, Nintendo, released its first home video game, this single company, by the year 2000, had sold over 1 billion video game units worldwide. One video game platform, Game Boy, in itself has sold over 110 million units (Nintendo n.d.). Sherry Turkle, a sociologist and psychologist who has done research on computer implications over many years and reports interviewing almost 1,000 people, including almost 300 children, as well as observing many while they used their computers, concludes, on the basis of this work,

> We are moving toward a culture of simulation in which people are increasingly comfortable with substituting representations of reality for the real.... In video games, objects fly, spin, accelerate, change shape and color, disappear and reappear.... The objects in a video game are made of information, not metal.... The heroes in the worlds of Nintendo can jump enormous heights and crush opponents with their 'weight,' yet suffer no harm to themselves. The youngest video game player soon learns that the game is always the same, unaffected by its particular surroundings. This is a socialization into the culture of simulation. (Turkle 1995, 25, 66–67)

On the basis of her interviews and observations, Turkle believes that the simulated world that is experienced in video games and on the Internet can prove so seductive that the real world comes to seem so boring that it loses appeal. Most of the examples that she provides are of high-school students and young adults, but she also thinks younger children are already at risk of developing that feeling. She also believes that the Internet allows people to play games in which they can assume many identities; she sees this as leading to the development of selves that are more flexible and less stable than previously. Children experience this flexibility when they play at "morphing," that is, games in which Power Rangers, a group of teenage martial-arts experts, turn themselves into "person/machine/animal hybrids with super-robotic powers ... children seem to understand that the Power Rangers have human bodies that are flexible enough to morph into cyborg ones" (Turkle 1995, 171).

Some researchers support Turkle in claiming that many children become addicted to video games. One study, surveying children aged 11 to 17 in the Canadian province of British Columbia, reports that "24 percent . . . felt that many were totally dependent on video games, [and] 34 percent believed that some kids played them too much" (Kline 1998, 16).

But all researchers do not agree. A team of research psychologists presents a view of video games that differs in two significant respects from Turkle's view. First, they argue that game playing is not as addictive as is widely believed. They cite a study that reports that only 21 percent of a national sample of boys aged 8 to 18 played games more than an hour a day on a stand-alone platform (such as Nintendo or Sony Play Station), and only 6 percent reported playing more than an hour a day on a computer (Subrahmanyam et al. 2001, 83). Second, they cite some research that suggests computer-game playing has some positive effects on cognitive development, such as improved ability to keep track of events going on in multiple locations. Another issue they take up is the gender discrepancy in game playing. Boys between the ages of 8 and 14 are five times more likely than girls in that age group to own a Genesis or Super

Nintendo game system. This gender difference carries over to school use of computers: Girls use them less than boys, and, according to one study, computers are seen as belonging more to boys than to girls (Subrahmanyam et al. 2001, 83–77).

Video games are not only played on computers and on in-home game platforms but also continue to be available in commercially operated video arcades. Sociologist Simon Gottschalk observed children and teenagers playing games in arcades located in the major casino/hotels in Las Vegas, Nevada. These arcades are segregated from gambling areas and are freely open to children. On the basis of his observations in the arcades, together with consideration of others' work, Gottschalk concludes that video games are organized on the basis of a set of ideological assumptions that he calls "videology." Most of the assumptions are about violence. He writes,

> The central organizing assumption of videology is unarguably that of violence. Although the humans, machines, robots, animals, and mutants that video-games simulate are technically capable of a wide range of activities, videology translates these objects into violent, dangerous, and destructive ones. . . . Of course, not all video-games contain violent themes, but in an overwhelming majority of them, violence is the basic assumption, the given. (Gottschalk 1995: 7)

Other assumptions are wrapped up in this central one. The game is played against a violent enemy, usually male and "often browner or yellower than the hero," who is battled in a Third World jungle, an inner city, or some other recognizably dangerous place (Gottschalk 1995, 8). Most of the most popular games are played by one person and thus contribute to a sense of individual violent conquest. Girls are underrepresented among players in the arcades; as figures depicted in the games, they are usually portrayed as objects of temptation and in need of rescue by violent male action, not as active participants. Some games encourage the player to use great violence against characters involved with drugs.

According to Gottschalk's analysis, the assumptions on which these video games are constructed lead the players into a fantasy world that borrows sights and sounds from the real world, a fantasy world in which the players are "subjects of a decidedly violent, paranoid, individualist, racist, sexist, militarized and oversaturated New World Order whose trigger-happy patriotic young white male agents brutally enforce a 'zero-tolerance' policy toward drug smugglers and a great variety of others, while keeping women 'in their place' " (Gottschalk 1995, 14). He regards these games as having a socializing consequence in that they reproduce a dominant cultural reality (Gottschalk 1995, 3–4). While he does not say so explicitly, he clearly suggests, when he comments that the video enemy is browner or yellower than the hero, that many of the games also communicate a racist message.

An interdisciplinary team of social scientists reviewed a number of experimental studies that, together, suggest that playing a violent game can have a number of aggressive effects on children, including increased aggressive behavior in free play, hostile responses on ambiguous open-ended questions, and having aggressive ideas (Subrahmanyam et al. 2002, 25). Psychologist Craig A. Anderson, reviewing another set of studies, reaches similar conclusions but states that the effects of playing these games are "small" to "moderate." However, he argues that this does not mean they are inconsequential. He says that "small effect sizes can yield large effects, especially when they accumulate across repeated occasions." As an analogy, he presents the relationship of cigarette smoking to lung cancer. It is almost impossible to measure the effect of smoking one cigarette or even a pack on lung cancer, but the accumulated effects of years of smoking can be very large. Likewise, the cumulative effects of long-term exposure to violent video games can have serious social consequences (Anderson 2002, 115).

Computers, Parental Authority, and Children's Autonomy

What is particularly striking about computers, compared to earlier media, is that they are interactive. And it is here that the implications for socialization are especially significant. Children can use them not only to play games and listen to music but also to send and receive email, chat with one another, or just browse and explore new fields. In these ways, the computer offers possibilities far beyond those of other media and suggests many questions for further socialization research.

Home computers are purchased by parents, often for the benefits they may offer their children. According to one Canadian survey, 55 percent of parents cited this reason (Gulens 2002). Once purchased, however, they raise many questions about the role they play in family relationships. We have already noted Joshua Meyrowitz's observation that one traditional form of parental discipline, sending a child to his or her room, is probably not much of a punishment for a child who has a computer there. And there are other ramifications. First, many children become much more knowledgeable and adept in the use of computers than their parents—and also their teachers—which may well give them a sense of autonomy and power. Strengthening this sense of independence—since the computer is generally used without supervision, sometimes in the privacy of a bedroom—they have access to information and relationships unknown to and possibly strongly disapproved by their parents. In a Canadian survey, four out of ten children between the ages of 9 and 17 said their parents know very little or nothing about the websites they visit, and more than one-third of them said they always or sometimes erased the history of the websites they visited (Media Awareness Network 2001). Frequently, too, the use of the computer becomes a topic for discussion and negotiations between parents and children and between siblings, negotiations that also have implications for socialization.

The studies we have cited provide preliminary glimpses into the way computers, the Internet, and video games are beginning to influence children's lives. As of now, there are many questions and few definitive answers concerning their impact on children's socialization. Unsatisfactory as that situation may be, that is where we have to leave it.

* * *

Mass media are increasingly pervasive in modern American society. Television has long been central, but video games, computers, and the Internet are gaining as occupiers of children's time. Children's involvement with all these media arouses parental and other adult concern, as did comic books in their heyday. Involvement with the newer electronic media is only beginning to be researched, but television's impact on children has been the subject of decades of research. The major concerns have been the sheer amount of time that children spend watching TV, the impact of watching violent programs, and the impact of advertising. There seems little doubt that children spend less time playing outdoors than in pre-TV days. The research on the impact of watching violent programs is less conclusive than many had hoped or claimed. TV advertising stimulates children's consumer appetites, but it also provides content for interacting and forming relationships with other children.

References

Altheide, David L. 1995. *An Ecology of Communication*. New York: Aldine de Gruyter.

Anderson, Craig A. 2002. "Violent Video Games and Aggressive Thoughts, Feelings, and Behaviors." In Sandra L. Calvert, Amy B. Jordan, and Rodney B. Cocking (eds.) *Children in the Digital Age*, 101–119. Westport, CT: Praeger.

Barcus, F. Earle. 1983. *Images of Life on Children's Television: Sex Roles, Minorities, and Families*. New York: Praeger.

Becker, Henry J. 2000. "Who's Wired and Who's Not: Children's Access to and Use of Computer Technology." *The Future of Children* 10(2): 44–75.

Blumler, Jay G., and Elihu Katz. 1974. *The Uses of Mass Communications*. Beverly Hills, CA: Sage.

Buckingham, David. 1993. *Children Talking Television: The Making of Television Literacy*. London: Falmer Press.

——. 2000. *After the Death of Childhood: Growing Up in the Age of Electronic Media*. Cambridge: Polity Press.

"Burning Books in New Mexico." 2002. *New York Times*.January 1, 1.

Comstock, Anthony. [1883] 1967. *Traps for the Young*. Cambridge, MA: Belknap Press of Harvard University Press. [New York: Funk and Wagnalls, 1883.]

Comstock, George, and Haejung Paik. 1991. *Television and the American Child*. San Diego, CA: Academic Press.

Comstock, George, and Erica Scharrer. 1999. *Television*. San Diego, CA: Academic Press.

Cook, Daniel Thomas. 2004. *The Commodification of Childhood*. Durham, NC: Duke University Press.

Dorr, Aimee. 1986. *Television and Children*. Beverly Hills, CA: Sage.

Felson, Richard B. 1996. "Mass Media Effects on Violent Behavior." In John Hagan and Karen S. Cook (eds.) *Annual Review of Sociology* 22: 103–128. Palo Alto, CA: Annual Reviews.

Fingerson, Laura. 1999. "Active Viewing: Girls' Interpretations of Family Television Programs." *Journal of Contemporary Ethnography* 28: 389–418.

Gerbner, George, and Larry Gross. 1980. "The Violent Face of Television and Its Lessons." In Edward Palmer and Aimee Dorr (eds). *Children and the Faces of Television*, Pg ??. New York: Academic Press.

Glick, Ira O. and Sidney J. Levy. 1962. *Living with Television*. Chicago: Aldine.

Gore, Tipper. 1987. *Raising PG Kids in an X-Rated Society*. Nashville, TN: Abingdon Press.

Gottschalk, Simon. 1995. "Videology: Video-Games as Postmodern Sites/Sights of Ideological Reproduction." *Symbolic Interaction* 18(1): 1–18.

Gulens, Mara. 2002. "The Kids They Are a-Changin." July 9, *www.backbonemagg.com*.

Gunter, Barrie, and Jill McAleer. 1997. *Children and Television*, 2nd ed. London: Routledge.

Heins, Marjorie. 2001. *Not in Front of the Children: 'Indecency,' Censorship, and the Innocence of Youth*. New York: Hill and Wang.

Hodge, Robert, and David Tripp. 1986. *Children and Television: A Semiotic Approach*. Stanford, CA: Stanford University Press.

Huston, Aletha C., and John C. Wright. 1996. "Television and the Socialization of Young Children." In Tannis M. MacBeth (ed.) *Tuning in to Young Viewers*, 37–60. Thousand Oaks, CA: Sage.

Joy, Leslie A., Meredith M. Kimball, and Merle L. Zabrack. 1986. "Television and Children's Aggressive Behavior." In Tannis MacBeth Williams (ed). *The Impact of Television: A Natural Experiment in Three Communities*. Orlando, FL: Academic Press.

Kershaw, Sarah. 2006. "Web Sites for the Brave New Electronic B@by." *New York Times*, Sunday Styles, January 16, sec. 9, 1.

Kinder, Marcia (ed.). 1999. *Kids' Media Culture*. Durham: Duke University Press.

Kline, Stephen. 1993. *Out of the Garden: Toys, TV, and Children's Culture in the Age of Marketing*. London: Verso.

———. 1998. "Video Game Culture: Leisure and Play Preferences of B.C. Teens." Media Awareness Network, August, *www.media=awareness.ca*.

Kunkel, Dale. 2001. "Children and Television Advertising." In Dorothy G. Singer and Jerome L. Singer (eds.) *Handbook of Children and Television*, 375–394. Thousand Oaks, CA: Sage.

Lewin, Tamar. 2003. "A Growing Number of Video Viewers Watch from the Crib." *New York Times*, October 29, 1.

———. 2005. "See Baby Touch a Screen. But Does Baby Get It?" *New York Times*, December 15, 1.

Liebert, Robert M., and Joyce N. Sprafkin. 1988. *The Early Window: Effects of Television on Children and Youth*, 3rd ed. New York: Pergamon Press.

MacBeth, Tannis M. 2001. "The Impact of Television: A Canadian Natural Experiment." In Craig McKie and Benjamin D. Singer (eds.) *Communications in Canadian Society*, 5th ed, 196–213. Toronto: Thompson Educational Publishing.

Media Awareness Network. 2001. "Young Canadians in a Wired World: The Students' View." June, 3. *www.media-awareness.ca*.

Meyrowitz, Joshua. 1985. *No Sense of Place*. New York: Oxford University Press.

Moores, Shaun. 1993. *Interpreting Audiences: The Ethnography of Media Consumption*. London: Sage.

Nintendo. n.d. *www.nintendo.com*.

OECD. 2002. "Education at a Glance." *OECS Indicators*, 2002 ed. *www.oecd.org*.

"Quick Facts: Computers and Internet Usage." 2000. *www.mediaawareness.ca*.

Roberts, Donald F., and Ulla G. Foehr. 2004. *Kids and Media in America*. Cambridge: Cambridge University Press.

Rubin, Rebecca, Alan M. Rubin, and Linda J. Piele. 1996. *Communication Research: Strategies and Sources*, 4th ed. Belmont, CA: Wadsworth.

Savage, William W., Jr. 1990. *Comic Books and America 1945–1954*. Norman: University of Oklahoma Press.

Schramm, Wilbur, Jack Lyle, and Edwin B. Parker. 1961. *Television in the Lives of Our Children*. Stanford, CA: Stanford University Press.

Seiter, Ellen. 1993. *Sold Separately: Children and Parents in Consumer Culture*. New Brunswick, NJ: Rutgers University Press.

Shanahan, James, and Michael Morgan. 1999. *Television and Its Viewers: Cultivation Theory and Research*. Cambridge: Cambridge university Press.

Shields, Margie K., and Richard E. Behrman. 2000. "Children and Computer Technology: Analysis and Recommendations." *The Future of Children* 10(2): 4–30.

Signiorielli, Nancy. 1990. *A Sourcebook on Children and Television*. Westport, CT: Greenwood Press.

Statistics Canada. 2002. "Computer Access at School and at Home." October 29. Ottawa: Statistics Canada.

Subrahmanyam, Kaveri, Patricia M. Greenfield, Robert Kraut, and Elishiva Gross. 2002. "The Impact of Computer Use on Children's and Adolescents' Development." In Sandra L. Calvert, Amy B. Jordan, and Rodney B. Cocking (eds.) *Children in the Digital Age*, 3–33. Westport, CT: Praeger.

Subrahmanyam, Kaveri, Robert Kraut, Patricia Greenfield, and Elisheva Gross. 2001. "New Forms of Electronic Media." In Dorothy G. Singer and Jerome L. Singer (eds.) *Handbook of Children and the Media*, 73–99. Thousand Oaks, CA: Sage.

Tapscott, Don. 1998. *Growing Up Digital*. New York: McGraw-Hill.

Thompson, Teresa, and Eugenia Zerbinos. 1995. "Gender Roles in Animated Cartoons: Has the Picture Changed in 20 Years?" *Sex Roles* 32: 651–673.

Turkle, Sherry. 1995. *Life on the Screen: Identity in the Age of the Internet*. New York: Simon & Schuster.

Turow, Joseph. 2002. "Family Boundaries, Commercialism, and the Internet: A Framework for Research." In Sandra L. Calvert, Amy B. Jordan, and Rodney R. Cocking (eds.) *Children in the Digital Age*, 215–230. *Westport, CT: Praeger.*

Valkenburg, Patti M., and Joanne Cantor. 2002. "The Development of a Child into a Consumer." In Susan L. Calvert, Amy B. Jordan, and Rodney R. Cocking (eds.) *Children in the Digital Age*, 201–214. Westport, CT: Praeger.

Wartella, Ellen A., and Nancy Jennings. 2000. "Children and Computers: New Technology—Old Concerns." *The Future of Children* 10(2): 31–43.

Wertham, Frederic. 1953. *Seduction of the Innocent*. New York: Rinehart.

Williams, Tannis MacBeth (ed.). 1986. *The Impact of Television: A Natural Experiment in Three Communities*. Orlando, FL: Academic Press.

Wolf, Mark J. P. 2001. "Introduction." In Mark J. P. Wolf (ed.)*The Medium of the Video Game*. Austin: University of Texas Press. ✦

Introduction

E very functioning society is held together in several ways. In the modern world, most are organized as nation-states. This means each occupies a defined territory, has a government that exercises authority over the people living in that territory, and has some public symbols of nationhood such as a flag, national holidays, and a national anthem. A government operates through its political institutions—a president or prime minister, a parliament or congress, a judiciary, and so on. These government institutions help to hold a society together by providing some orderly procedures and thus some predictability. In addition, a society has one or more official languages; official business is conducted in official languages, although people may speak other languages in their personal interactions. At least as important in holding a society together is its *culture*, which is created through the innumerable interactions of the members of society. Like any concept that tries to capture a complex reality, it has been variously defined and interpreted. The following definition captures, we believe, the central elements of what is widely understood as culture: *A culture is a way of life developed by people in adaptation to the physical and social circumstances in which they find themselves. It tends to be passed on from generation to generation, but it changes as circumstances change. It includes some elements that are highly valued by the people themselves and some elements that are accepted as necessary or "realistic" adaptations but are not especially valued.* A way of life includes, then, values and norms, but also, as our quotation from Ann Swidler pointed out in Chapter 2, skills, habits, and styles of action.

Any society that is large includes within it many different ways of life. But a moment's reflection makes clear that the concept *way of life* is somewhat fuzzy around the edges because it is not always possible to state where one way of life stops and another begins. Farmers and suburbanites and city people in the United States all recognize July 4 as Independence Day and take it as a holiday, but farmers have to get up early in the morning to look after their livestock, while the rest of the population does not. Farmers need some skills, habits, and styles of action that differ from those of bankers or bus drivers.

Another problem presented by the term *culture* is that of the unit that it represents. We may speak of cultures of nations, regions, social classes, ethnic groups, generations, religious groups, occupational groups, youth gangs, children's peer groups, or indeed any kind of organization or group, in each case focusing on the commonalities of thought, attitudes, behavior, skills, and material objects (such as houses, motorcycles, music players, sailboats, pickup trucks, video games, etc.). This question of what unit a culture refers to is of considerable importance in understanding differences in socialization. Does the child growing up in a poor rural hamlet in the mountains of Kentucky or West Virginia have the same culture as a child growing up in the middle of New York, Chicago, or Houston? Does the child growing up in the slum have the same culture as the child growing up in the affluent suburb? Does the child of Chinese immigrants in a Chinese section of San Francisco or Vancouver have the same culture as the child of long-established families of English descent?

The easiest answer to the above questions is "No." And this answer would be partially correct. In Part III we shall describe some differences of culture among different segments of society, what are generally known as *subcultures*. But before we say more about subcultures, we want to call attention to a trend that points to increasing uniformity of culture in the United States and, in fact, goes beyond its borders to Americanize other cultures. For this trend, sociologist George Ritzer has coined the term "McDonaldization of society." The growth of the McDonald's restaurant chain set in motion a trend that spread not only to other restaurant chains but to other types of businesses as well. The chains offer predictable, standardized products in multiple far-flung locations. "The Egg McMuffin in New York will be, for all intents and purposes, identical to those in Chicago and Los Angeles" (Ritzer 2002, 17). Local "mom-and-pop" stores, each with their distinctive local character, are driven out of business by the efficient and highly standardized chain unit. An executive of the toy-store chain Toys R Us is quoted as saying, "We want to be thought of as a sort of McDonald's of toys" (Ritzer 2002, 9). Ritzer argues that McDonaldization has several positive results, two of which are relevant here. One is that "[p]eople are more likely to be treated similarly, no matter what their race, gender, or social class," and the other is that "[t]he most popular products of one culture are more easily diffused to others" (Ritzer 2002, 20). So McDonald's—and Wendy's and Burger King and Taco Bell, and so on, and so on—are known to adults and children of all ethnic groups and all social classes. They are a component of a national American culture.

McDonaldization, then, is a trend toward cultural homogeneity in society. Yet that trend is not so powerful as to obliterate subcultural differences. The relationship between subculture and dominant culture can sometimes be subtle and complex. For example, there are people who, for various reasons, have lost all possibility for occupational success or even for a steady job. But they often know very well that American society judges people by their occupation. They may even share in the value that others hold, but the value has lost meaning for their own day-to-day lives because there seems to be no way in which they can implement it. Thus a value may be shared across many segments of society, but it may not be lived out in the same way in those various segments (Rodman 1963). Indeed, we saw in Chapter 5 that most parents want their children to get a good education, but there are variations in the skills, habits, and styles of action with which parents seek to fulfill the value.

Thus there is sometimes a complex relationship between being part of society yet being in some ways marked off from it, between participating in a larger culture yet having a distinctive version of it. Charles Valentine emphasizes both the distinctiveness of subcultures and their interplay with the larger culture:

> It is perhaps reasonable to assume that any subsociety may have a configuration of more or less distinguishable lifeways of its own. The configuration constitutes a subculture that is distinct from the total culture of the whole society in a . . . special and limited sense. The wider sociocultural system has its own coherence to which subsocieties and subcultures contribute even with their distinctiveness. (Valentine 1968, 106)

Valentine's general point can be illustrated with this example: African Americans have long been segregated, residentially and socially, from whites. This segregation was a particular type of "coherence" in the American sociocultural system. In their segregated communities they developed a subculture, which included new forms of music known as the blues, jazz, and, more recently, rap and hip-hop. These forms of music diffused into white society—distinctive contributions of the subculture to the larger culture.

What is the importance of subcultures for socialization? First, even granting McDonaldization, children are socialized into a particular subculture more than into a culture as a whole. This means that initially children learn the ways of a particular segment of society more than the ways of the wider society. They develop outlooks and assumptions that are not necessarily shared by those outside that segment. If they spend their entire lifetimes associating only with those who share the same subculture, they may have difficulty understanding the thoughts, actions, and situations of those from other subcultures. The point may be illustrated with a hypothetical example. We might imagine a child in comfortable circumstances meeting a very poor child and asking, "How much allowance do you get?"—not realizing that in some parts of society, children do not receive a weekly allowance. This is an example of a situation that affects all children in their early socialization but that most eventually leave behind as their experience widens. The things that are done and valued in one's own way of life lead to the implicit question "Doesn't everyone?"

A child's encounter with a different subculture can also take the reverse form. Instead of the revelation "I didn't know that everyone doesn't do what I do," the child may have an experience that takes the form of "I didn't know other people do that." Thus, a young black woman whose mother cooked for a white family reports a childhood discovery: "Sometimes Mama would bring us the white family's leftovers. It was the best food I had ever eaten. That was when I discovered white folks ate different from us. They had all kinds of different food with meat and all. We always had just beans and bread" (Moody 1970, 23). A child's "emergence" from her or his subculture into an awareness of diversity may come early or late in life, and for some living in isolated homogeneous communities, it may never come at all.

Of course, with increasing urbanization, mobility, and education, and the widespread influence of television, a smaller and smaller proportion of children grows up so completely insulated within a subculture as to be unacquainted with other ways of living in the same society. Even the very small towns come under the influence of urbanization (Vidich and Bensman 1969). These changes mean that more and more children are learning at some point in the course of their socialization that the answer to the question "Doesn't everyone?" is "No, everyone doesn't." Everyone does not belong to a country club; everyone does not go to church on Sunday morning; everyone does not live in a neighborhood of crowded apartments; everyone does not believe that the most important thing is to get a good job that leads to advancement and a house in a nice suburb; and everyone does not live in decaying houses in muddy hollows.

The general implication of the fact that socialization starts within a particular subculture is that *every child's socialization in some measure limits his or her ability to function in other segments of the larger society.* The values, beliefs, assumptions, skills, and ways of life that come to be "second nature" to children make it difficult for them to function effectively in some kinds of situations involving persons who have been socialized in other subcultures. The limiting effects of socialization are currently receiving considerable attention in the United States, Canada, and other Western countries. In the United States, for example, there has been a growing emphasis since the 1990s on *multiculturalism* (Buenker and Ratner 1992; Vecoli 1995, xxi–xxvii), an effort in education to familiarize children—and adults—with cultures other than their own.

Multiculturalism in the United States is a response to cultural conflicts that flared up earlier and, to some extent, continue, even if more quiescently. Very poor children are sometimes referred to by others as *lower class,* and they are thought to be socialized in such a way that they do not know how to function in middle-class society. In the 1970s and 1980s poor people began to be more assertive, and they argued that middle-class people are so "locked in" by their values and norms that they do not understand the different subculture of very poor people. An intense version of this occurred between black people and white people. Many whites had long believed (and some still do) that blacks cannot acquire many necessary kinds of competence because of their "inferior" way of life. Many blacks countered this with a growing insistence that the socialization of whites rendered them incompetent to meet the needs of blacks and to serve as socializing agents for black children. These antagonisms are more under the surface today than in the past, but from time to time they erupt openly. The same arguments were made by native Indians in Canada and the United States. These bitter problems are but a recent version of what early sociologist William Graham Sumner saw many years ago as a universal social characteristic, which he named *ethnocentrism:* "Each group thinks its own folkways the only right ones. . . . Ethnocentrism leads a people to exaggerate and intensify everything in their own folkways which is peculiar and which differentiates them from others" (Sumner 1906, 13). As two more recent sociologists have noted, ethnocentrism is one type of "trained incapacity"; it limits a child's ability to understand others and participate in the larger society (Shibutani and Kwan 1965, 109).

Although all cultures necessarily generate some measure of ethnocentrism, some do so more than others. Isolation from other subcultures intensifies ethnocentrism, but so also do conflict and discrimination. Ethnocentrism is, in principle, modifiable, and many programs designed for its reduction are carried out by agencies concerned with human relations. Many social scientists go so far as to affirm that all socialization outcomes that limit social competence are modifiable by appropriate action programs (for example, Foote and Cottrell 1955; Lippitt 1968; Weinstein 1969).

The importance of subcultures for socialization can be further appreciated by reference to concepts introduced earlier.

1. A person's *status* in society is partly determined by the subcultures in which he or she participates.

2. A child's earliest *role models* are drawn from her or his subculture, although by school age the child may have encountered some role models from outside it.

3. Since a child's *self* is formed in large part by taking the role of others, and since the child's earliest significant others tend to be from his or her own subculture, the child's self has an anchor in a particular subculture.

Subcultures are based on various types of social differentiation. In Chapters 9 and 10 we shall consider two of particular importance, social class and ethnic/minority group, and consider how each of these affects socialization. We shall also briefly discuss neighborhood communities, an emerging focus of research in children's socialization.

In Chapter 11 we examine another kind of diversity, one that exists in every social class and in every culture and subculture. Every society has construed the biological differences between males and females as a basis for socializing girls and boys differently in certain important ways. In some societies, the socialization differences are considered to be "natural" consequences of the anatomical and physiological differences between males and females. Such views often also provided a justification for maintaining male domination over females. This type of thinking was prevalent in the United States until the 1960s, when it began to change under the influence of a women's movement that challenged its validity and influenced thinking in sociology, psychology, and many other fields. Thus, until the 1960s, and even for some time thereafter, sociologists studying the different ways that males and females participate in society referred to them as *sex roles*—men were doctors and women were nurses, men were executives and women were secretaries, and wives did the cooking and husbands took out the garbage. The realization finally dawned that such roles are not inherent in sexual difference but are normative constructions that can be changed. Consequently, calling them *sex roles* perpetuates unjustified assumptions and expectations. Socially constructed roles that are differentiated on the basis of sex but that have no biological basis in sex are now referred to as *gender roles*, a term that recognizes they can change as cultural definitions change. But boys and girls are still socialized differently in certain respects, even though sex and gender are not as tightly linked as they once were. In Chapter 11, we examine the continuing complexities of this topic.

References

Buenker, John D., and Lorman A. Ratner. 1992. *Multiculturalism in the United States.* Westport, CT: Greenwood Press.

Foote, Nelson, and Leonard S. Cottrell Jr. 1955. *Identity and Interpersonal Competence.* Chicago: University of Chicago Press.

Lippitt, Ronald. 1968. "Improving the Socialization Process." In John A. Clausen (ed.) *Socialization and Society,* 321–374. Boston: Little, Brown.

Moody, Anne. 1970. *Coming of Age in Mississippi: An Autobiography.* New York: Delta.

Ritzer, George. 2002. "An Introduction to McDonaldization." In George Ritzer (ed.) *McDonaldization: The Reader,* 1–23. Thousand Oaks, CA: Sage.

Rodman, Hyman. 1963. "The Lower-Class Value Stretch." *Social Forces* 42 (December): 205.

Shibutani, Tamotsu, and Kian M. Kwan. 1965. *Ethnic Stratification.* New York: Macmillan.

Sumner, William Graham. 1906. *Folkways.* Boston: Ginn.

Valentine, Charles. 1968. *Culture and Poverty: Critique and Counter-Proposals.* Chicago: University of Chicago Press.

Vecoli, Rudolph J. 1995. "Introduction." In Judy Galens, Anna Sheets, and Robyn V. Sand Young (eds.) *Gale Encyclopedia of Multicultural America,* xxi–xxvii. Detroit, MI: Gale Research.

Vidich, Arthur, and Joseph Bensman. 1969. *Small Town in Mass Society.* Enlarged Edition. Princeton, NJ: Princeton University Press.

Weinstein, Eugene A. 1969. "The Development of Interpersonal Competence." In David A. Goslin (ed.) *Handbook of Socialization Theory and Research,* 753–775. Chicago: Rand McNally. ◆

Chapter 9

Social Class

In Chapter 2 we presented an overview of social class in the United States. There is wide agreement that a division of the American population into six social classes provides a reasonably good understanding of the American class structure. A fair amount of research is carried out focused on one or more of the classes identified in Chapter 2, although sometimes different labels are used for one or another of the classes. (A six-class scheme with somewhat different divisions than the Gilbert-Kahl model in Chapter 2 is presented by Kohn and Slomczynski [1990, 32–37].) We shall use the general classification from Chapter 2 to present discussions of how class subcultures affect socialization. From time to time we shall note variations within them, allowing for race or gender. Our major discussion of race will be reserved for the chapter following, on ethnic groups. Gender will be the focus of Chapter 11.

Classifying the American population into six social classes is a useful way of representing social reality. At the same time, the reader should be aware that divisions between classes are not absolute. Classes shade into one another, and the criteria for class membership are not always consistent. (For this reason, some researchers prefer the concept of *socioeconomic status*—SES—to the concept of social class because it is a little better at capturing shadings, although not as good at capturing cultural differences.) Consider, for example, the following, using only the criteria of education and income. For college graduates, it takes two years to earn a Master of Social Work (MSW) degree. It takes two years to earn a Master of Business Administration (MBA) degree. A new MSW will likely earn from $27,000 to $35,000 per year and, in the course of a career, will reach a peak of perhaps $80,000 to $90,000. A new MBA will probably earn $50,000 to $90,000 and, in the course of a career, may reach a peak of from $150,000 to $1 million or more per year. (There are regional variations as well as variations by employer in both fields.) Educationally, the MSW and the MBA are at the same class level. Economically, the experienced social worker and the early-in-career businessperson can be considered at the same class level. But if we take a life-course perspective, the incomes of long-experienced businesspeople will average far more than the incomes of long-experienced social workers. Both may be members of the upper-middle class, with high levels of education, but the incomes of the experienced businesspeople place some of them near the upper class (and sometimes in it), while the experienced social workers' income is near that of the middle class. Of course, a dual-career marriage or domestic partnership raises household income. Despite such complexities, the division into six classes captures some core differences in American society.

Upper Class

The upper class (or capitalist class) includes a relatively small proportion of the population, but they are people with the most wealth and power, and are often near the top in prestige. They may sit on the boards of directors of corporations and make decisions on opening or closing plants or the hiring or firing of hundreds of employees. As is true of all the social classes, there are variations within the upper class. Some members of the class are generous philanthropists who donate millions of dollars, while others are indifferent to social needs. Some work very hard at very demanding jobs, while others live on inherited wealth and don't work at all. Some are well-known publicly, while others are not. Generally, they manage to avoid being studied by social scientists, but there have been occasional studies that give us some information about their socialization of young children.

An illuminating view of upper-class children is provided by work done in the 1960s and 1970s by Robert Coles, an unusual research psychiatrist who traveled extensively talking to children and their parents. As he says, his work is "based upon the observations of a child psychiatrist who has placed himself at a remove from hospitals, clinics, consulting offices. Instead of children visiting him he visits them, tells them he is interested in their ideas, their observations, and tries later to portray them, to evoke their minds, hearts, spirits as pointedly and suggestively as he can" (Coles 1977, 49). (Whatever changes may have occurred in upper-class life since he wrote, there is no reason to believe that his basic observations of upper-class children are out of date. The family wealth of today's upper-class children continues to provide a luxurious lifestyle in which they are likely socialized. Some overlapping observations can be found in Wrigley [1995].) Originally, Coles went to the South to study African American children who endured the hardships of initial school desegregation. He wrote a book about those children, but while he was doing his work, some of the working-class parents said he ought to talk to the wealthy white people who controlled their lives (Coles 1977, 33). He decided to do so, began in New Orleans and Atlanta, then extended his work to other parts of the country.

Coles introduces upper-class lifestyle by describing some of the houses he visited. In the South, the house might be an old plantation manor that has been modernized with air conditioning and "tastefully decorated rooms." In Kentucky "bluegrass country," he went to horse farms in gentle hills with "an established tradition of leisure." In the suburbs and exurbs of northeastern and midwestern cities, there were "imitation English castles; French provincial, nineteenth-century American, contemporary one-levels." In Texas and New Mexico, the homes are big, sprawling ranch houses with many rooms in many wings. The owners of these and other large homes were plantation owners, corporation and business executives, bankers, lawyers, stockbrokers, doctors, architects, strip-mine operators, ranchers, and agricultural growers. Many have summer homes. Some have third homes in ski resorts (Coles 1977, 3–11).

Children's recreation involves learning certain skills and practicing them competitively. "Children take sailing lessons as well as tennis lessons, enter races or regattas, learn every trick they can to pull out front and stay there" (Coles 1977, 14). For many children, there is a considerable involvement with horses: "For some children and their parents the care of horses as well as the riding of them becomes one of the most important tasks of each day . . ." (Coles 1977, 13). The author presents a comparison of performance expectations between upper-class and working-class/middle-class children:

> On weekends there are rides, races, or a lot of care: the shoes, the coat, the mane, all in need of work. And a talk with the veterinarian. And a discussion to go here or there by van on such and such a weekend? . . . As with golf, there are clubs and clubs, hunts and hunts, horses and horses, stables and stables. Much has been made of Little League baseball—its searing effect on working- or middle-class children, who fight hard to win; so hard, some claim, that any loss becomes a devastating psychological experience and any victory an exercise in arrogant self-congratulation, accompanied, alas, by a haunting apprehension of future defeat. But among certain quite well-off children the performance at a show or on a hunt can be an occasion for fear, self-doubt, and fierce rivalry. (Coles 1977, 13)

Children of the upper class often go to private schools. They travel a great deal, including to foreign places. Their houses often have enormous playrooms, and the children have wider choices of toys and clothes than other children. In newspapers and on broadcast news programs, the news is sometimes about neighbors, friends, or acquaintances of their parents. They see their parents give orders to servants. "In a way, those servants . . . are for these American children a microcosm of the larger world as they will experience it. They are people who provide convenience and comfort. They are people, who, by and large, aim to please" (Coles 1977, 27).

The upshot of an upper-class childhood, according to Coles, is that children develop a taken-for-granted sense of entitlement to the privileged life they enjoy. Things and people are there for them, and they expect that that will be the case in the future. Further, "Even as a migrant child or a ghetto child learns to feel weak and vulnerable, a child of well-off parents learns to feel, in many respects, confident. . . . But let us not forget that entitlement is perfectly compatible with doubts, misgivings, despair. A child can feel—being realistic—entitled to a certain kind of life and yet have other reasons to be confused or hurt" (Coles 1977, 395, 397). What Coles is saying here is that a sense of privilege and entitlement becomes part of the upper-class child's self, but that there are other parts of the self. The child can be "in many respects" self-confident but in other respects, perhaps in his ability to achieve or in measuring up to his peers, he can also experience self-doubt.

When upper-class children reach the age of 14, many of them are sent by their parents away from home to boarding schools known as *prep schools*. The purpose of these schools is not only to give the children a good education but also to socialize these children to occupy positions of power. Two sociologists who have studied these schools note,

> The preservation of privilege requires the exercise of power, and those who exercise it cannot be too squeamish about the injuries that any ensuing conflict imposes on the losers. . . . The founders of the schools recognized that unless their sons and grandsons were willing to take up the struggle for the preservation of their class interests, privilege would slip from the hands of the elite and eventually power would pass to either a competing elite or to a rising underclass. (Cookson and Persell 1985, 24)

The boys' schools have very demanding curricula, and students are expected to become highly self-disciplined. They are being taught to be leaders. Girls' schools are more comfortable because girls are "not being socialized for power, but to be the helpmates of the powerful. . . . Unlike the boys' schools, where status was objectified by combat (real or symbolic), girls were taught to avoid open combat, because it was unladylike, and were encouraged to learn the fine art of persuasion through suggestion" (Cookson and Persell 1985, 25). No socialization agency succeeds with all those it seeks to socialize, and some prep school students "become playboys and playgirls more intent on squandering the family fortune than increasing it" (Cookson and Persell 1985, 26).

Upper-Middle Class

Upper-middle-class people are usually comfortably well-off, but they are not as wealthy or as powerful as upper-class people. They are, however, often more highly educated. Although some physicians, lawyers, architects, and other professionals have either been born into or "made it" into the upper class, most are upper-middle class. Most upper-class people are college graduates but are not as likely as upper-middle-class people to have gained advanced degrees. Upper-middle-class people are sometimes referred to as *the professional and business class*. Upper-middle-class families usually live in homes or apartments that are substantial, though not palatial, and are well stocked with a wide range of consumer goods, some of which are likely to be costly. The dwelling is usually large enough for each child to have a separate room; when this is not the case, the family is likely to look forward to the time when its income will increase sufficiently for this standard to be attained. Privacy is a value, and, in this class, children are entitled to some privacy. The children are also likely to have available expensive toys, sports equipment, computers, and other popular items of leisure and consumption.

The upper-middle-class way of life usually involves its members in a variety of institutions outside the family. Both the father's and mother's occupations (many families are dual-career) may require them to be in contact with many organizations in addition to the ones that employ them. If they are in business, they are involved in various financial relationships with people in other firms. If they are professionals, they are associated with hospitals or courts or universities or government agencies, where they meet others with whom they collaborate or whom they help, persuade, teach, or supervise, as the case may be.

In addition to occupational contacts with many organizations, both husband and wife are likely to have roles in numerous other formal organizations—associations of business or professional people (medical societies, law groups, chambers of commerce, and so on), church groups, country clubs or swimming clubs, and perhaps some civic betterment association. In addition to activities in these formal organizations, there is likely to be considerable entertaining at home, largely arranged by the wife, as well as much out-of-home entertainment such as dining in good restaurants and attending the theater, concerts, and the like.

The upper-middle-class child picks up information, knowledge, vocabulary, and attitudes concerning all this activity. At dinner and at other times, he or she is introduced to the world of business deals or court cases or giving lectures, as such matters are discussed or alluded to. The concerns, activities, and meetings of this or that association may also come up. Thus, in the upper-middle-class home, the child is likely to learn that life involves some kind of responsibility not only in an organization but also *for* the organization.

Children growing up in this class undergo what Bernard Farber (1964, 368–374) called *sponsored independence* and what Annette Lareau recently called *concerted cultivation* (Lareau 2002, 2003). Despite the difference in terminology, these two sociologists have arrived at virtually the same concept. The concept refers to the fact that children in this class participate in a wide range of activities that are sponsored and organized by adults (parents, teachers, and coaches), including various kinds of group activities (such as soccer practice and choir rehearsal) and private lessons (music, tennis, swimming, dance, etc.) to which the children are usually chauffeured by one or the other parent. Lareau adds that these parents see themselves as "developing their children" so that they cultivate their talents. Parents and children talk to each other a great deal about these activities—how things are going, what is happening, and what goals the child should set to reach for a higher level of skill. Interestingly, Lareau sees a sense of entitlement as an outcome, but it has a somewhat different focus than the sense of entitlement that Coles found in the upper class. Lareau writes, "From this [process of concerted cultivation], a robust sense of entitlement takes root in these children. This sense of entitlement is nurtured in all areas, but it is especially effective in institutional settings where these children learn to question adults and address them as relative equals" (Lareau 2003, 2).

Lareau's recent study of 88 children in three social classes is focused on how parents get children through the day. In addition to interviews that she and her assistants conducted with these families (equally divided between white and African American) with children aged 9 and 10, they conducted extensive in-home observations with 12 families, visiting each family for about 20 days. They went along on family errands and sat in on children's visits to doctors and dentists. They sat on the floor with the children when they watched television. They hung around outside while the children played with their friends. They had one overnight visit with each family. In addition to home visits, they also observed in the school classrooms of these children. These are probably the most comprehensive observations of children that any researcher has succeeded in making. We will present some of Lareau's findings about middle-class children here, and her findings on working-class and poor children in sections to follow. (Although she uses the term "middle-class," these families more nearly fit what Gilbert and Kahl (see Figure 2-1 in Chapter 2), and others, classify as upper-middle class.)

Both black and white middle-class children are given a great deal of individualized attention by parents who organize their own schedules as much as possible around their children's activities. Those schedules are often packed tight, and the pace is hectic as two or more children in a family are driven to different activities in different locations. Lareau observes that, in general, black and white middle-class children had more in common with each other than either did with working-class or poor children of their own race. However, black children sometimes experienced racism, as when a white first-grade boy told Alexander, a lawyer's son, that he could only be a garbageman when he grew up. Middle-class black parents have an extra burden in working to protect their children from such adversities.

Also captured in these observations of the home is the distinctive use of conversation. Middle-class parents generally avoid physical punishment; instead, they reason and negotiate with their children. Children, in turn, feel that they are entitled to have their opinions heard and even to challenge their parents. Parents consider this mode of interaction as fostering their children's reasoning power and negotiating skills. Fostering knowledge and encouraging opinion formation are also parental goals in conversation. Conversation is sometimes joking, not always serious. But an emphasis on reasoning in the home also can make family life exhausting, as children of all ages repeatedly seek to reason with their parents. The very same skills parents encourage in their children can and do lead children to challenge, even reject, parental authority, but the parents consider that their approach to child rearing advances their goals for their children (Lareau 2003, 116–133).

The families Annette Lareau studied did not have nannies or in-home hired caregivers for their children. However, according to one estimate, about one-third of parents with advanced degrees do have in-home hired caregivers (Wrigley 1995, 147), and sociologist Julia Wrigley focused on the consequences for socialization in this segment of the upper-middle class (and also upper class) with hired in-home caregivers. She and her assistants conducted 79 interviews with parents, 76 with caregivers, and 22 with the heads of domestic employment agencies in Los Angeles and New York (Wrigley 1995, x). Most of these parents were in dual-career families. We limit ourselves to one important aspect of her study, contrasting values of parents and caregivers.

Many of the caregivers hired by upper-middle-class parents are poor immigrant women, from developing countries in Latin America and the Caribbean, with little formal education. They bring with them values and beliefs about how children should behave and how adults should deal with them. These often differ greatly from those of the parents who employ them. This presents a serious dilemma to the parents who are out of the house at work and must leave their children with someone who does not share their ways. Generally, these caregivers consider the children to be overindulged, with little respect for adult authority. Whereas the caregivers, from an early age, helped their parents, they see that the children in their care have no family responsibilities. Children as young as 5 give them orders. There were some exceptions; some of the caregivers were favorably impressed by the parents' patience and focused attention to their children. Overall, parents try to instruct the caregivers to handle their children as the parents want, but this is often difficult for the caregivers to implement because it goes against their own deeply held beliefs (Wrigley 1995).

Middle Class

The ranking of social classes is clearest at the top and the bottom. In the middle, the distinction between classes is somewhat blurred (Gilbert 1998, 288). Part of the blurring occurs because of overlap in the criteria used to distinguish the classes. Adding to the blurring is the practice of politicians to speak to voters in a way that suggests they are all middle class. The term *working class*, although long used by sociologists, has been avoided by politicians and by many others who want to believe or pretend to believe that the United States is a classless society. (All citizens are equal before the law, and this legal equality is sometimes used to obscure differences in wealth, power, and prestige.) Government agencies sometimes also contribute to the blurring. The head of the Congressional Budget Office is reported as saying that any family of four with an annual income between $19,000 and $78,000 is middle class. This range is so broad that it obscures the problems faced by, and the differences in lifestyle among, families at different points in this range (Rubin 1992, xvii). Sociologist Lillian Rubin also points to the accumulation of consumer goods as contributing to blurring class lines. Since "everyone" owns a TV, VCR, washing machine, answering machine, dishwasher, and car, this shared material culture obscures the visibility of class distinctions (Rubin 1994, 38).

One basis for distinguishing between middle class (sometimes called the lower-middle class) and working class is type of occupation. Middle-class occupations usually require more knowledge, skill, and preparation than working-class occupations, and they also allow more autonomy in the work. Included, for example, are some professions such as teaching and social work, craft workers, and foremen (Gilbert 1998, 289). Also included are small business owners, middle-level managers in business, middle-level bureaucrats in government, secretaries, and paraprofessionals such as nurses, medical technicians, and legal workers (Marger 1999, 84). Another basis for distinguishing the two classes is type of remuneration. People in middle-class occupations (also known as *white-collar workers*) are usually paid a *salary* specified by the week or month or year, while those in working-class occupations (also known as *blue-collar workers*) are paid an hourly *wage*. Much white-collar work is office work, which once had a great deal more prestige and paid better than blue-collar work. In recent years, however, much white-collar office work has become more routinized and, in this respect, is not so different from blue-collar work. Further, the pay difference has narrowed (Gilbert 1998, 59–61). This contributes to the blurring.

One influential line of research contrasting middle-class with working-class child rearing has been carried out by sociologist Melvin Kohn and his colleagues over many years. Kohn argues and presents evidence that middle-class occupations require greater initiative, independence, and self-direction than do working-class occupations which involve closer supervision and more routinization (Kohn 1963, 1977, 1979; Kohn and Schooler 1983; Kohn and Slomczynski 1990). To carry on such middle-class occupations with even a moderate amount of success requires a certain kind of self: a belief in one's ability to face and solve problems that are not routine and to make judgments and decisions. Confidence that one's own actions make a difference in how things turn out is also required, even though there are uncertainties, anxieties, and disappointments. These are manifestations of self-efficacy (Gecas 1989, 2005), which we discussed in Chapter 4.

Kohn argues that the nature of their work leads middle-class people to value self-direction, and this value is transmitted to their children, while working-class people value obedience and demand it of their children. In applying discipline, middle-class parents are more concerned with motives and intentions of their children's acts, whereas working-class people are more concerned with the overt consequences. This hypothetical example illustrates the difference: A 5-year-old girl trips her younger sister, who falls and bursts out crying. The middle-class parent is likely to try to find out how it happened: whether it was accidental or whether the older girl deliberately tripped her. Only in the latter case would the child be punished, for the child must learn to internalize appropriate standards. The working-class parent is more likely to react to the outcome; the tripping is hurtful to the younger sister and disrupts the peace of the household, so the older girl should be punished.

It must be said that Kohn does not distinguish between upper-middle class and middle class in his writings. What we have just presented from his research is consistent with Lareau's characterization of the middle class, which we believe, on the basis of her evidence, is mostly upper-middle class. Kohn's analysis also, we believe, clearly applies to the upper-middle class as well as to much of today's middle class. It is in the nature of sociological research that researchers do not always use identical criteria for classifications. Therefore, trying to see the relationship of one study to another in order to learn something more general requires some interpretation based on clues from multiple studies. It is also necessary to recall that there is some overlap in values and practices between classes. At the upper end of the middle class, people may have many similarities to upper-middle-class people, while at the lower end they may be somewhat similar to working-class people.

The work of Kohn and his colleagues has certain limitations, which have been summarized by anthropologist Adrie Kusserow: (1) It is based only on men; (2) the nature of a person's work is not the only factor that links the self (or *personality*, the Kohn group's term) to the social structure; and (3) "each social class has too often been saddled into bipolar procrustean beds of conformity vs. self-direction, which hardly illuminate the varying individualistic and conformist styles present in all groups" (Kusserow 2004, 30). These comments are well taken. It would be worthwhile and interesting to see whether a study of women in the social class levels that Kohn and colleagues compared would yield similar or different results. The Kohn group does not claim that they are producing a comprehensive explanation of the relationship between the individual and the social structure but that they have identified a very significant link. And it is true that sociological generalizations do not capture the contours of individual variation. Although it is necessary to have some sociological research that shows aspects of human action that do not fit within generalizations, one basic thrust of sociology is to try to identify ways in which the features of a particular social position influence the actions and the very selves of those who occupy the position, whether it be social class level; membership in a minority or a majority category; marital status; sex category; age category of child, adolescent, or young adult; and the like. Such social positions influence the ways that people in them act, but none of them provides a total explanation. Further, studies of this kind do not capture human agency, the capacity and necessity of people to interpret their social situations, which means that some interpretations differ from or go against those of the majority in a particular position. Despite these limitations, studies of how social positions influence actions provide illumination, provided we do not expect them to explain every action of every individual in a social position. Indeed, as we shall see shortly, Kusserow herself offers a social class explanation of differences in the meaning of the American value of "individualism."

Working Class

Working-class occupations include primarily machine operators in factories, but also auto mechanics, truck drivers, construction workers (known as "hard hats" because of the protective headgear they wear), and such semiskilled workers as bus drivers, beauticians, and barbers. As American manufacturing companies shifted much of their manufacturing to other countries where workers are paid less than in the United States, American workers lost relatively well-paying jobs and had to settle for lower-paying ones.

In her recent study, sociologist Lillian Rubin points to a cultural difference between middle-class and working-class parents. Working-class parents are only slowly accepting changes, such as the open expression of premarital sex and living together without marriage, that middle-class parents accepted earlier. She attributes this to the fact that most working-class parents have not been exposed to the wide range of ideas that the middle class, especially the college educated, have experienced. The working-class parents remain more traditional in outlook for a longer time (Rubin 1994, 48).

As we noted in Chapter 2, some social mobility does occur, but generally classes reproduce themselves. How does that happen? Sociologist and economist George Farkas has carried out studies that led him to this formulation:

> [P]arental skills, habits, and styles determine the very early cognitive skills of their children and these influence the child's habits and styles via his or her estimation of the success they can expect from tasks that both require and increase cognitive skill. The resulting differential time-on-task and concentration-on-task . . . affect the level of cognitive skill itself, creating a powerful mechanism by which large cognitive skill gaps between groups of children from different backgrounds come into being by relatively young ages. In sum, skills, habits, and styles are central to stratification outcomes, but these are formed at young ages and essentially without conscious intent

on the children's part. Instead, they result from outcomes that are taught, modeled, and reinforced by events occurring in households and schools. These events may pass relatively unnoticed at the time but they constitute the central mechanisms by which stratification outcomes are determined. (Farkas 1996, 11–12)

A review of some 30 studies of mother-child interaction concludes that there are some consistent differences between the middle and working classes that support Farkas' conclusion. While working-class and middle-class mothers are not different in holding and touching their babies, middle-class mothers address more speech to their children, and, as the child's speech develops, they elicit more talk from their children and keep a conversation going longer. They also provide more informational labeling of objects for their children. Another finding is that working-class mothers tend to be more controlling, restrictive, and disapproving of their children than middle-class mothers (Hoff-Ginsberg and Tardif 1995, 174–179). This finding that working-class mothers are more controlling and disapproving is consistent with the earlier finding of Gans, reported in Chapter 5, that adult-centered families are likely to be found in the working class (Gans [1962] 1982).

Annette Lareau conceptualizes her observations of upper-middle-class and working-class parenting as two contrasting cultural logics. In contrast to concerted cultivation, the cultural logic of working-class parents she calls *the accomplishment of natural growth* (Lareau 2003, 3). Bernard Farber (1964) called the working-class approach *unsponsored independence*. Working-class parents do not consider the management of their children's leisure time activities as part of their parenting responsibilities. While working-class children may belong to some organized activities such as scouts or sports teams sponsored by neighborhood groups or school, they generally are more on their own after school, independent of the watchful eyes of their parents or other adults. "[W]hereas upper-middle-class children often are treated as a project to be developed, working-class and poor children are given boundaries for their behavior and then allowed to grow" (Lareau 2003, 67). They are less likely to participate in individualized sports or to take music or other fee-charging lessons, because of both financial limitations and the belief that children need to have free time with their peers. Lareau notes that, like some other researchers, she did not find extensive differences in attitude between upper-middle-class, working-class, and poor mothers. They all desired to be good mothers and have their children grow and thrive. What was different was the actions they took to carry out their idea of what it means to be a good parent. The *behavior* was different (Lareau 2003, 290, n.5).

The cultural differences show up in a number of ways. Family relationships differed. Upper-middle-class children whom Lareau observed were more competitive with and hostile to their siblings because of their often conflicting schedules and because of invidious comparisons of accomplishments (Lareau 2003, 55–57) than were the working-class and poor children. Also, they had less satisfying ties to extended family members.

We have noted the difference in activity patterns between the children of the two class groups. Lareau emphasizes the long-term implications of this difference for work success. Upper-middle-class children learn to work with different adults. She sees this as acquiring a basic job skill—learning to work smoothly with acquaintances. Since most of the adults whom working-class and poor children deal with are immediate or extended family members, they have fewer opportunities for what she terms a type of "pre-employment training" (Lareau 2003, 39, 62).

Another difference is that upper-middle-class parents look their children in the eye when conversing with them, and children are taught to shake hands with adult men to whom they are introduced and look them in the eye. This is not the practice in poor neighborhoods, and in poor black neighborhoods it can be dangerous to look people in the eye too long (Lareau 2003, 5, 63). Still another difference is that time is organized on a different basis in working-class and poor families than it is in upper-middle- and middle-class families. In working-class households, children's activities do not set the pace, whereas the array of children's activities in the middle class generates a hectic pace (Lareau 2003, 63–65, 72–73).

Because working-class and poor children have autonomy in their play activities, Lareau believes that they develop important life skills. The boys she observed "often play games they have devised themselves, complete with rules and systems of enforcement. Thus . . . [they have] opportunities to develop skills in peer mediation, conflict management, personal responsibility, and strategizing" (Lareau 2003, 80). These skills may well become useful if these children become upwardly mobile.

Working-class parents are glad to see their kids have fun, but, "In general, children's leisure activities are treated as pleasant but inconsequential. Of much greater importance are the many steps involved in getting children through the day: getting them up, showered, fed, dressed, bundled up in winter jackets, and out the door in time for school, and then at the end of the day making sure they get home safely, have dinner, complete their homework, and get to bed at a reasonable hour" (Lareau 2003, 83).

There are some significant differences in attitudes toward language and in how language is used by parents. Such differences were first brought to attention many years ago by British sociologist Basil Bernstein. He argued that in the upper-middle-class, language becomes the object of special attention and elaboration. The structure and syntax of middle-class speech are particularly complex and make possible a more subtle and complex grasp of reality than is the case in the working class. Bernstein illustrates with a homely example, an English middle-class mother saying to her child, "I'd rather you made less noise, dear." Middle-class children have learned to interpret *rather* and *less* as requiring a particular response. Bernstein believes that working-class children do not have available this kind of sentence structure and would have to translate the foregoing sentence into a form that they know from their own experience: "Shut up!" (Bernstein 1961).

In keeping with the fact that upper-middle-class parents live more in the realm of ideas and abstractions and give greater emphasis to verbal skills, they are more likely to explain and give reasons to the children for their actions; the working-class parents are more likely to express directly what they have in mind, without explanation. Thus, whereas the working-class parent may simply say, "No, you can't," to a child who wants to stay up late to watch a TV show, the middle-class parent may say, "It's probably not a good idea because if you stay up you won't get enough sleep and then you won't be alert for your test tomorrow" (Grimshaw 1981, 230). In her detailed observation of a working-class family, Annette Lareau observes that

> in poor and working-class families, a parent's key responsibility lies in providing important physical care for children, offering clothing and shelter, teaching the difference between right and wrong, and providing comfort.... [A parent] does not systematically and continuously try to enrich [a child's] vocabulary, or cultivate his verbal (or physical) talents, or cajole him, or attempt to persuade him to act in particular ways. She issues short, clear directives and she expects prompt, respectful compliance. (Lareau 2002, ch. 8, 9)

Thus, the working-class child is less likely to understand more subtle forms of personal communication.

Working Poor

The working poor include service workers such as supermarket cashiers, servers in fast-food restaurants, waitresses in small restaurants, as well as the lowest-paid workers in working-class occupations. In Annette Lareau's sample of 12 families, for example, one couple consists of a mother who works as a housecleaner and a father who is a housepainter. Neither finished high school; their combined annual income is $35,000. Another couple includes a mother with some college education who works as a clerk in a large company; her husband did not finish high school and is unemployed, and their income is between $15,000 and $25,000 (Lareau 2002, appendix B). Dennis Gilbert points out that the boundaries between the working poor and the classes above and below it are somewhat indistinct, and people can move between them in what he calls "oscillating mobility." The working poor tend to have less stable work histories than the working class (Gilbert 1998, 290). We do not have socialization studies of pre-adolescent children that focus specifically on the working poor. The presumption is that socialization in this stratum is not significantly different from that in the working class.

The Underclass

Members of the underclass are people with a low level of education and few or no marketable skills who work erratically or at part-time jobs. Some are single mothers who receive limited help from absent fathers. Many depend on government transfer programs (programs that transfer money from general tax revenues to those in need) such as public assistance or Temporary Aid to Needy Families (TANF), Supplemental Security Income (SSI), and veterans' benefits (Gilbert 1998, 290–291).

Not all researchers use the concept of underclass. Instead, a number focus on the consequences of *poverty* for children. Although their starting point is family income, their research is dealing with people whom others would include in the underclass, and we shall cite some of that research here. In 1996, and for the preceding decade, 20 percent of American children were living in poverty. Poverty was defined as an income of no more than $12,000 a year for a family of three. In addition to the poor, another 20 percent of children lived in families with an income between $12,000 and $22,000 per year; they are referred to as "near-poor" (Brooks-Gunn, Duncan, and Maritato 1997, 1–3). A more recent study, using a somewhat different research procedure, defines poverty as an income of $20,200 or less for a family of three, and $22,200 or less for a family of four. These criteria yield a result somewhat, though not exactly, comparable to the preceding study: According to this more recent study, 20.3 percent of American children were poor in 1997 (Rainwater and Smeeding 2003, 20–21, Table 1.1 and Figure 1.1). People with poverty incomes are in the underclass, in the Gilbert-Kahl classification, while the near-poor might be divided between the underclass and the working poor. In Canada, which uses a slightly different definition of poverty, about 19 percent of children were classified as in poverty in 1998 (National Council of Welfare 2001).

Poverty has numerous negative consequences for children. However, before we discuss them, the reader should recall the concept of risk, which we introduced in Chapter 6. Poor children are at greater risk than those from higher-income families. But, as some researchers point out, "Some children from poor families do well, while some children from more affluent families have difficulties. In the view of Garmezy and Rutter (1983), 'some children are resilient to the untoward consequences of negative conditions'" (quoted in Brooks-Gunn, Duncan, and Maritato 1997, 6). But poor children are less likely to do well, although some are resilient. The risks are greater the longer they live in poverty. More than 200 years ago Adam Smith, considered the first economist, showed awareness that poverty is a cultural as well as economic condition. "He defined economic hardship as the experience of being unable to consume commodities that 'the custom of the country renders it indecent for creditable people, even of the lowest order, to be without'" (Hernandez 1997, 18). But the consequences for children go beyond matters of consumption.

As early as age 3, on tests that measure intelligence at that age, poor children do not do as well as those from better-off families. Test scores at this age approximately predict performance in the later preschool years (Smith, Brooks-Gunn, and Klebanov 1997, 165). One study finds a difference between poor children in two-parent and in one-parent families. Parents in two-parent families who use "good parenting practices" (e.g., praising and hugging their child, as contrasted to yelling and spanking) have a positive effect on their child's well-being (as shown by the children's initiative and sociability, not being sad, and not being mean to others). However, the combination of economic deprivation and living in a one-parent family seems to reduce children's capacity to respond positively to good parenting practices (Hanson, McLanahan, and Thomson 1997). Another study concludes that children who grow up in poverty are less likely than other children to graduate from high school. Again, if they grow up with a single parent, their chances of graduation are further reduced (Haveman, Wolfe, and Wilson 1997, 442). An important overall conclusion from a series of studies emphasizes the importance of poverty during the early years: "Family economic conditions in early and middle childhood appear to be far more important for shaping ability and achievement than they are during adolescence" (Duncan and Brooks-Gunn 1997, 597).

There is some evidence that poor children who have the advantage of being in a good preschool program can lower the risk of negative outcomes. A review of studies of seven such programs finds that, compared to control groups who did not have the advantage, children in them improve their intellectual performance and IQ at the beginning of school. They are less likely to repeat a grade or to be placed in a special education class. They are less likely to drop out of high school. The study of one program that followed children beyond high school into early adulthood found that those who had the preschool education were less likely to be on welfare, have a teenage pregnancy, or be arrested. They were more likely to be in postsecondary education or be employed (Schweinhart and Weikart 1987). Such results suggest long-term stabilizing effects of a good early preschool program, effects that we have called (in Chapter 3) maintaining responsive participation in society and developing some forms of competence.

Social Class and Individualism

Individualism is an American value. It finds expression in such often heard comments as "Everybody is entitled to their own opinion" and "Everybody's different." Earlier research, such as the work of Kohn and his colleagues (Kohn 1963; Kohn and Schooler 1983; Kohn and Slomczynski 1990) credited the upper-middle class with being independent and self-directed, while finding the working class conformist and obedient, and not at all individualistic. Anthropologist Adrie Kusserow considers this too simplistic and too overdrawn. She proposes that all groups have what she calls individualistic and sociocentric orientations, "but in different styles and ratios, depending on the local worlds they inhabit." Her goal is to move beyond what she considers the too simplistic view of Kohn and others "by exploring the ways individualism is understood, taken up, and used in raising children among working-class parents and teachers" (Kusserow 2004, 23). She focused on the practices of individualism, which she defines as "any verbal or nonverbal encouragement of the child's independence, individuality, uniqueness, privacy, personal expressiveness, personal rights, self-assertiveness, self-reliance and self-confidence." She was also interested in sociocentric practices, which she defines as "any verbal or nonverbal encouragement of an identification of the child's self with her social role, the group, group activity, empathy, conformity, or knowing one's place in a hierarchy" (Kusserow 2004, 8–9). She found that individualism is interpreted differently in neighborhoods differentiated by social class. She studied three neighborhoods in New York City. Parkside is a neighborhood in the Borough of Manhattan of upper-class and upper-middle-class residents who are mostly white. Kelley is a white working-class neighborhood, and Queenston is a lower-working-class neighborhood with residents of different races; both are in the Borough of Queens. Kusserow interviewed parents, observed them interacting with their children, and observed in preschools in each neighborhood.

The most basic finding of her study is that there are two main patterns of individualism, which she calls *hard* and *soft*. The parents in the two Queens neighborhoods socialize their children into a hard individualism; that is, they view the child's self as being a unit that is "against" the world. The child's self requires toughening and hardening. The Parkside parents practice a soft individualism, meaning that they regard the child's self as "opening up"; the child is encouraged to express feelings and to open out into the world. It is a view of the child's self as fluid and flexible (Kusserow 2004, 26). The Kelley and Queenston parents put emphasis on their children being "tough," a word they used often in the interviews and a quality they saw as necessary for their children to be able to resist the negative influences of the street, such as gangs, peer pressure, violence, prostitution, drugs, and alcoholism. They believe that too much praise is not good for a child because it can lead to feeling "too full of himself" (Kusserow 2004, 35–36). The Parkside parents do not seek to toughen their children but to assist them to develop their unique qualities. They try to be warm and receptive to each child's individuality. They talk about a child "flowering" or "blooming." While they value being gentle and receptive to their children, some find their children to be stubborn or willful. This made parenting sometimes difficult, but the parents saw value in these qualities. Kusserow notes, "In contrast to some of the comments made by Queenston and Kelley parents on the problem of having a fresh kid who talks back too much stubbornness and willfulness were even described as healthy in Parkside" (Kusserow 2004, 101).

Kusserow found two versions of hard individualism. In Kelley, the working-class neighborhood, which was safer, neater, more cohesive, and at a slightly higher income level than Queenston, the parents' emphasis on hardness was not only so their children could resist violence or drugs but also so that they could be tough enough to strive to better themselves. In other words, they were trying to prepare their children to push for upward social mobility. A tough skin is necessary to survive the stresses of struggling to better oneself. She calls this *hard projective individualism*. In contrast to this emphasis on self-assertion and self-confidence, the Queenston parents were focused on having their children become self-protective and self-reliant. Theirs is a *hard protective individualism* that involves "putting up shields of armor through pride, self-sufficiency, privacy, independence, toughness, and self-resilience." Not trusting others too much is a parental caution and one aspect of being self-reliant (Kusserow 2004, 57, 73, 170–171).

In preschools in Parkside and Kelley, Kusserow found that teachers operated in ways that were congruent with the ways the children's parents did. Thus, in Parkside the teachers socialized children to "a psychologized individualism of feelings, rights, and uniqueness" (Kusserow 2004, 113). In the Kelley preschools, the emphasis was on self-reliance, coping with difficulties without help, not calling attention to yourself, and not expecting much sympathy or praise. The schools taught sociocentric values as well as their versions of individualism. The researcher notes that in Parkside preschools,

> Group life . . . was often taught by emphasizing how one's selfish act was hurting other children's feelings. Empathy, listening, and learning to articulate one's feelings in words were important skills for the child to learn. In the Queens preschools (and again mainly in Kelley) conformity to group life was taught mainly through practices such as teasing, public shaming, blaming, promotion of a sense of competition between children, and use of threats. (Kusserow 2004, 113)

The one Queenston preschool she observed had an upper-middle-class teacher trying to communicate a soft individualism to working-class children. Her observations of this specific situation are not detailed, but, drawing on observations she had made in other comparable situations, she notes a clash of cultures, the one the child brings from home and the one the teacher expresses and communicates. In such situations the children become silent, "as if mystified by the fairy-like teacher who moved around the classroom with a constant glow and smile, showering praise upon them" (Kusserow 2004, 178–179).

In concluding her study, Kusserow argues that she has presented a more nuanced picture of social class differences than is found in Kohn's long—and still—influential work. She finds a version of individualism in people of the social class level that he characterized as exhibiting conformity, and a fair amount of sociocentric socialization among those whom he characterized as self-directed. In all three communities that she studied, parents and teachers were concerned with socializing their children in both individualistic and sociocentric values (Kusserow 2004, 172). They differed in how they construed these values and in the practices they used to achieve their goals.

✻ ✻ ✻

In American society, as in most others, the benefits that it makes possible—notably income, wealth, prestige or social honor, and power—are distributed unevenly among people. Some have a great deal, some have little, and some are in between. People sort themselves according to how much they have, and interact socially primarily with people at their level. People of roughly similar income and wealth, prestige, and power can be regarded as constituting a social class, a certain level in the social hierarchy. Although there is no one exclusively correct way to describe the complexities of this distribution, a considerable amount of accumulated evidence has indicated the usefulness of understanding American society in terms of six social classes. Each tends to develop a class culture that is somewhat different from that of other classes; each is a somewhat distinctive version of the general American culture. Children are socialized by their parents, teachers, other adults, and peers into the culture of their class. The ways in which children live in their childhood, as well as their prospects for the kinds of lives they will have thereafter, are significantly influenced by the class into which they are socialized.

References

Bernstein, Basil. 1961. "Social Class and Linguistic Development: A Theory of Social Learning." In A. H. Halsey, Jean Floud, and C. Anold Anderson (eds.) *Education, Economy, and Society*, 288–314. New York: Free Press.

Brooks-Gunn, Jeanne, Greg J. Duncan, and Nancy Maritato, Nancy. 1997. "Poor Families, Poor Outcomes: The Wellbeing of Children and Youth." In Greg J. Duncan and Jeanne Brooks-Gunn (eds.) *Consequences of Growing Up Poor*, 1–17. New York: Russell Sage Foundation.

Coles, Robert. 1977. *Privileged Ones: The Well-Off and the Rich in America*. Boston: Little, Brown.

Cookson, Peter, and Caroline Persell. 1985. *Preparing for Power: America's Elite Boarding Schools*. New York: Basic Books.

Danziger, Sheldon, and Ann Chih Lin. 2000. *Coping with Poverty*. Ann Arbor: University of Michigan Press.

Duncan, Greg J., and Jeanne Brooks-Gunn. 1997. "Income Effects Across the Life Span." In Greg J. Duncan and Jeanne Brooks-Gunn (eds.) *Consequences of Growing Up Poor*, 596–610. New York: Russell Sage Foundation.

Farber, Bernard. 1964. *Family: Organization and Interaction*. San Francisco: Chandler.

Farkas, George. 1996. *Human Capital or Cultural Capital?* New York: Aldine de Gruyter.

Gans, Herbert. [1962] 1982. *The Urban Villagers: Group and Class in the Life of Italian Americans*. New York: Free Press.

Garmezy, Norman, and Michael Rutter. 1983. *Stress, Coping, and Development in Children*. New York: McGraw-Hill.

Gecas, Viktor. 1989. "The Social Psychology of Self-Efficacy." *Annual Review of Sociology* 15: 291–316.

——. 2003. "Self-Agency and the Life Course." In Jeylan T. Mortimer and Michael J. Shanahan (eds.) *Handbook of The Life Course*, 369–388. New York: Kluwer Academic/Plenum.

Gilbert, Dennis. 1998. *The American Class Structure*, 5th ed. Belmont, CA: Wadsworth.

Grimshaw, Allen D. 1981. "Talk and Social Control." In Morris Rosenberg and Ralph H. Turner (eds.) *Social Psychology: Sociological Perspectives*, 200–232. New York: Basic Books.

Hanson, Thomas L., Sara McLanahan, and Elizabeth Thomson. 1997. "Economic Resources, Parental Practices, and Children's Well-Being." In Greg J. Duncan and Jeanne Brooks-Gunn (eds.) *Consequences of Growing Up Poor*, 190–221. New York: Russell Sage Foundation.

Haveman, Robert, Barbara Wolfe, and Kathryn Wilson. 1997. "Childhood Poverty and Adolescent Schooling and Fertility Outcomes." In Greg J. Duncan and Jeanne Brooks-Gunn (eds.) *Consequences of Growing Up Poor*, 419–460. New York: Russell Sage Foundation.

Hernandez, Donald. 1997. "Poverty Trends." In Greg J. Duncan and Jeanne Brooks-Gunn (eds.) *Consequences of Growing Up Poor*, 18–34. New York: Russell Sage Foundation.

Hicks-Bartlett, Sharon. 2000. "Between a Rock and a Hard Place. The Labyrinth of Working and Parenting in a Poor Community." In Sheldon Danziger and Ann Chih Lin (eds.) *Coping with Poverty*, 27–51. Ann Arbor: University of Michigan Press.

Hoff-Ginsberg, Erika, and Twila Tardif. 1995. "Socioeconomic Status and Parenting." In Marc H. Bornstein (ed.) *Handbook of Parenting* 2: 161–188. Mahwah, NJ: Lawrence Erlbaum.

Kohn, Melvin. 1963. "Social Class and Parent-Child Relationships: An Interpretation." *American Journal of Sociology* 68: 471–480 (January 1963).

——. 1977. *Class and Conformity*, 2nd ed. Chicago: University of Chicago Press.

——. 1979. "The Effects of Social Class on Parental Values and Practices." In Davis Reiss and Howard A. Hoffman (eds.) *The American Family*, 45–68. New York: Plenum.

Kohn, Melvin, and Carmi Schooler. 1983. *Work and Personality: An Inquiry into the Impact of Social Stratification*. Norwood, NJ: Ablex.

Kohn, Melvin, and Kazimierez Slomczyniski. 1990. *Social Structure and Self-Direction*. Cambridge, MA: Basil Blackwell.

Kusserow, Adrie. 2004. *American Individualisms: Child Rearing and Social Class in Three Neighborhoods*. New York: Palgrave Macmillan.

Lareau, Annette. 2002. "Invisible Inequality: Social Class and Chldrearing in Black Families and White Families." *American Sociological Review* 67(5): 747–796.

——. 2003. *Unequal Childhoods*. Berkeley: University of California Press.

Marger, Martin N. 1999. *Social Inequality*. Mountain View, CA: Mayfield.

National Council of Welfare. 2001. *Child Poverty Profile 1998*. Summer. Ottawa, Canada: National Council of Welfare.

Rainwater, Lee, and Timothy Smeeding. 2003. *Poor Kids in a Rich Country*. New York: Russell Sage Foundation.

Rubin, Lillian. 1992. "Worlds of Pain Revisited: 1972–1992." In *Worlds of Pain: Life in the Working-Class Family*, Xv–xxxix. New York: Basic Books.

——. 1994. *Families on the Fault Line*. New York: HarperCollins.

Schweinhart, Lawrence I., and David P. Weikart. 1987. "Evidence of Problem Prevention By Early Childhood Education." In Klaus Hurrelman, Franz-Xaver Kaufmann, and Friedrich Losel (eds.) *Social Intervention: Potential and Constraints*, 86–101. Berlin: Walter de Gruyter.

Smith, Judith R., Jeanne Brooks-Gunn, and Patricia Klebanov. 1997. "Consequences of Living in Poverty for Young Children's Cognitive and Verbal Ability and Early School Achievement." In Greg J. Duncan and Jeanne Brooks-Gunn (eds.) *Consequences of Growing Up Poor*, 132–189. New York: Russell Sage Foundation.

Wrigley, Julia. 1995. *Other People's Children*. New York: Basic Books. ✦

Chapter 10

Ethnic Groups, Minorities, and Neighborhood Communities

A n ethnic group, in contemporary usage, is a distinctive minority segment of society. In the United States and in Canada, the dominant, white, native English-speaking group does not think of itself as an ethnic group, but that is because it is more prestigious not to apply that term. The members of an ethnic group have a *shared identity* based on (1) a *common ancestry*, and (2) a *common culture*. Each of these terms condenses several elements, which should be identified.

A *shared identity* can be based on the members' own beliefs and feelings, on the beliefs and feelings of nonmembers who attribute such an identity to others, or on the beliefs and feelings of both members and nonmembers. Most ethnic groups include some members who have minimized or are in the process of minimizing their identity with the group. Nevertheless, nonmembers as well as members may still consider them part of the group, and this attributed identity may continue to have some impact on the socialization of the children. But the core of an ethnic group is usually made up of members who choose to identify themselves as members.

The concept of a *common ancestry*, although widespread in popular usage, is more complex than it seems. It seems to imply a common biological background, and there is partial truth to this. However, relatively few people can trace their biological ancestry more than five or six generations, at which point they lose track of who contributed to their biological inheritance. People may say, "I'm mostly Irish, with a little English and German mixed in," by which they mean that they know of some specific English and German contributors to their biological inheritance, know of many more Irish contributors, and assume that their ancestors far back beyond their knowledge were mostly Irish, in conformity with the recent majority they know of. The point here is that the notion of a common ancestry shared by members of an ethnic group rests on (1) their *shared belief concerning their biological inheritance*, combined with (2) a sense of the group's having inhabited a given geographical area and, therefore, (3) sharing in a distinctive group history.

A *common culture* here means a culture that is distinctive to the minority group in the midst of a dominant culture. Ethnic-group cultures usually involve one or more of the following cultural elements: (1) a language that is different from the dominant language in the society; (2) a religion; (3) a shared awareness of a historical background that is preserved in stories, legends, songs, costumes, and holidays; and (4) some values and norms that are distinguishable from those of the dominant majority and other ethnic groups.

These diverse components of what has come to be called *ethnicity* combine in different ways to result in different kinds of ethnic groups. Nationality groups, such as Italian, Polish, and Lithuanian, are distinguished by their origin in and ties to a particular political unit, a country of origin. There is in such nationality groups a sense of common biological inheritance, but this is usually less prominent than the sense of coming from a politically designated geographic place where people spoke their own language and participated in a culture identified with that place. In contrast, a sense of biological distinctiveness is more prominent in what are thought of as racial minorities, such as blacks (African Americans), Indians (Native Americans), and Inuit (Eskimo). Groups such as Koreans, Vietnamese, Chinese, Japanese, Filipinos, Indians, Pakistanis, and Bangladeshis, while each having their own nationality background, are, in the United States, often lumped together in a racial category, Asian American. Mexicans, Puerto Ricans, Dominicans, Cubans, and people from other Spanish-speaking Latin American countries are often lumped together as Latinos or Hispanics, a category that is also sometimes treated as though it were a racial category. Some religious groups that escaped from European oppression, such as the Amish, Hutterites, and Mennonites, each have distinctive cultures and shared identities based on their distinctive religions, which serve as bases for distinctive ways of life. Arabs have a shared identity based primarily on their Islamic religion and Arabic language and a onetime common historical background. Jews have had a shared identity based on a distinctive religion—in this respect, they are like the religious minorities—but also based on a shared awareness of a distinctive historical background and language. In this respect, they are like the nationality groups. In fact, Jews are divided into various cultural groups, ranging from those who are ultra-Orthodox in religion, who retain much of the dress and other culture of their European forebears, all the way to those who are secular (nonreligious), who are aware of their ethnic identity but who have little or no distinctive culture.

Except for the Native Indians and Inuit, who were already here, and the blacks, who first came as slaves, the populations of the two northernmost countries of North America (the United States and Canada) derive from immigrants of many countries. First came the original colonizers, primarily from England, Scotland, France, Spain, and Holland; then immigrants from northern and western Europe and from China. Many Mexicans were incorporated into the United States in 1848 following the American victory in the Mexican-American War. Puerto Rico became an American possession (now called a commonwealth) in 1898 as a result of victory in the Spanish-American War. In the United States, free and open immigration was halted by legislation in the early 1920s, when it was replaced by a restrictive quota system based on national origins; some nationalities were preferred over others. In 1968 the national quota system was replaced by one giving priority to preferred occupational skills and to kinship ties. Also, from time to time, special acts of Congress have permitted refugees to come from countries in political turmoil. In recent years, relatively more immigrants have come from Latin America (especially Mexico and the Dominican Republic), the Philippines and other countries in Asia, and the Caribbean region. In Canada also, immigrants have come primarily from non-European countries—from Hong Kong, Jamaica, the Philippines, Latin America, the Near East, and other countries in Asia and Africa. Refugees have also been admitted in large numbers.

Blacks (African Americans), until recently the largest ethnic group in the United States, are not an immigrant group. In 1790, when the first U.S. census was taken, blacks made up 19.3 percent of the population. They numbered about 32 million (12 percent of the American population) in 1990 (Elo and Preston 2002, 183–184). Their number has grown to 36 million (13 percent of the American population) in 2002 (McKinnon 2003), but Hispanics are now slightly more numerous. For generations, whites regarded blacks as a distinctive minority group by virtue of their common African ancestry. Increasingly, in recent years, blacks have also come to so regard themselves, accepting the definition the larger society has thrust upon them. Accompanying the new self-definition has come a change in feeling from one of derogation to one of racial consciousness and pride. In the 1970s, the slogan "Black is beautiful" gained wide dissemination as a response to long-standing white derogation of blacks. A similar redefinition that focuses on an assumed common ancestry and on similarities rather than differences among individuals and subgroups has also been occurring among North American Indians who, generations past, saw themselves as Iroquois, Creek, Hopi, or whatever other particular tribal group they stemmed from. To indicate that they were the original inhabitants of the land, Indians have come to adopt the term *Native Americans* in the U.S. and *First Nations* in Canada.

Because there are some very important differences in the situations and experiences of African Americans, recent immigrant groups such as Hispanics (Latinos) and Asians, and long-established ethnic groups from Europe, it is necessary to discuss them separately. We will begin with socialization among African Americans, who have a unique history and position in American society. We will follow with a discussion of what seems to be happening now among ethnic groups who have immigrated from Europe. We will then discuss recent immigrant groups from south of the border and from Asia.

African American Socialization

Most African Americans are descendants of slaves who were captured in African countries and sold to European American slave owners. They are not identified by their countries of origin or by their African ethnic identities but by the color of their skin. The contrast with the skin color of European Americans has led to the common notion that these are two different "races," and that is the term also used by social scientists in their studies. A recent definition states that " '*race' is a social category based on the identification of* (1) *a physical marker transmitted through reproduction and* (2) *individual, group, and cultural attributes associated with that marker*. . . . The concepts of race and ethnicity are social realities because they are deeply rooted in the consciousness of individuals and because they are firmly fixed in our society's institutional life" (Smelser, Wilson, and Mitchell 2001, 3; italics in original).

Prejudice against African Americans and discriminatory practices expressing that prejudice, known as *racism*, have led to residential segregation. More than any other group in American society, socioeconomic advancement by African Americans has only modestly reduced their being excluded from living alongside whites of the same class level (Charles 2002, 272, 284–286). African Americans remain the most segregated racial or ethnic group in the United States. The segregation is largely involuntary, and there are three main reasons for it: (1) discrimination in the real estate and banking industries, (2) prejudice of whites against blacks as possible neighbors, and (3) discriminatory policies by government (local, state, and national) carried out by whites. These are, respectively, institutional actions, private behaviors, and public policies that combine to create what Douglas Massey and Nancy Denton term "hypersegregation" (Massey 2002, 319–320). In recent times, discrimination has lessened in spots, so that a small but growing number of blacks live among whites.

There are social class differences among African Americans. Racism is a factor in the lives of most of them. Even highly successful, upper-middle class blacks do not escape it, as illustrated in a work by Lawrence Otis Graham, who grew up in a predominantly white upper-middle-class setting, graduated from Princeton University and Harvard Law School, and is the author of 10 books. He recalls that at age 10 he stepped up to a swimming pool at a country club and saw several angry parents drag their children out of the water and run (Graham 1995, 2). His book is replete with examples of racism experienced by upper-middle-class blacks, but a couple of brief examples of his personal experiences as an adult illustrate some of the humiliation it inflicts:

> There is a second-floor Italian restaurant in the East Sixties in New York that I no longer patronize because the maitre d' is never at the second-floor entry landing upon a guest's arrival, which has left me on three occasions to fend off incoming patrons who handed me their hats, jackets, and umbrellas for the coat check. And I almost always avoid restaurants with valet parking because of the times I've been handed keys by incoming white patrons who assume that I am there to park their cars rather than waiting to have my own car delivered to the front door as I leave. (Graham 1995, 91)

Because of the color of his skin, whites in these settings automatically assumed that he was there to serve them. This is one manifestation of racism. It reflects a continuing view that blacks are inferior to whites and should be subordinate to them (Bobo and Smith 1998, 199–200, 209–213).

The black middle class has grown, a development facilitated by anti-discrimination legislation and affirmative action. According to one recent estimate, about one-third of the black population is now middle class. Fair housing legislation has enabled many to move away from inner-city ghetto neighborhoods into more desirable residential areas (Anderson 2002, 431). A study of black executives in one organization that began hiring blacks in other than lowly positions reveals that they experienced diverse treatment, ranging from being mentored effectively and accepted with open arms to receiving cold stares, hostile receptions, and persistent racial discrimination (Anderson 2002, 433).

Although less than 10 percent of black families live in predominantly white upper-middle-class suburban communities, this number is likely to slowly increase. According to one recent study (Tatum 1997) of 10 families in one such community, parents have two main socialization strategies for dealing with racism:

1. *Race conscious.* While the parents choose to live in such a community for educational and economic reasons, they also want their children to have a positive black identity. They want their children to perform well in school so that they can demonstrate competence in the larger society, but they also want them to develop competence in relating to their own ethnic community. Parents using this strategy make active efforts to create black peer groups for their children, because there are not enough black families in the community for such peer groups to occur naturally.

2. *Race neutral.* These parents make no special effort to influence their children's friendship relationships. These parents assume either that the situation cannot be altered or that it will change naturally when the children get older.

The author also interviewed 15 children in the community between the ages of 6 and 14. Generally, they were enthusiastic about their community and felt accepted. Citing other studies, the author speculates that when these children reach adolescence, they will encounter some hostility from whites and also from other blacks who will accuse them of being "too white" (Tatum 1997).

In a work reviewing other studies as well as presenting her own research, Shirley A. Hill argues that black parents have always racially socialized their children. "In the past those messages included teaching the customs and racial dissimulation required of blacks for survival in a racial caste system, but today racial socialization more commonly refers to teaching pride and self-acceptance" (Hill 1999, 101–102). Her study of middle-class and working-class black parents finds that parents usually discuss race with their children and tell them that they should expect to encounter racism and that they need to learn to cope with it. However, they do not focus on it or initiate discussions. Most parents tend to wait until their children become aware of racial issues and then try to provide information (Hill 1999, 93). Annette Lareau describes black parental disagreement over how best to socialize their children to deal with racism (Lareau 2003, 120–124).

While African American parents are trying to socialize their children to cope with racism, many white children are being socialized to be racist. As two researchers (Van Ausdale and Feagin 2001, 34) note, "being 'white' in the United States involves not only a privileged status and strong identity, but also the carrying out on a regular basis of a white performance that hems in, hurts, and frustrates the lives of Americans of color."

Our data show that while the cultural language of race and racial hierarchy is conveyed to children by adults, children internalize these ideas most thoroughly when they implement them repeatedly in their own actions and interactions with other children and with adult caregivers. Thus, the language and ideas of race empower white children to set themselves apart as 'better' than racialized others, and by so doing they learn and perform the social practices associated with being 'white American.' (Van Ausdale and Feagin 2001, 34)

The authors of the above statement studied for nearly a year a preschool with 58 children between ages 3 and 6, of whom 24 were white, 19 were Asian, four were black, three were biracial, three were Middle Eastern, two were Latino, and three were "other" (Van Ausdale and Feagin 1999, 38–39). They observed these nursery school children using racial categories to exclude some children from play situations and instances of white children using ideas of superiority and inferiority to dominate another child (Van Ausdale and Feagin 1999, 102). Thus, in contrast to other scholars who have said that children do not have a clear grasp of racial and ethnic distinctions until the age of 6, these authors conclude that children make such distinctions at even younger ages. They argue, "Well before they can speak clearly, children are exposed to racial and ethnic ideas through their immersion in and observation of the large social world. Since racism exists at all levels of society and is interwoven in all aspects of American social life, it is virtually impossible for young children either to miss or ignore it. Far from being oblivious to racial group[s] and racism, children are inundated with it from the moment they enter society" (Van Ausdale and Feagin 1999, 189–190). As a consequence, black children have to develop skills from an early age "that can guide them through life with a minimum of damage" (Van Ausdale and Feagin 1999, 191). They offer several illustrations from their observations of black children developing various strategies for dealing with racial comments made by other children.

African Americans have been a focus of social thought and political controversy for more than 200 years, beginning with slavery and its acceptance in the original American Constitution. This focus continued through the Civil War, the emancipation of the slaves, the Jim Crow period that followed and that lasted 100 years, down through the civil rights movement of the 1960s and down to the continuing disputes over affirmative action in the present day. In the last few years, some sociologists have turned the spotlight away from the minority and onto the majority to examine the meanings of being white. A major conclusion is that whiteness has been largely invisible to whites. Whiteness brings privileges that are unselfconsciously taken for granted. Sociologist Paula S. Rothenberg (2001) writes, in her introduction to a collection of writings that she has edited on this subject,

For the most part, these authors agree that whiteness has often gone unnamed and unexamined because it has been uncritically and unthinkingly adopted as the norm throughout society. When people of color are asked to reflect on their childhood and to try to remember when and how they learned about race, they usually have very specific memories of when and how they 'discovered' or were taught that they were "African American," "Korean," "Caribbean," "Chinese," "Puerto Rican," or "Latina." ... When whites are asked a similar question, they often draw a blank. Many cannot remember a time when they first 'noticed' that they were white because whiteness was, for them, unremarkable. It was always everywhere. They learned to remark on 'difference' by noticing what was not like them. From an early age race, for white people, is about everybody else. (Rothenberg 2002, 2)

Rothenberg argues that it is culturally normative for white people to think of others as different but not to include themselves in the universe of the different. Rather, they are ordinary, and others are different. In this way, they remain oblivious to the ways in which they are privileged because of their whiteness. "The power of whiteness is that it gives certain people an advantage without ever acknowledging that this is the case" (Rothenberg 2001, 2–3).

Whites usually do not need to deal with their whiteness. Blacks, living in a predominantly white society, find that they need to deal with racism. One of the resources that blacks have in dealing with racism and its effects is their churches. A recent study of an African American Baptist church in Salt Lake City, Utah, portrays the efforts of adult members to socialize their children so that they become resilient in dealing with the negative reactions they may encounter. They view the development of spirituality as protective: "Spiritual development is seen as a lifeline, most importantly to eternal life through belief in Jesus Christ, but also as a healthy way of coping with the trials of everyday life" (Haight 2002, 78). An important activity is telling personal stories to illustrate how biblical scriptures can have personal meaning. Sunday School teachers and children both participate in such storytelling.

In the United States, about 26 percent of blacks are poor, compared to about 11 percent of whites (Danziger and Lin 2000, 3). Most poor blacks live in dangerous, inner-city neighborhoods. Because the neighborhood context is coming to be understood as a very important factor in the socialization of poor black children, we present the discussion of socialization of children in this part of the population in a later section of this chapter, "Neighborhood Communities."

White European Ethnic Groups

During the nineteenth and twentieth centuries, immigrants from many European countries came in large numbers to the United States and to Canada. They brought with them distinctive cultures, which were maintained by residential clustering in ethnic neighborhoods, endogamous marriage (marriage within the in-group), continuing to speak the native language while also learning English, establishment of ethnic food stores and other ethnic businesses, clustering together in certain occupations (e.g., Irish became policemen and firemen, Greeks opened restaurants, and Poles worked in steel mills), and celebrating holidays of the homeland. These immigrants, known as the *first generation*, attempted to socialize their children, the *second generation*, to maintain at least some aspects of the original culture even while they were becoming acculturated and assimilated into American or Canadian society. But as the acculturation and assimilation processes proceeded, and children were acquiring the culture of the new country, they began—in varying degrees—to reduce or even entirely drop their parents' culture as they reached adulthood.

The distinction between acculturation and assimilation has been usefully drawn as follows: "(1) [A]cculturation is the loss of traditional cultural traits and the acceptance of new cultural traits (these can be two distinct processes), while (2) assimilation is the social, economic, and political integration of an ethnic minority into mainstream society. Obviously, the two processes are related, with most social scientists agreeing that acculturation must to some extent precede assimilation. . . ." (Keefe and Padilla 1987, 6). This distinction, while very useful for some purposes, is not always observed, and *assimilation* is often used to include both.

The assimilation process is captured in brief statements by two scholars. In his review of the relationship between socialization and ethnicity in Canada, Frederick Elkin writes, "As high proportions of the descendants of immigrant Ukrainians, Hungarians, Dutch, Greeks, Italians, Lithuanians, Portuguese, Germans, and others come to lose their language, traditional customs, and symbols of their groups; as they intermarry with men and women from other ethnic groups; as they come to feel 'Canadian' and participate in non-ethnically defined activities—we ask, what happens to their ethnic identity?" (Elkin 1983, 145). The answer is complex because it is not the same for all people. But an important part of the answer is captured when he notes that

> the ethnic child in Canada experiences many aspects of the larger society which differ from and tend to pull away from his ethnic identity, including teachers and the public school, television and movies, non-ethnic and sometimes ethnic peers, secular holidays, and many other facts of our popular culture and contemporary way of life. In some respects, the immigrant family, knowingly or unknowingly also contributes to this process by 'pushing' the child away from his ethnic and into an Anglo-Saxon world. (Elkin 1983, 153)

A similar view is expressed for the United States by Lillian Rubin:

> When people no longer live in the same neighborhood, work at the same occupation, socialize almost exclusively with members of their group, [then] language facility falters, manners undergo change, and ethnic identity wanes. Therefore, although some *subjective* sense of ethnic identity remains, recent researches in the field insist that it has little objective reality. And it certainly isn't strong enough to contain the soaring rates of intermarriage, which now involve roughly three in four American-born whites. (Rubin 1994, 8–9)

Recent researchers, studying third- and fourth-generation Americans, have come to some new understandings of ethnicity among white descendants of Europeans. Mary Waters (1990) first identifies two earlier views of what would happen to ethnicity. Scholars she refers to as "assimilationists" anticipated that ethnicity would decline with each generational remove from the original immigrants. In contrast to these proponents of the "melting pot" theory, "pluralists" argue that ethnic assimilation is not inevitable, and they point to evidence that ethnic identity is maintained by some of those in later generations. In her study of third- and fourth-generation "white ethnics" in suburban areas of San Jose, California, and Philadelphia, Pennsylvania, Waters comes to a basic conclusion that white people have a choice as to whether they want to have an ethnic identification or not, and which one. Her key finding is presented early in her book:

> . . . individuals who believe their ancestry to be solidly the same in both parents' backgrounds can (and often do) choose to suppress that ancestry and self-identify as 'American' or try to pass as having an ancestry they would like to have. The option of identifying as ethnic therefore exists for all white Americans, and further choice of which ethnicity to choose is available to some of them.
>
> Furthermore, an individual's self-identification does not necessarily have to be the same at all times and places, although it can be. Someone whose mother is half Greek and half Polish and whose father is Welsh may self-identify as Greek to close friends and family and as Polish at work, or as Welsh on census documents. An individual may change ethnic identification over time, for various reasons. . . . In a local situation where everyone knows one's believed ethnic origins—for example, a small town where everyone knows your mother and father—it would be more difficult to identify with one or the other. If one moved to another locality this would probably become easier. (Waters 1990, 19–20)

While she does not explicitly discuss socialization, it is clear from her study that, as a result particularly of intermarriage and of generational distance from immigrant forebears, these "white ethnics" have no clear ethnic culture and identity that were passed on to them or that they are passing on to their children. Some have information about some forebears, but some do not, and some have information about one side of their family but not the other. She notes, "Most respondents were not aware of ethnic differences in their neighborhood, but many were very aware of racial or minority groups and their presence or absence in the neighborhood. This also echoes the results of residential segregation studies, which show that neighborhoods are now defined by racial as opposed to ethnic lines" (Waters 1990, 101).

In his study of the descendants of European ethnic groups living in and around Albany, New York, Richard Alba (1990) begins by arguing that ancestry and identity don't always go together: "Although an individual may know his ancestry in considerable detail, he may not perceive it as relevant to himself, believing in effect, 'That was long ago, not today' " (Alba 1990, 38). Like Mary Waters, he notes a great amount of intermarriage among the area's descendants of early settlers who were English, Dutch, Irish, Scottish, German, Italian, Polish, and French. He found that the majority of parents, whether of mixed ancestry themselves or shared single ancestry, were not concerned whether or not their children identify themselves in ethnic terms. Only 27 percent of parents with children living at home made any effort to teach their children about their ethnic background, and even smaller percentages made efforts to teach about ethnic foods, customs, and traditions. The one exception that he finds is among Italians: Two-thirds of them strongly desire to impart some ethnic identity to their children (Alba 1990, 185–206).

Hispanic, Caribbean, and Asian Immigrants

In the last 40 years or so, major new waves of immigration into the United States have come from Mexico and the Spanish-speaking countries of Latin America, from the Caribbean islands, and from Asian countries. In 1997, about 10 percent of the U.S. population was foreign-born (26.8 million people out of about 270 million), and 90 percent of them immigrated since 1960. Fifty-two percent of the immigrants came from Latin America and the Caribbean; 29 percent came from Asia. One out of every five children in the United States is either an immigrant or the native-born child of immigrants (Portes and Rumbaut 2001, 19–21). In Canada in 2001, over 53 percent of the immigrants came from Asia and the Pacific region, about 19 percent from Africa and the Middle East, and about 17 percent from Europe and the United Kingdom (Statistics Canada 2001).

Although terms like *Latinos, Hispanics, Asian Americans* are in wide use, they do not represent clear ethnic identities as each includes people from several countries, each of which has its own distinctive culture and identity. The term *Hispanic* was created by the U.S. government in 1978 as a simplifying category to cover all people from Mexico, Puerto Rico, Cuba, and Central and South America (Garcia 1996, 197–198; Camarillo and Bonilla 2001, 119–120). The most recently available U.S. Census figure at this writing counts Hispanics in the United States at 37.4 million people, 13.3 percent of the population (Ramirez and de la Cruz 2003), now slightly more numerous than African Americans.

A study of Mexican American politicians in Monterey Park, a suburb of Los Angeles, reveals, "Although the majority of Latinos in Monterey Park are of Mexican origin, they identified themselves as Hispanic, Mexican American, Californio, Mexican, and Latino. While Hispanic was the most widely used term at the city hall level, Latino was most prominently used at the neighborhood level" (Calderon 1996, 188, n. 1). However, another scholar argues that "the diversity of the Latino population is so great that it can reasonably be said that there is no such person as a 'Latino' " (Rhea 1997, 69). The terms *Chicano* and *Chicana* were adopted in the late 1960s by young politically activist Mexican Americans who sought to define a new identity that emphasized their fused Spanish, Mexican, and Indian ancestry. *Chicano* had previously been an epithet for lower-class Mexicans, and therefore many older people refused to accept it for themselves. Some writers disregard this history and use *Chicano* and *Mexican American* interchangeably (Martinez 1999, 122; Rhea 1997, 73–80). These tangles of ethnic terminology suggest some of the complexities of continuing ethnic identity among descendants of Latin American immigrants.

The situation among Asian Americans is a bit different:

Without constant racist coercion, most members of the various groups which constitute Asian America now tend to think of themselves in specifically ethnic terms, as Chinese Americans, Korean Americans, Japanese Americans, and so on. Awareness of a shared Asian racial identity is episodic; it informs Asian Americans' self-understandings at specific times but has not become a stable way of seeing the world. In times of crisis, though, race does become a meaningful category. (Rhea 1997, 39)

A recent study of what Alejandro Portes and Ruben Rumbaut (2001) call "the new second generation" casts some light on their future positions as ethnic members of the larger society. Using a broad definition of *second generation* to mean "native-born children of foreign parents or foreign-born children who were brought to the United States before adolescence," the authors conducted a survey in 1992 of 5,262 middle school/junior high school children of immigrant parents in Miami/Ft. Lauderdale, Florida, and San Diego, California, two of the areas most affected by the new immigration. In 1995, they did a follow-up survey of the same children. They also surveyed parents at both times. Perhaps the most important general result of their study is conveyed in these words:

There are groups among today's second generation that are slated for a smooth transition into the mainstream and for whom ethnicity will soon be a matter of personal choice. They, like descendants of earlier Europeans, will identify with their ancestry on occasion and when convenient. There are others for whom their ethnicity will be a source of strength and who will muscle their way up, socially and economically, on the basis of their own communities' networks and resources. There are still others whose ethnicity will be neither a matter of choice nor a source of progress but a mark of subordination. These children are at risk of joining the masses of the dispossessed, compounding the spectacle of inequality and despair in America's inner cities. The prospect that members of today's second generation will join those at the bottom of society—a new rainbow underclass—has more than a purely academic interest, for it can affect the life chances of millions of Americans and the quality of life in the cities and communities where they concentrate. (Portes and Rumbaut 2001, 45)

Among the various factors that the authors present to explain these different outcomes, perhaps the most important are the human capital of the parents and how the particular ethnic group is received by the government and by the community. *Human capital* refers to the combination of education, skills, job experience, and language knowledge that the immigrants bring. But whether that human capital finds opportunity depends on what they call *modes of incorporation* into society. They point out that the government provided resources primarily to refugees escaping from Communism, which gave them advantages in establishing themselves and therefore in helping their children. Other immigrants may be largely ignored. Another factor is race. They argue that "the darker a person's skin is, the greater is the social distance from dominant groups and the more difficult it is to make his or her personal qualifications count." They say that Irish immigrants receive more favorable treatment than Haitians, although many of the Irish are illegal immigrants and many of the Haitians are here legally (Portes and Rumbaut 2001, 44–48).

To illustrate some of the problems experienced by these new immigrants and the light they cast on outcomes of socialization, we have selected the Mexican and Vietnamese immigrants to the United States for further discussion, with brief added references to Caribbean and Hong Kong immigrants.

Mexican Americans constitute almost two-thirds of the entire Latino population in the United States (Rhea 1997, 67). One study of Mexican immigrants and their children in San Diego, California, calls attention to the fact that Mexican immigrants have certain disadvantages that are greater than those that other recent immigrants face: Despite the fact that two-parent households and dependable employment are the norm, "in comparison with certain other immigrant communities, they lack the web of organizations and social practices that have allowed specific groups to utilize traditional culture to help children achieve" (Lopez and Stanton-Salazar 2001, 57). The immigrant parents, who mostly work at low-level jobs, emphasize to their children the importance of education, but internal processes within the family sometimes undermine what they say. They expect their adolescent children to share family responsibilities of child care of younger siblings, do housework, and broker for parents, that is, help them deal with landlords, government agencies, and other situations requiring greater English fluency than the parents have. Further, the parents have little understanding of the challenges the children face in school and are unable to give them much support. The result is that "educational success is valued by Mexican-origin children and their immigrant parents, but the scarcity of educational resources that parents bring to the table means that in many cases they are not able to translate those values into effective institutional support for their children" (Lopez and Stanton-Salazar 2001, 79–80).

A study in three small California cities—Santa Barbara, Oxnard, and Santa Paula—reveals some of the complexity of Mexican American adaptation to American culture and society. The authors note, for example, that ethnic loyalty need not be accompanied by cultural awareness. They write that "it is not uncommon to meet a third- or fourth-generation Mexican American who does not speak Spanish and knows relatively little about his/her cultural background, but retains pride in his/her Mexican heritage and enjoys associating with Mexican people. This phenomenon is not unique to Mexican Americans, for it is found among members of many ethnic communities throughout the world" (Keefe and Padilla 1987, 52).

Through case studies, the authors illustrate some of the issues of socialization. For example, 30-year-old Rosa Hernandez, who lived in a Mexico City slum until she came to the United States at age 20, speaks Spanish most of the time, and prefers Mexican food, music, and mass media, but believes her Oxnard-born daughters should be American. She has not taught them Mexican history or customs, and she celebrates only American holidays with them. She replied, "No opinion," when asked if Mexican American children should be taught Mexican history in school. While she would prefer that her daughters' future marriages be to Mexican men, she also has reservations because

Mexican men are too demanding (Keefe and Padila 1987, 77–78). Thirty-year-old Margaret Camacho, born in Santa Barbara, California, is four generations removed from Mexico on her mother's side and five generations removed from Ireland on her father's side (her maiden name was Callahan). She speaks no Spanish, knows little about Mexico or its customs, and has no feeling of attachment to the Mexican people, nor does her Mexican American husband. Although she cooks Mexican food periodically, she has not taught any Mexican customs to her children (Keefe and Padilla 1987, 111–114).

One important difference between Mexican Americans and Anglos is that Mexican Americans place a much greater emphasis on maintaining ties to extended family members, and this emphasis does not seem to fade along with other aspects of acculturation and assimilation. The authors find, "Even the fourth generation Mexican Americans in our study retain aspects of Mexican culture—significantly, their value of and involvement in large and local extended families" (Keefe and Padilla 1987, 7). Although the authors do not provide observations of how children are incorporated into these extended family activities, we can infer that children must be socialized into such family interactions if the ties remain into the fourth generation.

Immigrants from Caribbean countries—Jamaica, Trinidad, Barbados, Guyana, and smaller island countries—confront a distinctive problem. They are black, but unlike African Americans, they come from societies run by blacks rather than from a society in which they are largely subordinate to whites. Although they are aware of some of the problems of American race relations, they arrive with intentions to not focus on race. A study of them in New York found that they see themselves as superior to American blacks and do not wish to be seen as "black American" because they interpret such an identification as downward mobility (Waters 1999, 64 ff.). Although they are sometimes shocked and offended by experiences of prejudice, they are nonetheless critical of American blacks for emphasizing race in situations in which they believe race has nothing to do with the situation (Waters 1999, 181). Although middle-class immigrants are able to pass on to their children their values of hard work, disregard of racialism, high value on education, and saving for the future, the hard facts of race tend to overwhelm working-class and poor immigrants. They are seen as black Americans. Their children often develop "oppositional identities" to cope with that assigned status. As part of their opposition, they consider doing well in school as "acting white" and thus alienate themselves further from mainstream society (Waters 1999, 8, 241; see also Waters 1996).

One of the newest ethnic groups in the United States is the Vietnamese, who came as refugees beginning in 1975 after the United States abandoned the Vietnam War. The people of Vietnam consist of 54 different ethnic groups, of whom the most numerous are the Viet, but those distinctions do not seem to be maintained among those who have come to live the United States (Freeman 1995, 4–5). In the United States they are considered a single ethnic group. Over 1.2 million Vietnamese have settled in the United States (Thai 2002, 55). Many fled the Communist victory in that war and escaped in overcrowded, leaky boats, becoming known as *boat people* (Zhou and Bankston 1998, 27). The

American government first settled them in refugee camps and provided an Americanization program consisting of schooling for children and classes on English language and American culture for adults (Zhou and Bankston 1998, 29 ff.). One study notes that

> U.S.-born Vietnamese children and those who arrived in the United States as infants have no clear personal memory of life in Vietnam nor of the flight from the ancestral land, nor of life in the refugee camps. But the abruptness of the move from Vietnam to America has made life in Vietnam a continuing reality, even for the younger generation who have never been there. Parents often communicate to children with a strong sense of determination born of their struggle to survive. (Zhou and Bankston 1998, 38)

A study of Vietnamese who were resettled in a very poor neighborhood of New Orleans casts some light on how community organization can influence socialization. The adults have meager education and skills (human capital), and little money (financial capital). However, in time a number were able to start small businesses such as grocery stores, beauty salons, and the like, and the owners of these businesses led the way in forming community organizations such as the Vietnamese-American Voters Association, the Vietnamese Educational Association, and the Vietnamese Parent-Teacher Association. The Vietnamese Educational Association conducts after-school language instruction classes for children and teenagers in English and in Vietnamese. These classes emphasize reading and writing skills. This association also conducts an annual awards ceremony for children who have excelled in the public school system (Zhou and Bankston 1998, 81–83, 102–103, 155–159). There is also a high degree of interaction among community members resulting in "a small-town effect." There is much gossip and exchange of information about who is doing what, so that parents are shamed when a child flunks out or drops out of school, and they are honored when the child does well. These informal social networks (social capital) seek to maintain and enforce the traditional value of respect for elders (Zhou and Bankston 1998, 105–107).

Zhou and Bankston point out that ethnicity for Vietnamese children is not a barrier to becoming American but is rather the means of becoming American: "An ethnic identity based on social relations with other Vietnamese serves as a springboard for upward mobility by means of education. In contrast to traditional assimilationist theory, structural assimilation to a host country is occurring before cultural assimilation. Indeed, to some extent it appears that young Vietnamese are achieving structural assimilation in America precisely because they have not been fully acculturated" (Zhou and Bankston 1998, 235).

Although Vietnamese American children receive much support from their families and community, there is also considerable tension. The fact that children often have greater familiarity with American society and culture than their parents and serve as translators and intermediaries results in role reversals undermining the respect due elders (Zhou and Bankston 1998, 40). Parents and children also experience a clash in cultures between the strong traditional collective emphasis of the Vietnamese parents and the value of individualism acquired by the children. Vietnamese expect parent-child obligations to be mutual and lifelong. "The Vietnamese traditional family stresses disciplined authority of and obligation to the father, but also nurturance, sentiment, and affection, associated with the mother. An important family value is moral debt, the deep, unpayable obligation that children owe parents for bringing them into the world and for the sacrifices and unconditional love that parents give their children" (Freeman 1995, 89). Their children growing up in America often want to get out from under family obligations and to have greater freedom to live as they please (Zhou and Bankston 1998, 160 ff.; Detzner 1992, 85–102; Gold 1999, 233–234; Zhou 2001).

A study of second-generation Vietnamese in the San Francisco Bay area, however, presents a somewhat different picture. The author interviewed young adults between the ages of 18 and 27, most of whom had come to the United States around the age of 5 ½ and most of whom were college students or college graduates when interviewed. They told of their childhood, when they tried to blend into American society by "acting white," but they experienced what sociologists call *marginality*. That is, they did not feel at home in either their traditional Vietnamese culture or the new American culture. Parents urged them to make American friends so as to learn the language and culture rapidly, but they were also repeatedly cautioned against becoming too American, which they strongly wished to be. During their college years, however, they engaged in what one of them called "deprogramming the self." They became critical of what they saw as the extremity of American individualism. They formed new friendships with other Vietnamese, strengthened their commitments to their families and to the value of family collectivism, and regained a strong sense of Vietnamese identity (Thai 2002).

Although our primary focus is on the United States, a study of Hong Kong Chinese immigrants to Britain produces some findings of interest. Forty-two young adults in their early 20s, members of 25 families that run take-out food businesses, were interviewed about their work in them. Many started working as young as 7 or 8 years old. The children's labor was considered a necessary contribution to family survival. In many cases, parents "guilt-tripped" their children by emphasizing the sacrifices they had made for them and by comparing the child's work commitment to that of ideal Chinese children. Some now complain about a "loss of childhood" because of the sometimes heavy responsibilities they had to assume. Those who had lived and worked in Hong Kong before the family moved to Britain were less conflicted because there it was common for children to work. Those who had been born and grown up entirely in Britain were somewhat more resentful because their parents were not like other parents and because they compared themselves to English children, who did not have such intense family obligations (Song 1999). This study illustrates some of the ways in which children interpret their situation in their family by comparing it to what they observe in the wider community. It also suggests that some immigrant children are socialized to the role of worker at younger ages than children of established native families.

Neighborhood Communities

In recent years, sociologists have revived the formerly important but later neglected study of neighborhoods. The new researchers are finding evidence for and arguing for the importance of the features of the neighborhood for childhood outcomes. Most attention, so far, is on neighborhoods with high concentrations of poverty, racial isolation, and social disadvantage (National Research Council/Institute of Medicine 2000, 329). Neighborhoods are less significant for children in well-to-do families whose outside activities take place in many different locations. Parents may ferry them to school, music lessons, swimming classes, sporting games, and organized events with specialized facilities (Zeiher 2003). The research on neighborhoods is still in its early stages, but indications are that it is becoming a major focus of interest. We present here some early findings and conclusions.

When we talk about a social class or an ethnic group, we recognize that its members may live in a variety of places, even though they may be concentrated in certain neighborhoods. Studying a neighborhood starts with a specified space or territory and looks at the mix of people who live there and at certain characteristics of the neighborhood. Robert Sampson writes, "It is important to note that a focus on the capacity of communities to achieve common goals does not require cultural or sociodemographic homogeneity. Ethnically diverse populations can and do agree on goals such as safety for children" (Sampson 2001, 8). Building on ideas of James S. Coleman (1988) and others, Sampson points to the importance of *social capital*, which is defined as resources that are built into community relationships and that facilitate cooperation. Sampson points to "the social-organizational context of childrearing that extends beyond families 'under the roof.' " He illustrates the point in this way: "For example, when parents know the parents of their children's friends, they have the potential to observe the child's actions in different circumstances, talk to each other about the child, compare notes, and establish norms. Such intergenerational closure of local networks provides the child with social capital of a collective nature" (Sampson 2001, 9). In some neighborhoods, residents have the shared values and mutual trust (components of social capital) that enable them to work together to support children and to exercise informal social control. However, this does not always happen where it might. A study in a Nashville neighborhood found that even though living side by side, whites interacted mostly with white neighbors and blacks with black neighbors (Lee 2001, 35–36). The children in that neighborhood have less social capital than they would if there were more mutual trust that led to cross-racial neighborly interaction.

A study in Chicago contrasted a cooperative neighborhood inhabited largely by working poor (West) and an underclass neighborhood with high unemployment (North). In North, "The extremity of the negative features of the environment—poverty, violence, poor housing—seem to be matched by negative community climate—lack of community identity, and fragmented formal support system networks" (Garbarino and Kostelny 1993, 211–213). The rate of child abuse in North was twice as high as in West, as was the rate of child deaths from child abuse. There are other dangers in underclass communities such as North. A mother may not let her child play on the floor because there is poison to kill the rats that infest the apartment. Necessary as this is, it deprives the child of a chance to engage in exploratory play. A parent may keep a child indoors because of frequent shooting incidents; this protection has the unintended consequence of restricting the child's opportunities for social and athletic play A parent in a high-crime neighborhood may resort to a very strict and punitive form of discipline to keep the child out of danger. Such an approach is likely to make the child more aggressive and hostile. The authors conclude, "In all these examples, the parental adaptation is well intentioned and may appear to be practically sensible, but its side effects may be detrimental in the long run. The onus here is on the social forces that create and sustain danger in the family's environment, thus forcing the parent to choose between the lesser of two evils" (Garbarino and Kostelny 1993, 216).

Poor, dangerous neighborhoods sometimes make it very difficult for single mothers to take jobs. One study of a poor African American community—"Meadow View," near a large city—comments on the constant vigilance required of parents. Because of neighborhood violence, drug dealing, and sexual predators,

> During interviews, mothers habitually peek out the window. This seemingly small gesture is repeated in households throughout the community. Parents survey the landscape, tirelessly scanning the environment, monitoring slow-moving cars, scrutinizing suspicious gatherings—behavior all rooted in indisputable facts of daily life. Before going out, people caution each other to 'be careful.' . . . While protecting children is a universal parental behavior, in Meadow View it can require extreme measures; it is labor-intensive, emotionally draining work. The need to protect children and the vigilance this requires create major barriers to working and parenting, especially when the two are attempted simultaneously. (Hicks-Bartlett 2000, 32–34)

Many, perhaps most, underclass children live in inner-city neighborhoods that are characterized by frequent violence. Children live, objectively, in almost constant danger; subjectively, they feel in danger. In addition, "For inner-city children, the risks of living in the midst of violence are compounded by the risks of living in poverty—risks that include malnutrition, unsuitable housing, inferior medical care, inadequate schools, family disruption, family violence, and maladaptive childrearing patterns" (Garbarino et al. 1992, 52). Such a combination of risks results in outcomes such as poor school achievement, aggression, and self-destructive behaviors. Children are traumatized by violence they have witnessed or experienced, and they often become withdrawn or aggressive, and indifferent or apathetic. Their motivation to continue responsive participation in society is considerably diminished.

Recall our definition of *culture* as adaptation to the physical and social circumstances in which people find themselves. The above studies present examples of such adaptations—cultural practices for dealing with danger. These include not letting children play on the floor, keeping children inside, and "tirelessly scanning the environment." These practices are adopted to minimize danger to children, but, as some of the studies point out, they are maladaptive parenting strategies so far as the children's development is concerned. They make children aware of dangers that children in safer neighborhoods do not experience, and they impose limits on children's experiences that children in other neighborhoods do not have.

An exceptionally detailed and insightful study of an inner-city poor black neighborhood was conducted by sociologist Elijah Anderson. Over a 14-year period, he carried out an ethnographic study of a neighborhood he calls Northton in a metropolis he calls Eastern City. The neighborhood is dominated by a drug culture—people buying and selling drugs, and activities deriving from this activity, including prostitution, muggings, robberies, shootouts, and killings, as well as visibly addicted people walking around (Anderson 1990). The interpersonal violence that erupts so frequently gives rise to a special cultural pattern, the *code of the street,* "a set of informal rules governing interpersonal public behavior, particularly violence." The code of the street centers on people feeling that they receive respect from others. For example, if someone seems to maintain eye contact with someone else for "too long," the latter may feel disrespected or "dissed." Such hair-trigger sensitivity can lead to confrontation (Anderson 1999, 33–4).

All families in the neighborhood must try to cope with this violent, drug-infested scene. Anderson finds that residents distinguish two major types of adaptation among families. Most people are in "decent families." The members of these families usually have some concern with and hope for the future. The adults work, try to save, and try to raise their children to make something of themselves. They try to instill mainstream values in their children. Although intact two-parent families are in the minority in this neighborhood, the two parents usually both work at low-paying jobs, and each may hold down more than one job. They try to teach their children to be polite and considerate of others. Single mothers are particularly challenged by men of the streets who try to draw their children into the life of the streets, and the mothers have to be constantly on guard and show determination to prevent this (Anderson 1999, 37–45).

Families of the other type, "street families," show little consideration for other people. The adults are participants in the street culture and sometimes socialize their own children to become part of it.

> They may love their children but frequently find it difficult to cope with the physical and emotional demands of parenthood. . . . The lives of the street-oriented are often marked by disorganization. . . . The frustrations associated with persistent poverty shorten the fuse in such people, contributing

to a lack of patience with anyone—child or adult—who irritates them. . . . Street-oriented women tend to perform their motherly duties sporadically. The most irresponsible women can be found at local bars and crack houses, getting high. . . . (Anderson 1999, 49)

Their children often have to fend for themselves, getting food and money any way they can. "They often learn to fight at an early age, using short-tempered adults around them as role models. The street oriented home may be fraught with anger, verbal disputes, physical aggression, even mayhem. The children are victimized by these goings-on and quickly learn to hit those who cross them" (Anderson 1999, 49).

Because many immigrants are poor, they often have no choice but to live in dangerous neighborhoods. There they encounter behavior norms that are harmful to efforts at social mobility as well as great hostility to conventional standards of American society. Immigration scholars point out, for example,

In Miami inner-city schools, Haitian youths are often ridiculed because of their obedience to school staff, and some have been physically attacked. To survive in this environment, they must adopt the same tough aggressive stance of the ghetto and, along with it, a common rejection of their parents' expectations. Although some Haitian students . . . manage to survive and advance under these hard conditions, others assimilate. In this case, assimilation is not to the middle-class mainstream but downward to the attitudes and norms of the inner city. (Portes and Rumbaut 2001, 61)

The recognition of neighborhoods as significant contexts for socialization extends beyond the United States. The United Nations Education and Social Council (UNESCO) initiated a Growing Up in Cities study in cities throughout the world, and, in disadvantaged areas, reports problems similar to those found in American cities. Writing of Braybrook, Australia, a suburb of Melbourne, two specialists in environmental research report,

. . . young people in this neighbourhood suffered from the social stigma of living in a neighbourhood that historically identified its residents as *underclass*. This stigma contributed to young people's feelings of isolation and alienation, due in part . . . to their fear of public spaces . . . young people recited stories of being regularly harassed and told to 'move on' by police when they ventured into the streets. The high evidence of needles from drug use that littered the streets added to the evidence that the streets were a dangerous place. Owing to this fear of crime, many parents did not allow their children to move beyond the pavement outside their houses. (Chawla and Malone 2003, 130)

Poor, dangerous neighborhoods, then, present challenges to all parents and children living there. All have to deal with the dangers on the streets, dilapidated housing, and powerful influences of some neighbors and intruders that undermine efforts to join mainstream society. Most residents try to protect themselves from the dangers, while some are active contributors to them. Some children manage to enter mainstream society, while others grow up to be angry, hostile opponents of it.

* * *

Race and ethnicity influence how children are socialized, but the pattern is not uniform across racial and ethnic groups. African Americans, mostly descended from slaves, continue to experience discrimination in the form of racism, although it is much less virulent since the civil rights movement of the 1960s. Contemporary research indicates that African American parents find it necessary to socialize their children to deal with the particular problems that confront them because of their status as a disfavored minority. Other research, focusing on "whiteness," indicates that whites are mostly unselfconscious about being white and the advantages that taken-for-granted identity provides them. Descendants of European immigrants have great freedom to choose whether or not to continue ethnic heritage as part of their lives and to imbue their children with it. A strong effort to do so is found among Italian Americans but not among other European Americans. Vietnamese immigrants seek to maintain expected respect for elders, but their children, with some exceptions, increasingly seek to throw off the burdens that they feel the traditional expectation imposes on them.

References

Alba, Richard. 1990. *Ethnic Identity: The Transformation of White America*. New Haven, CT: Yale University Press.

Anderson, Elijah. 1990. *Streetwise*. Chicago: University of Chicago Press.

——. 1999. *Code of the Street*. New York: W. W. Norton.

——. 2002. "The Social Situation of the Black Executive: Black and White Identities in the Corporate World." In Elijah Anderson and Douglas Massey (eds.) *Problems of the Century: Racial Stratification in the United States*, 405–436. New York: Russell Sage Foundation.

Bobo, Lawrence, and Ryan A. Smith. 1998. "From Jim Crow Racism to Laissez-Faire Racism: The Transformation of Racial Attitudes." In Wendy F. Katkin, Ned Landsman, and Andrea Tyree (eds.) *Beyond Pluralism: The Conception of Groups and Group Identities in America*, 182–220. Urbana and Chicago: University Illinois Press.

Calderon, Jose Zapata. 1996. "Situational Identity of Suburban Mexican-American Politicians in a Multiethnic Community." In Roberto M. De Ande (ed.) *Chicanas and Chicanos in Contemporary Society*, 179–189. Boston: Allyn and Bacon.

Camarillo, Alberto M., and Frank Bonilla. 2001. "Hispanics in a Multicultural Society: A New American Dilemma." In Neil J. Smelser, William Julius Wilson, and Faith Mitchell (eds.) *America Becoming: Racial Trends and Their Consequences* 1: 102–134. Washington, DC: National Academy Press.

Charles, Camille Zabrinsky. 2002. "Socioeconomic Status and Segregation: African Americans, Hispanics, and Asians in Los Angeles." In Elijah Anderson and Douglas S. Massey (eds.) *Problem of the Century: Racial Stratification in the United States*, 271–289. New York: Russell Sage Foundation.

Chawla, Louise, and Karen Malone. 2003. "Neighborhood Quality in Children's Eyes." In Pia Christensen and Margaret O'Brien (eds.) *Children in the City: Home, Neighborhood, and Community*, 118–141. London: Routledge-Falmer.

Coleman, James S. 1988. "Social Capital in the Creation of Human Capital." *American Journal of Sociology* 94 (Supplement): 94–120.

Danziger, Sheldon, and Ann Chih Lin. 2000. *Coping With Poverty*. Ann Arbor: University of Michigan Press.

Detzner, Daniel F. 1992. "Life Histories: Conflict in Southeast Asian Families." In Jane F. Gilgun, Kerry Daly, and Gerald Handel (eds.) *Qualitative Methods in Family Research*, 85–202. Newbury Park, CA; Sage.

Elkin, Frederick. 1983. "Family, Socialization, and Ethnic Identity." In K. Ishwaran (ed.), *The Canadian Family*, 145–158. Toronto: Gage.

Elo, Irma T., and Samuel Preston. 2002. "The African American Population, 1930 to 1990." In Elijah Anderson and Douglas S. Massey (eds.) *Problem of the Century: Racial Stratification in the United States*, 168–223. New York: Russell Sage Foundation.

Freeman, James S. 1995. *Changing Identities: Vietnamese Americans 1975–1995*. Boston: Allyn & Bacon.

Garbarino, James, Nancy Dubrow, Kathleen Kostelny, and Carole Pardo. 1992. *Children in Danger: Coping with Consequences of Community Violence*. San Francisco: Jossey-Bass.

Garbarino, James, and Kathleen Kostelny. 1993. "Neighborhood and Community Influences on Parenting." In Tom Luster and Lynn Okagaki (eds.) *Parenting: An Ecological Perspective*, 203–226. Hillsdale, NJ: Lawrence Erlbaum Associates.

Garcia, Ignacio M. 1996. "Backwards from Aztlan: Politics in the Age of Hispanics." In Roberto M. De Ande (ed.) *Chicanas and Chicanos in Contemporary Society*, 191–204. Boston: Allyn & Bacon.

Gold, Steven. 1999. "Continuity and Change Among Vietnamese Families in the United States." In Harriette Pipes McAdoo (ed.) *Family Ethnicity*, 223–234. Thousand Oaks, CA: Sage.

Graham, Lawrence Otis. 1995. *Member of the Club: Reflections on Life in a Racially Polarized World*. New York: HarperCollins.

Haight, Wendy. 2002. *African-American Children in Church: A Sociocultural Perspective*. Cambridge: Cambridge University Press.

Hicks-Bartlett, Sharon. 2000. "Between a Rock and a Hard Place: The Labyrinth of Working and Parenting in a Poor Community." In Sheldon Danziger and Ann Chih Lin (eds.) *Coping With Poverty*, 27–51. Ann Arbor: University of Michigan Press.

Hill, Shirley A. 1999. *African American Children: Socialization and Development in Families*. Thousand Oaks, CA: Sage.

Keefe, Susan E., and Amado M. Padilla. 1987. *Chicano Ethnicity*. Albuquerque: University of New Mexico Press.

Lareau, Annette. 2003. *Unequal Childhoods*. Berkeley: University of California Press.

Lee, Barrett A. 2001. "Taking Neighborhoods Seriously." In Alan Booth and Ann C. Crouter (eds.) *Does It Take a Village?*, 31–40. Mahwah, NJ: Lawrence Erlbaum.

Lopez, David, and Ricardo D. Stanton-Salazar. 2001. "Mexican-Americans: A Second Generation at Risk." In Ruben G. Rumbaut and Alejandro Portes (eds.) *Ethnicities: Children of Immigrants in America*, 57–90. Berkeley and Los Angeles and New York: University of California Press and Russell Sage Foundation.

Martinez, Estella A. 1999. "Mexican American/Chicano Families." In Harriette Pipes McAdoo (ed.) *Family Ethnicity*, 121–134. Thousand Oaks, CA: Sage.

Massey, Douglas S. 2002. "Segregation and Violent Crime in America." In Elijah Anderson and Douglas S. Massey (eds.) *Problem of the Century: Racial Stratification in the United States*, 317–344. New York: Russell Sage Foundation.

McKinnon, Jesse. 2003. "The Black Population in the United States: March, 2002." In U.S. Census Bureau, *Current Population Reports P 20-541*. Washington, DC: Census Bureau.

National Research Council/Institute of Medicine. 2000. *From Neurons to Neighborhoods: The Science of Child Development*. Washington, DC: National Academies Press.

Portes, Alejandro, and Ruben G. Rumbaut. 2001. *Legacies: The Story of the Immigrant Second Generation*. Berkeley and New York: University of California Press and Russell Sage Foundation.

Ramirez, Roberto R., and Patricia de la Cruz. 2003. "The Hispanic Population in the United States March 2002." In U.S. Census Bureau, *Current Population Reports P 20-545*. Washington, DC: Census Bureau.

Rhea, Joseph Tilden. 1997. *Race Pride and the American Identity*. Cambridge, MA: Harvard University Press.

Rothenberg, Paula S. 2002. *White Privilege: Essential Readings on the Other Side of Racism*. New York: Worth.

Rubin, Lillian. 1994. *Families on the Fault Line*. New York: HarperCollins.

Sampson, Robert J. 2001. "How Do Communities Undergird or Undermine Human Development? Relevant Contexts and Social Mechanisms." In Alan Booth and Ann C. Crouter (eds). *Does it Take a Village?*, 3–30. Mahwah, NJ: Lawrence Erlbaum.

Smelser, Neil, Wilson, William Julius, and Mitchell, Faith. 2001. "Introduction." In Neil J. Smelser, William Julius Wilson, and Faith Mitchell (eds.) *America Becoming*, 1–20. Washington, DC: National Academy Press.

Song, Miri. 1999. *Helping Out: Children's Labor in Ethnic Businesses*. Philadelphia: Temple University Press.

Statistics Canada. 2001. *Facts and Figures 2001: Immigration Overview*. Ottawa: Statistics Canada.

Tatum, Beverly Daniel. 1997. "Out There Stranded? Black Families in White Communities." In Harriette Pipe McAdoo (ed.) *Black Families*, 3rd ed., 214–231. Thousand Oaks, CA: Sage.

Thai, Hung Cam. 2002. "Formation of Ethnic Identity Among Second-Generation Vietnamese Americans." In Pyong Gap Min (ed.) *The Second Generation: Ethnic Identity Among Asian Americans*, 53–83. Walnut Creek, CA: AltaMira Press.

Van Ausdale, Debra, and Joe F. Feagin. 2001. *The First R: How Children Learn Race and Racism*. Lanham, MD: Rowman & Littlefield.

Vecoli, Rudolph J. 1995. "Introduction." In Judy Galens, Anna Sheets, and Robin V. Sand Young (eds.) *Gale Encyclopedia of Multicultural America*, Xxi–xxvii. Detroit, MI: Gale Research.

Vidich, Arthur, and Joseph Bensman. 1969. *Small Town in Mass Society*, enlarged ed. Princeton, NJ: Princeton University Press.

Waters, Mary C. 1990. *Ethnic Options: Choosing Identities in America*. Berkeley: University of California Press.

——. 1996. "Ethnic and Racial Identities of Second-Generation Black Immigrants." In Alejandro Portes (ed.) *The New Second Generation*, 171–196. New York: Russell Sage Foundation.

——. 1999. *Black Identities: West Indian American Dreams and American Realities*. Cambridge, MA: Harvard University Press.

Zeiher, Helga. 2003. "Shaping Daily Life in Urban Environments." In Pia Christensen and Margaret O'Brien (eds.) *Children in the City: Home, Neighborhood and Community*, 66–81. London: Routledge-Falmer.

Zhou, Min. 2001. "Straddling Different Worlds: The Acculturation of Vietnamese Refugee Children." In Ruben G. Rumbaut and Alejandro Portes (eds.) *Ethnicities: Children of Immigrants in America*, 187–227. Berkeley and New York: University of California Press and Russell Sage Foundation.

Zhou, Min, and Carl L. Bankston III. 1998. *Growing Up American: How Vietnamese Children Adapt to Life in the United States*. New York: Russell Sage Foundation. ✦

Chapter 11

Sex, Gender, and Socialization

The first thing anyone is likely to say about a healthy newborn is either "It's a girl" or "It's a boy." Human newborns vary in several visible characteristics. Some are born with full heads of hair; others are bald. They vary in weight, height, and skin tone. Yet, none of those visible characteristics is given as much social importance as the shape of the newborn's external genitalia. It results in the newborn's assignment to perhaps the most fundamental social category, that of sex. The newborn's initial sex category assignment as female or male will influence how others treat her or him and what they expect of her or him. It may be the most fateful of all social identities.

The shape of the newborn's genitalia is given such social weight because we consider it a reliable predictor of her or his future. It forecasts the bodily shape and characteristics that she or he will acquire during puberty. It foreshadows her or his likely reproductive role. Beyond such physical characteristics and capabilities, we also consider the genitalia a reliable predictor of how aggressive or empathetic, gifted in mathematics or reading, and interested in different activities the infant will be in the future. As we will discuss later, it is an open and debatable question of just how much such predictions about male and female infants' future behavior, traits, and interests accurately reflect differences in the biological propensities of males and females or just how much they are self-fulfilling prophecies. If we expect different things of female and male children, we may treat them differently and confirm our own predictions. Whatever the case, the fates of female and male children in human societies have long differed and continue to do so.

Many social and other scientists distinguish between sex and gender in an attempt to disentangle biologically from socially and culturally produced differences between females and males. They use the term *sex* to refer to biological differences in anatomy and physiology and *gender* to refer to differences that result from psychological, social, and cultural influences. Others argue, as we will in the following examination of gender socialization, that biological, psychological, social, and cultural processes are complexly interrelated and not that easily distinguished (West and Zimmerman 1987; Fausto-Sterling 2000, 1–29). Some have proposed that we use the term *sex* to refer to the biological criteria generally used to identify individuals as males and females and the term *sex category* to refer to the social identities of male and female. The term *gender* then refers to psychological, emotional, and behavioral expressions of what are socially considered the different "natures" of males and females (West and Zimmerman 1987). That is the way that we will use these terms in the remainder of this chapter. Although many psychologists and social scientists use the expressions *sex role* or *gender role* to refer to the socially expected behaviors of males and females, others argue that the expression *role* belittles the importance of gender expectations in everyday social life (Lopata and Thorne 1978). The term *role* usually refers to socially circumscribed and situated activities such as occupation or position in a group, while gender expectations shape and color the performance of all social roles. Sex category is what the late sociologist Everett Hughes (1945) called a "master status" that influences how others view and treat the individual in almost every social situation. Hence, there are good reasons for simply calling the psychological, emotional, and behavioral expectations associated with sex categorical identities *gender* and more situated roles that are considered compatible with such expectations *gender-appropriate roles*.

Sex Category and Social Organization

Throughout human history, males and females have assumed different social roles as adults and often earlier in their lives. Men's and women's different social roles have been at least loosely associated with their biologically determined reproductive roles. The fact that, in general, women can bear and nurse children has fostered the belief and expectation that women *ought* to bear children. The expectation that women *would* bear children has shaped, in one way or another, the social roles considered appropriate for them. For example, both men and women have considered child care a "natural" sequel to childbearing and the maintenance of the domestic household a logical extension of child care. Thus, females' early socialization has commonly prepared them for these later social roles. In contrast, men's reproductive role has been less decisive in shaping the social roles considered appropriate for them. They have generally assumed less responsibility than women for child care, which has allowed them to assume roles that take them further away from the domestic household for longer periods of time than those of women. It was not until recently, and then primarily in affluent industrialized societies, that people started to question whether women's potential reproductive role should restrict the social roles open to them.

Sex and the Social Division of Labor

Most societies, both past and present, have made and make some distinction between work that is appropriate for females and males. The anthropologist George Murdock (Murdock and Provost 1973) analyzed how 185 human societies on which information was available allocated responsibility among females and males for 50 different kinds of tasks. He reports that in almost all societies, certain tasks were and are performed overwhelmingly by men and others by women. For example, in 144 societies that hunted large animals, males exclusively did so in 139 or 96 percent of them and mostly did so in the remaining 5. In contrast, women did all the cooking in 117 or 64 percent of societies on which information was available and did most of the cooking in an additional 63 of those societies. Societies vary widely in how and whether they assign responsibility for other tasks to males or females. For example, in the 141 societies that grew crops, only men planted crops in 27 (19 percent) of them and predominately did so in another 35 (25 percent) while only women planted crops in 20 other societies (14 percent) and predominately did so in 26 (18 percent) others. In the remaining 33 (24 percent) of these societies, women and men were equally involved in the planting of crops.

As these findings suggest, women's greater responsibility for child care would seem to provide relatively weak grounds for a sexual division of labor in settled agriculture societies in which people cultivate crops close to their domestic household and whose livestock graze nearby. Men's, on average, greater upper-body strength than women's may have made them more suitable for certain tasks such as plowing fields and clearing land. Yet, the division of labor between men and women in settled agricultural societies seems to have had, and have, as much to do with cultural beliefs about the "natural" talents and abilities of men and women as with relative differences in strength or child-care responsibilities. Even when work did not require anyone to venture far from the domestic household, women tended to have primary responsibility for tasks such as laundering, spinning, and milking (Murdock and Provost 1973) that kept them closest to home.

The industrialization of Western societies during the nineteenth century initially strengthened the association of women with the home and exaggerated differences between men's and women's social roles. An increasing number and variety of goods were manufactured in factories and workshops away from the domestic household. Because of women's historic association with domestic tasks, they commonly remained at home performing tasks like laundering and gardening while men went off to work in factories and offices for wages and profits. This drove a deep wedge between men's and women's daily activities and experience. Men tended to labor for money in a competitive market that valued individual autonomy and drive, while women labored in the direct care of their family. These very different social roles and spheres of activity—work and home—came to reinforce social beliefs about the personalities of men and women. Independence and assertiveness were considered masculine characteristics, and caring and empathy feminine ones (Cancian 1987, 15–27).

Yet, the affluence and technological progress that industrialization brought eventually undermined the sharp distinction between men's and women's appropriate spheres of activity that it initially fortified. Over time, children's labor was no longer needed on the family farm or to supplement the family's income, and women on average had fewer and fewer children (Davis 1988). It also took fewer pregnancies to have the same number of surviving children because of a steep decline in infant mortality. Commercial food and clothing production and so-called labor-saving devices like automatic washing machines also decreased the number and burden of tasks that needed to be done in the home. By the 1950s, in the more economically developed parts of the world, as Judith Stacey (1990, 9) has observed, "the full-time homemaker's province had been pared to chores of housework, consumption, and the cultivation of a declining number of progeny during a shortened span of years."

Hence, there were fewer reasons for women to stay at home, and, especially in North America, more and more of them joined the paid labor force during the second half of the twentieth century.

Although the entry of women into the paid labor force in more technologically advanced societies has eroded sharp distinctions between men's and women's social roles, many tasks and occupations continue to be performed primarily by either men or women. In the United States, over 60 percent of all women over 16 years of age, compared to about 75 percent of men, and almost 80 percent of those with children under 18 years of age were either working or looking for work in 2000 (U.S. Census Bureau 2001, 367, 373). Yet, these women, including those who work full-time, tend to have primary responsibility for the overwhelming majority of child care and domestic tasks at home (Hochschild and Machung 1989), and those tasks men typically do, such as home repair and lawn care, reflect long-standing gender expectations (Berk 1985). Similarly, while many women now work in occupations from which they were once largely excluded, other occupations remain almost exclusively male or female. For example, currently in the United States, over a quarter of all physicians and lawyers and over 40 percent of college and university teachers are women (U.S. Bureau of the Census 2001, 380). But in contrast, over 98 percent of automobile mechanics, 96 percent of firefighters, and 90 percent of engineers are still men, while over 98 percent of secretaries and prekindergarten and kindergarten teachers and over 92 percent of registered nurses are women (U.S. Bureau of the Census 2001, 380–382). Although the sexual division of labor has radically changed in some technologically advanced societies in recent decades, it has not disappeared. Most girls and boys still look forward to different futures.

Sex and Gender Hierarchies

Human societies not only tend to assign females and males different social roles but also tend to differentially value those roles. The different value societies place on women's and men's tasks also tends to be associated with the relative power and authority that women and men wield in those societies. Anthropologists refer to such sex categorical differences in status, power, and authority as *sex and gender hierarchies* (Miller 1993). In general, men are the beneficiaries of such social hierarchies.

Yet, scholars are divided over just how universal and extensive male social dominance or patriarchy has been and is among human societies. Some anthropologists maintain that men invariably wield more power and authority in human societies than do women, as the anthropologist Michelle Rosaldo (1980, 394–395) explains.

> My reading of the anthropological record leads me to conclude that human cultural and social forms have always been male dominated. By this, I mean not that men rule by right or even that men rule at all and certainly not that women everywhere are passive victims of a world that men define. Rather, I would point to a collection of related facts which seem to argue that in all known human groups—and no matter what prerogatives that women may in fact enjoy—the vast majority of opportunities for public influence and

prestige, the ability to forge relationships, determine enmities, speak in public, use or forswear the use of force are all recognized as men's privilege and right. . . . I know of no political system in which women individually or as a group . . . hold more offices or have more political clout than their male counterparts.

Others argue that such a focus on public pronouncements and roles often conceals the actual distribution of power and authority between the sexes. An often cited example is the Native North American Iroquois. Although a Council of Elders consisting of elected male chiefs held ultimate political authority, the so-called clan mothers or elder women who ran the affairs of extended-family "longhouses" appointed the members of the council and could revoke an appointment if their initial choice "proved unsatisfactory" (Tooker 1984, 112). Moreover, because the elder women of the longhouses controlled the goods their extended families produced, they could effectively void the council's decisions by withholding goods necessary to conduct their military adventures, hold religious festivals, or even convene council meetings (Harris 1993, 68). As this example illustrates, even when men hold official positions of authority, women may exercise indirect kinds of power that neutralize men's public authority.

In light of examples such as this, the anthropologist Peggy Reeves Sanday (2002, 236–237) argues that patriarchy, rule by men, and matriarchy, rule by women, should be defined not in terms of who occupies official positions of political authority but in terms of cultural symbols and practices. She maintains that the usual focus on official positions of authority reflects a Western bias that neglects the diffuse authority over affairs of daily life that is often far more important in non-Western societies such as the Minangkabau village that she studied in Sumatra, a region of Indonesia. There women inherited ancestral lands, including the home; kept the key to the family's rice house; and played leading roles in local ceremonies. Although men occupied official positions of authority, they generally deferred to senior women (Sanday 2002), as apparently did Iroquois men (Tooker 1984).

However prominent male power and authority may be, there can be little doubt that its character and extent have been and are cross-culturally quite variable. Today, most anthropologists agree that sex and gender hierarchies result from an interaction between "physical sex difference, particularly women's reproduction and men's size and strength," with "the demands of the socioeconomic system" (Eagly, Wood, and Diekman 2000, 130). For example, the anthropologist Marvin Harris (1993) provides a compelling account of how subsistence patterns and types of warfare may enhance or diminish men's usual social dominance over women. According to Harris (1993, 57–58), men's average greater height, weight, and upper-body strength made them more efficient than women with spears, spear throwers, heavy clubs, and bows and arrows. As previously noted, males consequently assumed primary responsibility for big game hunting in most foraging societies and for the manufacture and use of the weapons used to kill game. Their control of such weapons was a potentially influential source of power, especially when such weapons were also employed in warfare with neighboring bands and villages (Harris 1993, 61). Although local warfare among band and village societies arguably enhanced males' power and authority, Harris (1993, 66) contends that warfare with distant enemies generally detracted from it. That is because male warriors' routine and often lengthy absence encourages matrilocality, or the practice of married couples living in or near the household of the wife's family. Unlike partrilocal societies where married couples live with or near the husband's family, husbands in matrilocal societies become outsiders among women who have been living together all their lives. As Harris (1993, 67) observes, "where matrilocality prevails, therefore, women tend to take control of the entire domestic sphere of life," as was the case with the previously mentioned Iroquois. Harris (1993, 72) also argues that women are more equal to men in agricultural societies that rely on hoes to till the land than in those that use plows. Although women can use hoes as effectively as men, men's greater average upper-body strength enables them effectively to guide draft animals pulling a plow for longer periods of time than can most women and children. The importance of that task generally translates into social standing and authority for the males who do it.

Despite such associations between subsistence practices, patterns of warfare, and variations in male dominance, there is no evidence of a matriarchal human society where women ruled or rule over men (Martin and Voorhies 1975, 10). Peggy Sanday (2002, 228 ff.) argues that is because we define matriarchy as the opposite of patriarchy, as the overt domination of men by women, ignoring how the cultural dominance of maternal symbols and practices may alter the use of power and authority in a society. Others conclude that patriarchy or male dominance is inevitable and universal in human societies. For example, Steven Goldberg (1974; 1993) argues that males are biologically more aggressive than females because of the influence of male hormones and, therefore, more assertive and domineering. For Goldberg, males' biological propensity for aggression consequently results in male social dominance whatever the demands of the socioeconomic system. In contrast, Harris (1993, 75) argues "that today's hyperindustrialism is almost totally indifferent to the anatomical and physiological differences between men and women," resulting in women's growing power and influence in the hyperindustrial societies of North America, Europe, and, to a lesser degree, Asia. Still others argue that males' seeming aggressiveness is based more on cultural beliefs, perceptions, and practices than biology, and that, even if men are generally more aggressive than women, there is no inherent reason why aggressiveness necessarily results in social dominance (e.g., Johnson 1988, 21). This debate reflects the long-standing controversy about the relative influence of nature and nurture over the development of gender differences and the relative social positions of males and females. Before addressing that controversy, it is necessary briefly to consider the complex biological processes underlying the development of human sexual characteristics.

The Biology of Sex

According to the popular account of biological sex differentiation among humans, an individual's sex is determined at the moment of conception. A fertilized egg, or ovum, whose twenty-third chromosome pair is XX will become a "normal, natural" female and one with an XY chromosome pair will become a "normal, natural" male. However, this popular account neglects the complex biological processes involved in the development of sex-related characteristics among humans.

The Development of Sex-Related Characteristics

Whatever the composition of their twenty-third chromosomes, human fetuses are sexually indistinguishable until around the third month of pregnancy. Until that time, even their embryonic gonads, or so-called sex glands, are identical. The development of the sexually undifferentiated fetus into either a boy or girl infant, or a sexually ambiguous one, is the result of hormonal influence. For example, around the sixth or seventh week after conception, fetuses with a Y chromosome produce a hormone that causes the fetal gonads to develop into testes. In fetuses with a second X chromosome, rather than a Y, the fetal gonads develop into ovaries (Kessler and McKenna 1978, 47–48).

Until the differentiation of the fetal gonads into either testes or ovaries, human fetuses have identical external genitalia and the rudiments of similar internal reproductive organs. The development of testes or ovaries soon changes that. The developing testes in fetuses with an XY pair of chromosomes produce "androgens" or so-called male sex hormones that cause the fetal genitalia gradually to develop into a penis and scrotum (Lippa 2002, 105) and the internal reproductive ducts develop into seminal vesicles, ejaculatory ducts, and the vas deferens, transforming the fetus into a potential sperm producer (Kessler and McKenna 1978, 48). In fetuses with ovaries, the external genitalia develop into a clitoris and labia surrounding the vaginal opening and cavity, and the internal reproductive ducts develop into fallopian tubes, a uterus, and the upper vagina (Kessler and McKenna 1978, 48), transforming the fetus into a potential egg producer.

Much more is known about the fetal development of male anatomical characteristics than female characteristics. Many scientists concluded that without the influence of androgens, a fetus will develop female characteristics. Hence, male development became something needing explanation while female development was treated as a kind of "default" option. Scientists have only recently begun to examine closely the fetal development of female characteristics (Fausto-Sterling 2000, 349–350, n. 46), and their findings suggest that at least some minimal levels of so-called female sex hormones are necessary for normal female development (Lippa 2002, 82).

Although androgens (literally "to build a man") and estrogens (literally "to create estrus," or the periodic state preceding ovulation and menstruation) are often called the *sex hormones*, testes and ovaries produce both kinds of hormones, as does the cortex of the adrenal glands in both males and females (Kessler and McKenna 1978, 49). These hormones affect the development of not only external and internal reproductive organs but also tissues such as those of the bones, nerves, blood, liver, kidneys, and heart (Fausto-Sterling 2000, 186). In fact, men need estrogens for "normal development of everything from bone growth to fertility" (Fausto-Sterling 2000, 147). What hormonally distinguishes females from males is not the presence or absence of androgens or estrogens but their relative quantities, and the production of those substances varies widely over the life span. For example, the testes of developing males start to produce androgens in the seventh week after conception, and their production peaks around the eighteenth week of pregnancy (Lippa 2002, 82). From soon after birth until puberty, there is a low, steady production of androgens and estrogens in both girls and boys. Then at puberty, the pituitary gland signals the gonads to produce much higher levels of androgens, especially in males, and estrogens, especially in females, than had been produced in childhood. The first, prenatal surge in sex-related hormone production results in the development of typically male or female external genitalia and reproductive organs, while the second surge during puberty results in the development of so-called secondary sexual characteristics such as fuller breasts and hips among females and facial hair and deepening voices among males.

The profound effects that androgens and estrogens have on anatomical characteristics have led many to conclude that they have equally powerful effects on the development of the central nervous system. They argue that prenatal (or before birth) exposure to different levels of these substances has an "organizing effect" on the central nervous system, influencing the growth of nerve cells, connections among them, and the size of brain structures (Lippa 2002, 83). They attribute everything from differences in cognitive abilities to behavioral propensities; gender identity, or the individual's own sense of being male or female; and even sexual preference to the organizing effects of these hormones on the central nervous system. The obvious implication is that men's better performance, on average, on visual-spatial tasks than women's and supposedly greater propensity toward aggression; girls' and women's greater verbal fluency, on average, than boys' and men's; an individual's sense of being either female or male; and a person's sexual orientations are all biologically determined before birth. According to these scholars, gender is indeed an expression of males' and females' hormonally determined different natures.

Nature and Nurture

The claim that individuals' gender identities, sexual orientations, and sex-related differences in cognitive abilities and behaviors are hormonally determined before birth is highly contentious. Most of the evidence to support that claim comes from either animal research or research on individuals whose prenatal development did not follow the typical female or male path described above. There have been studies of possible differences in the structures of males' and females' brains, but their implications are far from clear. To date, scientists can only speculate about the causes of documented and hypothesized differences between the brain structures of males and females and about their possible relation, if any, to cognitive functioning and behavior.

The earliest and most consistent evidence regarding the effect of prenatal hormones on subsequent behavior has come from studies of animals, mostly rats and other rodents. Scientists manipulate such animals' early exposure to so-called sex-related hormones by either injecting their pregnant mothers with androgens or castrating newborn males. Research using these procedures indicates that early exposure to different quantities of androgens and estrogens does influence subsequent sex-related behaviors. For example, female rats that are prenatally exposed to high levels of androgens are more likely than untreated females to engage in typically masculine behaviors later in life, and male rats that are castrated early in life are more likely than untreated males to engage in typically feminine behaviors later in life. However, other research indicates that environmental factors can also change the normally sex-related behaviors of rats, independent of any hormone influence (Fausto-Sterling 2000, 195–232).

Scientists have not performed similar experiments on humans because of obvious ethical considerations and have instead focused attention on naturally occurring conditions that expose developing human fetuses to unusual quantities of so-called sex-related hormones. The fetal development of sex-related characteristics does not always follow the typical male and female paths described above. For example, the adrenal glands of some fetuses with an XX pair of chromosomes produce unusually high levels of androgens, which sometimes result in the development of ambiguous-appearing external genitalia. At birth, the clitoris may be enlarged to the point of appearing like a penis and the genital folds may be fused, forming an empty scrotum (Lippa 2002, 103–104). This condition is called Congenital Adrenal Hyperplasia, or CAH for short.

Many studies have compared CAH girls with more normal girls in an attempt to investigate the possible effects of prenatal androgens on behavioral propensities and preferences. Regardless of the appearance of their external genitalia, and those of many CAH girls appear unremarkably female, they are commonly raised as girls and develop a female gender identity. However, some studies suggest that compared to normal girls, CAH girls engage in more rough-and-tumble play, are more likely to prefer boys' toys, score higher on measures of aggression, show more visual-spatial abilities, and report a higher incidence of sexual attraction to females (Lippa 2002, 104). Other research challenges those findings, suggesting that CAH girls do not engage in more rough-and-tumble play than normal girls and almost never grow up to be exclusively homosexual in their sexual orientation (Fausto-Sterling 2000, 75).

A more remarkable condition called reductase-deficiency that occurs among individuals with an XY pair of chromosomes has also attracted scientists' attention. In these cases, the fetus lacks an enzyme necessary for processing the androgen that causes the prenatal masculinization of the external genitalia. These reductase-deficient individuals are consequently born with typically female or slightly ambiguous external genitalia, and are commonly raised as girls. However, the surge of androgens during puberty eventually causes the reductase-deficient individual's "clitoris" to enlarge into a sexually functioning penis and the testes to descend into a partially fused scrotum

(Lippa 2002, 105). Although rare, there is a relatively high incidence of this condition in several small villages in the Dominican Republic and among the Sambia people in the highlands of Papua, New Guinea (Fausto-Sterling 2000, 109). Studies indicate that although these reductase-deficient individuals are raised as girls, most choose to live as men after their anatomical masculinization during puberty (Lippa 2002, 106). Because these individuals' brains were exposed to high levels of androgens before birth, some scientists argue that this finding demonstrates that prenatal hormones are a more powerful determinant of gender identity than the appearance of the external genitalia or how individuals are raised. Others dispute that claim. They argue that both the Dominican villagers and Sambia have a special word to describe these individuals and often recognize them as such at birth. They consequently do not raise them exactly the same as other girls, anticipating their anatomical transformation at puberty. Moreover, in both Dominican villages and among the Sambia, men have more power and privileges than do women, so it is understandable why individuals who are given the opportunity to live as men rather than women would choose to do so (Fausto-Sterling 2000, 109).

Although suggestive, studies of animals and of individuals with unusual conditions have not yet definitively demonstrated that prenatal exposure to different levels of androgens or estrogens has an "organizing effect" on the central nervous system and, consequently, on subsequent behaviors and preferences. In addition to the kind of questions already reviewed, there is also much debate over the extent to which the findings of such studies can be generalized to typically male and female humans. The study of rodents and other animals may have limited applicability to human's varied and complex expressions of gender. Moreover, humans, unlike other animals, imbue anatomical characteristics and behavior with symbolic meanings, and those meanings may have as powerful an organizing effect on behavior as do hormones. For example, the findings of studies of individuals with unusual conditions may well reflect the organizing effect of meanings rather than hormones on behavior. As noted, reductase-deficient individuals may be recognized as different from normal girls soon after birth and treated differently as a result. Similarly, CAH girls are often diagnosed shortly after birth and, when necessary, their genitalia surgically "corrected." So parents, who almost always know about their CAH daughters' condition, may treat them differently from non-CAH girls (Lippa 2002, 173).

For a number of years, many scientists and other scholars considered the nature-nurture controversy regarding human gender development settled by a remarkable case of identical twin boys. At the age of six months, one of the boy's penis was severely damaged during an attempted circumcision. Scientists who were studying gender development in so-called intersexed children, such as CAH girls, subsequently convinced his parents that he should undergo sex reassignment surgery and be raised as a girl. At 22 months of age, the boy "Bruce" underwent surgical castration and reconstruction of his genitalia, becoming "Brenda." Over the following years, published reports indicated that Brenda, although a bit of a tomboy, was as well-adjusted a girl as her twin brother was a boy. The obvious implication was that nurture was a more powerful determinant of gender identity and gender than nature because Brenda and her brother were genetically identical and were prenatally exposed to similar levels of androgens.

However, Brenda was not as well-adjusted as the published reports indicated. Her behavioral and psychological problems escalated over the years, and, at adolescence, after learning of her early life, she rejected her female identity and chose to undergo surgical and medical procedures so that she could live as a man. The former Brenda eventually married a woman and adopted two sons. However, he continued to suffer bouts of depression, and in May 2004 committed suicide (Colapinto 2004).

Many now argue that the former Brenda's rejection of a female identity demonstrates that nature, in the form of prenatal hormones' organizing effect on the central nervous system, is the principal determinant of human gender and gender identity (Colapinto 2000). Yet, that is not the only conclusion that can be drawn from this remarkable and tragic case. The former Brenda was not assigned a female identity until she was almost 2 years old. She underwent a number of painful surgical procedures over the years and repeated interrogations by researchers that often traumatized her. Her rejection of her assigned female identity may, at least partially, have been a rejection of those she came to see as her tormentors and of what they had made her. The case that had supposedly settled the nature-nurture controversy first in favor of nurture and then in favor of nature has ultimately settled nothing. What it does provide is yet more evidence that human gender and gender identity are products of complex interactions among biological, psychological, social, and cultural processes. It is to that complexity that we now turn.

Socialization Processes and Agents

There can be little doubt that humans treat male and female newborns differently in many if not all human societies, giving them different kinds of names, often dressing them differently, and, perhaps, giving then different kinds of attention. For example, research indicates that while still in the hospital, Australian mothers spend more time breastfeeding newborn sons but more time talking to newborn daughters (Thoman, Leiderman, and Olson 1972). Similarly, research in North America suggests that until infants are around six months of age, mothers tend to hold and touch sons more than daughters but look at and talk to daughters more than sons. After about 6 months of age, mothers tend to interact both verbally and physically with daughters more than sons (Cahill 1986a, 168). It is unclear to what extent such subtle differences in the treatment of female and male infants result from mothers' attribution of different characteristics to sons and daughters or from subtle differences in male and female infants' behavior. If, for example, male infants are fussier or, in more scientific language, expend more physical energy than female infants, then mothers may hold them more when they are younger in an attempt to calm them but later allow them freely to exhaust some of that energy. Yet, whether or not there are biologically based differences between the behavioral propensities of female and male infants, their social experiences do influence their future behavior, preferences, and temperaments. Those experiences channel whatever biologically based propensities children may have in varied directions, sometimes exaggerating them and perhaps other times neutralizing them. Although much ink has been spilled debating whether nature or nurture is primarily responsible for observed differences between human males and females, it has resolved little. A more fruitful question might be to ask just how the two interact under different social circumstances to produce the varied expressions of gender found among humans. Addressing that question requires consideration of the varied agents and complex processes involved in children's gender socialization.

It also requires recognition that children are active agents in their own gender socialization. Even before infants understand sex categorization, they seem to practice it. Research suggests that by 7 months of age most infants, on the apparent basis of hair length, can distinguish between adult female and male faces. They also associate female and male voices with the corresponding faces (Bussey and Bandura 1999). Their repeated exposure to sex categorical labels like *mommy, daddy, girl,* and *boy* implicitly conveys that such distinctions are of considerable social importance, and young children quickly learn that lesson. By 3 years of age, the overwhelming majority of young children appropriately use such sex-categorical labels in reference to others and to themselves. That self-categorization is the cornerstone of the child's developing gender identity (Cahill 1986b). She or he begins to define herself or himself as a girl or a boy, a female or male, and incorporates that identity into her or his self-concept (Maccoby 1998, 157). Young children then actively seek out information about what it means to be a girl or a boy, female or male, form beliefs about the gender appropriateness of different objects, activities, and characteristics, and hold both themselves and others to the sex categorically relevant standards. Those beliefs constitute what some psychologists call a *gender schema* (Bem 1981; Martin and Halverson 1987) that influences the information that children subsequently attend to, perceive, and remember, partially insulating their developing understandings of gender from discrepant information. Children's understanding of gender undoubtedly varies in relation to the kind of information to which they are exposed, but, as the psychologist Eleanor Maccoby (1998, 152) has noted, such information is "in the air" and children can pick it up "from a host of sources," such as parents and other family members, mass media, caregivers and teachers, and peers. It is to those different sources of information or agents and agencies of gender socialization that we now turn.

Family Interaction

Most children's earliest social experiences revolve around the family, and scholars and researchers have devoted much attention to how parents may influence their children's gender-related behavior, beliefs, and identity. For example, following the lead of Freud and Parsons (see Chapter 1), some feminist scholars have proposed that nuclear families are the "factories which produce" not simply human personalities but also gendered—feminine and masculine—personalities. Perhaps the most influential of those scholars, the sociologist and psychoanalyst Nancy Chodorow (1978), attributes the development of feminine and masculine personalities to the very fact that women are primarily responsible for child care. She argues that although mothers tend to feel a sense of oneness with their infants, they identify more closely with daughters who are sex categorically like them than with sons whom they experience as different from them. They consequently encourage their sons to develop an identity separate from them at an early age. Feeling rejected by their mothers, sons reject the femininity she represents and define their own masculinity in contrast to whatever they consider feminine. Moreover, sons are not as close to their often absent fathers as they were to their mothers, so they do not develop their sense of masculinity through personal identification with their father but through cultural images and idealizations of masculinity, such as those personified by sport figures and fictional characters. Although little girls gradually develop an independent identity separate from their mothers', they remain closely identified with them and define their own femininity through this personal relationship with them. According to Chodorow, these very different processes of masculine and feminine personality development explain why men tend to be more impersonal and closely identified with their jobs and why women tend to be more interpersonally oriented, caring, and closely identified with their family and parenting roles. Although Chodorow's psychodynamic account of gender identification and personality development is intuitively appealing, it is based on assumptions about unconscious psychological processes that are difficult to investigate and empirically verify. And, there is little evidence to date that "mothers construct a more empathic or enmeshed relationship with daughters than with sons" (Maccoby 1998, 141).

Other scholars, like the sociologist Miriam Johnson (1988), argue that it is not mothers but fathers who are primarily responsible for children's acquisition of socially recognized feminine or masculine traits. She maintains that both boys and girls develop "their generic human qualities" in "interaction with the mother in a reciprocal relationship whose main content" is mutual love (Johnson 1988, 155, 129). Fathers then enter children's purview "somewhat later," treating boys and girls differently. Compared to theories like Chodorow's, those like Johnson's would seem to have the bulk of research evidence on their side. Much research evidence indicates that fathers tend to treat their children in more gender-stereotypic ways than do mothers (Bussey and Bandura 1998, 695). Yet, theories that attribute the development of gender differences primarily to either mothers' or fathers' influence arguably oversimplify and perhaps exaggerate parents' contributions to children's gender socialization.

Studies of parents' treatment of sons and daughters paint a complex and unclear picture of how and to what extent mothers and fathers influence their children's gender-related behavior, beliefs, and identity. Taken together, the results of those studies indicate that although parents are equally responsive to sons and daughters overall, they do treat girls and boys differently in some respects during the early years. For example, parents, especially fathers, are more likely to roughhouse with sons than with daughters. They also tend to assert more power over boys to get them to comply with demands. On the other hand, parents, especially mothers, talk more with girls about emotions and interpersonal relations than they do with boys. And, mothers and especially fathers tend to react positively to their children's gender-appropriate play, such as when a girl puts on dress-up clothes or a boy plays with toy trucks, and negatively to gender-inappropriate play, especially that of boys. As we noted in the discussion of the media (see Chapter 8), toy retailers often direct their advertising, especially on television, to boys or to girls, and parents tend to respond to those messages. Yet, most of the differences in parental reactions to sons and daughters are small in magnitude and not consistently found (Maccoby 1998, 145). Moreover, parents are equally affectionate toward young sons and daughters, place similar restrictions and demands on them, and are equally responsive to their bids for attention or help (Maccoby 1998, 124).

Those who study children's gender socialization and development have drawn very different conclusions from the findings of these studies. To some, the inconsistent findings and the slight and limited differences that are found in parents' treatment of sons and daughters suggest that parents have a more limited role in children's gender socialization than is commonly believed (Maccoby 1998, 151). Others disagree, arguing that even slight differences in how parents treat sons and daughters can have large cumulative effects on children's behavior and preferences. They point out that the inconsistent findings may merely reflect inconsistency in how different parents encourage or discourage gender-stereotypic beliefs and behavior. They also contend that research has neglected the behavior that parents model to their children and how consistent it is with the behavior they explicitly encourage and teach (Bussey and Bandura 1999, 698–699). These scholars maintain that parents have a profound influence on children's gender-related beliefs, behavior, and identity, but that existing research has failed to address how varied and complex that influence may be, including how varied and complex the separate influence of mothers and fathers may be.

Mothers and fathers undoubtedly influence their children's gender-related beliefs, behaviors, and identities, but so too may other family members, such as siblings. For example, a recent study of over 2,000 British 3-year-olds found that "having an older brother was associated with more masculine *and* less feminine behavior in both boys and girls, whereas boys with older sisters were more feminine but not less masculine and girls with older sisters were less masculine but not more feminine" (Rust et al. 2000, 299). The authors of that study speculate that older brothers may have a more profound influence than older sisters on the gender-related behavior of younger siblings because it is more acceptable for girls to engage in masculine activities than for boys to engage in feminine activities and that boys may exert more pressure on younger siblings than girls do to engage in activities that they prefer (Rust et al. 2000, 300). Moreover, an earlier study of 200 North American sibling pairs suggests that younger siblings may also have an influence on their older brothers' and sisters' gender-related behavior. For example, sisters with younger brothers tend to engage in more feminine activities than those with younger sisters, while brothers of younger brothers are slightly more likely to engage in masculine activities than those with young sisters (McHale, Crouter, and Tucker 1999). In any case, research has only begun to scratch the surface of how different family members and patterns of relationships may influence children's gender-related behavior, beliefs, and identity. Much is yet to be learned, but what is clear from available research is that the family is one among a host of agents and agencies of children's gender socialization.

The Media

In many parts of the world today, television is as much a presence in family households as other people. Children start watching television at an early age, and by the time they are school age, in North America at least, they spend more time on average watching television than they spend in school (Schneider 1995, 63). Children undoubtedly acquire much information about gender from their television viewing, and researchers have devoted considerable attention to the kind of information they are receiving. Content analyses of commercials, cartoons, and other television programs directed at children from a variety of countries have yielded remarkably similar findings. There are generally more male characters than female characters, and they are generally portrayed in gender-stereotypic ways. Male characters tend to be more courageous, aggressive, and enterprising than female characters, who tend to be more emotional, caring, and romantic than their male counterparts. Male characters are also depicted as exercising more control over events, whereas female characters are more often depicted as victims of circumstance (Bussey and Bandura 1999; Furham and Mak 1999; Lippa 2002, 143–145). There is some evidence that female characters are now being presented as more independent, intelligent, and assertive than in the past, but many gender stereotypical portrayals remain (Lippa 2002, 144).

Although content analyses cannot establish that what is shown on television influences children's gender-related beliefs and preferences, there is evidence that it does. For example, research has found that children who are heavy viewers of television have more stereotypical gender beliefs than do light viewers (McGhee and Frueh 1980). Even stronger evidence that television viewing encourages more gender-stereotypic beliefs comes from the Canadian study discussed in Chapter 8 on the impact of television on children in a town that previously had none. At the beginning of that study, the children in the town without television called Notel held significantly less gender-stereotypic beliefs than children in either Unitel, which received one television station, or Multitel, which received several television stations. Yet, when the research was conducted again after Notel had had television for two years, the children in Notel held as gender-stereotypical beliefs as the children in the other two towns (Kimball 1986). Those findings strongly suggest that television is an influential source of information about gender for children.

However, it is important to recognize that children are not passive receptacles of what is shown on television. They selectively attend to the flickering screens in front of them, transfixed by them one moment and totally ignoring them the next. They also actively interpret and make sense of what they watch. What they watch is not simply what entertains them but what informs them about matters of concern to them. And, once children acquire a gender identity, once they define themselves as boys or girls, they are interested in what it means to be a male or female. For example, one study found that 6- to 7-year-olds pay significantly more attention to programs dominated by characters who share their gender identity than to those dominated by characters who do not. It also found that children paid more attention to those characters who display more gender-stereotypical behavior than those who act in more gender-neutral ways (Sprafkin and Liebert 1974). Children apparently look to television for information about what distinguishes girls from boys, and television provides clear answers. For example, four- to nine-year-olds describe male cartoon characters as more active and violent than female characters, whom they tend to describe in terms of appearance, domestic activities, and their relationships to male characters (Thompson and Zerbinos 1997). From all indications, children do draw gender-stereotypic lessons from their television viewing, but it is doubtful that simply discouraging children from viewing television or gender-stereotypic programs would profoundly alter their gender-related beliefs.

There may be many reasons to encourage reading to and by children as an alternative to watching television, but discouraging gender-stereotypic beliefs may not be among them. Content analyses of award-winning picture books written for children have found that, as in television programs and commercials, male characters tend to be far more numerous than female characters and both tend to be depicted in gender-stereotypic ways (e.g., Weitzman et al. 1972). Although many feminist-inspired children books that challenge gender stereotypes have been published since those studies were conducted, there are reasons to suspect that they have not had their intended effect on children's gender-related beliefs. For example, in an innovative study, the Australian researcher Bronwyn Davies (1989) read such feminist-inspired books to preschoolers and then talked to them about what the stories meant. One story was about a boy who was considered a sissy because he wanted to dance but was hailed a star by other boys after he danced in a talent show, and another was about a princess who spurned a charming prince's offer of marriage in favor of independence. However, the children interpreted these stories in gender-stereotypical ways. They maintained that it was wrong for the dancing boy to want to do "girl things" and that the princess's rejection of the prince was a temporary interlude before they married and lived happily ever after. Although there has been no comparable research on children's reaction to television programming that challenges gender stereotypes, they may well interpret it in similarly gender-stereotypic ways. As previously mentioned, children form gender schemas or interrelated beliefs about what objects, activities, and traits are appropriate for females and males at an early age, and these subsequently influence the information they attend to, perceive, and remember, as well as how they interpret that information. Children recognize at an early age that sex-categorical identification is of fundamental social importance and actively seek information about what distinguishes males and females and how they can distinguish themselves as boys or girls. What children see on television and the stories they hear and read may encourage and reinforce gender stereotypic beliefs, but similar lessons are "in the air" and everywhere. It is easy to blame television, books, and other media for perpetuating gender-stereotypic beliefs, but doing so only ignores how pervasive gender-stereotypic messages are in everyday social life and how quick children are to recognize them.

It is also easy to overlook the fact, as much research does, that children seldom, in isolation, interpret what they see, hear, and read. Children commonly discuss with parents, peers, caregivers, and teachers what they watch on television and the stories that are read to them and they read. Those discussions surely influence how children interpret what they see and hear and the lessons that they draw from that information. Researchers have only begun to investigate how children collaboratively interpret such information in interaction with parents, peers, and other adults (e.g., Fingerson 1999) and how such collective interpretations influence their gender-related beliefs and preferences. Yet, it is essential to recognize that parents, peers, the media, and teachers are part of an interactive system of agents and agencies of gender socialization that includes inquisitive and clever children themselves.

Preschools and Schools

Like the media, schools and other organized group settings have become an increasing presence in children's lives over past decades. Today children spend more of their days, weeks, and years in school and school-like group care than in the not so distant past. Daycare providers, teachers, and classmates have correspondingly become increasingly important agents of children's gender socialization. And, as the variety of agents and agencies of gender socialization has increased, it has become increasingly difficult to assess the influence of any one apart from the influence of others.

During the earliest years when children have only limited understanding of media messages and little interaction with peers, adults (both family members and care providers outside the family) are probably most influential. Although, as previously discussed, research has found that parents tend to be equally responsive to boys and girls during their earliest years, caregivers outside the family may not be. For example, one study of 13- and 14-month-olds in a daycare setting found that girls and boys were equally likely to try and communicate with care providers and to be assertive with other children. However, the teachers were more likely to respond to girls' attempts to communicate with them and to respond more quickly and decisively to boys who pushed, hit, or grabbed toys away from other children. When these children were observed a year later in a different classroom with other teachers, girls talked with teachers more than the boys who were more aggressive toward other children (Fagot et al. 1985). Such different responses to girls' and boys' behaviors may well set a continuing process in motion. For example, a number of studies have found that teachers tend to interact with girls more than boys in preschools and during the early years of elementary school (Lippa 2002, 138). One possible explanation for teachers' greater attentiveness to young girls is that the girls tend to stay closer to the teachers than do boys and to work more steadily on tasks the teachers give them. In turn, young girls may be more attentive and responsive to teachers because teachers have been more responsive to them in the past.

On the other hand, research suggests that as children progress through the elementary school grades, boys get more of teachers' attention than do girls. Teachers tend to call on boys more, ask them more difficult questions, and listen longer to their responses (Sadker and Sadker 1995). Boys may get more of teachers' attention in the classroom because they are more verbally assertive or because teachers believe, for good reason, that it is harder to get and hold boys' attention. Whatever the reasons, some argue that elementary school teachers thereby encourage greater classroom participation and academic achievement from boys than from girls (Lippa 2002, 138). Others argue that teachers pay more classroom attention to boys than to girls in an attempt to control the boys whom they believe are more likely to be disruptive. Rather than encourage academic achievement, teachers' attempts to control boys' classroom behavior may actually encourage disruptive attempts to evade the teachers' control. These different interpretations of teachers' dissimilar treatment of girls and boys have spawned a debate over whether classrooms are biased against more assertive and potentially disruptive boys or more compliant girls. For example, an influential study by the American Association of University Women's Educational Foundation (1992) is subtitled *How Schools Shortchange Girls*, while others argue that boys' generally lower grades than girls', greater problems with reading, and much higher school dropout rate indicate that boys are the ones who are being shortchanged by the schools (Sommers 2000).

Those who argue that schools shortchange girls counter that, whatever boys' educational problems, schools discourage girls' achievement in more prestigious subjects like math and science and channel them into less valued fields of study. Although, in general, boys do score higher than girls on tests of mathematical achievement, such a gender difference does not appear until the middle or junior high-school years, suggesting that girls' school experiences are least partially responsible. Other research suggests that parents may be at least as responsible as schools for girls' declining math achievement relative to boys'. Many parents believe that boys are naturally better at math than girls, and those parents tend to overestimate their sons' math abilities and underestimate their daughters'. In turn, parents' perceptions of children's math abilities influence children's estimations of their own abilities, resulting in a self-fulfilling prophecy. Girls who believe that they are not that good at math tend not to value it and spend less time studying math than boys who believe they are talented at it. Girls' math achievement consequently falls behind boys (Eccles et al. 2000). Teachers who share parents' beliefs about the different academic abilities of boys and girls undoubtedly contribute to this self-fulfilling prophecy, but even if they do not, parents' perceptions of their children's academic abilities and their effects on children's own self-perceptions will fulfill the prophecy. Hence, what may first appear a result of schools' gender bias may actually be more a consequence of parents' influence.

Peers, like parents, also influence children's academic performance and their school experiences in general. In a comparative study of British primary schools, Barbara Lloyd and Gerard Duveen (1992) demonstrate that there is considerable variability in "local gender cultures," in the meanings and salience of sex categorical identities, among schools and even among classrooms within schools. Although teachers clearly influence what role gender plays in their classrooms, Lloyd and Durveen show that students can be just as influential. As one teacher-researcher has noted (Gallas 1998, 32), the gender dynamics of the classroom are "only partially in the hands of the teacher, and in many ways [are] more clearly within the control of small numbers of influential children." It is important to recognize that children are often as concerned with impressing their peers as their teacher in the classroom. What children themselves consider appropriate for boys' and for girls' and their gender-related responses to one another largely define the local gender cultures children confront both inside and outside the classroom. Children's peer groups are, therefore, centrally important to their gender socialization.

Peer Relations and Cultures

Compared to the past and many societies still today, children in technologically advanced, urbanized societies spend a considerable amount of time from early in their lives in the company of similarly aged peers. Many start attending group daycare or nursery schools at 2 to 3 years of age, and then graduate to kindergarten and elementary school classrooms and organized group activities that are restricted to children no more than 12 months older or younger than they are. Neighborhood playmates, too, are likely to be in the same general age group. Children consequently interact regularly with similarly aged peers, share information with one another, and develop and enforce collective standards of conduct, including gender-appropriate conduct. Children's own collective understandings of gender and standards of gender-appropriate conduct are undoubtedly influenced by parents and other family members, the media, and teachers, but they are more than mere mirror reflections of what they have been taught and seen. Children collectively and creatively interpret and elaborate upon information gathered from varied sources, developing their own distinctive understandings of gender, standards of gender-appropriate conduct, and gender-related peer practices.

One of the most notable and consistent characteristics of children's peer groups is the extent to which they tend to be separated by gender. From early in their lives, children show a marked preference for playmates who share their gender identity. For example, research indicates that by the age of 3 years, girls initiate interaction with other girls significantly more often than with boys. Although 3-year-old boys are as likely to play with girls as with boys, by the age of 4, they spend most of their time in the company of other boys (Maccoby 1998, 19). The resulting gender segregation of children's play groups increases with age, at least up to the immediate preteen years, a pattern found in a range of diverse societies. For example, one study observed children at play in 10 different villages and neighborhoods in Africa, India, the Philippines, Mexico, and the United States, and found that in each case children over 3 years of age spent most of their play time with peers who shared their gender identity. Moreover, when only play with peers who were not siblings was considered, the study found that 3- to 6-year-old children spent about two-thirds of their play time with peers who shared their gender identity, while 6- to 10-year-olds spent more than three-fourths of their play time with such peers (Whiting and Edwards 1988).

The gender segregation of children's peer groups seems largely of children's own making. Children's preference for playmates who share their gender identity is unrelated to their parents' encouragement of gender-stereotypic behavior (Maccoby 1998, 146), and there is little evidence that parents or other adults directly encourage young children to play with peers who share their gender identity. On the contrary, adult supervision tends to decrease the extent to which children segregate themselves by gender (Thorne 1993, 55–56). There are a number of factors that might lead children to choose playmates who share their gender identity. In general, boys as young as 2 years of age tend to play more roughly and be more assertive with peers than girls, whether because of prenatal hormonal influences, fathers' tendency to play more roughly with infant sons than with infant daughters, adults' greater tolerance of such play among boys, or some combination of these influences. In any case, girls, who tend to prefer more cooperative forms of play, may avoid playing with boys because of their more assertive style of play (Maccoby 1998, 186–187). It is also notable that children start to prefer playmates who share their own gender around the same age that they start to recognize their own and peers' sex categorical identities (Maccoby 1998, 161). For them, gender may be as much a collective as a personal identity, as much identification with girls or boys as identification of oneself as a girl or boy (Maccoby 1998, 164), which would explain their growing preference for playmates who are sex categorically like "me." Finally, as children start to develop their own standards of gender-appropriate conduct, the content of girls' and boys' play is likely to increasingly differ and seem increasingly inappropriate for members of the other sex category.

Whatever the reasons for children's gender segregation of their peer groups, that very segregation heightens gender differences. Although individual boys may be only slightly more forceful with peers than individual girls, their rougher and more assertive play seems to provoke even rougher and more assertive play on the part of other boys (Maccoby 1998). For example, a recent study of 3- to 5-year-olds found that boys' play tends to be notably more "actively forceful" when playing with other boys than when playing either with girls or in mixed-sex groups (Fabes, Martin, and Hanish 2003). All-boy groups are consequently more competitive and explicitly hierarchical or characterized by status differences than are all-girl groups, and perhaps mixed-sex groups as well. There is also more open and obvious conflict in boys' groups, but that is largely because conflict among girls tends to take the form of *relational aggression*, such as excluding one another from the group, withdrawing friendship, or breaking up friendships through gossip (Maccoby 1998, 40). Compared to girls' groups, boys' groups also tend to separate themselves more strongly from adults, to test adults' rules and authority, and to discourage their members from tattling (Maccoby 1998, 288).

Groups of boys and of girls also tend to engage in different kinds of activities. Boys tend to engage in team sports and to organize other activities along the line of team competition, while girls tend to engage in smaller-scale, turn-taking kinds of play like jump rope (Thorne 1993, 92–94). Boys consequently tend to play in larger groups than girls, large enough to make up two teams, and their play tends to have more diverse roles, such as baseball positions, and to have more elaborate rules (Lever 1978). Although boys' play is often characterized as competitive and girls' as cooperative, that characterization is somewhat misleading. When boys compete against members of other teams, they do so by cooperating with their teammates. Girls are less likely to organize their play in terms of such team competition, but they do attempt to outlast one another jumping rope or outdo one another's performance on playground bars. Moreover, girls often engage in a kind of teamwork, developing "group choreographies" such as counting and jumping rope in unison, swinging around the bars together, or performing complex cheerleading routines and dance steps (Thorne 1993, 95).

According to some scholars, the different interpersonal dynamics, types of activities, and themes of fantasy play of boys' groups and girls' groups constitute separate peer cultures (e.g., Maccoby 1998, 56). Living essentially in different worlds, boys and girls supposedly become increasingly strange and foreign to one another during the elementary school years, making subsequent contact between them vulnerable to cross-cultural misunderstanding (Maltz and Borker 1983). Others argue that this separate cultures model exaggerates the extent of gender segregation among children and the differences between boys and girls while neglecting the differences among boys and among girls (e.g., Thorne 1993, 89–109).

These scholars note that the extent of gender segregation among children varies across different kinds of settings, that such segregation is seldom total and is periodic rather than continuous, having a kind of "with-then-apart" rhythm. For example, gender segregation tends to be more extensive in settings where a large number of children are present, such as school playgrounds, than in settings where fewer children are present, such as neighborhoods (Thorne 1993, 52). That in part reflects the fact that when children have a choice, they choose to play with those who share their gender identity, but it is also an effect of children's own public enforcement of gender segregation. In settings where many children are present, girls and boys who play together are often teased publicly for "liking" each other or ridiculed for engaging in gender-inappropriate activities (Thorne 1993, 52–53). Boys who engage in girls' activities are especially likely to be ridiculed, by both boys and girls. However, girls who are athletically talented are often accepted into boys' groups as kind of honorary boys and are sometimes admired by other girls. Hence, they may move freely between boys' and girls' groups (Thorne 1993, 111–134). Like parents, especially fathers, and other adults, children seem more tolerant of "tomboys" who join in boys' activities than "sissies" who attempt to participate in girls' (Thorne 1993, 11–134).

The separate cultures model of boys' and girls' peer groups also tends to neglect the diversity of those groups. Both girls' and boys' groups tend to be divided into distinct cliques based on popularity, such as the "populars," the "wannabes," the middle group, and the "dorks" or social isolates (Adler and Adler 1998, 74–97). The popular boys and girls are much less likely to play with members of the middle group or with isolates than with one another. Depictions of boys' and girls' cultures most accurately describe the activities and behaviors of popular boys' and girls' groups, often ignoring the less gender-stereotypical activities and conduct of less popular children (Thorne 1993, 96–103). Class and ethnicity are also implicated in the popularity hierarchies and divisions among boys and girls, and influence children's gender-related definitions of one another. For example, popular girls often consider fashionable, brand-name clothing a badge of social standing and of femininity (Adler and Adler 1998, 48–50), excluding girls from less affluent backgrounds from their inner circle and implicitly defining those girls as less feminine than they are. Ethnicity also excludes some children from popular cliques and affects how others view their gender. For example, at one of the elementary schools that the sociologist Barrie Thorne (1993, 98) studied, most of the boys routinely ignored two boys who were recent immigrants from Mexico and who commonly played with Spanish-speaking girls. In a related vein, a study of a multi-ethnic British primary school found that both teachers and children tended to view black boys as highly masculine because of their athletic ability and assertiveness and considered quieter and more compliant South Asian boys less masculine or "boy-like" (Connolly 1998). Yet, however diverse boys' and girls' peer groups, the most popular children often set the standards, including the standards of gender-appropriate conduct, in terms of which other children are judged and may judge themselves. Like it or not, less popular children must adapt to the standards of gender-appropriate conduct a few popular children may set, including the knowledge that they do not live up to those standards (Maccoby 1998, 58).

Although gender segregation commonly divides children's peer groups, boys and girls are not completely foreign to one another. They often interact casually with one another in classrooms and play together in neighborhoods. However, some interactions between boys and girls actually strengthen the gender boundaries that commonly separate them. Barrie Thorne (1993, 64) refers to such interaction as "borderwork." It includes such activities as contests between boys and girls, chasing games like "chase and kiss," playful rituals of pollution like "cooties," and invasions of the other group's activities and territories, almost always by boys' of girls' activities and territories (Thorne 1993, 63–78). Although boys and girls comfortably interact with one another as often as they engage in these forms of borderwork, borderwork is more memorable because it is particularly dramatic and emotionally charged. It also tends to exaggerate gender differences by defining girls and boys as opposing teams. For example, during chasing games, "gender terms blatantly override individual identities" as children call out, "Help, a girl's chasin me," or, "C'mon Sarah, let's get that boy" (Thorne 1993, 68). Children thereby increase the salience of gender identities and reinforce the boundaries separating girls and boys, regardless of their other characteristics.

Although the separate cultures model of boys' and girls' peer relations oversimplifies the complexity of those relations, it does draw attention to how children themselves define and enforce standards of gender-appropriate conduct and proper contact between girls and boys. Teachers sometimes pit boys and girls against one another in spelling and math contests, reinforcing the gender divisions that the children themselves draw. However, they usually do so as a convenient way of dividing the children into teams that evoke enthusiasm because of their collective identity with those who share their gender identity (Thorne 1993, 66–67). Adults and media messages undoubtedly influence children's conceptions of gender, but children themselves are the ones who most vigilantly police one another's gender-related conduct and relations. And most children probably look first and foremost to their peers for confirmation of their gender identities. Children's peer groups are, then, centrally important agents of their gender socialization.

The Complexities of Gender Socialization

As the preceding discussion suggests, children's gender development is not a simple process that can be clearly attributed to one factor or another. Female and male infants may be born with different behavioral and cognitive propensities because of the organizing effect of prenatal hormones on their nervous systems. Even slight differences in their behavior may cause others to respond to them differently and reinforce or even strengthen those differences. On the other hand, infants' behavior is often very unclear, and people tend to fall back on stereotypes when faced with ambiguity (Fagot, Rodgers, and Leinbach 2000). Hence parents' and other adult caregivers' treatment of female and male infants is not simply in response to the infants' behavior but is also influenced by how parents and caregivers expect male and female infants to act. For example, fathers may play rougher with their sons than with their daughters not because their sons invite such play but because fathers expect them to enjoy it more than their daughters would. Similarly, daycare providers may respond more quickly to young boys' interpersonal aggression than to girls' because they expect boys to be more aggressive and, therefore, believe that they must quickly counter that tendency. In doing so, both fathers and caregivers may fulfill the prophecy of their own gender expectations. Fathers encourage their sons to play roughly, and caregivers teach young boys that they can quickly get adults' attention by acting aggressively. Girls consequently may be wary of playing with boys because of their rough and aggressive style of play and prefer to play with other girls. The resulting gender segregation then concentrates individual differences in same-gender groups, strengthening the contrast between boys' and girls' styles of play and interpersonal dynamics.

Moreover, by the time children are 3 years of age or so, they begin routinely to sex categorically identify others and themselves as boys and girls, men and women, male and female. Once they recognize the fundamental social importance of sex-categorical identification, they look to their environment for answers as to its meanings, and those answers are everywhere. Parents' and others' discouragement of what they consider gender-inappropriate conduct and appearances provide direct answers while the media and examples of parents, teachers, and older peers provide indirect answers. Children actively interpret and integrate information from these varied sources, forming their own beliefs and standards regarding gender-appropriate objects, appearances, and activities. They then hold both themselves and others to the sex categorically relevant standards, policing both their own and their peers' gender-related conduct. Any doubts they have about gender differences are suppressed. As children increasingly interact with similarly aged peers, collective gender-related beliefs and standards of conduct emerge that guide relations both within and between girls' and boys' often distinct peer groups.

In recent years, many researchers have concluded that the peer group is the principal agent of gender socialization, but that conclusion neglects that children's peer groups are embedded in a web of social and cultural influences. Peer standards of gender-related conduct clearly do not originate in the peer group but are based on information gathered both directly and indirectly from other sources. For example, peer affiliation "does not disembody a child from the family" (Bussey and Bandura 1999, 700). Children bring information and concerns that originate in the family to the peer group and bring information and concerns from their peer group to family members. Children's peer groups are influential agencies of gender socialization, often emphasizing and exaggerating gender differences, but they do not exist in a social and cultural vacuum. Rather, they are one component of what the psychologist Richard Lippa (2002, 196–203) calls a "causal cascade" of interlocking influences that promotes gender differences among children.

Gender socialization is a not only complex but also highly variable process. Parents vary in how much they encourage or discourage gender-stereotypical behaviors in their offspring. Children with and without older or younger sisters and brothers are exposed to different gender influences. Different children watch different television programs, read different books, play with different boys and girls, and draw different lessons about gender from what they watch, read, and hear, often in collaboration with others. Teachers, both knowingly and unwittingly, set different tones for classroom interaction by either emphasizing or diminishing the salience of gender in the classroom. And, although children's peer groups may enforce their own collective standards of gender-appropriate conduct and relations, children vary in how much they subscribe and conform to those standards. Popular kids may gain at least some of their social standing by most clearly conforming to peer standards of gender appropriate conduct, but kids in the middle and lower levels of the peer status system may have little interest in popularity and develop their own alternative, less stereotypical expressions of gender (Adler and Adler 1998, 84–88).

Gender socialization results in both gender differences and differences among females and males. The traditional focus on gender differences has revealed the complex thicket of biological, psychological, social, and cultural factors involved in the development of such differences among children and the challenges facing those who want to change how children are raised so as to lessen such differences and the gender inequality that often accompanies them. Should they concentrate their efforts on parents, toys, the schools, or the media, or should they try to intervene directly in children's peer relations; and, if so, how might they do so without provoking defensive reactions against their efforts? Research suggests that there are no easy answers to such questions. However, we might better understand gender and its development in childhood if we paid more attention to the wide variation in gender-related conduct among girls and among boys and in their relations to one another. We must at least be sensitive to variable expressions of femininity and masculinity among children, among different groups of children, and under different circumstances. We must also recognize that gender differences are statistical, not absolute, differences. For example, a study may report that boys in general are more interpersonally aggressive than girls because 20 percent of boys were more aggressive than the most aggressive girls even though 80 percent of the boys were no more aggressive than most girls (Jacklin 1981). We must be careful not to confuse our own binary thinking about gender with the complexity and variability in children's everyday lives. Only then will we fully understand children's diverse gender socialization and development.

References

Adler, Patricia, and Peter Adler. 1998. *Peer Power: Preadolescent Culture and Identity.* New Brunswick, NJ: Rutgers University Press.

American Association of University Women. 1992. *The AAUW Report: How Schools Shortchange Girls.* Washington, DC: American Association of University Women.

Bem, Sandra L. 1981. "Gender Schema Theory: A Cognitive Account of Sex Typing." *Psychological Review* 88: 354–364.

Berk, Sarah. 1985. *The Gender Factory.* New York: Plenum.

Bussey, Kay, and Albert Bandura. 1999. "Social Cognitive Theory of Gender Development and Differentiation." *Psychological Review* 106: 676–713.

Cahill, Spencer. 1986a. "Language Practices and Self-Definition: The Case of Gender Identity Acquisition." *The Sociological Quarterly* 27: 295–311.

——. 1986b. "Childhood Socialization as Recruitment Process: Some Lessons from the Study of Gender Development." In Patricia Adler and Peter Adler (eds.) *Sociological Studies of Child Development* 1: 163–186. Greenwich, CT: JAI Press.

Cancian, Francesca. 1987. *Love in America: Gender and Self-Development.* New York: Cambridge University Press.

Chodorow, Nancy. 1978. *The Reproduction of Mothering.* Berkeley: University of California Press.

Colapinto, John. 2000. *As Nature Made Him: The Boy Who Was Raised as a Girl.* New York: HarperCollins.

——. 2004. "Gender Gap: What Were the Reasons Behind David Reimer's Suicide?" *http://slate.msn.com/id/2101678.*

Connolly, Paul. 1998. *Racism, Gender Identity, and Young Children.* London: Routledge.

Davies, Bronwyn. 1989. *Frogs and Snails and Feminist Tales.* Boston: Routledge and Kegan Paul.

Davis, Kingsley. 1988. "Wives and Work: A Theory of the Sex-Role Revolution and Its Consequences." In Sanford Dornbusch and Myra Storber (eds.) *Feminism, Children, and the New Families,* 67–86. New York: The Guilford Press.

Eagly, Alice, Wendy Wood, and Amanda Diekman. 2000. "Social Role Theory of Sex Differences and Similarities: A Current Appraisal." In Thomas Eckes and Hanns Trautner (eds.) *The Developmental Social Psychology of Gender*, 123–174. Mahwah, NJ: Lawrence Erlbaum.

Eccles, Jacquelynne, Carol Freedman-Doan, Pam Frome, Janis Jacobs, and Kwang Suk Yoon. 2000. "Gender-Role Socialization in the Family: A Longitudinal Approach." In Thomas Eckes and Hanns Trautner (eds.) *The Developmental Social Psychology of Gender*, 333–350. Mahwah, NJ: Lawrence Erlbaum.

Fabes, Richard, Carol Martin, and Laura Hanish. 2003. "Young Children's Play Qualities in Same-, Other-, and Mixed-Sexed Peer Groups." *Child Development* 74: 921–932.

Fagot, Beverly, R. Hagan, M. D. Leinbach, and S. Kronsbert. 1985. "Differential Reactions to Assertive and Communicative Acts in Toddler Boys and Girls." *Child Development* 1499–1505.

Fagot, Beverly, Carie Rodgers, and Mary Leinbach. 2000. "Theories of Gender Socialization." In Thomas Eckes and Hanns Trautner (eds.) *The Developmental Social Psychology of Gender*, 65–89. Mahwah, NJ: Lawrence Erlbaum.

Fausto-Sterling, Anne. 2000. *Sexing the Body*. New York: Basic Books.

Fingerson, Laura. 1999. "Active Viewing: Girls' Interpretations of Family Television Programs." *Journal of Contemporary Ethnography* 28: 389–416.

Furham, Adrian, and Twiggy Mak. 1999. "Sex-Role Stereotyping in Television Commercials: A Review and Comparison of Fourteen Studies Done on Five Continents Over 25 Years." *Sex Roles* 413–437.

Gallas, Karen. 1998. *Sometimes I Can Be Anything: Power, Gender, and Identity in a Primary Classroom*. New York: Teachers College Press.

Goldberg, Steven. 1974. *The Inevitability of Patriarchy*. New York: William Morrow.

——. 1993. *Why Men Rule*. Peru, IL: Open Court Press.

Harris, Marvin. 1993. "The Evolution of Human Gender Hierarchies: A Trial Formulation." In B. D. Miller (ed.) *Sex and Gender Hierarchies*, 57–79. New York: Cambridge University Press.

Hochschild, Arlie, and Anne Machung. 1989. *The Second Shift: Working Parents and the Revolution in the Home*. New York: Penguin.

Hughes, Everett C. 1945. "Dilemmas and Contradictions of Status." *American Journal of Sociology* 50: 353–359.

Jacklin, Carol Nagy. 1981. "Methodological Issues in the Study of Sex-Related Differences." *Developmental Review* 1: 226–273.

Johnson, Miriam. 1988. *Strong Mothers, Weak Wives*. Berkeley: University of California Press.

Kessler, Suzanne, and Wendy McKenna. 1978. *Gender: An Ethnomethodological Approach*. Chicago: University of Chicago Press.

Kimball, Meredith. 1986. "Television and Sex Role Attitudes." In Tannis MacBeth Williams (ed.) *The Impact of Television: A Natural Experiment in Three Communities*, 265–301. New York: Academic Press.

Lever, Janet. 1978. "Sex Differences in the Complexity of Children's Play and Games." *American Sociological Review* 43: 471–483.

Lippa, Richard. 2002. *Gender, Nature, and Nurture*. Mahwah, NJ: Lawrence Erlbaum.

Lloyd, Barbara, and Gerard Duveen. 1992. *Gender Identities in Education*. New York: St. Martin's.

Lopata, Helena, and Barrie Thorne. 1978. "On the Term 'Sex Roles.' " *Signs* 3: 718–721.

Maccoby, Eleanor. 1998. *The Two Sexes: Growing Up Apart, Coming Together*. Cambridge, MA: Harvard University Press.

Maltz, Daniel, and Ruth Borker. 1983. "A Cultural Approach to Male-Female Miscommunication." In John Gumperz (ed.) *Language and Social Identity*, 195–216. New York: Cambridge University Press.

Martin, Carol Lynn, and C. Halverson. 1987. "The Roles of Cognition in Sex Role Acquisition." In D. B. Carter (ed.) *Current Conceptions of Sex Roles and Sex Typing*, 45–57. New York: Praeger.

Martin, M. Kay, and Barbara Voorhies. 1975. *Female of the Species*. New York: Columbia University Press.

McGhee, P. E., and T. Frueh. 1980. "Television Viewing and the Learning of Sex-Role Stereotypes." *Sex Roles* 6: 179–188.

McHale, Susan, Ann Crouter, and Corinna Tucker. 1999. "Family Context and Gender Role Socialization in Middle Childhood: Comparing Girls to Boys and Sisters to Brothers." *Child Development* 70: 990–1004.

Miller, B. D. ed. 1993. *Sex and Gender Hierarchies*. New York: Cambridge University Press.

Murdock, George, and C. Provost. 1973. "Factors in the Division of Labor by Sex: A Cross-Cultural Analysis." *Ethology* 13: 203–225.

Rosaldo, Michelle. 1980. "The Use and Abuse of Anthropology: Reflections on Feminism and Cross-Cultural Understanding." *Signs* 5: 389–417.

Rust, John, Susan Golombok, Melissa Hines, Katie Johnston, Jean Golding, and the ALSPAC Study Team. 2000. "The Role of Brothers and Sisters in the Gender Development of Preschool Children." *Journal of Experimental Child Psychology* 77: 292–303.

Sadker, Myra, and David Sadker. 1995. *Failing at Fairness: How Our Schools Cheat Girls*. New York: Touchstone.

Sanday, Peggy Reeves. 2002. *Women at the Center: Life in a Modern Matriarchy*. Ithaca, NY: Cornell University Press.

Schneider, Dona. 1995. *American Childhood: Risks and Realities*. New Brunswick, NJ: Rutgers University Press.

Sommers, C. H. 2000. *The War Against Boys*. New York: Simon & Schuster.

Sprafkin, Joyce, and Robert Liebert. 1974. "Sex Typing and Children's Television Preferences." In Gayle Tuchman, Arlene Kaplan Daniels, and James Benet (eds.) *Hearth and Home: Images of Women in the Mass Media*, 228–239. New York: Oxford University Press.

Stacey, Judith. 1990. *Brave New Families*. New York: Basic Books.

Thoman, Evelyn, P. Herbert Leiderman, and Joan Olson. 1972. "Neonate-Mother Interaction During Breast Feeding." *Developmental Psychology* 6: 110–118.

Thompson, Teresa, and Eugenia Zerbinos. 1997. "Television Cartoons: Do Children Notice It's a Boy's World?" *Sex Roles* 37: 415–432.

Thorne, Barrie. 1993. *Gender Play: Girls and Boys in School*. New Brunswick, NJ: Rutgers University Press.

Tooker, Elizabeth. 1984. "Women in Iroquois Society." In Michael Foster, Jack Campisi, and Marianne Mithun (eds.) *Extending the Rafters*, 109–123. Albany: State University of New York Press.

U.S. Census Bureau. 2001. *Statistical Abstract of the United States*. Washington, DC: U.S. Government Printing Office.

Weitzman, Lenore, Deborah Eifler, Elizabeth Hokada, and Catherine Ross. 1972. "Sex-Role Socialization in Picture Books for Preschool Children." *American Journal of Sociology* 77: 1125–1149.

West, Candace, and Don Zimmerman. 1987. "Doing Gender." *Gender and Society* 1: 125–151.

Whiting, Beatrice, and Carolyn Edwards. 1988. *Children of Different Worlds*. Cambridge, MA: Harvard University Press. ✦

PART IV
Continuities With and Discontinuities From Childhood

Introduction

We have defined *socialization* as the process by which we learn and adapt to the ways of a given society or social group so as to adequately participate in it. Socialization is an enormously broad and complex process that may be approached from many different perspectives, including its biological foundations, the patterns of different cultures, the historical changes over the years, the psychological development of individuals, the agencies and institutions acting on and responding to children, and by the differences in social class, ethnicity, gender, locality, and other major groupings by which we divide a society. These approaches help us to break up the process of socialization into more analytical and understandable units, and each contributes to our understanding of how children become functioning members of the society. Our focus has been on the social and interactional aspects of the process. Adding to the complexity of analysis, of course, is the fact that these perspectives are all related to one another.

In this volume, our major concern has been the socialization of children in North America: how, in growing up, they gain the ability to function according to accepted standards in some part of the larger society. Our interest includes outcomes. An unsocialized child cannot function adequately, or functions contrary to some accepted standard. ✦

Chapter 12
Looking Back and Looking Ahead

Children are born into an ongoing world with its various patterns, social groupings, and institutions. It is a society constantly in change. The infant is completely dependent on others for care but is himself or herself active, feeling, and interpreting. Without social interaction, a child is isolated and will remain unsocialized. In interaction with others, the child learns a language, comes to develop a self, and is thus able to respond to symbols as others do, which allows for cooperative behavior.

A child in our society is expected to follow a more or less orderly sequence in development, moving from the family through the school system to the labor force, possibly to marriage, a family, and retirement. Many have a role in the child's continuing socialization—first the mother and father, then the siblings and other family members, neighbors, teachers, perhaps religious leaders, coaches, and numerous other adults. Peers almost always become especially important. The media likewise may have a strong impact.

The surrounding world is a complex and varied environment with many physical settings, material objects, groupings, institutions, and means of communication. A child belongs to only certain segments of the society—a given sex category, neighborhood, social level, and ethnic group—and is socialized into only a small part of the total larger scene.

Socialization, we have stressed, is not just a childhood phenomenon; it continues throughout a person's life until his or her dying days. Throughout our lives, we are constantly experiencing new developments. We change physically, respond to new and changing events, meet new individuals, enter different social worlds, and constantly evaluate the world around us and reinterpret the lives we have led. All of these developments involve modifications in socialization, varying from the slight to the momentous. In this chapter, we will touch briefly on socialization in the life course beyond childhood. Socialization in later years is, of course, a continuous process; however, to clarify our discussion, we shall divide the life course into the general stages of adolescence, adult life, and aging. Our thread will be a focus on the continuities and discontinuities of the socialization process.

Socialization in Adolescence

Socialization has a biological foundation, a foundation that interacts constantly with features of the environment. This interaction begins in the growth of the fetus and continues through early childhood development. The very development of the child's brain structure, we have observed, is partially determined by the social world the child experiences. This is especially evident, for example, in the relationship between learning a language and a critical period.

This close link between the biological and the social is strikingly evident again in the period of adolescence. To physiologists, adolescence begins with puberty, the dramatic changes in physical stature and the increased secretion of hormones. Recent research suggests that the brain too continues to undergo structural changes well past puberty (National Institute of Mental Health 2001). Girls grow, begin to menstruate, and develop enlarged breasts and broader hips. Boys grow, produce sperm, and develop body hair and deeper voices. But even here, life conditions play a role. In the past century, for example, puberty in girls, with changing life conditions, has begun at an increasingly younger age, and the trend has continued to the present day (Susman and Rogol 2004, 17–19; Brooks-Gunn and Reiter 1990, 32). Some societies have recognized this transition to adolescence with an initiation ceremony. In our own society, confirmation and bat (or bar) mitzvah roughly mark the transition.

To social scientists, adolescence is less a physical development than a social construction It is a period that different societies variously define (Brown and Larson 2002, 4) but one that we and many other societies have chosen to distinguish from childhood and adulthood (Schlegel and Barry 1991, 36–37). It ranges roughly from 11 to 19 years of age. Some, using the term *youth*, extend the age to the early 20s.

Adolescence has not everywhere been recognized as a period of life distinct from childhood and adulthood. In many societies, including our own until about the seventeenth century, children, when they become physically mature—say, ages 12 to 14—moved almost directly into an adult world. Some worked on farms, and some apprenticed to skilled workers; girls often were married and soon bore children. With the development of the industrialized society and later compulsory education, these children were removed from the labor market and adolescence became recognized as a distinct stage of life. Children were now dependent on their families for longer periods and not expected to participate fully in an adult life until increasingly older ages (see Chapter 3).

In some simpler stable societies, anthropologists have found the transition from childhood to adulthood to be relatively smooth. (The classic study suggesting a smooth transition is Margaret Mead's *Coming of Age in Samoa* [Mead 1928].) In recent years in our own society, however, we have tended to emphasize the discontinuities. Social scientists have long spoken of the need for adolescents to break away from their families and develop a sense of independence and autonomy. Instrumental in gaining this independence was a strong identification with peers and peer culture. Psychologist Stanley Hall and psychoanalyst Sigmund Freud spoke of adolescence as a period of *Sturm und Drang*, storm and stress, (Schulenberg, Maggs, and Hurrelmann 1997, 3–4). Talcott Parsons in the 1940s, with a widely disseminated reprint in the 1960s, spoke of a "youth culture" in which the main concerns of adolescents were to "have a good time," engage in heterosexual activities and also, for males, participate in athletics (Parsons [1942] 1964). Two decades later, James

Coleman, studying high schools in Illinois, reinforced the idea of a youth culture, stressing the general opposition to the world of adults and the great emphasis the students placed on athletics, reputation, and popularity (Coleman 1961). Parents may see benefits from adolescents' participation in sports and social activities and worry about their future, but the adolescents themselves focus more on the present.

These values, of course, as Bennett Berger writes in a review of Coleman's work, are not solely characteristic of adolescents (Berger 1963). Parents too are concerned about popularity and prestige, and support athletics in the high schools. And the schools themselves sponsor athletic programs, extracurricular activities, and social events, considering them to be training grounds for adult responsibilities.

The apparent discontinuities in adolescent socialization continue to be most striking. Peer groups loom large in almost all studies of adolescents. Adolescents spend a considerable amount of time with their peers. They may gossip, joke and goof about, talk of sports and relationships, listen to music, watch television or videos, participate in sports, and generally relax. Through their peers, they may more freely express their own ideas and feelings, gain confidence, and resist the demands and attempts of discipline of their parents. Peer groups here represent a major area of support and comfort and something of a safety zone (Savin-Williams and Berndt 1990, 279). Mothers too, research suggests, are also often sources of comfort (Call and Mortimer 2001; Ch 3). Compared to adolescents in many other countries, adolescents in the United States have large amounts of unregulated time and they party more (Larson and Sepersad 2003; Ch 4). The peak years of television and media exposure are ages 11 to 14; older adolescents watch less TV because they find that school-related and social activities make more demands on their time (Roberts and Foehr 2004, 140).

Considerable attention has also been devoted to delinquency among adolescents, although there is no consensus on causes. One criminologist characterizes delinquent groups as having "unclear and shifting role assignments and role definitions, predominantly same-sex composition, constantly changing membership" (Warr 2002, 5–6). Since delinquent behavior is predominantly group behavior and almost always among friends, some authors in discussing the topic stress the influence of peers (Warr 2002; Ch 2). The researchers who have studied the social characteristics of delinquents have often stressed their neighborhoods, their social class origins, and measures of economic disadvantage such as poverty and welfare (Thornberry and Krohn 2003, 318). Although gangs represent only a small proportion of delinquent groups, they, often ethnically distinguished, have received special attention. Janowski, who spent over 10 years studying gangs, primarily through participant observation, says individuals become members of gangs because they see a personal advantage in doing so. Gangs are "composed of individuals with defiant individualist characters who make decisions on the basis of what is good for them" (Janowski 1991, 62). The gangs in general often fit in well with the lower-income communities in which they operate; their relationship is not necessarily one of antagonism or apathy. Rather, following a generally accepted code of behavior, they are a recognized organization with a "working relationship" (Janowski 1991, 78–79). Because youth offenders are considered immature and less responsible, special efforts are generally made for possible reform through separate youth justice policies (Zimring 2000).

Peer groups have their own values, interests, standards, and role models. Popularity, attractiveness to the opposite sex, friendships, conforming behavior, fashions, and musical taste, and sometimes toughness for boys, can be of great importance in adolescent life. For some, also, it may be membership in gangs or a common interest in athletics, television, video games, popular music, or even academic success. In school, there may be cliques with some groups having higher status than others. For some, the youth culture, as expressed in punk, hip-hop, and rap, expresses defiance and resistance to mainstream culture. Such topics have all been widely reported in the literature (Eder 1995; Giordano 2003; Furman, Brown, and Feiring 1999; Bennett 2000; Nayak 2003; Grasmuck 2005).

Peers can also give what adults consider to be negative messages to one another—don't be too compliant with parents, and don't "show off" your intelligence. Some adolescents reject the common norms and values of their age mates and form their own alternative culture (Kinney 1999). Not that peer relationships always go smoothly. There are shifts in friendships, and some do not last long (Cairns and Cairns 1994, 98). Disagreements and conflicts too are an inherent part of relationships with both same-sex friends and romantic partners. But such differences do not generally lead to disruption; rather, the problems are resolved through negotiation. This is to be contrasted with relationships with nonfriends, where there may be aggression and coercion (Laursen 1996, 194–195). Numerous reports, often followed by advice on policies to be followed, have been reported on aggression, bullying, and rejection among teenagers (Tatum and Herbert 1997; Williams, Forgas, and von Hippel 2005).

Peer group relationships, it is evident, may involve intense feeling and emotion. For individuals, psychological and health problems may accompany conflicts, including anxiety, depression, drug use, obesity, anorexia, and attempted suicide (Blum and Nelson-Minari 2004, Ch 18; Brumberg and Striegel-Moore 1993, Ch 6; Schulenberg, Maggs, and Hurrelmann 1997, passim).

Some trends in the larger society are mirrored by similar trends among adolescents. With generally freer sexual behavior in the society at large have come changes in adolescent sexual behavior. For some years, the percentage of teenagers who had engaged in sexual activity steadily increased and then took a turn downward. For example, among females ages 15 to 19, the percentage who had had sexual intercourse rose from 29 percent in 1970 to 55 percent in 1990, and then declined in 2002 to 47 percent. Among males, the percentage reached 60 in 1988, then declined to 46 percent in 2002. For girls below the age of 15, the percentage who had engaged in sex declined from 19 percent in 1995 to 13 percent in 2002. For males under 15, the percentage in those years declined from 21 percent to 15 percent (National Center for Health Statistics 2004). The pregnancy rate for teenagers has also decreased from 117 per 1,000 in 1990 to 84.5 in year 2000, primarily because of more effective contraception (Planned Parenthood Federation of America 2005). Pregnancy rates for teenagers vary by neighborhoods, and the teenagers themselves generally experience poverty and reduced opportunity (Mauldon 2003).

Also notable in recent years, following a trend in the larger society, has come an increasing interest among adolescents in new technology. Aided by school programs, many have become knowledgeable about computers and the Internet, often more so than their parents. They may play a range of computer games, but also have free access to a wide range of information (see Chapter 8). The computer is also an instrument affecting social relationships—the most common use of computers by adolescents is email (Anderson 2002, 191). Information and communication technology continue to advance with such recent developments as digital video and audio. In all these developments, one problem continues to stand out—that of the digital divide: Access to information and communication technology varies considerably across income and ethnic groups, and this seems unlikely to change (Roberts and Foehr 2004, 33–37; Anderson 2002, 197).

Other societal trends such as the greater independence of women, the rise in divorce rates with an increase in the number of single mothers and blended families, the greater number of immigrants from Asian and Latin American countries, and increasing attention to multiculturalism and homosexuality have all affected adolescents and are also now often included in adolescent awareness. Some youth, supported by foundations and specialists in adolescence, are active in civic and community-building activities (Lerner 2004).

The general characteristics and trends in peer groups, of course, are generalizations. We recognize that there are tremendous variations in peer group patterns in different segments of the society—in the different social classes, ethnic groups, religions, and residential areas. And there are many variations as well within these groups. The editors of one recent collection of reports on youth cultures write,

> Significant among these tales is the unchallengeable fact that young people constitute a highly differentiated group and any attempts to totalize the identity of youth elide notions of class, gender, ethnicity or 'race' as well as other social, economic, and political factors, Thus, youth cannot be seen as a fixed, preexisting entity or a unified image. Rather, it is a complex mercurial signifier offering mixed messages and resisting a single interpretation or positioning. (Mallan and Pearce 2003, x)

Socialization of adolescents in families that are mobile, geographically or socially, merits particular attention. Immigrant adolescents may have to be socialized into a new language and a very different way of life. The recent immigration of Muslims from the Middle East represents a notable example of cultural difference. If families move from one locality to another, the adolescents change schools, adjust to a new neighborhood, and develop new friendships. Moving upward to a new neighborhood generally has favorable results (Leventhal and Brooks-Gunn 2004, 457–462). A working-class adolescent who moves up the social scale through his family's progress or his own achievement in school may have to become aware of a different social world, with different standards, aspirations, and values. Manners, friendships, cultural knowledge, and the parents' personal characteristics may all become matters of concern. The socialization also requires a changed self-image, which may now include expectations of a university education and a middle-class job. For some adolescents, of course—those who live in depressed, lower-class communities with little cultural capital—such mobility is extremely difficult to achieve (Macleod 1997).

In all these activities involving adolescents, the adolescents are not passive participants or mere followers of group patterns. They are always active, interpreting, feeling, and interacting with others, responding in their own unique ways. They are constructing their own patterns and relationships. They are viewing and judging their own behavior and creating their own identities (Pufall and Unsworth 2004, passim). Two editors of a work on youth cultures write that

> youth's identities are in a continual process of formation and reformation as young people engage with the images, texts, and practices that are available for consumption, appropriation, and reinterpretation. . . . Youth are also savvy consumers, manipulators, and producers capable of subverting, resisting and transforming the popular images that attempt to fix and define their existence. (Mallan and Pearce 2003, xviii)

In their families and in relations with other adults, the picture is never one of simple conflict. The parents and others, with their own norms, values, perspectives, and problems, are also actively interpreting, responding, and modifying their own behavior. In moving toward greater independence, adolescent relationships with others are always multidimensional.

Continuities

Most research on adolescence has dwelt on the discontinuities in adolescence, on the changes in interests, concern with the opposite sex, relationships with peers and parents, and problem areas. However, underlying these changes are fundamental continuities that temper these changes. Throughout the transitional period, adolescents generally remain at a given social level, continuing to live with their family and having available its social contacts and cultural resources. Nor do the ethnic group, religion, and most affiliations change. The neighborhood and some friendships often stay the same. Continuing in school, the basic aspirations, and general career orientation will probably not be greatly modified.

Parents still have a crucial role. In one intensive longitudinal study, the researchers found that the youth sample had similar values and life choices as their parents in their youth and that the parents served as models for occupational and educational aspirations (Bengtson, Biblarz, and Roberts 2002). Unfortunately, the sample underrepresents ethnic minorities and the less educated. Peggy Giordano summarizes the research on the continued family relationships: ". . . there is now rather wide consensus that parents continue to be critically important sources of support, control, and socialization, even as autonomy is negotiated and peers take on a heightened salience" (Giordano 2003, 258).

Continuities, along with changes, are also evident in particular types of behavior. Speaking of a series of longitudinal studies in delinquency, two researchers write, "The results from the summarized research confirm that there is a significant amount of continuity in deviant behavior. Early aggression predicts later delinquency and the early onset of delinquency predicts later criminal behavior" (Thornberry and Krohn 1993, 322).

Distinguishing between continuities and discontinuities of adolescence is helpful in understanding many of the issues of socialization, but the "adolescent period" remains a social construction. We are speaking of a long period of transition with constant movements in many directions. Michael Shanahan, attempting to put some organization into the period, speaks of "Pathways to Adulthood" (Shanahan 2000, 667–692). Adolescence here is viewed as part of a life course in which the adolescent is functioning in a social structure and roughly following particular directions. Throughout, there is an interplay between agency, the activities of the adolescent, and features of the social structure. These pathways have changed historically and have become more and more varied in our own society.

Gerald Handel has considered the transition from childhood through adolescence to adulthood from a symbolic interactionist perspective. Since all human action is based on interpretation—of oneself, one's situation, one's understanding of what has happened, and one's estimation of and hopes for what lies ahead—he argues that a person moving through adolescence into adulthood interprets his or her childhood in setting a direction for the life course. The person who likes the kind of childhood and upbringing that he or she had will generally try to lead a life with similar kinds of experiences, one that is an elaboration of major aspects of childhood—what may be called an *elaborative life course*. A person who is very unhappy with his or her childhood upbringing and seeks a total break from that kind of life will try to lead a very different kind of life, one that is nothing like the complex of childhood experiences, and will seek a *dissociative life course*. A person who has some major childhood grievance, a sense that something went on that should not have, will work on trying to undo or repair what happened and will lead a *restitutive life course*. Finally, through a series of chance events that are not specifically motivated by unhappiness or resentment but lead to new interpretations of situations that arise, a person may drift away from his or her childhood into an *innovative life course* (Handel 2003, 104–107). Although these are presented as distinctive types of life course, blends are possible, and a person may shift direction.

The transition period to adult roles has gradually lengthened over the years, leading authors to speak more often of *youth* and *postadolesence*. With 85 to 90 percent of adolescents in the United States and Canada completing high school, increasing numbers attending college, and generally longer training periods for many occupations, young people are postponing their entry into the full-time labor market, marriage, parenthood, and other adult roles (Mortimer and Larson 2002, 10–11; Fussel 2002, 18–51).

Socialization in Adult Life

Socialization, we have observed, is never a static condition; it continues throughout one's lifetime. One primary reason is that we are constantly entering new statuses with new role expectations—we take on and change occupations, some of which may be new in our lifetime; we become spouses; we have children; we join organizations, or change positions within an organization; we become customers, patients, pet owners, and so on. With each of these statuses comes new role expectations with their new norms, adaptations to other people, and changed self-images.

In some instances there may be *anticipatory socialization*, with a perception of participation in statuses to come. Apprentices in skilled labor programs anticipate their activities as skilled workers, golfers anticipate joining a particular club, young people anticipate living with particular partners or becoming spouses, prisoners look forward to parole and release from jail, and 60-year-olds anticipate living in retirement. But it is only when they are actually in the new statuses that the true socialization occurs.

The image of the new status in reality may not turn out to be as expected, in which case we sometimes speak of *reality shock*. A new schoolteacher, for example, may anticipate an interested, cooperative class with respectful students and instead find disinterest, resistance, and defiance. Reality shock, in one way or another, is not uncommon in the adoption of new statuses.

Another possible reason for continued adult socialization is an identification or relationship with a significant other, which may come about through a leisure activity, a job, a family relationship, the media, a stray meeting, or any of innumerable ways. The significant other could be a peer, a neighbor, an older mentor, a celebrity, or even one's own children. Many a parent's new interest has stemmed from the school and recreational activities of their children. The significant other attachment can lead to modifications in attitude or feeling, and can cover a wide range of activity—a new hobby, working on a community project, playing the stock market, taking drugs, soliciting funds, following a new sport, considering a different occupation, and so on, all of which involve taking on new or modified interests and/or values.

Socialization in later life, of course, is also initiated by personal developments in someone's life. Illness or involvement in an accident, for example, may lead to socialization into aspects of the hospital and medical world; suing for divorce leads to new knowledge and experience in legal matters; becoming a union member requires learning its norms of solidarity. The possibilities are endless.

Underlying all the reasons for the importance of socialization in adult life is the point made earlier in the book—childhood socialization endows the child with the capacity for participating in adult society in limitless ways. Adult socialization makes possible participation in specific ways through particular associations and institutions of the society.

In the ideal-type stable community, socialization would move smoothly through the expectations of the life course, members having internalized the correct beliefs and knowledge of appropriate behavior. In our contemporary society, however, new, often unanticipated events constantly occur that require a more complex socialization. New social movements, for example, require us to modify our expectations and behavior. The women's movement of recent years is a prime example. In recent decades, women in North America have become more independent and autonomous. A wider range of jobs is open to them; they can move up more easily to executive-level positions; they can divorce more easily; they may more easily become political candidates; in some religions, they can become clergy; and they are admitted to organizations from which they had previously been excluded. Such developments, though often not without intense struggles, have led to a generally wide acceptance of the changes in the society at large and the accompanying socialization in our attitudes, behavior, and expectations. Even our language has changed: *Mailman* has been replaced by *letter carrier, airline hostess* by *flight attendant, actress* for many by *actor.* The term *old maid* with its stigma has almost been dropped from our vocabulary.

The social movements of blacks, Native Americans, and homosexuals (now widely known as *gays*) represent other developments that have required widespread socialization. Such movements may take some time to become diffused, and not all groups accept the changes at the same time or in the same way. Sharp conflicts may arise between the followers and opponents of the movement, but the movements affect us all. Everyone sooner or later becomes socialized to the changed society.

Technology is another area in which we have experienced many new developments, each in its own way affecting our behavior, relationships with others, and self-images. Laptop computers, cell phones, DVDs, digital cameras, radio wave signals to lock and unlock doors, and cell phones joined with cameras or handheld computers are examples. And we have every expectation that these will be further developed or replaced by technologies more advanced, and we will modify our expectations and behavior accordingly. . . .

Particular temporary events in the larger society likewise affect socialization in the society. War, economic depressions (Elder 1974), and natural disasters represent extreme examples that require us to give up some aspects of our lives and become socialized to the new social contexts. We adapt and develop a new base that might be quite different from the one we had before. Some movements of longer duration, such as globalization with its shifting work patterns and populations, may require continuing socialization.

Sometimes, the socialization to particular statuses in adulthood, especially occupational, takes place in formally organized settings such as colleges, trade schools, work organizations, professional associations, and military services. The organization's goal in such cases is to prepare the person who enters the organization for new statuses and roles. This person, who may be called a *recruit*, moves through the organization in a series of steps until the program is completed, each step contributing further to the recruit's socialization. The recruit in this program not only gains knowledge to practice the occupation, but also is socialized to the language, attitudes, feelings, and self-images intrinsic to the job. A nurse in training, for example, is expected to learn that the job is of great value to the society, to be caring to patients, to follow the bidding of doctors and supervisors, and to understand that, at times, the conditions of work will be difficult and stressful. These also all become part of the accompanying self-image.

In the organization, the recruits may develop attitudes and norms that go beyond the formal training—learning from peers and immediate predecessors. Howard Becker and fellow authors, speaking of students in medical school, for example, report that the students originally looked forward to learning everything taught to them, but soon found themselves so overloaded with work that their expectation changed to learning essentially only what might be asked on examinations (Becker et al. 1961). It is common that students and others in organizations learn much informally from their peers.

There may follow further specific training, procedures, and qualifying examinations, in accounting, medicine, or dentistry, for example, culminating in a degree and a new status. The socialization continues with still further socialization into the actual practice of the occupation, with possibly, as we noted, some reality shock.

There are other formal institutions in the society devoted to *resocialization*, to changing the attitudes and/or behavior of individuals in whom the earlier socialization process has been judged unsuccessful. Thus delinquents and criminals are sent to reformatories or prisons, and those judged very psychologically disturbed may be sent to mental hospitals. One major goal in these institutions is, through punishment, retraining, medication, or therapy, to resocialize the inmates and modify their attitudes and behavior so they can function in the society in an acceptable way. The task is often enormously difficult. Recidivism of criminals and setbacks for mental patients are common. Speaking of the transition of prisoners from prison to community, Visher and Travis of the Justice Policy Center in Washington, DC, cite some of the complications for the prisoner:

> [Prison and community] are both embedded in the life experiences of the prisoner as he or she enters prison, completes the prison term, and is released, and they change over time. . . . Prison reentry and reintegration experiences vary considerably based on individual characteristics, family and peer relationships, community concerns, and state 'policies.' (2003, 91)

Continuities

The discontinuous aspects of our lives do have limits, however, partly because of the consistency of our personalities and partly because of the social structure and our social relationships. Erik Erikson long ago spoke of a core identity coming after the period of adolescence (Erikson 1959). This core identity in later life will be further developed and modified, and in certain extreme conditions, such as battlefield fighting, imprisonment, religious conversion, or mental illness, may be drastically altered. But it does provide a kind of platform from which a person may launch himself or herself into further socialization. The core identity also provides the person, within the limits of the economy and the social structure, with the opportunities and capacities for choice. People make major decisions, whether to work or go to college, move from one community to another, live or not live with someone, and so on. With each significant choice, people are also choosing environments in which they will be further socialized, although they may have only a vague idea of what these socializing experiences may be.

Yet, the choices people make often reflect their earlier socialization. The French sociologist Pierre Bourdieu ([1979] 1984) coined the term *habitus* to refer to the predispositions that people acquire through their varied social experiences as members of different social classes, ethnic groups, and the like. For example, we acquire different tastes in food, entertainments, and other activities due to those experiences. Our subsequent choices often reflect these tastes and predispositions and lead us, sometimes quite inadvertently, into occupations, statuses, and family situations similar to those of our parents and other adults around whom we grew up. According to Bourdieu, we thereby tend to reproduce the structures of social class, status, and ethnicity across generations.

Further limits to discontinuity arise because of homophilly, which stems from the very structure of our society. *Homophilly* refers to social relations in which there is a similarity of some kind among the participants. It tends to underlie and set bounds to the constant discontinuities in our lives. Throughout our lives—in our families, our work, our marriages, our leisure, our organizations, and our friendships—we tend to be with people who share our characteristics. A team of reviewers summarize the major areas of similarity (McPherson, Smith-Lovin, and Cook 2001, 415):

> Homophilly in race and ethnicity creates the strongest divides in our personal environments, with age, religion, education, occupation, and gender following in that order. Geographic propinquity, families, organizations, and isomorphic positions in social systems all create contexts in which homophilious relations form.
>
> The result is that people's personal networks are homogeneous with regard to many sociodemographic behavioral and intrapersonal characteristics. Homophilly limits people's social worlds in a way that has powerful implications for the information they receive, the attitudes they form, and the interactions they experience.

Socialization in Aging and Death

Aging, like other biological developments, is also a social construction, with varied cultural conceptions of the process. In some societies in Asia, and Africa, and among Native American tribes, for example, the elderly were socialized to expect to be respected, revered, and cared for by their younger families, although sometimes this prestige was not matched by actual practice (Smith 2000, 147; Keith 1985, 233). In other societies, the elderly were not expected to receive such care and attention. Among the Inuit, at one time, it was expected that those who thought they were no longer useful to the society because of their age or infirmity might kill themselves or ask close relatives, perhaps a son, to do it for them (Hoebel [1964] 1968). Other societies have different expectations for elderly behavior, often distinguishing between men and women. The variations are many. In our contemporary society, and even in the European and North American past, the image of elderly statuses and roles is varied and not so clear. One historian speaks of the status as often quite uncertain (Laslett 1985).

We are generally socialized in anticipatory socialization to think we should be less active, give up some roles, and take on others. Sixty-five has been a common age for retiring from work and some social positions. From another perspective, retirement from work is given an assist by social systems that withdraw work roles for the aged whether or not they wish to retire. Recent trends suggest that the elderly, besides living longer, are having more flexible options with fewer cases of mandatory retirement. Women, commonly marrying men older than themselves and having a higher life expectancy (Connides 2001), also may well anticipate a period of widowhood.

At one time in our North American society, especially among many ethnic groups, people were often socialized to think that, when they became old, their families would assume responsibility for them. But many changes over the years have tended to modify this expectation. We now have more private pension plans, collective agreements that provide for pensions, government savings plans and programs to help the needy, retirement and nursing homes, and segregated retirement communities. Many retirement homes are specifically created for members of a particular ethnic group. Also contributing to the range of possible patterns are such technological developments as improved transportation, recreation vehicles, and new communication devices, all of which allow for greater mobility. The lives and incomes of most elderly may not allow such a free choice, and they are vulnerable to failures of institutional obligations and pension funds, but we are socialized to know that our lives will be different and we may well have alternatives.

It is apparent that there is no single pattern of aging and no single lifestyle the elderly must follow. The patterns and roles followed will depend on many variables, especially health, income, and family ties including the number and proximity of children, grandchildren, and siblings (Connides 2001). Other relevant considerations include locality, ethnic traditions, social capital, distinctive interests, participation in voluntary groups, and even productive labor. The family and kin networks are especially important (Philipson 2003; Sussman 1985). Ethnicity, too, especially among Hispanics and blacks, can be a major source of support (Smith 2000; Sussman 1985). There is almost always some uncertainty and choices to be made.

The final and inevitable step for the elderly, as well as for younger people with terminal illnesses, is death. Death, like all aspects of our lives, is variously viewed in different cultures. In some societies, for example, the dead are revered. In Japan, altars are set up in homes in their memory, and family members continue to be in touch with them (Lemme 1999, 485). Buddhists believe in rebirth after death, "the dynamic and constantly changing continuity of the individual from one life to the next" (Keown 2003, 235). We are not generally socialized to such beliefs in our Western industrialized society, although our common religions do teach of a generally undefined afterlife for our souls.

Until recently in our North American society, death was surrounded by numerous taboos and was a topic to be avoided in conversation, if not in thought.

Those who were dying were encouraged to think they would recover, and when they died, others spoke of their "passing away," "breathing their last," or "departing this life." Children were protected from death by excluding them from attendance at funerals and the emotional experiences of surrounding adults. In attempts to lighten the tension, people have sometimes joked about "kicking the bucket" or going to "Davy Jones's locker."

In recent years, for social scientists and many in the public at large, the taboos have been lifted. Researchers and popular writers now openly discuss the fear of death, the grief of the dying, and the relationships among the dying, their families, and the attending personnel. Programs of "death education" have been developed for professionals to help patients with their concerns and to prepare people both to die and to accept death in others (Leviton 1977). Many now go to hospices or palliative care units to die (Novak and Campbell 2006), and many now prearrange their own funerals. Ceremonies following a death are now often "celebrations" of a life. Socialization for dying and death has been given a legitimacy unknown a generation or two ago.

We are socialized to expect others to die and to die ourselves. "Nothing is more certain than death and taxes" is a popular expression. Almost everyone has the experience of knowing elderly relatives and/or friends who die, besides becoming aware of terminal illness, deathbed scenes, the grief of families and friends, and the rituals that follow We have also often heard of suicides. These experiences all add to our socialization regarding death.

Continuities

Again, as with all later life socialization processes, we do find some continuities in aging, death, and dying. Those who in the past have identified with and been affiliated with particular religions are likely to continue to identify with these religions and perhaps receive support from them. Their funerals will be appropriately religious. Those who had the income to live well will, when they retire, continue to live in relative comfort, be it in their own homes or at retirement residences. Their friends will be of the same social level. Likewise, for those who have been working class, their retirement conditions will be simpler, with less material comfort and medical support. Those members with significant ethnic ties are likely to continue to maintain these ties and possibly receive support from their communities.

* * *

We have referred to the complexities of socialization and the many perspectives from which it may be viewed. Our perspective has been social and interactional. Throughout as well, we have viewed socialization through the lens of a life course, as an ongoing life activity in which earlier life experiences are the precursors of later developments. We ask, "What are the relationships between the past, the present, and the future?" The early family life, role models, economic position, ethnic affiliation, cultural capital, and neighborhood—these and other factors are relevant in understanding later progress at schools, activities with peers, occupational alternatives, memberships in organization, sexual preferences, social class, and other aspects of an ongoing life. The children of single mothers will face different hurdles from those of couples that stay together. The number of years that one spends in school will affect one's transition to work, social mobility, age of marriage, and future number of children. The mother's treatment of a sickly son or daughter may affect their interpersonal relations for the rest of their lives.

Also, as we go through life, depending on our individual characteristics and experiences and the period in which we live, we undergo constant changes. Few would argue, as Freud once did, that the self is established in early life and that only limited basic changes can occur thereafter. These changes, as we move through different positions, will involve continuities in some respects and discontinuities in others. The changes may be relatively smooth or abrupt; they will involve general movements in particular directions and back-and-forth movements in others. We are constantly being socialized, socializing others, and actively participating in our own socialization. Thus socialization in childhood, our focus in this volume, is far from being a determining process, yet it is always the foundation on which subsequent development and growth are based. It covers the early stages of an ongoing life course.

References

Anderson, Ronald E. 2002. "Youth and Information Technology." In Jeylan T. Mortimer and Reed W. Larson (eds.) *The Changing Adolescent Experience*, 175–207. Cambridge, UK: Cambridge University Press.

Becker, Howard S., Blanche Geer, Everett C. Hughes, and Anselm I. Strauss. 1961. *Boys in White: Student Culture in Medical School*. Chicago: University of Chicago Press.

Bengtson, Vern L., Timothy J. Biblarz, and Robert E. L. Roberts. 2002. *How Families Still Matter: A Longitudinal Study of Youth in Two Generations*. Cambridge, UK: Cambridge University Press.

Bennett, Andy. 2000. *Popular Music and Youth Culture: Music, Identity and Place*. New York: St. Martin's.

Berger, Bennett M. 1963. "Adolescence and Beyond." *Social Problems* 10: 394–408.

Blum, Robert W., and Kristin Nelson-Minari. 2004. "Adolescent Health from an International Perspective." In Richard M. Lerner and Laurence Steinberg (eds.) *Handbook of Adolescent Psychology*, 2nd ed, 553–586. Hoboken, NJ: John Wiley.

Bourdieu, Pierre. [1979] 1984. *Distinction*, translated by Richard Nice. Cambridge, MA: Harvard University Press.

Brooks-Gunn, Jeanne, and Edward O. Reiter. 1990. "The Role of Pubertal Processes." In S. Shirley Feldman and Glen R. Elliot (eds.) *At the Threshold: The Developing Adolescent*, 16–53. Cambridge, MA: Harvard University Press.

Brown, B. Bradford, and Reed W. Larson. 2002. "The Kaleidoscope of Adolescence: Experiences of the World's Youth at the Beginning of the 21st Century." In Bradford B. Brown, Reed W. Larson and T. S. Saraswathi (eds.) *The World's Youth: Adolescence in Eight Regions of the Globe*, 1–20. Cambridge, UK: Cambridge University Press.

Brumberg, John Jacobs, and Ruth Striegel-Moore. 1993. "Continuity and Change in Symptom Choice: Anorexia." In Glen H. Elder, John Modell, and Ross D. Parke (eds.) *Children in Time and Place: Developmental and Historical Insights*, 131–146. Cambridge, UK: Cambridge University Press.

Cairns, Robert G., and Beverly D. Cairns. 1994. *Lifelines and Risks: Pathways of Youth in Our Time*. Cambridge, UK: Cambridge University Press.

Call, Kathleen Thiede, and Jeylan T. Mortimer. 2001. *Areas of Comfort in Adolescence: A Study of Adjustment in Context.* Mahwah, NJ: Lawrence Erlbaum.

Coleman, James S. 1961. *The Adolescent Society: The Social Life of the Teenager and the Impact on Education.* New York: Free Press.

Connides, Ingrid Arnet. 2001. *Family Ties and Aging.* Thousand Oaks, CA: Sage.

Eder, Donna. 1995. *School Talk: Gender and Adolescent Culture.* New Brunswick, NJ: Rutgers University Press.

Elder, Glen H. 1974. *Children of the Great Depression: Social Change in Life Experience.* Chicago: University of Chicago Press.

Erikson, Erik H. 1959. *Identity and the Life Cycle.* New York: International Universities Press. Also 1980, New York: Norton.

Furman, Wyndol, B. Bradford Brown, and Candice Feiring, eds. 1999. *The Development of Romantic Relationships in Adolesence.* Cambridge, UK: Cambridge University Press.

Fussell, Elizabeth. 2002. "Youth in Aging Socieies." In Jeylan T. Mortimer and Reed W. Larson (eds.) *The Changing Adolescent Experience*, 18–51. Cambridge, UK: Cambridge University Press.

Giordano, Peggy C. 2003. "Relationships in Adolescence." *Annual Review of Sociology* 29: 257–281. Palo Alto, CA: Annual Reviews.

Grasmuck, Sheri. 2005. *Protecting Home: Class, Race and Masculinity in Boys' Baseball.* New Brunswick, NJ: Rutgers University Press.

Handel, Gerald. 2003. *Making a Life in Yorkville: Experience and Meaning in the Life Course Narrative of an Urban Working-Class Man.* New York: Aldine de Gruyter.

Hoebel, E. A. [1964] 1968. "The Eskimo: Rudimentary Law in a Primitive Anarchy." In J. Middleton (ed.) *Studies in Social and Culural Anthropology*, 93–127. NY: Crowell. (Cited in Kotak, Conrad Philip. 1987. In *Anthropology: The Explanation of Human Diversity*, 350. New York: Random House.)

Janowski, Martin Sanchez. 1991. *Islands in the Street: Gangs and American Urban Society.* Berkeley: University of California Press.

Keith, Jennie. 1985. "Age in Anthropological Research." In Robert H. Binstock and Ethel Shanas (eds.) *Handbook of Aging and the Social Sciences*, 2nd ed., 221–263. New York: Van Nostrand Reinhold.

Keown, Damen. 2003. *Dictionary of Buddhism.* New York: Oxford University Press.

Kinney, David A. 1999. "From 'Headbangers' to 'Hippies': Delineating Adolescents' Active Attempts to Form an Alternative Peer Culture." In Jeffrey A. McLellan and Mary Jo V. Pugh, (eds.) *The Role of Peer Groups on Adolescent Social Identity: Exploring the Importance of Stability and Change*, 21–35. San Francisco: Jossey Bass.

Larson, Reed, and Sean Sepersad. 2003. "Americans' Leisure Time in the United States: Partying, Sports, and the American Experiment." In Susan Verma and Reed Larson (eds.) *Examining Adolescent Leisure Time Across Cultures: Developmental Opportunities and Risks*, 53–64. San Francisco: Jossey Bass.

Laslett, Peter. 1985. "Societal Development and Aging." In Robert H. Binstock and Ethel Shanas (eds.) *Handbook of Aging and the Social Sciences*, 2nd ed., 199–220. New York: Van Nostrand Reinholdt.

Laursen, Brett. 1996. "Closeness and Conflict in Adolescent Peer Relationships: Interdependence with Friends and Romantic Partners." In William M. Bukowski, Andrew F. Newcomb, and Willard W. Hartup (eds.) *The Company they Keep: Friendship in Childhood and Adolescence*, 186–212. Cambridge, UK: Cambridge University Press.

Lemme, Barbara Hansen. 1999. *Development in Adulthood*, 2nd ed. Boston: Allyn & Bacon.

Lerner, Richard M. 2004. *Liberty: Thriving and Civic Engagement Among America's Youth.* Thousand Oaks, CA: Sage.

Leventhal, Tana, and Jeanne Brooks-Gunn. 2004. "Diversity in Developmental Trajectories across Adolescence: Neighborhood Influences." In Richard M. Lerner and Laurence Steinberg (eds.) *Handbook of Adolescent Psychology*, 2nd ed., 451–486. Hoboken, NJ: John Wiley.

Leviton, Daniel. 1977. "Death Education." In Herma Feifel (ed.) *New Meanings of Death*, 253–272. New York: McGraw-Hill.

Macleod, Jay. 1997. *Ain't No Makin' It: Leveled Aspirations in a Low-Income Neighborhood*. Boulder, CO: Westview Press.

Mallan, Kerry, and Sharyn Pearce (eds.) 2003. *Youth Cultures: Texts, Images and Identities*. Westport, CT: Praeger.

Mauldon, James. 2003. "Families started by Teenagers." In Mary Ann Mason, Arlene Skolnick, and Stephen D. Sugarman (eds.) 2003. *All Our Families: New Policies for a New Century*, 2nd ed., 40–65. New York: Oxford University Press.

McPherson, Miller, Lynn Smith-Lovin, and James M. Cook. 2001. "Birds of a Feather: Homophilly in Social Networks." *Annual Review of Sociology* 27: 415–444. Palo Alto, CA; Annual Reviews.

Mead, Margaret. 1928. *Coming of Age in Samoa*. New York: William Morrow.

Mortimer, Jeylan T., and Reed W. Larson. 2002. "Macrostructural Trends and the Reshaping of Adolescence." In Jeylan T. Mortimer and Reed W. Larson (eds.) *The Changing Adolescent Experience*, 1–17. Cambridge, UK: Cambridge University Press.

National Center for Health Statistics. 2004. "Teenagers in the United States: Sexual Activity, Contraceptive Use, and Childbearing, 2002." Series 23, no. 4. *www.cdc.gov/nchs/data/series/sr_23/sr23_024.pdf*.

National Institute of Mental Health. 2001. "Teenage Brain: A Work in Progress." *www.nimh.nih.gov/publicat/teenbrain.cfn*.

Nayak, Anoop. 2003. *Race, Place and Globalization: Youth Cultures in a Changing World*. Oxford, UK: Berg.

Novak, Mark, and Lori Campbell 2006. *Aging and Society*, Canadian Edition. Toronto: Nelson.

Parsons, Talcott. [1942] 1964. "Age and Sex in the Social Structure of the United States." *American Sociological Review* 7: 604–616. (Reprinted in Parsons, Talcott. 1964. *Essays in Sociological Theory*, Rev ed., 89–103. New York: Free Press.)

Philipson, Cliff. 2003. "From Family Groups to Personal Communities: Social Control and Social Change in the Family Life of Older Adults." In Vern L. Bengtson and Ariela Lowenstein (eds.) *Global Aging and Challenges to Families*, 54–74. New York: Aldine de Gruyter.

Planned Parenthood Federation of America. 2005. "Pregnancy and Childbearing Among U.S. Teens." *www.plannedparenthood.org/library/teenpregnancy*.

Pufall, Peter B., and Richard P. Unsworth, eds. 2004. *Rethinking Childhood*. New Brunswick, NJ: Rutgers University Press.

Roberts, Donald F., and Ulla C. Foehr. 2004. *Kids and Media in America*. Cambridge, UK: Cambridge University Press.

Savin-Williams, Ritch C., and Thomas J. Berndt. 1990. "Friendship and Peer Relations." In S. Shirley Feldman and Glen R. Elliott (eds.) *At the Threshold: The Developing Adolescent*, 277–307. Cambridge: Harvard University Press.

Schlegel, Alice, and Herbert Barry III. 1991. *Adolescence: An Anthropological Inquiry*. New York: Free Press.

Schulenberg, John, Jennifer Maggs, and Klaus Hurrelmann. 1997. "Negotiating Developmental Transitions During Adolescence and Young Adulthood: Health Risks and Opportunities." In J. J. Schulenberg, L. Maggs, and K. Hurrelmann (eds.) *Health Risks and Developmental Transitions During Adolescence*, 1–19. Cambridge, UK: Cambridge University Press.

Shanahan, Michael J. 2000. "Pathways to Adulthood in Changing Societies: Variability and Mechanisms in Life-Course Perspective." *Annual Review of Sociology* 26: 667–692. Palo Alto, CA; Annual Reviews.

Smith, Olivia, ed. 2000. *Aging in America*. New York: H. W. Wilson.

Susman, Elizabeth J., and Alan Rogol. 2004. "Puberty and Psychological Devlopment." In Richard M. Lerner and Laurence S. Steinberg (eds.) *Handbook of Adolescent Psychology*, 2nd ed., 15–44. Hoboken, NJ: John Wiley.

Sussman, Marvin B. 1985. "The Family Life of Old People." In Robert H. Binstock and Ethel Shanas (eds.) *Handbook of Aging and the Social Sciences*, 2nd ed., 415–449. New York: Van Nostrand Reinhold.

Tatum, Delwyn, and Graham Herbert, eds. 1997. *Bullying: Home, School, and Community*. London: David Fulton.

Thornberry, Terence P., and Marvin D. Krohn, eds. 2003. *Taking Stock of Delinquency: An Overview of Findings from Contemporary Longitudinal Studies*. New York: Kluwer Academic/Plenum.

Visher, Christy A., and Jeremy Travis. 2003. "Transitions from Prison to Community: Understanding the Individual Pathways." *Annual Review of Sociology* 29: 89–113. Palo Alto, CA: Annual Reviews.

Warr, Mark. 2002. *Companions in Crime: The Social Aspects of Criminal Conduct*. Cambridge UK: Cambridge University Press.

Williams, Kipling D., Joseph P. Forgas, and William von Hippel, eds. 2005. *The Social Outcast: Ostracism, Social Exclusion, Rejection, and Bullying*. New York: Psychology Press.

Zimring, Franklin E. 2000. "Penal Proportionality for the Young Offender: Notes on Immaturity, Capacity, and Diminished Responsibility." In Thomas Grisso and Robert G. Schwartz (eds.) *Youth on Trial: A Developmental Perspective on Juvenile Justice*, 271–289. Chicago: University of Chicago Press. ✦

Author Index

335

Subject Index